AUTOCOURSE

60 *Years*

OF
WORLD CHAMPIONSHIP
GRAND PRIX
MOTOR RACING

icon
PUBLISHING LIMITED

AUTOCOURSE

60

Years

OF WORLD CHAMPIONSHIP
GRAND PRIX MOTOR RACING

By ALAN HENRY

Photography by **BERNARD CAHIER** and **PAUL-HENRI CAHIER**

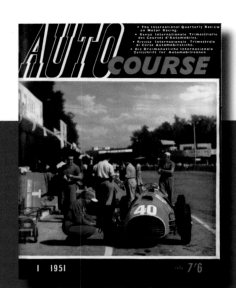

CONTENTS

Publisher
Steve Small
steve.small@iconpublishinglimited.com

Commercial Director
Bryn Williams
bryn.williams@iconpublishinglimited.com

Text Editor
Ian Penberthy

Statistics
David Hayhoe
dh1@gpworld.fsnet.co.uk

Photography
Cahier Archive
phc@f1-photo.com

AUTOCOURSE 60 YEARS OF WORLD
CHAMPIONSHIP GRAND PRIX MOTOR RACING
is published by: Icon Publishing Limited,
Regent Lodge, 4 Hanley Road, Malvern,
Worcestershire, WR14 4PQ

Tel: +44 (0)1684 564511

Website: www.autocourse.com

Printed in England by:
Butler, Tanner and Dennis Ltd,
Caxton Road, Frome, Somerset, BA11 1NF

First published as AUTOCOURSE 50 YEARS
OF WORLD CHAMPIONSHIP GRAND PRIX MOTOR
RACING by Hazleton Publishing Ltd 2000.
This edition has been completely revised and
updated.

ISBN:978-1-905334-56-8

DISTRIBUTORS
Gardners Books, 1 Whittle Drive
Eastbourne, East Sussex, BN23 6QH
email: sales@gardners.com

NORTH AMERICA
Motorbooks International
PO Box 1729 Prospect Avenue
Osceola, Wisconsin 54020, USA
Telephone: 1 715 294 3345
Fax: 1 715 294 4448

FOREWORD
By BERNIE ECCLESTONE

WHEN I first became involved in Formula 1, I was a good friend of the talented young British driver Stuart Lewis-Evans, team-mate to Stirling Moss and Tony Brooks in the Vanwall squad, and one of the sport's brightest rising stars of the 1950s. I helped him in his career. We travelled together to races and I was with him when he had the accident in Casablanca. Stuart suffered fatal burns when he crashed during the 1958 Moroccan Grand Prix after the sort of impact, if suffered by one of today's drivers racing on a contemporary circuit, that would quite possibly have seen him climb from the car without injury.

Much has changed over the 60 years during which the official FIA World Championship has been in existence, and not simply welcome improvements in safety. Many people within the sport, including drivers, team owners, engineers and administrators, have all worked tirelessly to expand what was once a specialist niche sport, attracting very much a specialist audience, into one of the world's great global sporting spectaculars right up there on a par with the Olympic Games, World Cup and the Super Bowl. I have always believed that the sport needs to grow and expand if it is not to be left behind, and believe passionately that expansion outside Europe, while not forgetting some of the so-called 'traditional' races, is absolutely crucial for the sport's longer-term strength and prosperity.

Within the pages of this book, you will read how Grand Prix racing evolved and developed over that 60 years, supplemented by a remarkable selection of photographs, many of which author Alan Henry tells me have not been published before. I must confess that I have never been a great one for history, always preferring to look to the future rather than dwelling on the past. But I hope you enjoy this book and finish it feeling that perhaps you know a little more about the traditions of our remarkable sport, and the drivers, cars and races that contributed so much to it over the decades.

THE DRIVER'S WATCH

The Oyster Perpetual Cosmograph Daytona is the ultimate reference chosen by professionals. On and off the track. Iconic from the moment it was introduced in 1963, the Daytona can perfectly measure elapsed time and calculate average speed. It is as essential as a driver's on-board controls. The Cosmograph Daytona sets the standard for those with a passion for driving and elegance. Visit ROLEX.COM. And explore more.

— THE COSMOGRAPH DAYTONA —

ROLEX

INTRODUCTION
By ALAN HENRY

AT first glance, this might seem like a book published ten years ago with another decade added to the narrative. Yet it is far more than that, as the text has been supplemented by significant additions to ensure a smooth transition into the first decade of the 21st century, a deeply significant period for this global sport, not least because it yielded an unparalleled run of five consecutive World Championships for Michael Schumacher at the wheel of a Ferrari, but also because it saw the emergence of British stars Lewis Hamilton and Jenson Button as successful title contenders.

Yet the overall keynote for this book has been a determination to keep the contents relevant and in perspective in the context of the individual periods being examined and analysed. Although the official FIA Drivers' World Championship was not inaugurated until 1950, I have described how the international Grand Prix scene developed before and immediately after the war to set the scene for what followed.

I have tried hard to capture the mood of each period, rather than simply providing the reader with a series of potted race reports. I have attempted to highlight trends, and focus on star drivers and particular events of significance to the sport itself. In particular, the great safety crusades of the 1960s and early 1970s are dealt with in detail, as is the sport's dramatic commercial expansion to all corners of the globe under the direction of Bernie Ecclestone, F1's energetic commercial rights holder, who has also been kind enough to contribute the Foreword.

I have also included some abbreviated features and interviews from past editions of the *AUTOCOURSE* annual, which now is owned by Icon Publishing.

Needless to say, it is a source of much personal pride that I have been entrusted with the editorship of *AUTOCOURSE* for 23 years, and I like to think that much of the annual's reputation and gloss has rubbed off on this current production.

Flip through this book, and you will be struck by the quality and diversity of the photography. Thanks to the efforts of Paul-Henri Cahier, we have again been able to trawl through the splendid archive built up by him and his legendary father, the late Bernard Cahier, over the past decades. Sadly, Bernard died in 2008, but his work lives on within these pages, and his reputation as one of the most talented and well-connected photojournalists in the F1 pit lane is further embellished by the use here of a large number of his previously unseen images.

In passing, I would like to thank some of the key personalities within the sport who have enhanced my journalistic career and, by direct association, added to the quality of this volume. They include long-time friends and associates such as Sir Frank Williams, Ron Dennis CBE, Sir Jackie Stewart, Luca di Montezemolo, Bernie Ecclestone and Max Mosley to name but a few; also journalistic colleagues Maurice Hamilton, Nigel Roebuck, Doug Nye, David Tremayne, Simon Arron and Mark Hughes. Finally, for Steve Small and Bryn Williams at Icon, this has involved a huge hands-on effort to what was a bruising schedule. Thanks to both of of them.

Alan Henry
Tillingham,
Essex, UK
June 2010

Full-circle. World Champions from the past 60 years were invited to Bahrain for the opening round of the 2010 World Championship.

Pictured are (back row, l to r) Alain Prost, Alan Jones, Nigel Mansell, Mika Häkkinen, Jacques Villeneuve, Keke Rosberg, Jody Scheckter, Michael Schumacher and Damon Hill; (front row, l to r) Fernando Alonso, Jenson Button, Niki Lauda, Bernie Ecclestone, Mario Andretti, Jean Todt and his wife Michelle, Sir Jack Brabham, Sir Jackie Stewart, John Surtees, Emerson Fittipaldi and Lewis Hamilton.

Photo: Paul-Henri Cahier

CHAPTER ONE
BEFORE THE WAR

THIS book celebrates the 60th anniversary of World Championship Grand Prix motor racing, six decades of a dramatic, colourful and ever-expanding global contest that has evolved almost beyond recognition during that period. Today, Grand Prix racing is arguably the world's most prestigious and cosmopolitan sport. More significantly, it is also more structured and regulated than any comparable international sporting spectacular.

With an annual programme approaching 20 races around the world, it captures a global audience far more frequently than either World Cup football or the Olympic Games. Yet it would be a mistake to believe that Grand Prix history began in 1950 with the inauguration of the official World Championship. Motor racing coughed and spluttered into life in the early years of the 20th century, and was already rich in tradition and achievement before everything was put on hold for six years while humanity became embroiled in the Second World War.

The first recorded motorised competition was the Paris-to-Rouen trial in 1894, which was followed by a rash of road races between European capitals. The 1903 Paris-to-Madrid event wrought such carnage among competitors and spectators, however, that the marathon was halted. A succession of accidents, caused by primitive machines plunging into the crowds who lined the very edge of the route, prompted the subsequent development of international racing on closed, albeit not very short, circuits.

The first Grand Prix, as such, took place in 1906, when two days of racing were staged on a 65-miles-to-the lap road course near the French city of Le Mans, each competitor facing the challenge of completing six laps of the circuit on each of the two days.

The event was won by Hungarian driver Ferenc Szisz, who took over 11 hours to complete the course at an average speed of 63mph, quite remarkable when one considers how his car's solid tyres and cart-sprung suspension must have reacted to the bumpy, rutted and

badly surfaced roads on which the event took place.

All this seems prehistoric by the high-tech, space-age standards of the current era, when Grand Prix drivers are as much highly qualified technocrats as committed professional competitors. It is also worth adding another perspective. Today, a Grand Prix field is whisked around the world loaded into half a dozen Boeing 747 jet airliners. By the time Szisz won at Le Mans, only three years had passed since Wilbur and Orville Wright had made their first, faltering powered flight at Kitty Hawk, North Carolina. And the development of the jet engine was still almost 40 years away.

Technical development proved as painfully slow and unco-ordinated as the evolution of the rule book in the early years of the 20th century, yet by 1907 the idea of a Grand Prix 'formula' was becoming established. Initially this was based on fuel consumption considerations, with around 30 litres per 100km being permitted.

This was followed variously by a piston area re-

striction, then a 300cc 'voiturette' formula, and later a 14mpg fuel-consumption limitation. Not until after the First World War, however, did Grand Prix racing seriously develop an identifiable pattern that would form the foundation on which the subsequent evolution of the sport would be based.

In 1921, Grand Prix racing was revived under a 3-litre/800kg minimum weight limit, which was reduced to 2 litres/650kg from 1922 to 1925 inclusive. The 1922 season also saw the construction of the world's first permanent Grand Prix circuit in the former royal park at Monza, on the northern fringes of Milan. Seven years later, Monaco would host its first race, and names such as Delage, Bugatti, Mercedes-Benz and Alfa Romeo would become increasingly familiar thanks to their on-track achievements.

The potential of international motor racing as a vehicle for enhancing national prestige abroad was quickly recognised by those two despots with a taste for self-publicity and a tendency to megalomania,

Above: **Pioneering days for the fledgling sport. The 1906 French Grand Prix at Le Mans was held over open roads and was won by Ferenc Szisz in a Renault, seen here leading the Hotchkiss HH of Elliot Shepard.**
Photo: **LAT Photographic**

Above: Tazio Nuvolari's giant killing performance to win the 1935 German Grand Prix at the Nürburgring, where he beat the massed forces of Mercedes and Auto Union in his underpowered Alfa Romeo Tipo B P3, is regarded as the high spot of the legendary Italian driver's distinguished career.

Photo: LAT Photographic

Benito Mussolini and Adolf Hitler. Thanks largely to the splendid achievements of Alfa Romeo engineer Vittorio Jano throughout the 1920s, Mussolini decided that Italy's sporting prowess could be demonstrated to great advantage following the inauguration of a new 750kg Grand Prix formula, which was introduced in 1934.

MOTOR RACING AND PROPAGANDA

Unfortunately the prospects for the P3 Alfa Romeo and the corresponding 2.9-litre Maserati took a dive when Auto Union and Mercedes-Benz – backed strongly by Hitler's Nazi regime – joined the fray. Originally it had been Hitler's intention to pay the massive state subsidy of around 450,000 Reichsmarks (about £40,000, which today would have the equivalent purchasing power of £1.5 million) exclusively to the long-established Mercedes Benz company, but Auto Union's chief designer, Professor Ferdinand Porsche, persuaded the government to split the contribution equally. In many ways, the subsidy was symbolic, as the overall operating cost of each team was several times the total received from the government.

Mercedes would be responsible for this new generation of German Grand Prix cars being dubbed 'The Silver Arrows'. The technical regulations in force at the time of their 1934 debut did not place any restriction on engine capacity, but imposed a maximum weight limit of 750kg. During scrutineering for their first race, that year's Eifel Grand Prix at the Nürburgring, the eight-cylinder, 78 x 88mm, 3360cc supercharged Mercedes W25s were found to tip the scales fractionally

over the limit. This deeply alarmed the team's racing manager, Alfred Neubauer, but someone – reputedly driver Manfred von Brauchitsch – cleverly suggested that it might be a good idea to strip off the cars' white paint prior to the race. This inspired piece of improvisation left the W25s, which developed 345bhp at 5800rpm, just inside the maximum weight limit. Now sporting bare silver aluminium bodywork, they soon received their new nickname, which was also applied to the Auto Unions for the remaining years in the run-up to the Second World War. Indeed, the soubriquet would continue to be applied to Mercedes Grand Prix entries for many years after the war.

The achievements of the Mercedes-Benz and Auto Union teams left precious little room for anybody else to enjoy the limelight, although the Italians picked up a few crumbs from the German table, most notably when Tazio Nuvolari stole victory from under their noses in the 1935 German Grand Prix. Nuvolari had been motivated by a passionate desire to upstage the German teams on their home patch, believing as he did that a conspiracy between fellow Italian Achille Varzi and German driver Hans Stuck had kept him out of the Auto Union team.

Yet it was Mercedes who had arrived at the 'Ring in confident mood, having already won seven major races that season to Auto Union's one. On a glistening, ominously damp track, the legendary Rudolf Caracciola stormed away into an immediate lead. However, although the Mercedes driver led at the end of the opening lap, the remarkable Bernd Rosemeyer soon took up the challenge in his Auto Union. But after seven laps, he was forced to make a precautionary pit stop, having damaged a rear wheel by hitting an earth bank earlier in the race.

It was not long, however, before the focus of attention fell on Nuvolari in the Scuderia Ferrari Alfa Romeo P3. By lap seven of the 22-lap race, he was up to third, trading fastest laps with Rosemeyer. Then on lap ten, he stormed ahead of Caracciola to take the lead. The crowds fell silent. This was not part of the script by any stretch of the imagination.

At the end of lap 12, it was time for the mid-race spate of routine refuelling stops. The Mercedes W25 of Manfred von Brauchitsch went through into the lead when Tazio Nuvolari lost two minutes while topping up his Alfa. However, the frail-looking Italian had not finished yet.

Having resumed in sixth, Nuvolari climbed relentlessly back to second place, and only von Brauchitsch lay between his Alfa and an astounding victory. Nevertheless, it looked as though Mercedes had it made. The German driver started the final lap just under 30 seconds ahead, and it all seemed over bar the shouting.

Von Brauchitsch had been caning the W25's tyres in his determination to stay ahead, though, and midway around that final lap, the left rear tyre flew apart, leaving the German driver a sitting duck. Nuvolari roared past to post possibly the most remarkable victory of his career.

There was an amusing postscript to this episode, which aggravated Nuvolari's rivals' embarrassment. Understandably, the organisers had anticipated nothing but a win for one of the German teams. Consequently, they had no recording of the Italian national anthem. No matter, said Nuvolari, who produced his own, which he carried with him to all the races. Best to be prepared.

NUVOLARI: THE SPEED-HAPPY LEGEND

Tazio Nuvolari was a racing driver cast in the heroic mould. As this story unfolds, it will become clear that the role and prestige of the Grand Prix driver changed subtly over the six decades in question. In Nuvolari's heyday, the drivers were motivated by a passion for racing that seems almost reckless and ill-judged by the structured standards of the 21st century.

Today a racing driver is regarded as a committed, polished and professional sportsman. He may have a burning competitive spirit and enormous motivation, but he tends to assess the overall situation shrewdly, considering carefully whether or not a risk is worth taking. In reaching a conclusion, he is buttressed by a generally supportive governing body, in the sense that the FIA – under the presidency of both Max Mosley and Jean Todt – is very aware that Grand Prix racing must be seen to be as safe as possible. Fatal accidents involving racing drivers have become no more acceptable in the public psyche than permitting NATO soldiers to be killed during a peace keeping operation.

The notion of safety was simply not part of the equation in Nuvolari's day. Born in 1892, originally he had made a living as a motorcycle racer, although his underlying ambition had been to race on four wheels. In 1925, he was quite badly injured after crashing during a test run in an Alfa Romeo

PROFESSOR PORSCHE AND THE AUTO UNION

PROFESSOR Ferdinand Porsche started his first technical drawing office in Stuttgart, where he produced two designs for the Wanderer company, which – along with Audi, DKW and Horch – was one of the constituent members of the Auto Union combine. Prior to that, he had worked for Daimler-Benz, where, shortly before he left in 1928, he had outlined a new racing car design. With its supercharged, eight-cylinder inline engine and rear mounted gearbox, it was, in essence, the machine that Mercedes would produce in 1934 at the start of the 750kg formula.

The new formula set no restriction on power, and Porsche, impressed by his business manager Alfred Rosenberger's memories of racing the mid-engined Mercedes Tropfenwagen in the mid-1920s, decided on a similar layout for his proposed supercharged V16 powered racer for the new regulations. This would become the spectacular Auto Union that was destined to go head-to-head with the Mercedes opposition for six memorable seasons.

The cars were designed at the Porsche headquarters, but assembled at the Horch plant at Zwickau, which, after the Second World War, would be stranded in the eastern zone of a divided Germany. Both Professor Porsche and his son, Ferry, were passionately involved in the entire project in a very hands-on manner, developing the cars technically at a relentless pace through to the end of 1937, when Porsche Senior's contract with Auto Union came to an end.

For the following two years, Porsche worked for Mercedes, developing a land speed record challenger, and, of course, is well known for his contribution to the design of the original Volkswagen, which was very much a pet project of Hitler's.

Professor Robert Eberan von Eberhorst, who had been invited by Porsche to join Auto Union in 1933, was promoted to take charge of the company's Grand Prix project. Unquestionably, von Eberhorst was a Porsche fan. "He was the presiding genius," he said. "He seemed to have a sixth sense. He could smell success and knew how to avoid mistakes."

Above: **The formidable sight of three Auto Unions being fettled in the paddock at Monza in preparation for the 1936 Italian Grand Prix. From left to right, the cars are to be driven by Ernst von Delius, Achille Varzi and Bernd Rosemeyer.**
Photo: **Robert Fellowes/LAT Photographic**

P2. Yet only a matter of weeks later, he ordered his doctors to strap him up into a compromise riding position to race his Bianchi in the Italian motorcycle Grand Prix. He won.

In 1930, when they were both members of the Alfa Romeo works team, Nuvolari successfully duped Varzi into giving away victory in the Mille Miglia by the simple expedient of closing on to his tail in the dark, having switched off his headlights. Almost within sight of the finishing line, he pulled out and passed his astonished rival to take the win. Varzi was not amused.

In 1933, the Alfa Romeo works team withdrew from international racing, and the Scuderia Ferrari effectively became the Milan car company's nominated team. In 1935, Nuvolari attempted to join Auto Union, but Varzi paid him back for the Mille Miglia trick. Not until 1938 did he finally get his break with Auto Union; he duly won the Italian Grand Prix at Monza and the second Donington Grand Prix, an event that had been taken the previous year by his predecessor, Bernd Rosemeyer, who had been killed during a speed record attempt on a German autobahn near Frankfurt in January 1938.

The rivalry between Mercedes-Benz and Auto Union was intense. The Auto Union was a mid-engined machine, powered by a 4360cc (68 x 75mm), 16-cylinder engine initially developing 295bhp at 4500rpm. By

1936, it would be enlarged to 6 litres, in which form it produced 520bhp at 5000rpm, although Mercedes topped this with the ultimate development of its inline eight-cylinder car – the sensational W125 – which had grown to 5.6 litres by the end of the 750kg formula in 1937, offering 610bhp at 5800rpm.

If Nuvolari and Rosemeyer were regarded as the stars of the Auto Union show, then the ace Mercedes exponent was surely Rudolf Caracciola. Despite starting this golden era on a low note, having been out of action for more than a year after fracturing his right thigh and hip during practice for the 1933 Monaco Grand Prix, he went on to win three European championship titles and no fewer than 15 Grands Prix before the Second World War intervened.

Varzi was another Auto Union great, but his career was almost wrecked prior to the war by drug addiction. He would heroically kick the habit and return to the Formula 1 front line in the immediate post-war era, only to be killed during practice for the 1948 Swiss Grand Prix.

In 1938, new technical rules were introduced that limited supercharged machinery to a capacity of 3 litres, and both German manufacturers opted for the V12 engine configuration. By then, Mercedes had secured the services of the dynamic young English driver Dick Seaman, who had impressed team manager Alfred Neubauer with his competitiveness in both an ERA and a ten-year-old Delage.

Seaman was destined to become Britain's first world-class driver, scoring a politically rather awkward victory in the 1938 German Grand Prix. He would surely have thrived in the post-war era, but his career was cut tragically short when he crashed in the 1939 Belgian Grand Prix at Spa-Francorchamps and succumbed to serious burns.

There is an anecdote that amusingly puts a social perspective on this era of German motor racing domination. It recalls an occasion when the aristocratic Manfred von Brauchitsch led Caracciola and their team-mate, Hermann Lang, into Berlin's swanky Roxy bar in the late 1930s. Lang was regarded as somewhat working class, having been unemployed during the early 1930s. He originally joined the Daimler-Benz company as a mechanic and had previously competed on motorcycles.

Von Brauchitsch settled down into a chair and hailed a waiter. "A bottle of champagne for Herr Caracciola and myself," he said, "and a beer for Lang."

Of course, in setting the scene for what came after the war, no account of European motor racing in the 1930s would be complete without mention of the 'voiturette' categories, which thrived during that decade with 1100 or 1500cc engines. Bugatti and Alfa Romeo competed in this category along with the British-built ERAs, with which Raymond Mays and others would lay the foundations for the post-war BRM operation.

Late on the afternoon of 3rd September, 1939, Tazio Nuvolari took the chequered flag to win the Yugoslavian Grand Prix in Belgrade. The Second World War was already a few hours old, and by the time Nuvolari reappeared in the austere post-war world, he would be over 50 and beset by bronchial problems, a shadow of his former self. A golden era for racing was at an end.

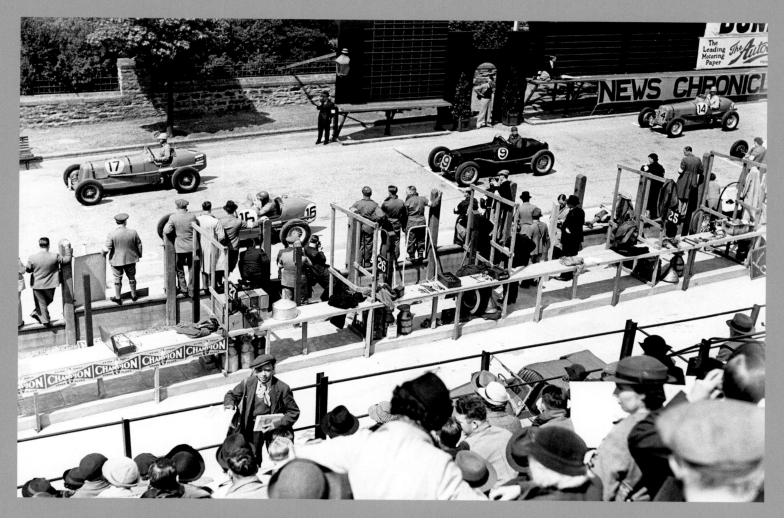

RAYMOND MAYS AND THE CONTRIBUTION OF ERA

IF there was a pivotal personality on the British motor racing scene, whose influence straddled the war years, then unquestionably it was Raymond Mays. A dignified, unstuffy and charismatic man in his own way, Mays had been born in the Lincolnshire fenland town of Bourne in 1899, and he never lived anywhere else until his death 80 years later.

Mays served in France in the closing months of the First World War, having been commissioned into the Grenadier Guards in 1918; he began his racing career three years later while still a Cambridge undergraduate. In the mid-1920s, he made his name competing with a Bugatti, but then switched to a 3-litre TT Vauxhall, updated by distinguished engineer Amherst Villiers.

Next came a highly tuned Riley, success with which prompted him to encourage the wealthy Humphrey Cook to fund the construction of the ERA (English Racing Automobiles) single-seaters to compete in the 'voiturette' category. The company established its factory in premises adjacent to the Mays family home in Bourne, Eastgate House, where Ray lived in some style with his mother and Peter Berthon, a former RAF pilot, who became an indispensable friend and confidant, as well as a key engineer in the forthcoming BRM project.

The Mays family businesses included the wool, tannery and fertiliser trades. They were certainly comfortably off, if not dramatically rich. Ray was an only child and had been brought up insulated from the harsh economic realities of life that blew through the homes of all too many English families during the first half of the 20th century, particularly during the 1930s.

Although ERA sold several Riley-engined cars to private entrants, Mays was effectively the number-one works driver, and he recorded the marque's first Continental victory in the 1935 Eifelrennen at the Nürburgring. The pressure of development and reported poor preparation standards at Bourne meant that Mays did not win another international event until 1937, when he really got into his stride, scoring three more victories.

Mays had the ability to charm the birds off the trees, a quality that aided him enormously when it came to romancing potential backers for his various motor racing projects. Famous names such as Dick Seaman, Pat Fairfield and the enormously talented Siamese prince, Birabongse Bhanudej Bhanubandh, popularly known as 'B. Bira', all purchased ERAs and helped add further gloss to the image of the marque.

Unfortunately it seems that, by 1939, Humphrey Cook was tiring of his role as ERA's benefactor. He had spent around £95,000 – a truly massive sum by the standards of the day, which would equate to almost £3 million at today's values – over five years and felt that increasingly he was being taken for granted by Mays and Berthon, who seemed to be hogging the limelight.

There was considerable acrimony behind the scenes because Cook resented the way in which he had been treated, although Mays's innate sense of good manners prevented him from making any overt criticism of his former colleague: when he published his memoirs, *Split Seconds*, in 1950, he talked about Cook in affectionate terms as a close and valued friend. Yet there was very real rancour between the two men, as evidenced in the correspondence published in *BRM, The Saga of British Racing Motors* by Doug Nye with Tony Rudd (Motor Racing Publications, 1994).

The whole tone of Mays's letters suggested that he delivered rather more to the enterprise in terms of intangible prestige than Cook did with hard cash. Ultimately it became an irreconcilable issue, but Mays's somewhat cavalier approach to financial and organisational matters

would resurface when it came to establishing the BRM team immediately after the war.

Some members of the racing fraternity regarded Mays as something of a social butterfly, determined to look after number one. A great fan of the theatre, he was an unashamed 'stage door Johnny'. Those who worked with him, however, testified to his loyalty and steadfast friendship. He was not a man to give up easily on any project he undertook.

When the war came to an end, Mays was still anxious to float his plan for a British national Grand Prix car, the project that eventually would turn into the BRM and initially establish itself as a countrywide joke, or disgrace, depending on one's sense of humour and the absurd. Mays continued sprinting and hill-climbing throughout the late 1940s, finally retiring in 1949 when the BRM project was getting into top gear.

Mays, and the influence and interest prompted by his ERAs have been widely credited for the expansion of interest in the 'voiturette' category during the 1930s. Latterly, his faith in the BRM project seemed dramatically misplaced, as we shall see, but ultimately he was vindicated when Graham Hill won the marque's first and only World Championship title in 1962.

GREAT DRIVERS: DICK SEAMAN, BERND ROSEMEYER

DICK SEAMAN was a rich young man whose family had the resources to fund his progress up the rungs of the motor racing ladder. Although his mother and father disapproved of his aspirations behind the wheel, they had no joy when it came to influencing him to pursue a career in the diplomatic service.

By the time he left Cambridge in 1934, at the age of 21, Seaman was already absolutely determined that he would become a professional driver, and he bought an MG K3 Magnette, which his fellow student Whitney Straight – later to become chairman of the British Overseas Airways Corporation – was all too willing to sell to him.

Despite parental disapproval, Seaman secured sufficient finance to clinch a deal to drive a factory prepared ERA in 1935. Unfortunately this coincided with a downturn in the standards of preparation at Boume, and Dick soon decided to cancel the agreement, preferring to have his car prepared by the highly respected Giulio Ramponi, whom he hired as his personal mechanic.

In 1936, frustrated by the ERA's performance, he was coaxed into acquiring the nine-year-old Grand Prix Delage that had been driven in its heyday by Earl Howe. The car was extensively reworked and lovingly fettled by Ramponi,

and Seaman drove it to four prestigious wins in 1936, sealing his reputation as the most impressive 500cc driver in Europe. It was on the strength of that achievement that he was offered a place in the Mercedes-Benz factory team for the following year.

Seaman accepted the Mercedes offer. This was an unmissable opportunity to make the 'big time', but his contract had to be rubber-stamped by Adolf Hitler himself, a measure of just how seriously the Nazi government regarded its investment in Grand Prix racing during the 1930s. Hitler had always been a fan of the English and clearly would have had no reservations whatsoever about approving Dick's appointment.

However, little success came his way during his first season with Mercedes. Indeed, his first test after signing his contract resulted in an accident at Monza, from which he was fortunate to escape with relatively minor injuries. By all accounts, Alfred Neubauer, the portly Mercedes team manager, was very philosophical about such incidents, feeling that they were something of an occupational hazard.

Later in the year, Dick was involved in a very serious accident in the German Grand Prix at the Nürburgring, on the long straight that leads back to the start/finish line and runs parallel with the main road to Koblenz. His Auto Union rival, Ernst von Delius, attempted to overtake his Mercedes, but inadvertently clipped the dense hedge and was thrown across in front of the Englishman. The Auto Union careered into the opposite hedge and was catapulted back through the left-hand hedge, after which it rolled several times before landing in a field on the opposite side of the public road. Meanwhile, Seaman struck a kilometre post and was thrown out of his car, losing most of the skin from his nose and breaking a thumb. The hapless von Delius died of his injuries that night.

Later that year, Seaman was disappointed not to have posted a good result in the first Donington Grand Prix, having been pushed off by a rival Auto Union early in the race. Amazingly, he did not race again until the following year's German Grand Prix at the Nürburgring, which he won. Then he was faced with the embarrassing situation of having to give a Nazi salute on the rostrum – which he did, albeit tentatively.

In December 1938, Dick Seaman married Erica, the 18-year-old daugh-

ter of BMW founder Franz-Joseph Popp. They would have less than a year together, as Dick crashed heavily on a rain soaked Spa-Francorchamps circuit while leading the 1939 Belgian Grand Prix. He succumbed to fatal burns that evening. The entire Mercedes team attended his funeral at Putney Vale cemetery in south London.

Seaman had died at the age of 26, but had he lived his very real talent would have continued to shine on the post-war racing scene. He would have been just 37 when Alfa Romeo brought its dominant 158s to Silverstone for the very first round of the official World Championship on 13th May, 1950. On that occasion, Reg Parnell was given the third entry and rounded off a Portello 1-2-3, much to the delight of the organisers. But for that skid on a rain drenched circuit 11 years earlier, the bright red car might well have been driven by Dick Seaman.

If Seaman was the best and most accomplished racing driver to emerge from Britain in the 1930s, then Bernd Rosemeyer was Germany's most dazzling, charismatic star from the same era. Born in 1909, Rosemeyer began

motorcycle grass-track racing in 1930 and made such dramatic progress that he had been recruited as a member of the Auto Union team by the start of the 1935 season.

As well as great charm, Rosemeyer had terrific car control, and his technique with the daunting rear-engined Auto Unions was truly magical. In only his second race, the Eifelrennen, he acutely embarrassed established star Rudi Caracciola, and the Mercedes ace had to draw on all his considerable experience to keep the new lad back in second place at the chequered flag.

Later Rosemeyer would finish second in the Coppa Acerbo at Pescara and round off the 1935 season with victory in the Czech Grand Prix at Brno. The 1936 season would see him win the Eifel GP ahead of Tazio Nuvolari's Alfa, and score a hat trick of wins in the Coppa Acerbo and the Swiss and Italian Grands Prix.

The 1937 season would yield repeat wins in the Eifel GP and Coppa Acerbo, and he would round off the year with victory in the inaugural Donington GP, the first of two memorable occasions when the 'Silver Arrows'

would compete on tracks in the UK.

Bernd Rosemeyer married the aviatrix Elly Beinhorn in the summer of 1936, and they became one of pre-war Germany's most glamorous and attractive couples. Their idyllic life together was torn apart, however, when Bernd was killed during a record attempt in a streamlined Auto Union on the Frankfurt–Darmstadt autobahn on 27th January, 1938. To this day, a handsome memorial stands in the woods close to a lay-by on this same autobahn at the point where he crashed more than 70 years ago.

Above: **The flaming wreckage of Dick Seaman's Mercedes W154 after the crash that left him fatally burnt in the 1939 Belgian Grand Prix at Spa-Francorchamps.**
Photo: LAT Photographic

Top: **The high spot of Dick Seaman's Mercedes career was his memorable victory in the 1938 German Grand Prix at the Nürburgring.**
Photo: Robert Fellowes/LAT Photographic

CHAPTER TWO
THE POST-WAR SCENE

Above: **Grand Prix racing gets back into top gear in the aftermath of the Second World War. Here, at the start of the 1947 Belgian Grand Prix, the Alfa 158s of Achille Varzi and Jean-Pierre Wimille accelerate towards Eau Rouge, ahead of Raymond Sommer's Maserati 4CM, Count Trossi's Alfa and Louis Chiron's Lago-Talbot T26C. Varzi would win the race from Wimille.**

Photo: LAT Photographic

AS Europe dusted itself down and surveyed the destruction wrought by six years of war, one might have been excused for thinking that motor racing would be low on the collective agenda. But that thought would have ignored the passion and purpose of the engineers, drivers and fans who had been starved of their favourite sport for so long.

Once the heady fever of relief had passed, there was a burning desire to re-establish normality as quickly as possible. Thus the first flickers of racing enthusiasm began to be nurtured in the dying embers of the conflict. But it was still a rough and ready game.

Crash helmets were optional until the early 1950s, safety facilities non-existent. A generation of young men who had endured the suffering and danger of wartime just wanted to compete in their chosen sport, so it was hardly surprising that nobody gave much thought to safety.

Before the war, a change in Formula A regulations – effectively Formula 1 – had been pencilled in for 1941. These rules would call for 4.5-litre unsupercharged or 1.5-litre supercharged engines, and in 1945 the newly titled Fédération Internationale de l'Automobile (FIA) quickly adopted these regulations for those who felt able to take part.

The Alfa Romeo 158s, eight-cylinder, 1.5-litre supercharged machines that had made their race debut in the 1938 Coppa Ciano at Leghorn – and which allegedly had spent the war walled up in a cheese factory – were the most obvious contenders to re-emerge. Naturally there was nothing from Auto Union or Mercedes-Benz, but there were some old French Talbots, the odd Delahaye, British ERAs and Italian Maseratis to fill out the field.

FERRARI TAKES THE CHALLENGE TO ALFA

More significantly, there was a new name on the block. Enzo Ferrari had forged his reputation by operating what was, in effect, the works Alfa Romeo team from 1929 through to 1938. At this point, he had had a major breach with the company after falling out on a personal level on matters of strategy with its director, Ugo Gobatto, and his nominee, Spanish engineer Wilfredo Ricart.

Ferrari said of Ricart, "When we shook hands, it was like grasping the cold, lifeless hand of a corpse." He certainly had a way with words, although he would be less appreciative when firm criticism was aimed in his direction over the next two generations by a succession of car-crazy Italian scribes.

In 1938, Alfa wanted to take back control of its works team to the company headquarters at Portello in Milan. Ferrari would have none of this and decided to go his own way, although he was somewhat hamstrung in his ambitions by a severance clause that prevented his participation in any races with a non-Alfa product for the next four years.

Despite this, by the end of 1939, the new company Ferrari had formed, Auto Avio Construzioni, was working on a couple of eight-cylinder sports cars – simply dubbed '815s' – for the following year's Mille Miglia. After Italy entered the war, Ferrari concentrated on specialist engineering work, and in 1943 he moved his base from Modena to a new factory at nearby Maranello.

By 1947, Ferrari was free to build cars under his own name. Two Ferrari 125s, fitted with 1.5-litre V12 engines, made their debut in a sports car race at Piacenza, where they were driven by Franco Cortese and Giuseppe Farina. A Ferrari took part in a classic Grand Prix event for the first time the following May, when Igor Troubetzkoy, later to gain fleeting celebrity status as one of the many husbands of Woolworth heiress Barbara Hutton, competed with a 2-litre version of the same machine.

Not until September 1948 did the first of the supercharged Ferrari 125s make their race debuts. Driving in the Turin Grand Prix were Raymond Sommer, Farina and the Siamese prince, 'Bira'. The cars had been designed by former Alfa Romeo engineer Gioacchino Colombo – the man responsible for the legendary 158 – and Sommer finished third on this occasion, behind Jean-Pierre Wimille's Alfa and Luigi Villoresi's Maserati.

The 1949 season saw Ferrari concentrating on the

development of the 125s and, crucially, generating extra income by selling a couple of cars into private hands. Both went to British owners: one to privateer Peter Whitehead and the other to Tony Vandervell, the engine bearing magnate, who raced the car under the title 'Thinwall Special Ferrari'.

By the mid-1950s, of course, Formula 1 would be well supported by many teams and manufacturers, but this was far from the case in 1949, when Alfa Romeo temporarily withdrew from the Grand Prix arena. The Milanese firm was worried by opposition from the emergent Ferrari and BRM teams.

In addition, Alfa's efforts had been undermined by the loss of three of its top drivers. Achille Varzi had been killed the previous year, while Jean-Pierre Wimille had lost his life at the wheel of a little Simca-Gordini in Buenos Aires on 28th January, 1949. In addition, Count Carlo-Felice Trossi had been laid low by cancer and eventually would die on 9th May, 1949, following a long illness.

Alfa Romeo's decision to stand aside, albeit fleetingly, meant that Ferrari pretty well had the scene to himself. Not that things went smoothly by any means, for Tony Vandervell soon returned his Ferrari 125 to Maranello with a stiff note to the effect that he was not satisfied with the new car's performance.

Nevertheless, Vandervell's decision to buy that Ferrari in the first place had not only been his first step towards building his own Vanwall cars, but also a clear signal that he had grown tired of his involvement in the complex 'management by committee' BRM project.

The first BRM was a 1.5-litre, centrifugally supercharged V16, which was not only late off the mark, but also beset with mechanical problems almost from the moment of its very first test outing. By the time its complicated and very temperamental engine had been massaged into some semblance of competitive trim, such was the dearth of cars available generally that conformed with the F1 regulations that the 1952 and 1953 title battles were turned over to Formula 2 machinery.

As a result, the BRM would eke out a faintly pathetic twilight existence in British domestic events, and those motor industry backers who had rallied to

Below: **First Ferrari outing in a Grand Prix. Prince Igor Troubetzkoy's Ferrari 166C goes wide at Station hairpin during the 1948 Monaco GP to make room for the Lago-Talbot 150C of Yves Giraud-Cabantous.**
Photo: Robert Fellowes/LAT Photographic

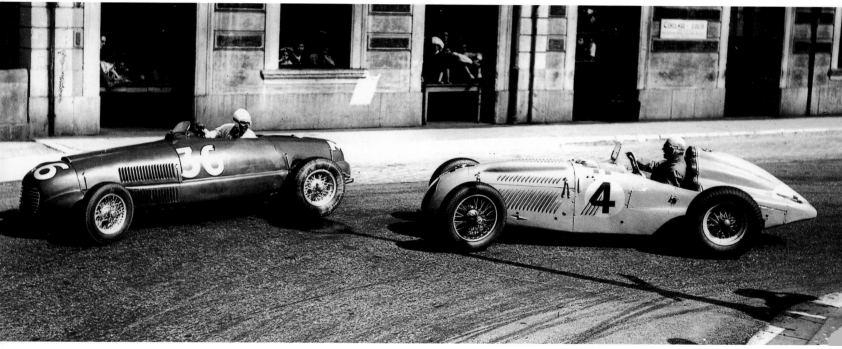

Left: **Drivers' briefing for the 1949 British GP at Silverstone.
From left: Philippe Étancelin, Yves Giraud-Cabantous, Lord Selsdon, Baron de Graffenried, Fred Ashmore, Philip Fotheringham-Parker, John Bolster and Peter Walker.**
Photo: LAT Photographic

Right: Louis Chiron's Lago-Talbot 26C laps the similar car of Pierre Bouillin, who raced under the name 'Pierre Levegh', on his way to victory in the 1949 French GP at Reims. His fellow Frenchman would retire from the race.

Below: 'Toulo' de Graffenried wins the 1949 British Grand Prix at Silverstone in his Maserati 4CLT/48.

Photos: LAT Photographic

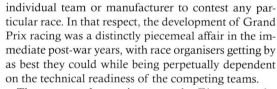

the cause, energetically supporting the call for a new national British Grand Prix car, suddenly found themselves pilloried for its lack of success.

Eventually the original British Motor Racing Research Trust foundered and the project was bought by the Owen Organisation, one of the country's largest privately owned industrial empires. At its head was a serious-minded, but very human and popular, Methodist by the name of Alfred Owen, whose cars eventually would be pitted against Tony Vandervell's Vanwalls.

Much was made of the personal rivalry between these two very different 'millionaire industrialists'. In reality, however, they seem to have enjoyed a formally cordial relationship. They were very different personalities, but both were, in effect, second-generation members of major commercial dynasties. The difference was that while Alfred Owen accepted the custody of his father's engineering empire, Tony Vandervell – the son of Clive Vandervell, founder of the CAV electrical concern – preferred to strike out on his own.

Meanwhile, at Ferrari, a great deal of technical consideration had gone into the V12 engine configuration. Ferrari admitted that his enthusiasm for this layout had been fired originally by the American Packard V12 engines, but there were firm practical reasons not to follow the Alfa Romeo eight-cylinder route.

The short-stroke configuration chosen by Colombo for the Tipo 125 offered potential for higher revs, and the additional advantages of a stiffer crankcase, reduced bearing loads and a lighter, lower cylinder block. Alfa Romeo's 158s were clearly the main opposition at this time, although Maserati's supercharged 4CL was regarded as the next best challenger, giving away around 50bhp to the 'Alfettas', which developed a claimed 275bhp at 7500rpm from their two-stage supercharged engines.

Talbot continued to campaign a 4.5-litre unsupercharged machine, which was definitely inferior to the Italian opposition, but fields were unpredictable in size and there was no obligation on the part of any

individual team or manufacturer to contest any particular race. In that respect, the development of Grand Prix racing was a distinctly piecemeal affair in the immediate post-war years, with race organisers getting by as best they could while being perpetually dependent on the technical readiness of the competing teams.

There were other aspirants on the F1 stage at the time, yet most appeared only fleetingly. The futuristic Cisitalia-Porsche would never start a race; the French CTA Arsenal was seen briefly in 1947 and 1948 before disappearing for good; and, as far as Britain was concerned, efforts to build a national racing car resulted in the BRM project getting off the ground, albeit shakily.

FRANCE TAKES A BACK SEAT

Of course, France had made a substantial contribution to the international motor racing scene in the pre-war years. Bugatti had won the inaugural Monaco Grand Prix in 1929, with William Grover-Williams at the wheel, and had followed up that success with a repeat victory thanks to the efforts of René Dreyfus the following year.

Dreyfus later produced one of the most startling upsets in established form at the 1938 Pau Grand

Prix, run around the splendid road circuit through the streets of the picturesque town in south-western France. Driving a 4.5-litre, naturally aspirated Delahaye against the 3-litre supercharged works Mercedes-Benz, Dreyfus took advantage of lower fuel consumption to win the race and beat Rudolf Caracciola into second place.

Forty-five years later, Dreyfus recalled, "Finally Rudi came in for fuel and got out of his car. His hip hurt, he said, he wanted Hermann Lang to take over. Rudi had suffered a bad accident five years before at Monaco, which had left him with a tender hip, but that wasn't the real reason he didn't want to finish Pau. We both knew, without ever saying it, that he just didn't want to be beaten by me."

That year also saw the Talbot company joining in, buoyed in its optimism after winning the previous year's Grand Prix de l'ACF for sports cars. Despite originally planning an ambitious 3-litre supercharged engine, Antony Lago's factory in Suresnes preferred to develop a 4.5-litre six-cylinder unit, which, as things turned out, would see racing action through to the early 1950s.

The French constructors were also very much in at the start of the post-war racing renaissance. Jean-

Pierre Wimille won the very first race to take place after hostilities had ceased in 1945, piloting the single-seater 1939 Bugatti to victory in the Liberation Grand Prix through the Bois de Boulogne in Paris.

By 1947, there were just four major international Grands Prix on the calendar. Wimille won the Swiss and Belgian races, while Count Trossi added a third success for the Alfa Romeo 158s in Italy. But Louis Chiron, 17 years after winning at Monaco in a Bugatti and as old as the century, gave Talbot a historic victory in the GP de l'ACF.

The 1947 season would see Maserati throw its hat into the ring with an uprated version of its 1939-built 4CL. Powered by a four-cylinder, single-stage supercharged, 1.5-litre four-cylinder engine, the car had been steadily developed to produce the 4CLT that year and later the 4CLT/48 – or 'San Remo' model after the memorable victory posted in its debut race by Alberto Ascari.

ASCARI BIDS FOR THE BIG TIME

Ascari would become one of the great post-war Grand Prix drivers, although his career would be ended prematurely, at the age of 37, in 1955, when he crashed fatally in a borrowed sports Ferrari during a leisurely

test session at Monza. His father was the legendary Antonio Ascari, who had been killed when his Alfa Romeo crashed during the 1926 French Grand Prix on the Montlhéry circuit near Paris.

Alberto's competition career started on motorcycles just before the Second World War, when he raced for the factory Bianchi team. He also tried his hand at car racing with the first '815' – the very first Ferrari-made car – in the 1940 Mille Miglia.

Ascari finished ninth in the 1940 Tripoli Grand Prix before the war put a stop to any further motorsporting activities. During the conflict, he managed to establish a thriving road transport business with his friend, Luigi Villoresi, hauling fuel to Mussolini's army in North Africa. This had the additional benefit of exempting him from military service. He picked up the threads of his racing career after the war with a Cisitalia, and won his first car race with a Maserati sports car at Modena on 28th September, 1947.

By that time, Ascari was married with a son and had seriously considered the idea of giving up racing altogether, but Villoresi persuaded him to continue. Together they raced under the Scuderia Ambrosiana banner through 1948 in a pair of Maserati 4CLTs; Alberto took the runner-up spot in the British Grand Prix at Silverstone.

Also in 1948, Tony Lago and his chief engineer, Carlo Marchetti, raised the tempo of the marque's challenge with the production of the new Talbot 26C, which, with 240bhp on tap, was expected to come close to challenging the rival 260bhp Maseratis. That year, Maserati and Alfa Romeo carved up the six Grands Prix equally, scoring three wins apiece. Louis Rosier drove the new Talbot at Monaco, and the team eventually managed to produce creditable fourth, fifth and sixth places in the Grand Prix de l'ACF at Reims.

That season also saw the death of the legendary Achille Varzi during wet practice for the Swiss GP at Bremgarten, his Alfa 158 toppling over at relatively modest speed after a spin. Varzi, wearing a linen helmet, did not have a chance. In addition, the race claimed the life of German driver Christian Kautz, third at Monaco in 1937 for Mercedes, when he crashed his Maserati.

The absence of Alfa Romeo in 1949 split the Formula 1 scene three ways. Baron Emmanuel de Graffenried won the British Grand Prix at Silverstone for Maserati, then Rosier triumphed in the Belgian Grand Prix at Spa-Francorchamps and Alberto Ascari's Ferrari took the Swiss Grand Prix at Berne. Chiron scored a second Talbot victory in France, while Ascari won again at Monza and Peter Whitehead's private Ferrari 125 clinched the distant Czechoslovakian Grand Prix at Brno.

It would be another 30 years before the French crowd would see their home Grand Prix won by a French driver and an all-French car. For that treat, the fans would have to wait until 1979, when Jean-Pierre Jabouille would drive to victory at Dijon-Prenois with the Renault turbo.

The 1949 season saw Ascari and Villoresi receive the pay-off for their efforts at the wheels of their private Maseratis when they were invited to join the works Ferrari team. It was then that Ascari's career really began to take off, notably when he led his old friend Villoresi to a 1-2 in the Swiss Grand Prix at Berne's spectacular Bremgarten circuit, thus achieving the Ferrari team's first international success with the 1.5-litre Tipo 125. Undeniably it was a victory made easier by the absence of Alfa Romeo from the stage, but nevertheless it was an important success.

A new face had appeared on the international motor racing stage in 1948, and it belonged to someone who eventually would break all the records and gain legendary status over the following decade. Driving a 1.4-litre Simca-Gordini, Juan Manuel Fangio made his European debut in the Coupe des Petites Cylindres at Reims on 18th July, followed by the French Grand Prix on the same day. The 37-year-old finished neither event, but he would be back in 1949 at the wheel of a Maserati 4CLT/48.

Equipped with the Maserati, which had been purchased by the Argentine Automobile Federation, Fangio won in front of his home crowd at Mar del Plata before returning to Europe, where he won again at San Remo, Pau, Perpignan, Marseilles, Monza and Albi. These successes led to an invitation to join the Alfa Romeo factory team for the 1950 season, the first year of the official World Championship for Drivers.

After that unobtrusive outing at Reims with the Simca-Gordini, Jean-Pierre Wimille invited Fangio to accompany him to the *L'Équipe* newspaper reception at which he was to be interviewed after his victory in the Grand Prix. On this occasion, the number-one driver of the Alfa Romeo team took the opportunity to introduce the new arrival from Argentina. "He is the one you'll be writing about one day," said the Frenchman to the newspaper's editor as he patted Fangio on the back. Later, he added, "If Fangio ever gets behind the wheel of a good car, he will do great things."

Wimille was killed barely six months later, ironically driving a Simca-Gordini in Buenos Aires, capital of Fangio's homeland. And the not-so-youngster from the provincial town of Balcarce would, by popular consensus, emerge as the man who took over the baton from the Frenchman as the finest driver of his era.

JEAN-PIERRE WIMILLE: FRANCE'S UNCROWNED CHAMPION

FRANCE would have to wait until 1985 before hailing its first official World Champion driver in Alain Prost. Yet in the first few seasons after the war, Jean-Pierre Wimille established himself as one of the greatest drivers of his era. Had he lived, say his fans, he would have won the first official title in 1950 instead of Giuseppe Farina.

Wimille was the son of a pioneer motoring and aviation journalist. Born in 1908, he was variously described as austere, aloof, withdrawn, stylish and deeply religious. He was accustomed to a wealthy lifestyle. Prior to the Second World War, he had raced Bugattis, starting as early as 1930, then had tried his hand with an Alfa Romeo 8C-2600 before joining the Bugatti works team, for whom he shared victory in the 1937 Le Mans 24-hour race with Robert Benoist.

During the war, Wimille had served energetically in the French resistance movement, together with his young wife, the 1938–9 ski champion Christiane de la Fressange. Their resistance group was headed by Wimille's racing colleague, Benoist, who ultimately was betrayed to the Gestapo and executed at the Buchenwald concentration camp in the closing months of the war.

Wimille was cheered generously by the crowds who flocked into the Bois de Boulogne in September 1945, where he won the Coupe des Prisonniers meeting at the wheel of his old 4.7-litre Bugatti *monoplace*. In 1946, he drove an ancient Alfa Romeo 308 Grand Prix car, in which he showed typically competitive form, and was invited to join the Alfa factory team for the Grand Prix des Nations at Geneva, where he finished third in the final. Then he took second in Turin's Valentino Park.

In 1947 and 1948, Wimille consolidated his brilliant reputation in the Alfa 158s, winning the 1947 Swiss GP at Bremgarten and the Belgian race at Spa-Francorchamps, where he topped 180mph on the Masta straight

Wimille's Alfa Romeo team-mate, Consalvo Sanesi, would remember him for a particularly symbolic gesture in the 1948 Autodrome Grand Prix at Monza, a race held to celebrate the re-opening of the famous circuit after the war. Sanesi was the test driver, a mechanic who had been promoted, and it was agreed that he would be the man to win this race.

He recalled watching in his mirrors as Wimille and his other team-mate, Count Trossi, held back, but eventually Trossi could contain himself no longer and shot past into the lead. Wimille followed him through and won, against team orders, to teach Trossi a lesson for overtaking Sanesi in the first place. "Wimille was a great man," recounted Sanesi.

On 28th January, 1949, Wimille was killed while driving one of the 1.4-litre Simca-Gordinis during an early-morning practice session for the Buenos Aires Grand Prix on the Palermo Park circuit. He was 41 years old and, ironically, wearing a crash helmet for the first time in his long career instead of a linen cap.

The start of the 1950 French GP at Reims, with the Alfa 158s of Juan Manuel Fangio (6) and Giuseppe Farina (2) surging away into the lead, chased by the rest of the pack, headed by Louis Rosier's Talbot-Lago (20), and the similar cars of Philippe Étancelin (16) and Yves Giraud-Cabantous (18).

Photo: LAT Photographic

Main photo: 13th May, 1950, the first Grand Prix counting towards the World Drivers' Championship. Fangio (1) and Fagioli (3) lead away, but Farina (2) would emerge victorious.

Inset above: Reg Parnell (left), with Farina (centre) and Fagioli took the first three places for Alfa Romeo.

Photos: LAT Photographic

THE official Drivers' World Championship began at the start of the 1950 season. The sport would have to wait until 1958, however, before the efforts of the constructors were similarly rewarded, so for the moment the men behind the wheel went into battle to sort out who was the best in the world. If not officially, then certainly mathematically.

The points system rewarded the top five finishers in each qualifying round on a sliding scale of 8-6-4-3-2, with an extra point awarded for the fastest lap. This would be amended in 1960, when an additional single point was added for sixth place and the point for fastest lap was dropped; the winner's points were increased from eight to nine in 1961. The practice of drivers being able to share points if they shared a car was abandoned after 1958.

With the exception of the introduction of an extra point for the race winner in 1991, the scoring system remained the same from 1961 until 2003, when points were awarded to the top eight finishers, the only qualification being the number of races that counted towards a driver's overall total. This has been altered and amended from time to time, as we shall see. Finally, there was another major anomaly from 1950 to 1960: the Indianapolis 500 was included as a round of the World Championship, even though the crossover between the F1 and US 'roundy-round' boys was virtually nil.

Thus it was with Alfa Romeo as the established pacesetter, Ferrari as the challenger and BRM as the no-hoper that the official World Championship began with the grandly titled Grand Prix of Europe – otherwise the British Grand Prix – at Silverstone.

This historic event enjoyed the patronage of King George VI and Queen Elizabeth, subsequently the Queen Mother, and much was made of the fact that this was the first time a reigning monarch had attended such an event. With bunting, brass bands and all the panoply of a state occasion, their Majesties were entertained by an Alfa Romeo grand slam, Giuseppe Farina winning from Luigi Fagioli second and Reg Parnell in third.

Further back, the elderly Frenchman, Yves Giraud-Cabantous, plodded on his lonely way to fourth place in a 4.5-litre Talbot – two laps behind. It was the sort of domination we would see many years later from the likes of the Honda-engined Williamses and McLarens. Except the Alfas were even more dominant, facing, as they were, decidedly makeshift opposition.

On race morning, the Alfas had been driven to Silverstone on the road from Banbury – strictly illegal, of course, but nobody cared. They managed to avoid becoming tangled up in the entry of their Majesties, who had arrived by train at the now long-defunct Brackley railway station, whence a Royal Daimler transported them to the track.

The King and Queen were duly presented to the drivers, and every aspect of their behaviour was scrutinised with good-mannered charm by William Boddy, the editor of *Motor Sport* magazine, who wrote:

Earl Howe sat between the King and Queen, and as the flag was about to fall the King looked up from his programme and eagerly down towards the starting grid. As the cars roared away, he appeared to be heavily interested, but the noise and the smoke took the Queen a trifle unawares as the mass-start of a race does to those close to the course ... Princess Margaret seemed to want to concentrate solely on what was happening, and to regard conversation as merely incidental. But this is to anticipate.

In the aftermath of the race, a Mr A.P. Bird wrote to the magazine mentioning that "the lavatory accommodation was nothing short of disgusting". Meanwhile, *Motor Sport* commented on the customary Silverstone gridlock that endures to this day:

We feel sure that those who arrived late because of traffic congestion, those who spent four hours or so getting out of the car parks, those who received the wrong passes and those honorary club marshals who had to sleep the Friday night in old tents because the RAC patrols had taken the beds in the huts, will readily concur.

Continued on page 32

GIUSEPPE FARINA: THE FIRST CHAMPION

FARINA was the first man to win the official Drivers' World Championship in 1950. He was tough and unforgiving towards his rivals out on the circuit, and his sheer reckless driving on the road – to which Fangio attested many years later – ended with his death at the wheel of a Lotus Cortina near the French town of Chambéry, a few months after his 60th birthday in 1966.

The son of one of the founders of the Farina coachbuilding dynasty, 'Nino' was born in Turin in 1906. After obtaining an engineering doctorate, he began his competition career in an Alfa Romeo 1500 in the Aosta-Grand St Bernard hillclimb. It was not an auspicious debut, ending with a broken shoulder and facial lacerations.

In 1934, Farina scored his first major victory when he drove his Maserati 4CM to victory in the 'Voiturette' race that supported the Czech Grand Prix at Brno. In 1938 and 1939, he was recruited to drive the Scuderia Ferrari Alfa 158s, and his final victory of the pre-war era came at Tripoli in 1940.

He picked up the threads of his career at the end of the war, racing his own Maserati 4CLT in 1947 and 1948. He won the 1948 Monaco Grand Prix and then rejoined the works Alfa squad in 1950, when he won the British, Swiss and Italian Grands Prix to beat team-mate Fangio to the first drivers' title.

In 1951, he won a single victory in the Belgian GP and then he switched to Ferrari, where he stayed to the end of his career in 1955, a season during which he drove only a handful of races after battling the after-effects of burns suffered in the previous year's Mille Miglia – an event in which he crashed again during his final season.

In 1956 and 1957, Farina made a couple of halfhearted attempts on the Indianapolis 500, and later he became a Jaguar importer for Italy before becoming a main agent for Alfa Romeo, the marque with which he had managed to achieve such great success.

Farina was popularly credited with having pioneered the 'arms-stretched' driving style so favoured by Stirling Moss. He was also regarded by more than a few as a ruthless and uncompromising driver, whose aggressive style would have been more at home in the 1990s than the 1950s.

BRM'S RIGHT ROYAL EMBARRASSMENT

In an embarrassing and rather contrived footnote, the BRM – still unready to race – was demonstrated for a few laps in front of the Royal Family. Still, at least it turned up, which is more than could be said of the Ferrari team. But Maranello was regrouping, laying a firm F1 footing for the future, which meant developing a naturally aspirated machine in addition to its 1.5-litre supercharged V12s, which were being driven by Ascari and Villoresi.

Ferrari engineer Aurelio Lampredi was pressing on with the development of a 4.5-litre non-supercharged engine, reflecting the fact that it would be quite possible to beat the Alfas by the simple expedient of making fewer refuelling stops.

Meanwhile, Alfa had the stage to itself. Fangio won at Monaco, Spa and Reims, with Farina adding triumphs at Monza and Bremgarten to his Silverstone victory. Thus the granite-like Farina became the first official World Champion driver with 30 points, ahead of Fangio (27) and Fagioli (24). Four out of the seven races counted towards his title.

The 1951 season would mark the gloriously memorable swansong of the Alfa straight-eights, which were now heavily revised and designated Tipo 159s. Their power output had been boosted to a remarkable 404bhp at 9500rpm, more than twice the claimed 190bhp with which they had reputedly competed before the war.

However, there was a distinct downside to this performance increase. The Alfas' consumption of alcohol laced fuel was down to a punishing 1.5 miles per gallon, which meant that the 70-gallon fuel load represented almost one-fifth of the car's all-up weight on the Grand Prix starting grid.

Alfa and Ferrari stalked each other in the pre-season non-championship races at the start of 1951, avoiding any direct confrontation. Ascari's new 4.5-litre Ferrari 375 won at Syracuse, Pau and San Remo, but Alfa's record remained intact when it came to the Swiss Grand Prix at Berne. Fangio won immaculately in pouring rain, but Piero Taruffi's Ferrari took second.

Ferrari consolidated its challenge in the French Grand Prix at Reims, a race extended to 77 laps – 374.9 miles – which evened up the balance between the two Italian teams by ensuring that the Ferraris would have to stop at least once. Taruffi was unwell and his place in the Ferrari squad, alongside Ascari and Villoresi, was taken by the tubby, but immensely tough, Argentine driver José Froilán González.

Despite his build, González had proved himself to be a well-rounded athlete from a young age. A first-rate swimmer, a crack shot and an accomplished cyclist, he had started motor racing in rough-and-ready open road races like his compatriot, Fangio. His father set him up in the trucking business, and by 1949 he was ready to join Fangio on their first European tour together.

After an undistinguished first couple of seasons, González had made his name in Buenos Aires at the start of the 1951 campaign. Mercedes-Benz had dusted down a trio of pre-war, two-stage supercharged W163s and shipped them to Argentina for a couple of high-profile Formule Libre races. But González had trounced them all in both events, driving a supercharged 2-litre Ferrari 166. This was his passport to the works Ferrari squad.

In the event, at Reims in 1951, Ascari had to take over González's Ferrari 375 after his own suffered a gearbox failure, and he finished second behind Fangio's victorious Alfa. There was a fascinating footnote to this race. Enzo Ferrari had actually approached the 21-year-old British rising star, Stirling Moss, to drive at Reims. However, the telegram inviting him to do so had arrived at the Moss family home at Tring, in Hertfordshire, after Moss had left for Berlin's Avus circuit, where he was scheduled to race his underpowered HWM.

Moss's manager, Ken Gregory, knew that Stirling was in Berlin, but he didn't know where. In desperation, he telephoned the British consul in the German city, getting him out of bed at some ungodly hour. The diplomat eventually managed to find Moss and give him the message.

Stirling was enormously flattered, but felt that he had to decline due to his commitment to the HWM team. That said, most believe that HWM team chief John Heath would have released him from his commitment. It says much for Moss's sense of obligation

that he did not bother even to ask to be released.

Another non-starter at Reims was the elusive BRM, prompting *Autosport* editor Gregor Grant to write in the issue of 6th July: "The failure of the BRM to come to the line at Rheims (sic) was a bitter disappointment to its thousands of well wishers.

"In the opinion of many people D-day for the BRM is 14 July. If the car fails to appear at Silverstone for the British Grand Prix, there is grave danger that the not inconsiderable amount of support gained for the venture will dwindle to such an extent that it will vanish – for evermore!"

The BRM's failure to appear at Reims was also symptomatic of the difficulties presented to race organisers by the haphazard nature of the F1 business. No promoter could be certain from one week to the next who would turn up for which event.

With that in mind, it's perhaps worth noting that on the same day that Fangio won at Reims, a 21-year-old was competing in the 500cc F3 race at the old Boreham airfield in Essex. In the first heat, he diced wheel-to-wheel with future Ferrari Grand Prix winner

Above: Fangio, having taken over Fagioli's sister Alfa (8), heads for victory in the 1951 French GP at Reims. He is seen here rounding the Thillois right-hander, ahead of the Talbot-Lago of Eugène Chaboud.

Left: Reg Parnell drove Tony Vandervell's 'Thinwall Ferrari Special' to fifth place at Reims, planting the seeds that would lead to Vanwall success later that decade.

Photos: LAT Photographic

33

Peter Collins, only losing the lead on the last lap. In the final, he finished third behind Eric Brandon and Alan Brown. His name was Bernard Ecclestone.

PRANCING HORSE AND THE PAMPAS BULL

Finally, at the bleak airfield wasteland of Silverstone, Ferrari made history on 14th July, 1951. González was still in the team for the British Grand Prix and, despite the fact that he was only allocated one of the earlier 1950 12-plug-specification 375s, he stormed around to take pole by over a second from Fangio's Alfa.

The big and heavy Alfa 159s found the relatively short straights at Silverstone insufficient for them to become fully wound up. It's funny how perceptions change – today, even with several extra corners, Silverstone is regarded as a relatively high-speed track.

González consolidated his place at the front of the field, but then Fangio began to come back at him. Ferrari and Alfa Romeo were amazingly closely matched on this occasion and, although Fangio got ahead, González – "a fat, dark little man, bare arms at full length" – clawed his way on to the Alfa's tail and re-took the lead on lap 48.

González went on to score a commanding victory, breaking the mould of contemporary Grand Prix racing for good. Enzo Ferrari sent an emotional telegram to Alfa Romeo's managing director, saying, "I still feel for our Alfa the adolescent tenderness of first love." What an old actor manager he was!

Thankfully for British fans, the BRM V16s duly made their appearance. Reg Parnell finished fifth, Peter Walker seventh "suffering intense agony from burns in the latter part of the race. No praise can be enough for their unforgettable performance."

The effusive *Autosport* editorial was supplemented by the words of its technical editor, John Bolster, also a BBC commentator. He wrote: "In conclusion, I would like to thank Reg Parnell for consenting to give me a broadcast interview when he was in great pain from his burns."

Another interesting footnote. The British GP supporting F3 final was won in commanding style by Stirling Moss. Into tenth place came B.C. Ecclestone. Nearly 60 years later, anybody wanting a broadcast interview with any F1 driver would have to go through Mr Ecclestone's Formula One Administration empire. The consent of the driver concerned would be neither here nor there!

Ferrari could now sense a realistic possibility of actually winning that year's World Championship, a prospect further enhanced by Ascari's dominant victory in the first post-war championship German GP, held at the Nürburgring. Having been defeated by Ferrari twice, Alfa Romeo was very definitely on the run. Ascari and González scored another 1-2 at Monza, where five Tipo 375s were ranged against the supercharged challengers from Milan.

A single round of the World Championship remained, the race scheduled for Barcelona on 20th October. Somewhat questionably, given what was at stake, Ferrari decided to experiment with Pirelli tyre

sizes for this crucial event, and the decision to employ smaller 16in-diameter tyres, rather than the 17in covers used previously, caused the 375s to start throwing treads once the race began.

Thus Fangio won the race for Alfa Romeo, with the gallant González second – and Ferrari had missed out on his first title crown. With four out of his eight scores counting, Fangio took the first of his five titles with 31 points (net), ahead of Ascari on 25 and González on 24.

ALFA QUITS, F1 TOTTERS

At the end of the season, Alfa Romeo withdrew from racing after failing to secure any financial support from the Italian government. This left race organisers across Europe in an acutely nervous frame of mind, wondering how many fully fledged F1 cars would actually be ready for the start of the 1952 season.

The answer was expected to come at the Turin Grand Prix on 6th April, where it was optimistically believed that the BRM team, which had spent much time over the winter testing at Monza, would attend to offer Ferrari some worthwhile opposition. Yet BRM withdrew at the last moment.

It had been the story of the BRM's life ever since the start of the official World Championship. Never good enough to go head-to-head with Alfa and Ferrari, the BRM spent much of its career in minor-league club races. Take the rain soaked Goodwood meeting in September 1950 as an example. The car was entered for Reg Parnell to drive, and you would be forgiven for imagining that the crowd would have dismissed its appearance with derisive laughter. Far from it.

There was admirably little scepticism among race fans in those days, and the sodden crowds cheered stoically as Parnell won the Woodcote Cup race by 13 seconds from Prince Bira's Maserati.

Supporting the BRM, and its originator, Raymond Mays, was regarded as a matter of faith by some sections of the media, and those who even hinted that the whole thing was a disgraceful failure were regarded rather sniffily as being unpatriotic. It was certainly a sign of the times that Movietone News devoted a considerable amount of coverage to Parnell's Goodwood success in the dank conditions.

Yet if the Goodwood crowds had really longed for a taste of sophisticated international competition, they certainly got it in 1951 when the September international meeting saw reigning World Champion Giuseppe Farina turn out to drive one of the legendary supercharged 1.5-litre Alfa Romeo 159s. Against makeweight opposition, it was not surprising that Farina won all three of his races that afternoon, duly receiving the *Daily Graphic* trophy from the Duchess of Richmond and Gordon.

The BRM's failure to perform on an international stage could be viewed as the last straw for motor racing's governing body, the Commission Sportive Internationale (CSI), the sporting arm of the FIA. The decision was taken to hold the official 1952 and 1953 World Championships under the 2-litre Formula 2 regulations, leaving Ferrari's Tipo 375s, along with the supercharged BRMs, to justify their existence with outings in a handful of non-championship F1 events.

In October 1952, the paddock at Goodwood echoed to the raucous crackle of BRM V16 engines yet again

Continued on page 38

Above: Ascari gives the Ferrari T375 V12 its final victory at Monza.

Left: The Alfa team drivers at Monza, 1951. From left: Fangio, Farina, Bonetto sucking on his briar, and de Graffenried

Photos: LAT Photographic

35

RACING FOR BRITAIN: THE BRM

THE passion displayed by Raymond Mays for the ERA project in the 1930s found fresh focus in the post-war years with his plan to design and build a state-of-the-art British national Grand Prix car to carry the prestige of British industry to the international race tracks of the world.

Taken at face value, this was an admirable ambition. Yet the BRM project would be dogged by chaotic management, inept engineering and poor quality control almost from the word go. It may have been an idea that captured the imagination of the public, but its actual execution left a great deal to be desired. The concept was just too complicated for the technology available.

Mays persuaded leading figures in British industry to form the British Motor Racing Research Trust, tasked not only with funding the BRM, but also helping with the sourcing of high-technology components and manufacturing techniques.

The 1.5-litre, centrifugally supercharged BRM V16 was an ambitious project indeed. Demonstrated at the 1950 British Grand Prix, the car suffered the embarrassment of breaking its drive shafts on the starting grid for that year's International Trophy race, much to the resigned dismay of its driver, the great Raymond Sommer – and, remarkably, it only finished in the World Championship points once, when Reg Parnell was placed fifth in the 1951 British GP.

Towards the end of 1951, rising star Stirling Moss drove the V16 and, while impressed with the raw power, identified a huge number of shortcomings.

In 1987, Moss would tell author and historian Doug Nye: "It was a classic example of a small concern convincing itself it was Mercedes-Benz and going into the high-technology racing car business deeper than either its competence or finances would allow."

While conceding that the BRM engine was a "fantastic device", he was less complimentary about other aspects of the car.

"Its chassis and suspension design was not really capable of putting its power through to the ground," he said. "Its steering was simply dreadful and its cramped-up, short-arm driving position was straight out of the ark… [and] its management was a shambles."

In failing to turn out for the 1952 Turin Grand Prix, despite an intensive programme of winter testing at Monza, the BRM management effectively scuppered the 4.5-litre/1.5-litre supercharged F1 regulations. It was also a massive own-goal. The star-struck Raymond Mays was more interested in letting Fangio test the car on an airfield in Lincolnshire than in racing in Turin. That was the story of BRM's life up to that point.

The BMRR Trust was unwieldy and difficult to steer. By the end of 1950, a big effort had been made to trim its membership and an executive council had been established, which consisted of Tony Vandervell, Alfred Owen and Bernard Scott of Lucas, in addition to Raymond Mays and Peter Berthon. Soon afterwards, Vandervell walked out to start his own F1 project. Eventually the entire BRM programme was purchased by the Owen Organisation under its patriarchal chairman, Alfred Owen.

It would take another decade, but eventually BRM would win the World Championship. That it survived at all was down to Alfred Owen's commitment, loyalty and extraordinarily patient way with people.

The Owen Organisation was one of the country's most diverse and wide-ranging engineering conglomerates. It had been founded by Alfred Owen's hard-working and diligent father, Ernest, in partnership with J.T. Rubery, in 1893, and the group's headquarters were established at Darlaston in Shropshire.

Ernest Owen died at the relatively early age of 61, leaving a fortune in excess of £1 million, which, thanks to some shrewd and careful financial husbandry, enabled the group he had founded to ride out the economic slump that followed on the heels of the First World War. This ensured that his sons, Ernest and Alfred, and his daughter, Jean, would inherit a thriving industrial empire.

Jean and her husband, Louis Stanley, would later run BRM after Alfred Owen was sidelined due to the effects of a stroke in 1969. Stanley was a larger-than-life personality who was no fool. Among his many observations in connection with the motor racing team, he once said that "had the BRM project coincided with his [Ernest Owen Senior's] heyday, success would have come twice as quickly at half the price."

Far left: **Reg Parnell wrestled the BRM V16 to fifth place in the 1951 British GP, finishing the race with badly burnt feet due to inadequate cockpit ventilation.**

Left: **Sir Alfred Owen, the saviour and bankroller of BRM, who kept alive Raymond Mays's early dream.**

Below: **Reg Parnell makes a refuelling stop in the vulnerable Silverstone pits. It would be more than another decade before the pit lane was separated from the track proper.**

Below right: **Fangio driving the BRM V16 in a Goodwood sprint race in 1953, the absence of a proper F1 series forcing the cars to eke out a twilight existence in such minor-league events.**

Photos: LAT Photographic

THE SAVIOUR OF THE BRM

ALFRED Owen inherited his father's astuteness and enthusiasm, but also was a kind and warm-hearted man. Perhaps he indulged his employees too much, and that was why it took until 1962 for BRM to win the World Championship with Graham Hill.

In fact, by the start of that season, even Alfred's patience was wearing thin. He informed the team management that unless they won at least two Grands Prix in 1962, they would be closed down. Hill duly obliged with a first win in the Dutch Grand Prix at Zandvoort, scene of Jo Bonnier's first ever BRM victory three years earlier, after which designer Tony Rudd felt sufficiently confident about the future to pen a note to Alfred raising the subject of plans for 1963.

Back came a letter reminding Rudd that his chairman had meant what he said. Subsequently Hill ensured the team's future with wins at the German Grand Prix at the Nürburgring and the South African race at East London, where he clinched the title.

Thus was Alfred Owen's confidence and support for BRM vindicated at long last. Louis Stanley would later write, "He showed unbelievable patience, sometimes to the point of weakness, and there were occasions where stern actions would have produced results. But he was reluctant to upset the ties of friendship."

Reg Parnell's son, Tim, who rose to take over the job of BRM team manager in 1969, described Alfred as "quite the most amazing and remarkable man I have ever met in my life."

He continued, "He was the chairman of over 1000 subsidiary companies all round the world, yet he also found time to be a committed Methodist lay preacher and a great family man, and worked on many public boards and charities such as Dr Barnardo's and the YMCA. The list was incredible.

"He had an army of secretaries keeping tabs on his appointments and work programme, which used up every minute of his day. People talk about workload, but, my goodness, he was absolutely unbelievable. He was an extremely nice man and, of course, my family knew him well from the time my father drove for the team.

"Then in the mid-1960s I managed the BRM Tasman team for three consecutive years and Reg Parnell Racing ran what was effectively a 'B' team for the BRM factory with people like Richard Attwood, Piers Courage, Mike Spence and Chris Irwin driving. But if I ever had to see Sir Alfred on business, it was usually a few moments squeezed into the back of a taxi while he was en route between board meetings…"

Sir Alfred Owen died on 29th October, 1975. That meant he was spared the embarrassing death throes of the BRM team a couple of seasons later. Yet without his foresight and determination, a whole chapter of British motor racing history would have ended in 1952. And the BRM would have been nothing more than a brief footnote in post-war F1 history.

as the *Daily Graphic* International meeting was held for a mixed bag of Formula 1 cars.

The tubby Argentine driver, José Froilán González, a great favourite with British fans since scoring Ferrari's first ever World Championship Grand Prix victory at Silverstone the previous year, won both the Woodcote Cup and the Goodwood Trophy, heading the sister BRMs of Reg Parnell and Ken Wharton across the line in the latter event.

"It was most impressive, but hardly epoch-making," noted *Autosport* founder-editor Gregor Grant, referring to the fact that the BRMs were now redundant.

FERRARI'S LONG-TERM PLANNING

Ferrari, of course, had been prepared for every eventuality. Not only had he developed his Grand Prix cars assiduously, but also in the 1951 non-championship Bari Grand Prix, Piero Taruffi had appeared behind the wheel of a 2490cc four-cylinder Ferrari. This was followed by a 2-litre version in time for the Modena Grand Prix, so it was clear that the *Commendatore* had things covered for the F2 World Championships in 1952 and 1953, as well as having an engine that he could use for the planned 2.5-litre F1 regulations, which would take effect at the start of 1954.

Aurelio Lampredi was the man behind these large-capacity four-cylinder engines. Although he knew they would have a longer stroke and a bigger piston area than a corresponding V12, he was more concerned about better torque characteristics and the overall lightness of the unit. In his estimation, a reduction in total engine weight from 400 to 348lb would equate to an increase in power-to-weight ratio of around 15 per cent.

This new Ferrari was dubbed the Tipo 500, reflecting its individual cylinder capacity. It would give ster-

ling service across two action-packed international seasons, during which the list of non-championship races it contested would far exceed the World Championship qualifying rounds. It would also represent the heyday of the brilliant Alberto Ascari, who competed in far more races than simply the title qualifiers.

Ranged against the Ferraris in 1952 were the new Colombo designed six-cylinder Maserati A6GCMs, to be driven by Fangio, González and Felice Bonetto, plus the six-cylinder French Gordinis handled by Robert Manzon and Jean Behra.

Four major non-title races took place on the European calendar prior to the Swiss GP at Bremgarten, which opened the World Championship contest. Three of these events fell to Ascari. The brilliant Italian headed a Maranello 1-2-3 at Syracuse, ahead of Taruffi and Farina, while at Pau he led French privateer Louis Rosier's Ferrari across the finishing line.

Next up, Ascari survived to win the Marseilles GP on the Parc Borély circuit, a race notable for Farina's reluctance to acknowledge Ascari's status as team leader. Only when Farina spun off shortly before the finish, lightly damaging his car against the straw bales, could Ascari be certain of victory.

The Swiss Grand Prix saw another works Ferrari demonstration, with Farina, Taruffi and André Simon on the driving strength, as Ascari was away at Indianapolis and Villoresi was convalescing following a road accident. Farina led initially before being sidelined by magneto failure, after which Taruffi had a relatively easy run to victory.

On 8th June, the works 500s appeared at the Autodrome Grand Prix at Monza, sporting a small number of detail improvements, including revised inlet trumpets and a longer nose section. This race also saw the debut of the new Maseratis, driven by Fangio, González and Bonetto, but Ferrari's rivals received a

Opposite: **Formula Two hopefuls at the 1952 Swiss Grand Prix held at the daunting Bremgarten circuit near Berne. Alan Brown (Cooper T20-Bristol) leads Stirling Moss (HWM 52-Alta), Emmanuel de Graffenried (Maserati 4CLT/48-Plate), and George Abecassis and Peter Collins in their HWM 52-Altas.**
Photo: LAT Photographic

Below: **The Siamese driver Prince Birabongse raced under the pseudonym 'B. Bira' and continued as a popular competitor into the 1950s, having first raced at Brooklands before the war.**
Photo: Bernard Cahier

shattering setback in the first of the event's two 35-lap heats. On the previous day, the reigning World Champion had competed in the Ulster Trophy at Dundrod with the largely redundant V16 BRM, then had missed a lift in Prince Bira's aeroplane and been forced into a gruelling overnight drive from Paris to Monza to compete with the Maserati.

Exhausted, Fangio started from the back of the grid without having practised, then crashed badly on the second lap. He fractured a vertebra in his neck and was invalided out for the rest of the season. His next Grand Prix success would not occur until Monza the following year, when he dodged through a last-corner pile-up to win the Italian GP for Maserati.

The 1952 season also saw the French Gordini marque deliver a rare knock-out blow to Ferrari in the non-title Reims Grand Prix. In the hands of Behra, the blue car out-ran Ascari in highly impressive style, the Italian eventually being forced into the pits with overheating problems after slipstreaming the French machine too closely.

Inevitably, many detractors were quick to suggest that Behra might have been using an engine of larger capacity than the regulation 2 litres. Perish the thought! Farina finished second, while Ascari sprinted back to third after taking over Villoresi's car.

Ascari won the 1952 Drivers' World Championship with 36 points (net), 12 ahead of Farina. The four best scores from the eight races (including Indianapolis) counted. He went on to retain the title the following year with 34.5 points (net), ahead of Fangio on 27.5. A race in Argentina was added to the calendar, but again only the four best scores counted. However, the real point about Ascari was the fact that he won nine straight Grandes Épreuves between the 1952 and 1953 Belgian Grands Prix. It was quite an achievement.

MOSS AND HAWTHORN: FLYING THE FLAG FOR BRITAIN

British drivers began to appear with distinction on the World Championship stage at this time. The most famous were Stirling Moss and Mike Hawthorn, who carved their respective paths to the upper echelons of motor sport by two distinctly different routes.

Stirling's father, Alfred, was a prosperous dentist and had raced at Indianapolis as a keen amateur in 1925, while Hawthorn's father, Leslie, had moved from Yorkshire to Farnham, where he bought a car repair and sales business, in the 1930s to be closer to Brooklands for his motorcycle racing.

Moss started racing in 1948, rising to prominence thanks to his exploits in the closely contested 500cc F3 category. Hawthorn started two years later, driving a couple of Riley sports cars owned by his father. Mike hit the headlines in 1952 when a family friend bought

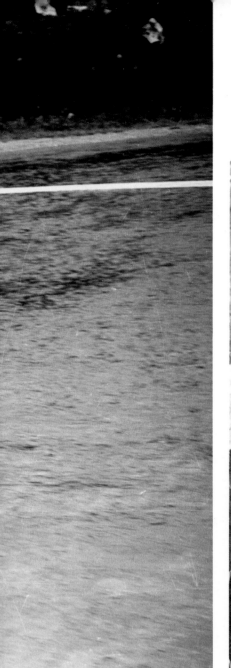

Left: No mod-cons. Alberto Ascari washes away the grime after his win in the 1952 British Grand Prix at Silverstone.

Below: Mike Hawthorn put his name on the map as an emergent talent by finishing fourth in the 1952 Belgian GP in this Cooper-Bristol.

Photos: LAT Photographic

Below: **Jean Behra demonstrated his fighting spirit with some great drives in the little F2 Gordini.**
Photo: Bernard Cahier

him a Cooper-Bristol F2 car. It was his passport to the 'big time'.

Mike rocked the establishment on its heels by planting his Cooper-Bristol on the front row of the grid for the first World Championship Dutch GP to be held at Zandvoort. There was no way he could stay with the Ferraris once the race started, however, even on what was regarded as a medium-speed circuit at the time, but he finished in fourth place, just as he had done earlier in Belgium.

Before the end of the 1952 season, Ferrari invited Hawthorn for a test drive. This was scheduled to take the shape of an entry in the non-championship Modena Grand Prix, but Mike rather blotted his copybook by rolling his Cooper-Bristol – which had been brought along for fellow-Brit Roy Salvadori to drive – during an unplanned test run. However, Enzo Ferrari had been won over as much by Mike's open, easy-going personality as by his talent at the wheel and made it clear that this little incident would not stand between him and a full-time Ferrari Grand Prix drive.

For the 1953 season, the Ferrari 500's power output was boosted to around 180bhp. Hawthorn had a shaky start to the year, and Ascari again did the lion's share of the winning. Mike's great day finally came in the 1953 French GP at Reims, although he and the rest of the Ferrari team very nearly failed to start at all.

The Grand Prix was preceded by a 12-hour sports car race, from which the 4.5-litre Ferrari of Umberto Maglioli and Piero Carini was withdrawn after the

organisers announced that no more times would be recorded for it following an apparent rule infringement. Enzo Ferrari responded by threatening to withdraw his cars from the Grand Prix, but the cracks arising from this dispute were eventually papered over and the Ferrari 500s duly took up their positions on the grid.

José Froilán González set a cracking pace in the opening stages of the race, but he was running a light fuel load and would have to stop for a top-up. Fangio and Hawthorn were wheel-to-wheel for second place, and when González duly made his scheduled stop after 30 laps, he just failed to resume ahead of the battling duo.

From then on, it was a straight fight between the Argentine driver and the young Englishman, each crouched low behind his windscreen, almost willing the last ounce of speed from his car. It was clear that the issue would only be sorted out on the final lap, and Hawthorn timed everything perfectly, slipping through on the inside of the final corner as Fangio briefly struggled to select a gear. Hawthorn duly won what *Autosport* magazine billed as "the race of the century" by just a single second.

It is fair to say that the Reims win was the making of Hawthorn, but he had to live on that reputation for much of his career. F1 success would come his way infrequently. In fact, his six-year Grand Prix career netted only three victories, including just one – in the

Above: **Replete with bow tie and blouson jacket, Mike Hawthorn after his epic win at Reims.**
Photo: Bernard Cahier

Left: **Mike Hawthorn's Ferrari wheel to wheel with the Maserati of Juan Manuel Fangio as they battle for the lead of the 1953 French GP at Reims, a race in which the Englishman memorably triumphed.**
Photo: LAT Photographic

Continued on page 46

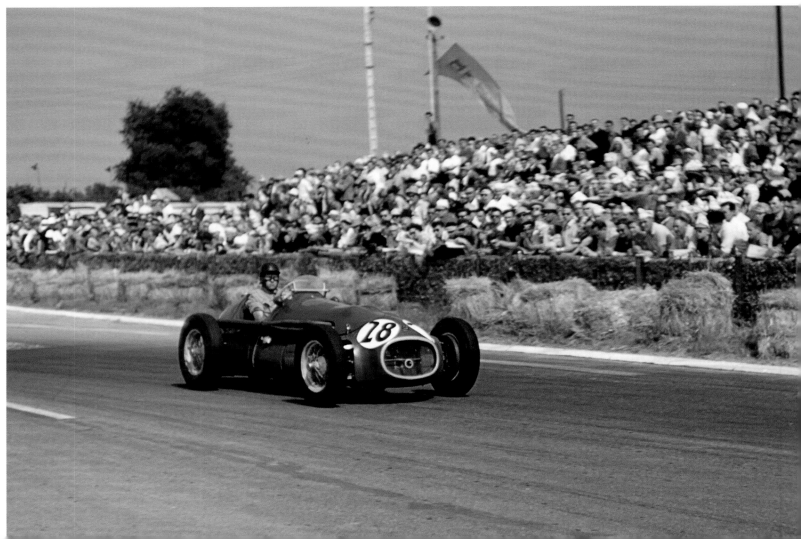

Bernard Cahier used a roll of Koda-chrome to capture the colour of a hot and sunny French Grand Prix at Reims in July 1953.

Left: A charging Froilán González rounds Thillois hairpin in his third-placed Maserati A6GCM.

Below: A relaxed Stirling Moss aboard the Cooper-Alta.
Photos: Bernard Cahier

Above: Maurice Trintignant on the pit straight with his Gordini T16.

Left: Peter Colllins had his sleeves rolled up for a long race in the HWM-Alta. He would end up eight laps down on the winner.
Photos: Bernard Cahier

1958 French Grand Prix – during his World Championship year.

Incidentally, Hawthorn's 1958 World Championship success would prompt Vanwall driver Tony Brooks to remark – many years later – that he "never felt quite the same about the World Championship scoring system, given that in 1958 Stirling [Moss] won four races, I won three and Mike won one – and the championship!" Many people could understand his point.

Moss, meanwhile, graduated to F1 via HWM, a determined, grossly underfinanced team that was run by John Heath and George Abecassis from their business, HW Motors, in Walton-on-Thames. In 1950, Moss first drove their dual sports/single-seater car, fitted with an underpowered 2-litre Alta engine, which developed around 140bhp at 5500rpm. With these cars, he raced across the Continent in a wide variety of events, allowing him to get to grips with road racing in the raw, rather than simply chasing around the straw bales on abandoned aerodromes, which was very much the style of racing available to post-war British competitors.

That year, Moss was fortunate to survive a big shunt at Naples, when a brush with a slower car burst one of the HWM's tyres. In the ensuing accident, Stirling broke his knee and lost two teeth, but he still had sufficient wit to leap from the car as best he could at the first opportunity.

In 1951, HWM produced a pukka F2 car, which Stirling used to take part in his first World Championship GP at Bremgarten; he contested the same race the following year, followed by the Belgian, British and Dutch races, with an uncompetitive ERA. Then he had two outings in a Connaught and three in a Cooper-Alta in 1953, before getting his big break with a private Maserati 250F in 1954.

Of course, the most celebrated British Formula 1 effort of the 1950s would eventually gel in the form of

Tony Vandervell's magnificent Vanwalls, which would win the first official Constructors' World Championship in 1958. The BRM struggled on, however, dogged by management and technical problems, only to come to full flower after the 2.5-litre era had come to an end. Yet there was another important British F1 project in the mid-1950s, which achieved a remarkable amount with very limited resources.

CONNNAUGHT'S DRIVING AMBITION

The Connaught grew from modest roots shortly after the war, when Rodney Clarke set up business in a small garage on the Portsmouth Road at Send, a few miles from Guildford. At that time, his speciality was the preparation of Bugattis, which brought him into contact with Kenneth McAlpine, heir to the construction family.

McAlpine was a keen amateur competitor at the wheel of a Maserati, but he was anxious to expand his involvement in the sport and asked Clarke whether he would be interested in building him a car. Clarke agreed to the proposal and came up with the design for a two-seater sports car using a 1.7-litre Lea Francis engine, which developed 98bhp at 5500rpm. The Connaught L3 put the company's name on the map, and a total of 24 such cars had been built by the end of 1953. But Clarke and McAlpine quickly developed a taste for more ambitious projects, producing their first Formula 2 Connaught 2-litre as early as 1950; it made its race debut at the Castle Combe meeting in October that year, McAlpine finishing a strong second in one of the ten-lap events behind rising star Stirling Moss in an HWM.

Although the main purpose of Connaught Engineering was to provide Kenneth McAlpine with racing cars – reasonable enough, since he had underwritten the whole project – it was also intended to produce

Above: **Fangio, hard at work in the winning Maserati, leads the Ferraris of Ascari and Farina.**

Right: **Ascari celebrates on the podium once more, after winning at Bremgarten in 1953.**
Photos: Bernard Cahier

Left: **Wealthy amateur Dennis Poore with his Connaught A-type in the 1952 British GP at Silverstone.**
Photo: LAT Photographic

Formula 2 cars for sale to private owners. In 1951, a total of nine such cars were sold. Over the next couple of seasons, the Connaughts tended to have their racing activities confined to British domestic events, while the rival HWMs and Cooper-Bristols were raced abroad.

In 1952 and 1953, of course, the World Championship was staged for 2-litre Formula 2 cars, and in the 1952 British Grand Prix at Silverstone, privateer Dennis Poore's Connaught at one point held down third place behind the Ferrari 500s of Alberto Ascari and Piero Taruffi. Unfortunately, the need for an extra pit stop dropped Poore back to fourth place, behind Mike Hawthorn's Cooper-Bristol, but the press gave favourable mention to the Connaught as a credible rival to both the Cooper-Bristols and the HWM team, which at that time also enjoyed the services of another rising star in Peter Collins.

The early 1950s were certainly a hectic and busy time for the young British drivers. Moss was invited to drive a Ferrari, at Bari in 1951, where he was due to appear in the 2.5-litre-engined Tipo 500, which was effectively a technical rehearsal for the 1954 F1 World Championship regulations. Unfortunately, after making the trip, Moss found that he had been replaced without warning by Taruffi. Stirling was furious and never seriously spoke to Ferrari again for ten years.

CHAPTER FOUR: 1954–60
THE 2.5-LITRE FORMULA

THE start of the 1954 season brought with it the new 2.5-litre F1 regulations, which opened the doors to one of the most fascinating and diverse periods in Grand Prix racing history. By the time the formula came to an end after the final race of 1960, the sport's senior category would have been revolutionised.

Of the front-running teams in existence at the start of 1954, only Ferrari would endure to the end of this period. Maserati, Mercedes-Benz, Vanwall, Connaught and Gordini would bow off the stage, to be replaced by the likes of Cooper and Lotus, who would usher in the mid-engined revolution.

On the face of it, Ferrari started the new era in a very strong position, having tested its new 2.5-litre four-cylinder engine for more than two years. With a driver line-up of Hawthorn, Farina, González (back from Maserati) and Maglioli, the team initially relied on its 1953 Tipo 500 chassis powered by the new 94 x 90mm engine derived directly from its F2 unit. This evolutionary design was dubbed the 625, and the team also had a totally new machine, the 553 'Squalo' with distinctive side tanks, but this would not make its debut until the Syracuse GP in Sicily during April.

However, there were definitely worries on the horizon for the Ferrari team, in the form of the planned return to F1 by Mercedes-Benz and the much-anticipated Lancia Grand Prix effort. As if those prospects were not enough, Fangio, who had been signed to lead the Mercedes team, was loaned to Maserati for the opening race of the year and duly won the Argentine Grand Prix.

FANGIO SWITCHES HORSES MIDSTREAM

Fangio's mount on that occasion was the elegant Maserati 250F. If any car came to represent the 2.5-litre Grand Prix formula, it was surely this well-balanced and versatile machine, which carried the Trident of Bologna – the Italian city's emblem – as its badge. Never mind the fact that in the late 1930s, the company had been taken over by Adolfo Orsi and moved to Modena. The name, image and reputation survived this reorganisation. The surviving Maserati brothers – Ernesto, Bindo and Ettore – were retained as designers and engineers until 1947, when they left to start their own new company, OSCA, back in Bologna.

Under the stewardship of Adolfo Orsi's son, Omer, Maserati thrived into the 1950s. The 250F was a direct descendant of the A6GCM in which Fangio had dodged through to win the 1953 Italian Grand Prix at Monza. Its six-cylinder engine had a bore and stroke of 84 x 75mm and, running on a mix of methanol and benzol, developed 240bhp at 7400rpm.

Fangio used the works 250F to win the 1954 Belgian GP at Spa-Francorchamps, ahead of Maurice Trintignant's Ferrari 500 and the private Maserati 250F driven by Stirling Moss. When Mercedes had announced its return to F1 for the 1954 season, Moss's manager had contacted the German company's racing manager, Alfred Neubauer, to see if there was any chance of securing Stirling a drive alongside Fangio.

Neubauer wisely replied that Moss should get some experience in a really powerful F1 car, with the result that his father, Alfred, agreed to purchase a Maserati

Opening spread: **The sensational Mercedes W196 streamliners of Juan Manuel Fangio and Karl Kling on the front row of the grid for the 1954 French GP at Reims. Double World Champion Alberto Ascari, guesting in a Maserati 250F, completes the front row, doubtless wishing his Lancia D50 was ready.**

Opposite: **Variations on a winning theme. Fangio (top) on his way to a convincing and decisive win in the 1954 French GP in the streamlined Mercedes W196; (bottom) Juan Manuel in the more conventional open-wheeler, winning the Swiss GP at Bremgarten.**

Below: **Alfred Neubauer was a tough racing manager for Mercedes, but he had a keen sense of humour and an irreverent streak!**

Photos: Bernard Cahier

Right: **At the 1954 French GP meeting, the popular Onofré Marimón offers a cooling drink to Prince Bira, while Mercedes drivers Fangio and Kling look on indulgently.**
Photo: Bernard Cahier

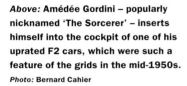

Above: **Amédée Gordini – popularly nicknamed 'The Sorcerer' – inserts himself into the cockpit of one of his uprated F2 cars, which were such a feature of the grids in the mid-1950s.**
Photo: Bernard Cahier

250F with the aid of sponsorship from the Shell Mex & BP fuel and lubricants firm, for whom Stirling was contracted to drive.

After the Belgian race, Maserati found itself short of top-calibre drivers now that Fangio was due to make his debut for the emergent Mercedes-Benz team in the French GP at Reims, round three of the World Championship. Maserati was impressed by Moss's progress, however, and began to offer tacit factory support, suggesting that he could rev his car up to 8000rpm and if the engine broke, it would be replaced free of charge.

This was a fantastic offer for the English privateer, who, up to then, had been driving with something in reserve. Later in the season, Moss would become an official factory entry with his private car, being promoted to number-one driver on the understanding that, if his own 250F was not ready on schedule for any race, he would be loaned a works car.

Moss made full use of this unexpected promotion, and although he failed to score any victories, he was well in charge of the Italian Grand Prix until mechanical failure intervened. By the end of the 1954 season, both he and Mercedes-Benz were ready for each other.

By then, of course, the Mercedes W196 had rewritten the parameters of contemporary F1 car design. Although the Mercedes factory had been razed to the ground by Allied bombing during the Second World War, West Germany's economic resurgence in the early 1950s continued at a remarkable rate, and nothing symbolised that recovery more graphically than the sight of three sleek 'Silver Arrows' lined up in front of the pits for the 1954 French Grand Prix.

Ranged against the Ferrari 625 and Maserati 250F, the Mercedes W196 was an extremely sophisticated and technically advanced machine, perhaps matched only by the Lancia D50, which at the time was still undergoing a protracted development phase and would not make its race debut until the end of that season.

The Mercedes was built around an advanced tubular spaceframe, which carried an inline eight-cylinder engine that incorporated desmodromic valve gear and was canted over at a 70-degree angle to keep the car's profile as low as possible. Designed by a team under the direction of Professor Fritz Nallinger, Dr Lorenscheid and brilliant engineer Rudolf Uhlenhaut, the W196 featured inboard drum brakes and Bosch fuel injection. With a capacity of 2496cc, it developed 260bhp at 8500rpm as a starting point in what was originally anticipated to be a five-year development programme, which would see the engine developing more than 300bhp by the end of 1958.

Fangio was the only world-class driver in the Mercedes line-up, which also included Karl Kling and Hans Herrmann. Moreover, time has tended to throw many people's memories into soft focus – the W196s were not quite the all-conquering titans they were expected to be, at least not as far as the 1954 season was concerned.

Below: **A dramatic moment at the start of the 1954 Belgian Grand Prix, with the Maserati of Roberto Mières making life unexpectedly hot for its driver by bursting into flames.**
Photo: Bernard Cahier

MERCEDES SETS NEW F1 BENCHMARK

Fangio and Kling finished 1-2 at Reims, using cars fitted with streamlined all-enveloping bodywork, but this configuration was not the ideal choice for Silverstone, where concrete-filled oil drums delineated the insides of the corners. As a result, Fangio could only struggle home fourth, his car's silver bodywork displaying ungainly dents by the time he took the chequered flag, in a race won by José Froilán González's four-cylinder Ferrari 625, the uprated version of the Tipo 500 F2 car that had carried Alberto Ascari to the previous two World Championship titles.

For Mercedes's home race at the Nürburgring, Fangio was allotted a W196 prepared to conventional open-wheel specification. He won this race in commanding style, but with a heavy heart. During practice, his young friend and compatriot, Onofré Marimón, had crashed his Maserati 250F at the Wehrseifen curve and suffered fatal injuries. González was so distraught that Mike Hawthorn had to take over behind the wheel of his Ferrari, going on to finish the race second, behind Fangio.

At Monza, Fangio again scraped home the winner in the W196 streamliner, two key rivals having fallen by the wayside. The Ferrari team was determined to do well on its home turf and negotiated for Alberto Ascari to be released from his Lancia contract for this specific event. The Italian driver, who had been sitting around for much of the year, vainly waiting for the new high-tech Lancia D50 to be readied, jumped at the chance of displaying his legendary skills.

Driving brilliantly in a Ferrari 625 powered by the later type 553 'Super Squalo' engine, Ascari shook himself free of Fangio and pulled out a nine-second lead until a valve broke. That let Stirling Moss through to the front in his Maserati, which then suffered a fractured oil pipe, allowing the Merc to win, ahead of Mike Hawthorn's Ferrari.

Hawthorn then gave the Italian team a win in the Spanish GP at Barcelona's Pedralbes circuit, followed home by Luigi Musso's Maserati and Fangio's Mercedes. It was sufficient to clinch Fangio's second World Championship crown with 42 points (net), ahead of González (25) and Hawthorn (24.5). Five scores out of nine counted.

The English driver would remember that race with particular satisfaction. After seeing off an early challenge from privateer Harry Schell's Maserati, he recalled, "The Squalo was going beautifully, while the Mercedes was giving trouble and Fangio was struggling on, covered in oil and black dust... The pit signalled each lap to tell me what the gap was between Fangio and I, but towards the end the Mercedes began to trail a smokescreen and was beaten into second place by Musso's Maserati."

Left: **After one of the drives of his life in his private Maserati 250F at Monza in 1954, Stirling Moss waits to push his stricken car across the finishing line. Pirelli was so impressed that it paid him the bonus he would have got for winning!**

Below: **Froilán González is almost lost in a crowd of well-wishers after taking a victory for Ferrari in the 1954 British Grand Prix.**
Photos: Bernard Cahier

LANCIA'S LOST CLASSIC

For 1955, Moss duly gained his promotion to the Mercedes works team, but that season the German manufacturer was scheduled to face possibly its most formidable opposition in the form of Lancia's new D50, in the hands of Ascari. It didn't show in the race results, but on the car's debut in the 1954 Spanish GP, Ascari was pulling away at two seconds a lap before retiring with what was officially described as clutch trouble.

Respected journalist Denis Jenkinson wrote, "The whole conception of the Lancia Grand Prix car was one of normal Grand Prix design, but with great attention paid to detail, excellent finish on the mechanical parts and a keen eye to weight saving."

The original concept had been approved in principle in 1953 by Gianni Lancia, after which he left his chief designer, Vittorio Jano, to get on with the project. After a year of speculation, the Lancia D50 finally turned out to do battle in the 1954 Spanish GP, where Ascari was absolutely bursting to show Fangio what he was really up against.

It was about time. The prototype D50 had first turned a wheel within the courtyard of Lancia's com-

petitions department on Turin's Via Caraglio on 8th February, 1954. Just over two weeks earlier, Ascari and Villoresi had signed their contracts, but, while the car was briefly tested at the Caselle airport in Turin during mid-February, it took another eight months before it was signed off as ready to race.

The Lancia D50 was striking indeed. It was powered by a 73.6 x 73.1mm, 2487cc, twin-overhead-camshaft 90-degree V8 engine, itself mounted at an angle of 12 degrees within the chassis with the propshaft running to the left, alongside the driver's seat to keep the overall package as low as possible.

The engine was a semi-stressed unit, in effect doubling for the upper tube of what otherwise would have been a complete spaceframe chassis, and the car was distinguished by long pannier fuel tanks fitted between the wheels: the right-hand tank contained only fuel, while the left-hand tank included an oil cooler towards the front.

Weighing in at 1367lb (620kg), the Lancia D50 was one of the lightest Grand Prix cars of its era. The Mercedes W196 tipped the scales at 1587lb (720kg) in aerodynamic trim and 1521lb (690kg) in open-wheel form, while the Ferrari 625 weighed in at 1433lb (650kg),

the 553 'Squalo' at just over 1300lb (590kg) and the Maserati 250F at 1389lb (630kg).

The history of Mercedes's 1954 'domination' might have been very different had Ascari been able to debut the car at Reims on the same day as the W196, but it was not until he lapped Monza during testing a full three seconds faster than Fangio's best in the Mercedes streamliner that Gianni Lancia gave the green light for its racing debut.

Yet in 1955, Ferrari would inherit the superb D50s when Gianni Lancia's team hit the financial rocks shortly after Alberto Ascari's untimely death in May of that year.

By the time of this disaster, the writing seemed to be very clearly on the wall for Ferrari. Not only had Moss joined Mercedes, but also Hawthorn had opted to switch to the British based Vanwall team, reasoning that such a move would enable him to spend more time concentrating on his family's garage business in Farnham, Surrey, in the wake of his father Leslie's death in a road accident the previous year.

Ferrari began the 1955 season in a precarious state, using the two-year-old, now-coil-sprung Tipo 625s equipped with five-speed gearboxes and driven by the journeyman Trintignant and Farina, the Italian veteran now well past his best.

Fangio and Moss scored a Mercedes 1-2 in the Argentine GP season-opener at Buenos Aires, with Trintignant a solid third, sharing his 625 with Maglioli and Farina. For the start of the European season, there was another revamped machine available, the Tipo 555 'Super Squalo', which was built around a completely different chassis frame; the new machine made its debut in the Turin GP at Valentino Park.

Ascari, Villoresi and new signing Eugenio Castellotti delivered a 1-2-3 grand slam for the Lancia D50s, and Ascari rammed home the message by winning at Naples and dominating the Pau GP before he retired, allowing Jean Behra's Maserati through to win.

Amazingly, considering how outclassed the 625 had become, Trintignant bagged a fortuitous win at Mo-

naco, but only after the Mercedes entries of Fangio and Moss had retired, and Ascari had taken an unscheduled ducking in the harbour just when his Lancia had been poised to take the lead. Castellotti finished second, ahead of the Behra/Cesare Perdisa Maserati and the arthritic Farina.

Further back in the field, Piero Taruffi became so fed up with the handling of his 'Super Squalo' that he came into the pits and handed it over to Paul Frère, the Belgian semi-professional racer who was the team's reserve driver. Frère later shed some light on the way in which the Ferrari team operated, having failed to persuade manager Mino Amarotti that changes should be made to improve the 555's handling.

"That car was a real beast round Monaco," he remembered, "as it just wanted to plough straight on at the two tight hairpins. I hinted that it might be a good idea to disconnect the front anti-roll bar, but Amarotti was responsible for technical matters at the races and I am sure he was really upset by my suggestion.

"He did not want to take the responsibility for modifying something which was part of the original design – for which he was not responsible. If he had taken my advice, and then something had gone wrong, then he most certainly would have been held responsible for it back at the factory. He just wasn't prepared to do it."

Four days after Monaco, Ascari was killed testing a sports Ferrari at Monza. Lancia's most crucial human asset had been snatched away, and Gianni Lancia, together with the entire Italian motorsporting fraternity, was bereft. Although Castellotti was allowed to take a single D50 to the Belgian GP at Spa-Francorchamps, financial problems were weighing heavily on Gianni Lancia's shoulders and he decided that he would have to retire from F1 racing thereafter.

Thanks to the combined efforts of the Italian automobile federation and Fiat, a deal was struck whereby Ferrari took over the entire inventory of Lancia D50s, plus the associated spares, with the promise of the equivalent of £30,000 a year in financial support

Continued on page 60

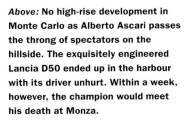

Above: No high-rise development in Monte Carlo as Alberto Ascari passes the throng of spectators on the hillside. The exquisitely engineered Lancia D50 ended up in the harbour with its driver unhurt. Within a week, however, the champion would meet his death at Monza.

Right: "How much for Alberto?" Mercedes team manager Alfred Neubauer gets out his wallet while Ascari (centre) grins broadly, and Lancia D50 designer Vittorio Jano (left) looks smugly confident.
Photos: Bernard Cahier

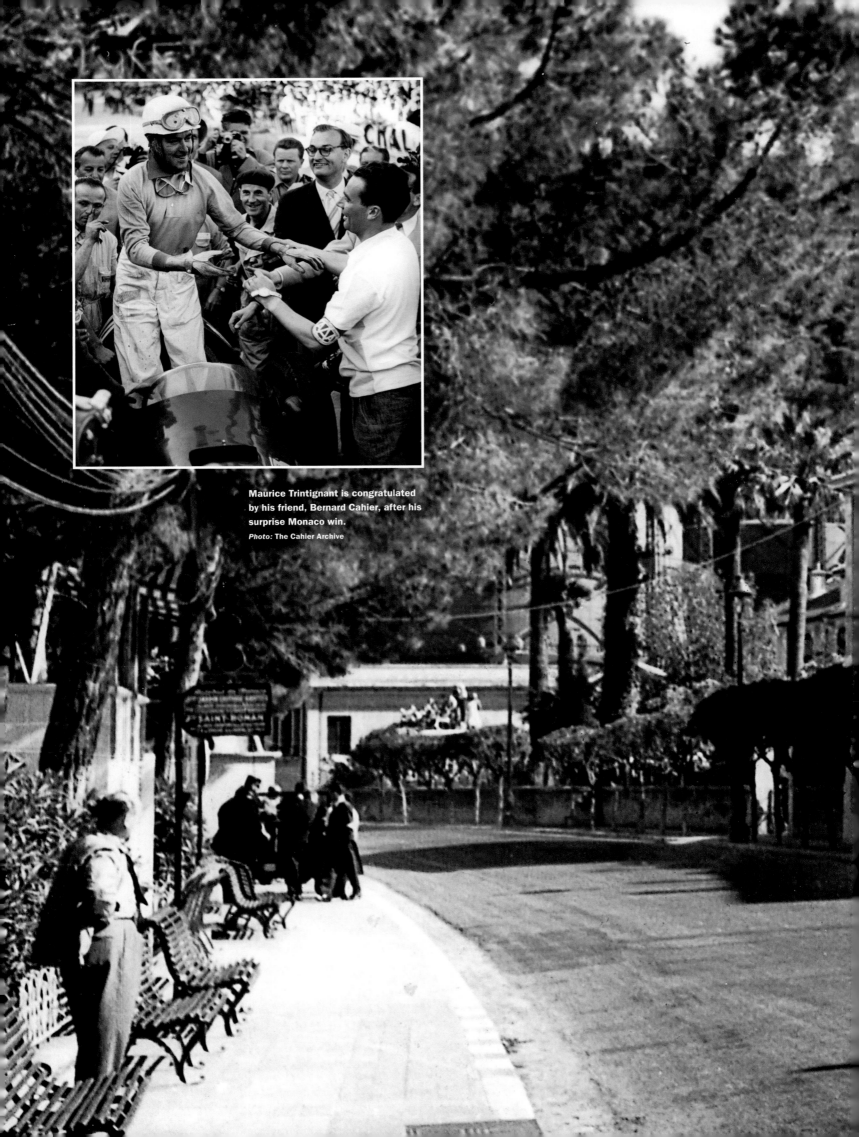

Maurice Trintignant is congratulated by his friend, Bernard Cahier, after his surprise Monaco win.
Photo: The Cahier Archive

Fangio leads Moss in tight Mercedes formation during the 1955 Monaco GP. Neither of the W196 cars made it to the finish.

Photo: Bernard Cahier

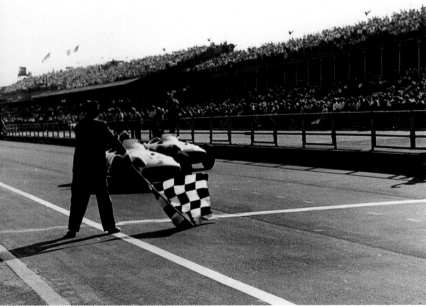

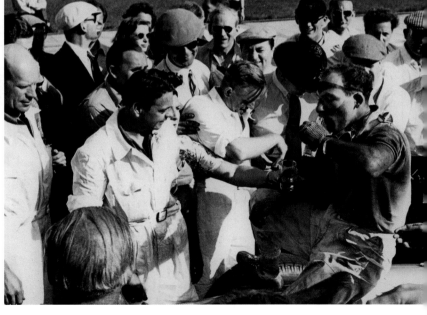

for as long as the Maranello team continued to race the cars.

Enzo Ferrari may have privately thought that this was Christmas for his team, but did a very good job of imitating somebody who really believed he was doing the Italian federation something of a favour by taking over what he would have liked to suggest was an outdated pile of junk – but it was far from being that. The old myth-maker had landed on his feet once more.

On 26th July, 1955, the formal hand-over of six cars and a host of other equipment took place. Neither Ferrari nor Gianni Lancia was present on this symbolic occasion, Enzo perhaps keenly appreciating his good fortune and not allowing his pride to be publicly dented by what, in truth, amounted to a fairly comprehensive, if oblique, humiliation for his organisation.

MOSS MAKES HISTORY AT AINTREE

Thereafter, the Mercedes W196s finished first and second in the four remaining races on the World Championship calendar. Fangio led Moss across the line at Spa-Francorchamps and Zandvoort, but in front of Stirling's home crowd in the British Grand Prix at Aintree, the positions were reversed. Britain's 'Golden Boy' – who had insisted on carrying the Union Flag on the tail of his silver Mercedes – won by a nose from the canny Argentine ace.

Was it staged? Did Fangio throw the race? If he did so, then it was a performance delivered with such subtlety that even Stirling has his doubts to this day. Karl Kling and Piero Taruffi rounded off a Mercedes grand slam by taking third and fourth places.

Transmission problems caused Moss to retire at Monza, where Fangio led Taruffi home to the final 1-2 of the season, thereby clinching his third World Championship with 40 points to Moss's 23, counting five scores from seven races. But it was all over now for Mercedes-Benz, whose management had been numbed by the Le Mans disaster in which Pierre Levegh's 300SLR had collided with Lance Macklin's Austin Healey, triggering the carnage that cost the lives of more than 80 spectators.

Moss's move to Mercedes had frustrated the Maserati team, which had been left without a first-rate number-one driver for the 1955 season. Instead it had the tenacious Jean Behra as team leader, backed up by Luigi Musso and Roberto Mières. To keep pace with the Mercedes on the fastest circuits, Maserati also developed a distinctive, all-enveloping 'streamliner' body for its car. As Denis Jenkinson remarked from first-hand observation, "it was not at all successful, having been designed by intuition rather than according to any aerodynamic theories, and was little faster than the normal 250F."

Maserati also began experimenting with Bosch fuel injection, a development that would start to pay off in 1956, but the 1955 season saw extremely important developments on the British Fomula 1 scene as well. While BRM was struggling to develop its 2.5-litre four-cylinder P25, Tony Brooks took the opportunity to write his own distinctive entry in the history books with an unexpected victory. And Tony Vandervell's new Vanwalls were demonstrating the first signs of genuine promise.

BROOKS WINS FOR CONNAUGHT AT SYRACUSE

Two developments were responsible for propelling Connaught into the motor racing spotlight, albeit briefly. The decision was taken to build a proper 2.5-litre Formula 1 car for the new regulations, which came into force in 1954. Then, in 1955, a quiet 21-year-old dental student turned in some impressive drives at the wheel of a privately entered Formula 2 Connaught. This, together with his performances for the factory Aston Martin sports car team, prompted Connaught to give him his first taste of Formula 1. His name was Tony Brooks.

The B-series Connaught Formula 1 car had been designed with the 2.5-litre Coventry-Climax 'Godiva' V8 engine in mind, but since this never materialised as a serious project, a four-cylinder Alta unit was used instead. Although this engine had its origins before the war, it still managed to produce a respectable 240bhp at 7000rpm.

The Connaught was promising, but by international standards it was definitely 'second division'. By the end of 1955, more than £15,000 had been poured into the F1 project by Kenneth McAlpine, and both he and Rodney Clarke were feeling tempted to close down the whole company. But at the end of the season, they put in a couple of entries for the non-championship Syracuse GP in distant Sicily. A streamlined B-type was entered for the seasoned Les Leston, while Tony Brooks would drive a regular car. What happened next went straight into the pages of the Formula 1 history books.

"I honestly think they invited me because most of the regulars couldn't manage it," said Brooks, who'd never so much as sat in the cockpit of a Formula 1 car prior to arriving at Syracuse, where he faced stiff opposition from the Maserati 250Fs of Luigi Musso, Luigi Villoresi and Harry Schell.

Yet to the amazement of the onlookers, Brooks planted the Connaught on the outside of the front row, alongside the two fastest Maseratis. "I never even managed a practice start," he remembered. "Firstly, I was anxious not to jigger up the 'box, and secondly I was very conscious of my instructions not to over-stress the engine."

Nevertheless, after a poor getaway behind the Maseratis, Brooks took the Connaught through into the lead on lap 11. At a time when the drivers of British cars were only supposed to watch Italian Ferraris and Maseratis disappear into the distance, this was a truly memorable change of script.

Musso tried his very hardest, regularly outbraking the Connaught into the tight hairpin on this challenging road circuit, but Brooks was always in a position to out-accelerate him. In fact, by the finish, he had outpaced the works Maseratis by almost one minute.

Back in Britain, it was Motor Show time, and the Connaught victory was greeted with remarkably little in the way of editorial attention. Even Brooks was somewhat downbeat about his achievement

"Only I knew how easy I had been on the car," he explained. "In a straight line, we definitely weren't faster than the Maserati, but I'd always tended to go rather well on circuits like Syracuse, with long, sweeping corners and brick walls [waiting] if you make a mistake, so I managed to get away.

"There are plenty of other circuits where this just wouldn't have worked. I think everyone was carried away and thought that Britain had a World Championship winner [in the Connaught], but, with respect, I was the best person to know that, unfortunately, we hadn't."

Yet Rodney Clarke's team remained a great favourite with the fans. In 1956, the Connaught Supporters' Club returned to Syracuse on a package tour to visit the scene of the marque's greatest triumph. Apart from the airline getting its wires crossed and booking the Dakota a day late for the nine-hour flight to Sicily, the coach bringing the fans – and some of the drivers – back from Syracuse to Catania airport contrived to burst its radiator.

Depressed as they might have been after the best Ivor Bueb could manage was a distant fifth in the race, the sight of Alfred Moss – Stirling's father – lying flat on his back beneath the coach, attempting to plug the holes with blocks of wood must have raised more than a few smiles. Meanwhile, the drivers stood in a line stretching down to a nearby stream and used their trophies to pass up water to Stirling, who was sitting astride the bonnet, filling up the radiator. Difficult to imagine Jenson Button doing the same today.

Eventually Connaught became overwhelmed by consistent lack of finance, so Clarke and McAlpine agreed to call a halt to proceedings shortly after Stuart Lewis-Evans won the 1957 Easter Monday Goodwood F1 race in the aerodynamic 'toothpaste tube' B-series.

Above: **A young Tony Brooks and his Connaught team-mate, Les Leston (right), celebrate after the dental student had pulled off a surprise victory in Syracuse.**
Photo: Autocourse archive.

In 1972, Clarke told the author, "Here I was, having been cut down on expenses ever since 1954, and the team was winning races with a three-year-old car. I got on the phone to McAlpine and said, 'Let's stop while we're on top.' And we did." The team's final race was at Monaco, a few weeks after the Goodwood victory, where Lewis-Evans's fourth place closed the book on a heroic effort to put Britain on top in Grand Prix racing.

By 1958, the Vanwalls were ahead, but the 'toothpaste tube' and the last of the conventional B-types were acquired by a Bexleyheath based wheeler-dealer, who subsequently sent them to Australia and New Zealand at the end of 1957 for Lewis-Evans and Bueb to drive.

The motor racing entrepreneur would have quite a future ahead of him on the Grand Prix scene. His name was Bernie Ecclestone, and he did a few laps at Monaco in the B-type in practice for the 1958 Monaco Grand Prix, where Paul Emery and the American, Bruce Kessler, also took a turn at the wheel. None of them qualified to start.

VANWALLS MAKE THEIR MARK

Tony Vandervell pursued his Grand Prix success with the same zeal and determination that he applied to his business ventures. In 1930, almost by chance, he had discovered that a new replaceable car engine bearing was being manufactured in the USA. Quickly appreciating its implications for reducing cost and manufacturing complexity in production cars, he hurried across the Atlantic and successfully concluded a deal with the Cleveland Graphite Bronze Company – inventor of the new technique – for its British licence. With the enthusiastic financial advice and assistance of his father, Tony set up Vandervell Products Ltd in a purpose-built factory on Western Avenue, Acton, on the western fringes of London.

The production of Vandervell 'Thinwall' bearings made a significant contribution to the war effort between 1939 and 1945, after which the company's immensely patriotic head quickly became involved with the new BRM project. Yet the vague, rudderless manner in which the BMRR Trust imposed 'management

by committee' on the team grated with Vandervell's direct manner.

It soon became clear to him that the 1.5-litre BRM V16 was going to be hopelessly late, so he struck out on his own. In 1949, as we've seen, he purchased a 1.5-litre supercharged Ferrari 125 as a test bed for the Vandervell Thinwall bearings, racing the car under the title of 'Thinwall Special', and in 1951, he replaced that with a 4.5-litre Ferrari 375, by which time he had convinced himself that he should go it alone.

Mike Hawthorn was signed to race for the team in 1955, but Vanwall was not quite ready for front-line action. As Hawthorn recalled, "When Tony Vandervell invited me to sign a contract to drive the Vanwall, with a regular retainer as an added inducement, I was very tempted, for it would give me the chance to spend more time in England. The Vanwall was improving fast." Hawthorn was right – but it wasn't improving fast enough.

Things came to a head for Hawthorn at the Belgian Grand Prix, where just a single Vanwall was entered for him to drive. Unfortunately, Tony Vandervell exer-

cised his *droit de seigneur* over the team by driving the Vanwall out to the circuit prior to Saturday practice, with the result that Hawthorn found that the clutch was slipping.

Hawthorn was extremely angry about the whole episode and, after retiring from the race, apparently bumped into team manager David Yorke in a bar, where tempers got heated and Mike made some intemperate remarks about Vanwall's operation. The 'Old Man' had clearly compromised his team's efforts by indulging his passion and taking a turn at the wheel of his car, but it was decided that he and Hawthorn should go their separate ways after this unfortunate debacle.

Hawthorn commented that, while everybody admired the immense drive and effort that Vandervell had put into his cars, it was difficult for him to accept the fact that they were still not ready for top-line international racing. "But that was the hard truth and there was still a great deal to be done," he noted.

By 1956, however, the 2.5-litre four-cylinder Vanwalls were beginning to show genuine promise.

Above: Élie Bayol looks apprehensive in the Gordini that he shared with André Pilette to take sixth in the 1956 Monaco Grand Prix.

Top: An Englishman abroad. Mike Hawthorn cruises around to the pits in his BRM P25, prior to the start at Monaco, 1956.

Photos: Bernard Cahier

After initial experimentation with chassis designed by Cooper, Tony Vandervell commissioned Lotus chief Colin Chapman to produce a new chassis, which was clothed in a strikingly slippery body conceived by aerodynamicist Frank Costin.

The 1956 season saw Ferrari concentrating all its efforts on uprated versions of the Lancia D50 – dubbed the 'Lancia-Ferrari' – although there were already signs that Maranello was starting to make a muddle of the exquisite Jano-designed car that had originated from Turin.

With Mercedes-Benz withdrawing from F1 at the end of 1955, Fangio signed for Ferrari, although he was clearly in two minds until quite late in the day.

"At the end of 1955, I considered the possibility of retiring," he later admitted, "but the Argentine government had fallen during the summer and there were great changes going on in my country. In fact, things began to go not so well in Argentina, so I decided to postpone my retirement for another year. As

Mercedes-Benz had withdrawn, I returned to Europe to race with Ferrari in 1956, but I wasn't very happy about that.

"Since I first raced in Europe, I had always been in a team opposing Ferrari. Now I was joining him, with Castellotti, Musso and Collins. But he would never say who was to be number-one driver, although the younger men told me, 'Juan, you are the leader.'

"Ferrari was a hard man. His team raced in every category and his drivers drove always for him. He wanted victory primarily for his cars and this suited my attitude, because I have never raced solely for myself, but for the team as a whole. But a driver must have a good relationship with his mechanics, and I found this rather difficult to achieve within the Ferrari team. I suppose it was because I had been their opposition for so many years and now here I was as their driver."

Meanwhile, over at rival Maserati, there was definite optimism in the air, with Stirling Moss leading the

Above: Despite the bonhomie, Enzo Ferrari and Fangio enjoyed an uneasy relationship.

Left: Maserati team-mates Jean Behra and Stirling Moss who carried the fight to Ferrari during 1956.
Photos: Bernard Cahier

team and opening the European season with a splendid victory at Monaco with the 250F.

Unfortunately, things went downhill from then onwards, and the best result Moss could post in the next six races was a second place to Fangio in the German GP at the Nürburgring. In its efforts to satisfy Moss's high standards and at the same time keep its number two, Jean Behra, as happy as possible, the factory spent too much time experimenting with various technical developments on a random and intermittent basis. These included trying various controlled air-flow concepts, ducting the radiator and improving the flow around the cockpit, a variety of different fuel injection systems and some experimentation with Dunlop disc brakes. However, in the final race of the season, the Italian Grand Prix at Monza, Moss managed another splendid victory, and the lessons learned there were incorporated into the very successful 250F derivative for 1957.

Meanwhile, Fangio had won his fourth World Championship title, thanks to the incredible generosity and sporting spirit displayed by British driver Peter Collins. Earlier in the year, Collins had taken his Lancia-Ferrari to victory in the Belgian and French Grands Prix, and had looked well placed to become Britain's first World Champion driver. At Monza came the grand gesture.

On lap 19 of the Italian Grand Prix, Fangio wobbled into the pits with a broken steering arm on his Lancia-Ferrari, and when Collins came in for a precautionary tyre check, he unhesitatingly gave his car to Fangio to keep open his colleague's title chances.

It was a generous, prompt and open action that attracted a deal of attention at the time, marking Collins as a gentleman. The fact that he was a Ferrari team driver and was obliged to obey such an instruction from the management was not altogether the point. The nice thing about Collins's attitude was his willingness to oblige without any sort of debate, in contrast to Luigi Musso, who had declined a similar suggestion that he might hand over his car to Fangio.

In the end, Fangio won the 1956 World Championship with 30 points (net) to Moss's 27 and Collins's 25. The Argentine ace then moved to Maserati in 1957, while Moss signed for Vanwall and Hawthorn returned to Ferrari after a season with BRM.

Moss would be joined in the Vanwall team by Tony Brooks. Connaught had offered Brooks a deal for the 1956 season, but the promising young English driver was being pursued with rival offers. "I couldn't see the Connaught being competitive, so it was with considerable regret I refused their offer," he recalled. "I joined BRM in 1956. They'd got a tremendously fast car in a straight line, but the only problem was that it was completely undrivable around corners.

"If Connaught had used the BRM engine, it would have been a seriously competitive car. But, as it was, the Connaught had a wonderful chassis and an uncompetitive engine, while the BRM had a first-class engine and diabolical chassis – and I *mean* diabolical. It was an absolute danger."

The BRM P25, designed by Peter Berthon, had a four-cylinder 2.5-litre engine and developed 270bhp at 8000rpm. It was extremely fast, but painfully unreliable – as emphasised in the British GP, where Haw-

Continued on page 71

Below: **Italian playboy Eugenio Castellotti, was a temperamental and tempestuous talent who lived life to the full.**

Bottom: **Fangio looks exhausted after taking his fourth World Championship at Monza in 1956.**

Photos: Bernard Cahier

Above: Few drivers coaxed the best out of the Lancia-Ferrari D50 after Maranello had got hold of it, but Fangio was in a class of his own, winning the 1956 German GP at the Nürburgring in one of these elegant 'pontoon tanked' cars.

Left: Ferrari with the selfless Peter Collins after the English driver had deferred to Fangio and allowed him to take over his car at Monza.
Photos: Bernard Cahier

A fine study of **Stirling Moss at work
in his Maserati 250F in the 1956
German Grand Prix.**
Photo: **Bernard Cahier**

ENZO FERRARI: F1'S LAST LONER

Above: **Enzo Ferrari, the last of the automotive titans.**
Photo: **Bernard Cahier**

WHEN Enzo Ferrari died at the age of 89, in August 1988, he had not been present to see one of his own cars racing for almost 31 years. After the death of his first son, Dino, Ferrari vowed never to attend another race. But he made an exception for the 1957 Modena event, as it marked the debut of the Dino 246s, named in memory of his son, who had collaborated in their design with the respected former Lancia technician, Vittorio Jano.

For the remaining years of his life, the Old Man lived in the shadow of that grief, his Maranello office regarded by many as a shrine to his much-missed offspring. Yet for many years, he would turn up at Monza for final practice prior to the Italian Grand Prix, but never the race.

In the space of 40 years, Enzo Ferrari transformed a tiny business making specialist sports cars into one of the most famous brand names in the world. He achieved this not only by building some of the most aesthetically beautiful and successful racing cars ever seen, but also by virtue of the continuity represented by the distinctive Prancing Horse motif, which had originally been presented to him by the parents of the famous Italian First World War fighter pilot, Francesco Barracca.

The Ferrari image has magical connections that reach back to the pioneering days of motor racing. Ferrari himself ran what amounted to the factory Alfa Romeo team in the 1930s. In his heyday, he was the man in absolute charge. Team managers would often shudder at the prospect of having to telephone him with news of the practice times, particularly when the red cars had done badly. More than one gave him incorrect times simply for a peaceful life.

This dictatorial tone was part of the man's compelling attraction. As the 1950s turned into the 1960s, and rival Italian makes faltered, so Ferrari increasingly became regarded as Italy's international flag bearer on the sporting scene. When Ferrari won, the whole of Italy cheered. When it failed, which it did often, the country was plunged into gloom.

Enzo Ferrari also had an illegitimate son, Piero Lardi, who was born just after the war. Only after Dino's mother, Laura, died in 1978 was Piero formally acknowledged by the Old Man, although he had been working in the company for many years. By the late 1970s, he was fully integrated into the senior management with "Piero Lardi Ferrari" on his office door at Maranello.

Having rebuffed an approach from Ford to buy his company in 1963,

six years later Enzo Ferrari was on his financial knees. Fiat Chairman Gianni Agnelli stepped in with a rescue package, shrewdly judging how much the car company would benefit from an association with what had become a national institution.

In essence, the deal was that Fiat would control the road car business, while Enzo Ferrari would continue to have complete control over the racing cars until the day he died. In the mid-1970s, Ferrari had its most sustained period of F1 success to date, when Niki Lauda won the Drivers' World Championship in 1975 and 1977, while the team took a hat trick of Constructors' Championships between those two years.

The man who masterminded the revival was Luca di Montezemolo, then a young lawyer, now president of arguably the most famous car company of all. Yet no matter how much Ferrari tries to reinvent itself, it can never be the same.

The heritage remains to this day, but by 1999 there was a raw, almost desperate, urgency about the need to win. Enzo Ferrari always liked winning – even though his cars were perhaps not as successful as he might have liked to recall. Had he been alive, he would have been a happy man over the next few years.

thorn and Brooks led in the opening stages. After 30 laps, Brooks was running smoothly in fourth place only for the BRM's throttle linkage to come adrift ten laps later. He pulled off at Club Corner, effected a temporary repair and successfully returned to the pits. After losing over nine minutes, Brooks rejoined, but got only as far as Abbey Curve. There the throttle stuck open and he crashed heavily, being flung out of the BRM, which promptly rolled and burst into flames. "Which was the best thing that could have happened to that particular motor car," he told the author some 17 years later. If BRM was still struggling, then Vanwall was certainly advancing towards maturity. With the gutsy Franco-American driver, Harry Schell, at the wheel, the Vanwall drove into the thick of the action in the French GP at Reims, where Schell mixed it determinedly with the Lancia-Ferraris of Fangio, Collins and Castellotti on this ultra-fast circuit. In the event, the Vanwall failed and Schell took over the sister car driven by Mike Hawthorn, briefly back in the fold, having made up his differences with Tony Vandervell.

Jean Behra stayed on in the Maserati works team for 1957, but this was to be Fangio's year yet again. The 250F was now entering its fourth season of front-line F1 competition and further modifications were incorporated.

Moss's Italian GP winning car from the previous year was one of two 250Fs that were significantly lower and lighter, this being achieved by setting the engine at an angle of five degrees to the centre-line of the chassis, allowing the propshaft to run diagonally across the floor of the cockpit to a revised final drive unit with the input bevel gears offset more to the left. This had enabled a much lower seating position to be achieved for the driver, while the frontal area was much reduced.

For 1957, it was decided to go back to the original central engine position and use a chassis frame of tubing that was much smaller in diameter and of thinner gauge, while the engine was now developing around 285bhp at 8000rpm. Even more importantly, if Fangio had experienced a troubled relationship with Ferrari, he was back in his element at Maserati, for the Argentine driver was, if anything, even more popular with the workforce than Moss had been because his association with the team went back to 1948, when he first began racing in Europe.

FANGIO SIGNS OFF ON TOP

The 1957 season started with Maserati posting a remarkable 1-2-3-4 grand slam in the Argentine Grand Prix at Buenos Aires, where Fangio led home Behra, Carlos Menditeguy and Harry Schell. Then Fangio won the Monaco and French Grands Prix – sensationally at Rouen-les-Essarts – before he was stopped in his tracks by a historic victory for Stirling Moss, who won the British Grand Prix at Aintree with the Vanwall.

The Colin Chapman-designed Vanwall, clothed in Frank Costin's very high, distinctively aerodynamic bodywork, had been steadily refined since it had first appeared in 1956. Its 96 x 86mm, 2490cc four-cylinder

Continued on page 74

Below: : **The works Maserati squad, all polished up and ready for action, in the cobbled Monza paddock prior to competing in the 1957 Italian GP.**
Photo: Bernard Cahier

The 1957 French Grand Prix, Rouen. Fangio and Behra at work in their Maseratis at the Nouveau Monde hairpin. The Argentine's car shows minor damage after hitting the rear of his team-mate's car. Who said there was no trackside advertising until Bernie Ecclestone's day?
Photo: Bernard Cahier

Above: Back with Maserati, Fangio won the 1957 Monaco Grand Prix.
Photo: Bernard Cahier

engine had been developed by Leo Kuzmicki, incorporating Norton motorcycle cylinder-head technology with a Rolls-Royce industrial bottom end.

It was Britain's first seriously competitive Grand Prix car of the post-war, or indeed any, era. Moss would gain great success in its cockpit, and the image of the impassive young man sitting far away from the steering wheel with his laid-back – in every sense of the expression – driving position somehow came to encapsulate the best of the front-engined 2.5-litre era.

Yet the Vanwall was not perfect. Its four-cylinder engine was prone to flat-spots, it had a bad gearbox and its handling bordered on the knife-edge, tending towards understeer and requiring the deft touch of a top driver. With Moss and his team-mates, Tony Brooks and the outstandingly talented rising star, Stuart Lewis-Evans, Vanwall certainly had the requisite resources at its disposal during 1957 and 1958.

Yet before the British cars could achieve that memorable breakthrough at Aintree, Behra's Maserati had moved into the lead after Moss's car had hit trouble and he took over Brooks's sister machine. Behra was a good number two, who for some reason felt more relaxed at Maserati supporting Fangio than perhaps he had the previous year with Moss. This may have been because he was closer to Stirling in age; in any event, all the drivers acknowledged Fangio as the best of his era in much the same way as rivals conceded Ayrton Senna's superior status just over four decades later.

Mike Hawthorn, for his part, was having a good race in the Ferrari 801 and was closing on Behra when the Maserati's clutch blew apart, showering the track with debris on which the Englishman picked up a puncture. That caused Hawthorn to make a stop for a fresh tyre, so he ended up in third place, behind Luigi Musso's Ferrari, allowing Moss a clear run through to his second World Championship victory at Aintree in two years.

The German Grand Prix at the Nürburgring followed, and it was there that Fangio produced what is widely regarded as the most remarkable victory of his career. Qualifying gave a taste of what was to come. Fangio had managed a 9m 41.6s fastest lap with a Lancia-Ferrari en route to victory in the 1956 Grand Prix, but when he did a 9m 25.6s to claim pole in the Maserati 250F, it was clear that the Argentine ace was in a class of his own.

The best Hawthorn could manage was a 9m 28.4s for second on the grid, but he actually got away first at the start, pursued by Peter Collins. Second time around, Mike did a 9m 37.9s to post a new lap record, but by the end of lap three, Fangio – running a light fuel load and intending to make a pit stop – had torn through into the lead; by lap eight, he had pulled out almost half a minute's advantage.

At the end of lap 12, Fangio came in with a 28s lead, but this was squandered disgracefully as the Maserati crew shambled their way through the stop, taking 52s to refuel the car and fit two new rear tyres.

That left Hawthorn and Collins swapping the lead, while Fangio spent the next couple of laps getting into the swing of things again. After that, he put the two Ferrari drivers on red alert for a ferocious counterat-

Below left: Fangio after his win in the 1957 French Grand Prix.

Below: Moss and Brooks after their shared victory in the 1957 British Grand Prix.

Bottom: Victory for a British-built car at last. Moss takes his Vanwall past the Aintree grandstands.
Photos: Bernard Cahier

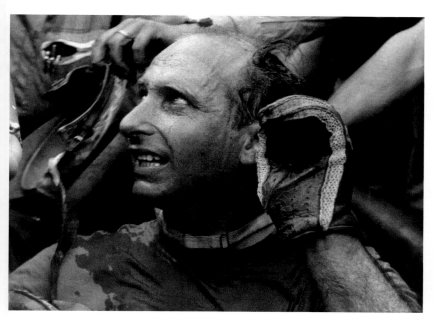

tack. Down, down came the gap. On lap 16, it was 33s; on lap 17, it was 25.5s; on lap 19, it was 13.5s; and on lap 20, it was just 2s.

Fangio then dived past Collins going into the North Curve, shattering one of Peter's goggle lenses in the process. Going down to Adenau, he forced his way ahead of Hawthorn, but the British driver fought back magnificently and went into the final lap only three seconds behind the Maserati, dropping just one more second on that final 14-mile blast.

"It was now a straight fight between Fangio and I once again," said Hawthorn, recalling the French GP four years earlier, "and I was driving right on the limit as we rushed through the endless tree-lined curves to Hocheichen and on to the Quiddelbacher Hohe, but just as I was going into a slow left-hander, Fangio cut sharply inside me and forced me on to the grass and almost into the ditch

"As we started the last lap, he had the vital yards in hand which prevented me from getting to grips on the corners and he crossed the finishing line 3.6s ahead of me. This time the race had been every bit as exciting for the drivers as for the spectators, and even though Peter and I had been beaten, we enjoyed

every moment of it."

The Vanwalls had an utterly dismal time at the Nürburgring. They may have performed to splendid effect on the relatively smooth surface at Aintree, but on the bumps and humps of the epic German track, they were well off the pace.

Stirling told Doug Nye, "The Vanwall's taut suspension was totally unsuitable for the Nürburgring, where they took a fearful hammering. Stuart crashed, I finished a distant fifth and Tony was ninth, having been sick in the cockpit. But my engine never missed a beat."

Moss would follow that up with momentous drives to victory at both Pescara and – perhaps most satisfyingly – Monza, where he finally realised the gruff Tony Vandervell's ambition to "beat those damn' red cars", winning the Italian Grand Prix in *una macchina Inglese*.

In the face of all this achievement on the part of Maserati and Vanwall, Ferrari faced up to a bleak 1957 season indeed with its type 801, the ultimate bastardisation of the Lancia D50, which now had close-fitting bodywork, no trace of the original pannier tanks and a rear-mounted fuel tank.

The magnificent 25.579km Pescara road circuit, on the fringe of the Adriatic, hosted just a single World Championship qualifying round in 1957. The race was won in commanding style by Stirling Moss (above) in his Vanwall.

Top right: **Tony Vandervell (in hat) stands in front of his sleek Vanwalls at Pescara.**

Centre right: **Mike Hawthorn (right) may have been defeated in the 1957 German Grand Prix, but he still congratulated the winner Fangio warmly once the race was over.**

Right: **The master at work. Juan Manuel Fangio put in a devastating performance to win the 1957 German Grand Prix for Maserati.**

Photos: Bernard Cahier

DINO 246 BOOSTS FERRARI FORTUNES

At the same time, Ferrari was developing a new 65-degree F1 V6, which saw the light of day initially as a 1.5-litre F2 engine, but later would be developed into the engine that would power one of the most famous F1 Ferraris of all time into the 1958 season, the Dino 246.

This, of course, was named after Ferrari's first-born son, Alfredino, who died from nephritis, a kidney complaint, in the summer of 1956, at the age of 24. This personal tragedy was a pivotal moment in Enzo Ferrari's long life and would result in his becoming increasingly reclusive, although no less a showman for that.

By the time the Italian Grand Prix at Monza came around, Fangio had long been crowned World Champion for a fifth time, clinching that unique distinction with his victory at the Nürburgring. This was also a memorable achievement for Maserati, and the famous Italian company was hard at work on a V12 engine project, which had been started originally in 1956, when it was envisaged that the powerplant would be installed in a totally new car. This was rethought for the 1957 season, and the new 60-degree V12 was eventually finalised in time to race at Monza.

The 68.5 x 56mm, 60-degree V12 had a capacity of 2476cc and was designed originally to run at up to 10,000rpm with a massive 320bhp at 9500rpm being developed during test runs on the dynamometer during the summer of 1957. Unfortunately, the downside to all this was a very narrow power band and acute lack of torque at anything below peak revs.

Behra agreed to drive the V12-engined 250F in the Italian Grand Prix, and for the first 28 laps he was right in the thick of the action, helping Fangio all he could in his battle against the Vanwall team. Unfortunately, he overtaxed his rear tyres and had to stop to change them, after which he thrashed his way back through the field, only for the engine to fail.

At the end of that memorable Italian Grand Prix, Moss and Fangio, separated by 40s, were the only competitors on the same lap. Into third place came Wolfgang von Trips's Ferrari 801, ahead of the private Maserati 250F driven by Masten Gregory.

The final points tally for the Drivers' Championship saw Fangio on 40 (net), comfortably ahead of Moss on 25 and Ferrari's Luigi Musso on 16. Only the best five results out of the eight races – which again included the Indianapolis 500 – counted for the ultimate outcome.

HAWTHORN AND VANWALL MAKE IT FIRSTS FOR BRITAIN

For the 1958 season, the F1 technical regulations were changed, largely at the prompting of the fuel companies, who were anxious to make as much advertising capital as possible out of their involvement in this increasingly prestigious sport. It was decided to introduce a requirement for pump petrol in place of the alcohol-based fuels used previously, but this posed immediate difficulties when it came to establishing and maintaining minimum acceptable standards on an increasingly global basis. As a result, it was eventually decided that 130-octane aviation fuel (AvGas) would

be adopted as the only available fuel governed by the appropriate international standards and regulations.

Adopting AvGas also had the effect of putting the brake on power outputs, at least temporarily. Ferrari would go into battle with the new 85 x 71mm, 2417cc Dino 246 V6, which now was developing around

Below: **Stirling Moss in the Rob Walker Cooper dives inside Mike Hawthorn's Ferrari Dino 246 to snatch second place in the 1958 Argentine Grand Prix.**

Photo: Autocourse archive

270bhp at 8300rpm. The Vanwall four-cylinder engines were nudging the 290bhp mark, while the BRM P25s were producing around 280bhp at 8800rpm.

Driver line-ups were broadly the same. Mike Hawthorn, Peter Collins and Luigi Musso were in the Ferrari front line; Vanwall retained its talented British trio; and BRM signed Jean Behra and Harry Schell. Juan Manuel Fangio began the season driving a Maserati 250F in the Argentine GP, but his long-term plans were uncertain.

There was, however, another major factor injected into the F1 equation, which would transform the Grand Prix scene in a period of barely 18 months. It was the arrival of the small British Cooper company with its spindly little rear-engined cars.

The 1958 season was scheduled to start in Buenos Aires with the Argentine GP on 19th January, but neither Vanwall nor BRM was ready. Moss had concluded a deal with Rob Walker to drive his Coopers in any race not contested by Tony Vandervell's cars, so he drove the 1960cc Climax-engined Cooper instead. What happened next would change the face of F1 for ever.

The story has been told time and time again: Moss won the race after a non-stop run in a close finish ahead of Musso's Dino 246. Having been lulled into a false sense of security that Moss would have to stop for fresh tyres, Ferrari's confidence turned first to disbelief and then to anguish as it became clear that he was going through without any delay.

Musso began his counterattack too late in the day and failed to catch the in-control Moss by just over two seconds; Mike Hawthorn was a distant third. The Ferrari pit became embroiled in a huge row at the end of the race over the Italian driver's failure to get the job done. For his part, Musso shouted back that he hadn't been kept fully informed about Moss's progress, but Peter Collins knew full well that he himself had held out several signals to his Italian team-mate after retiring his own car. It was all extremely unsettling.

Opposite: **Luigi Musso (top) finished second in the 1958 Monaco Grand Prix, but the surprise winner was Maurice Trintignant, who took Rob Walker's Cooper to victory. The Frenchman (left) is pictured with Princess Grace and Prince Rainier as the national anthem is played.**

Photos: Bernard Cahier

Moss, in fact, had inherited the lead on lap 35 of the 80-lap race, when Fangio's Maserati had stopped for fresh tyres, and thereafter he took things as gently as he dared. He was particularly keen to keep going, as he knew only too well that the four-bolt fixing on the Cooper's wheels would destroy his chances if he had to stop. He held on – and delivered.

The 1958 World Championship developed into a two-horse race between Ferrari and Vanwall. The 1958 Monaco Grand Prix was the second round of the title battle and proved to be a washout for both front-runners. Hawthorn and Moss both had spells in the lead, but retired, allowing Rob Walker's Cooper – this time driven by Maurice Trintignant – through to win again. The race was also marked by the debut of the distinctive front-engined Lotus 12s driven by Graham Hill and Cliff Allison. It was a starting point for another F1 legend, with Allison managing to squeeze home in sixth place.

Then came the Dutch Grand Prix at Zandvoort, where the three Vanwalls buttoned up the front row of the grid and Moss won easily. The Ferraris were nowhere, Hawthorn wrestling his way home to a frustrated fifth.

The Belgian GP at Spa-Francorchamps should have provided another win for Moss, but inexplicably he missed a gear while pulling away in the lead on the opening lap. The Vanwall's engine failed as a result

and Stirling was absolutely aghast at his mistake, which he freely and promptly admitted. But there would be no joy for the Ferraris here either. Moss's team-mate, Tony Brooks, took over stylishly at the head of the pack and drove away to post Vanwall's second win of the year.

Had the race been a lap longer, it might well have been won by Cliff Allison's Lotus 12. As he took the chequered flag, Brooks pulled off with gearbox problems. Hawthorn's engine blew up as he came down the hill to take second place, and Stuart Lewis-Evans's Vanwall wobbled past the chequered flag with a broken steering arm to take third. Allison followed them home in fourth place.

TRAGIC TIMES FOR MARANELLO

The harsh reality of the 1958 season was that the Vanwalls were generally superior and, had it not been for their intermittent unreliability, the Ferraris would have been decisively outclassed for much of the season.

Even so, Hawthorn won commandingly at Reims, where Musso, over-driving wildly in the hope that a big payday might enable him to clear his reputed gambling debts, flew off the road and was killed.

"On the eve of the race, he had, in fact, received a message, a few words typed on a buff telegram that urged him to make an all-out effort," Ferrari would

later reflect. Many believe this dark speculation to have been well founded.

Peter Collins, meanwhile, was experiencing some problems with his employer. The Englishman had been one of Enzo Ferrari's favourites, the team chief admiring his open and sunny disposition. However, the relationship changed distinctly after Peter married an American girl, Louise King. Ferrari hinted that the romance had taken the edge off his hunger in the cockpit. Or perhaps he was just resentful that Peter was no longer simply star-struck by the Ferrari team as a whole.

Just prior to the Reims race, team manager Romolo Tavoni announced that Collins would only be driving the Dino 156 in the F2 supporting race. This was absolutely typical Ferrari agitation, but the Old Man found himself up against a tough adversary in Collins.

Supported by his pal, Hawthorn, Peter replied that if he wasn't going to be allowed a run in the Grand Prix, then he wouldn't be driving in either race. Tavoni relented, so Collins also drove the F2 race and finished second, before coming fifth in the Grand Prix.

Carlo Chiti later suggested another reason behind Collins's apparent demotion. Mino Amarotti, who had been responsible for managing the works Ferrari Testa Rossa squad at Le Mans in 1958, reported that Hawthorn and Collins had deliberately destroyed their gearbox. Amarotti, who'd been a prisoner of war in East Africa, reportedly hated the British and somehow got it into his mind that Collins and Hawthorn were trying to help the rival Aston Martin squad, an absurd piece of lateral thinking by any standards.

Hawthorn's victory in France would be the last such success of his F1 career. It was also the final race for Fangio, who finished fourth in his Maserati 250F, Mike respectfully easing his pace in the closing

Continued on page 87

Below: Luigi Musso perished at Reims after overstepping the mark.
Photo: Bernard Cahier

Evocative moment as the Ferrari Dino 246s of
Mike Hawthorn (closest to camera) and Luigi
Musso line up on the grid at Reims prior to the
1958 French GP. Within an hour of Bernard Cahier
taking this photograph, Musso would be dead,
fatally injured as he tried to keep up with the winning Hawthorn. Mike would die in a road accident
in February 1959, and Schell would be killed in a
practice accident at Silverstone in 1960. It was a
dangerous and precarious business.
Photo: Bernard Cahier

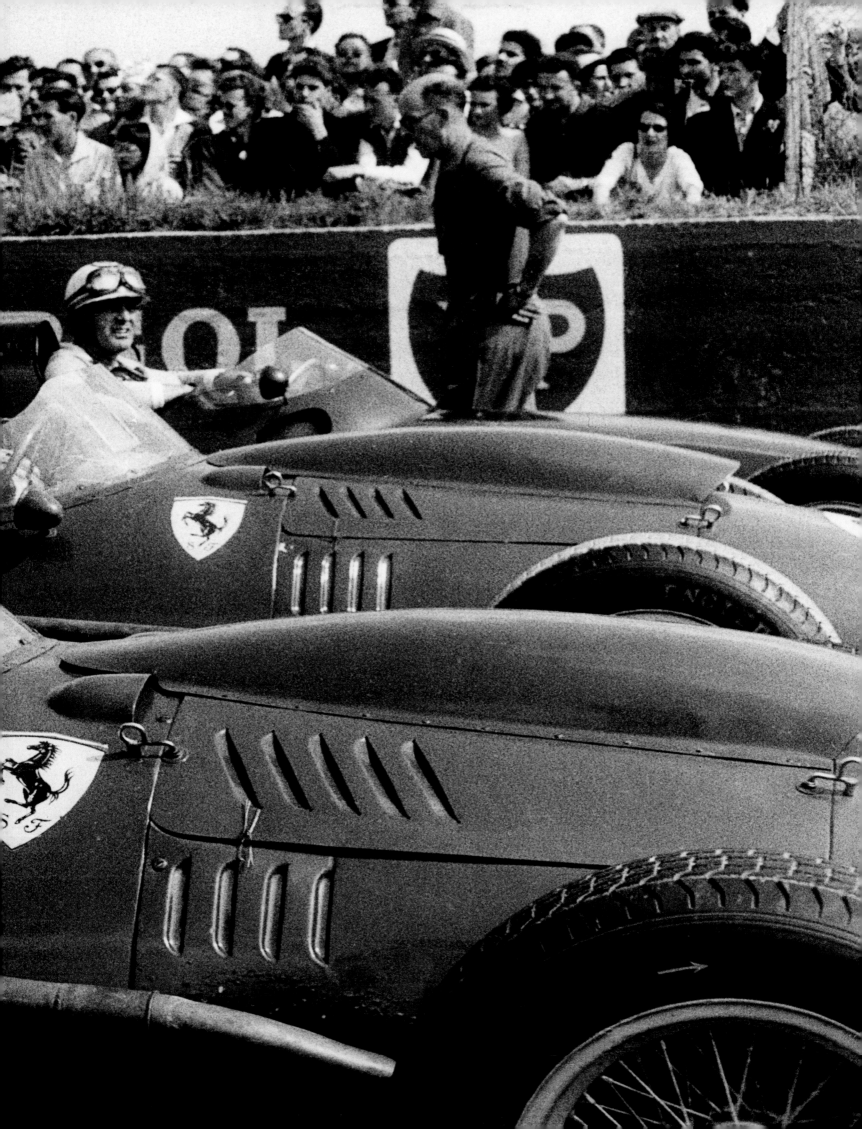

THE MAESTRO – JUAN MANUEL FANGIO

A moving tribute to the great Argentine driver was written by the late Denis Jenkinson and published in AUTO-COURSE 1995–96. This is an edited version of Jenks's first-person text.

I FIRST saw Juan Manuel Fangio race in 1949, when he won the Pau Grand Prix on the street circuit around the Basco-Béarnais city in south-west France, within sight of the Pyrenean Mountains. I had gone to Pau not to see a future five-times World Champion, but to race a motorcycle. The Grand Prix was traditionally held on Easter Monday, with motorcycle racing the day before. We practised on Saturday morning, and the Grand Prix cars practised in the afternoon, so naturally I stayed behind to watch.

Fangio did not disappoint, for he was known as a natural winner before he left Argentina, being champion in that country's national races with home-made specials, and a winner of marathon stockcar events in which he displayed remarkable stamina and endurance. More important was the impression he made on good European Grand Prix drivers of the time when they went out to the winter races in South America. They returned to Europe with the simple words: "He is good, a future champion."

Fangio came to Europe with a pretty good CV, but went back to Argentina about half-way through the '49 season with a much better one! He had won his first three Grand Prix races and totalled six victories in all. It later transpired that before he left his hometown of Balcarce for the first time, he had said to his friends, "I hope for one victory."

At the end of that season, I wrote in one of my motor racing books: "To those of us who have been fortunate enough to see this Fangio in action, the fact that he scored a hat trick with his first three appearances in European racing does not come as such a surprise, for he really 'motor races' with his Maserati in a manner that is a joy to behold."

The greatest demonstration of his ability to keep calm in times of crisis was during the 1951 Belgian Grand Prix on the very fast Spa-Francorchamps circuit when he was driving for the Alfa Romeo team. Two stops for fuel and tyres were planned and, after setting a new lap record at over 120mph, Fangio made his first stop while in the lead.

Drama then intervened when the left-rear wheel would not come off its hub. It was fourteen and a half minutes before Fangio rejoined the race, during which time the Alfa mechanics had to remove the entire wheel, hub and rear brake from the driveshaft, take the assembly into the pits, remove the tyre from the rim, fit and inflate a new tyre, and then fit the whole assembly back on the rear axle.

Throughout this, Fangio stood by, watching, but not saying a word to anyone and displaying no outward emotion, cleaning his goggles, cleaning the windscreen of the car and, above all, not making a fuss like some well-known drivers of that and even the current era.

When he rejoined, all hope of regaining the lead was gone, but he was determined to finish the race and protect his lap record if need be, thus preserving the World Championship point earned by fastest lap in

those days. His big handicap now was that he could not make his second scheduled tyre change and had to preserve the rubber on his car for the rest of the race as well as going fast enough to be classified as a finisher. He finished ninth and retained his lap record.

In later life, when telling us about this incident, he said, "That day people said how calm I was in the pits as I saw my chances of a win slipping away. It was not me they were slipping away from. I had done everything as it should be done, and made no mistakes. I believe that someone might well get nervous, or at least uneasy, when he has made a mistake. That was not the case with me. I was calm, even though Farina was at the top of the championship table. The second race of the championship was soon to come."

I watched that drama from the grandstand opposite the Alfa pits, not on a television screen, and joined in the applause and cheers from the spectators as this remarkable man from the Argentine went back into the race.

During his ten years of racing in Europe, Fangio seemed to create at least one magical legend each year. Many racing drivers would have been content to win one World Championship in that time, but Fangio won five. He entered motor races to win; if you won more than anyone else, you were justified in being called World Champion. He said, "If you are World Champion, it is up to you to always be the best and to show that you are champion."

The interesting thing about Fangio during that time was the way in which he would return to Argentina as soon

as the Grand Prix season was finished. No world publicity tours, no hype and bullshit in those days. If you did not know who the World Champion racing driver was, then you were not paying attention to your sport. He was born in Balcarce in 1911 and Argentina was his home; when he finished his season of work, he went home. He had no desire to live in Monte Carlo, or in a tax haven, or even in a beautiful part of Europe. It was always "better in Balcarce, where my friends and family are."

After he retired, Fangio would often return to Europe on business trips, principally connected with his Mercedes-Benz dealership in Buenos Aires. If it could be combined with a visit to a Grand Prix, he would take the opportunity and arrive at Monza, for example, before Saturday practice, often accompanied by his old sparring partner, Froilán González. Ten or fifteen years after his last race, his presence was magical and "FANGIO!" was the word that rippled through the crowd and along the pit lane.

On such occasions, he would make a tour of the pits with various officials, pausing to shake hands with old racing friends or acquaintances, or with current drivers like Jim Clark, Graham Hill or Jackie Stewart, and, more particularly, with mechanics and engineers from his Alfa Romeo and Maserati days.

Fangio was Fangio. There was no need to embellish his name. It was powerful enough on its own.

Top: The final curtain. Fangio in his Maserati about to be lapped by Stirling Moss driving the Vanwall.
Photo: Bernard Cahier

Above: Number one takes number one. The prophetically numbered Dino 246 of Peter Collins heads for victory in the 1958 British Grand Prix at Silverstone.

Right: Mike Hawthorn struggles to keep pace with Tony Brooks's Vanwall in the fateful 1958 German Grand Prix, where Peter Collins lost his life.
Photos: Bernard Cahier

stages of the race so as not to lap the World Champion.

Collins later scored a beautifully executed victory in the British GP at Silverstone, but was killed a fortnight later chasing Brooks's Vanwall around the Nürburgring in the German Grand Prix.

Moss had taken an early lead on the daunting mountain track, only for his Vanwall to stop with magneto trouble. That left Hawthorn and Collins running first and second, but Brooks swooped past on lap 11 and began to pull away.

Battling fading dampers and erratic drum brakes on his Ferrari Dino 246, Collins was chasing the leading Vanwall for all he was worth as they came out of the Pflanzgarten dip and into the climbing right-hander that followed. From third place, Hawthorn saw the drama unfold a matter of yards in front of him. As they went into that right-hander, Collins was slightly off-line, running wide to the left by little more than the width of his car.

The Ferrari's left wheel rode up the small bank on the outside of the corner and, just as Mike was thinking of telling Peter what a bloody fool he was, the car flipped over and threw out its driver. Hawthorn almost stopped, looking backwards to see Collins's Dino bounce upside down in a cloud of dust. Thereafter, Mike drove on like a robot, uncaring about the race and worried sick about his friend. Next time around, he retired when the clutch expired. Brooks won the race and a shattered Hawthorn later learned that his great friend, "Mon ami mate, Pete", had succumbed to serious head injuries in hospital.

From here on in, Hawthorn just wanted the season over. He determined that he would stop driving at the end of the year and that would be it. Done, decided. No more.

Above: A delighted Peter Collins poses for his friend Bernard Cahier's camera with the winner's trophy after his victory at Silverstone.
Photo: **Bernard Cahier**

Opposite: **Mike Hawthorn strolls across the paddock at Oporto in 1958. After the Portuguese Grand Prix, there would be just two more races to go before he could retire from the sport.**

Opposite, inset: **Stirling Moss takes the chequered flag in Portugal to keep his title chances alive**
Photos: Bernard Cahier

The crucial race in the World Championship battle between Moss and Hawthorn was the Portuguese GP at Oporto on 24th August. Mike led early on, but his Dino's drum brakes were no match for Moss's disc-braked Vanwall, and Stirling won easily.

After losing second place to Jean Behra's BRM when he came in to have his brakes adjusted, Hawthorn then set a new lap record as he chased after the Frenchman. It was at that point that the Vanwall pit signalled "HAWT REC" to Moss, indicating that Mike had set the fastest lap. Stirling read it as "HAWT REG" – Hawthorn regular – meaning that Mike hadn't made any progress.

On the last lap, Mike shot up an escape road, but turned the car around himself, fending off outside assistance from officials (which would have been illegal). Subsequently there was a protest to the effect that he had pushed his Ferrari against the direction of traffic on the track, but this was rejected thanks to the evidence of Moss, who correctly pointed out that Hawthorn had been on the pavement at the time of the alleged offence. So Mike took second place and that crucial extra point for fastest lap.

Then came the Moroccan Grand Prix on Casablanca's daunting Ain Diab circuit, where again Stirling would win convincingly for Vanwall. But Ferrari new boy Phil Hill had moved over to allow Hawthorn to take second place and become Britain's first World Champion driver by the margin of a single point.

Tony Vandervell's smart green Vanwalls had, for their part, won Britain the first Constructors' World Championship, but the celebrations were muted in the aftermath of another serious accident that left Vanwall driver Stuart Lewis-Evans with 70-per-cent burns.

Vandervell realised that motor racing was a dangerous game, but couldn't rid himself of the notion that poor Lewis-Evans wouldn't have been in this terrible state "if it wasn't for my bloody silly obsession with racing cars".

Poor Stuart was flown back to Britain in Vandervell's chartered Viscount airliner, the other drivers taking turns to talk to the amazingly cheerful young man who lay on a stretcher at the back of the passenger cabin. He was admitted to the famous McIndoe burns unit at East Grinstead hospital, where he succumbed just over a week later.

Grand Prix racing in those days was nothing if not predictably dangerous. Lewis-Evans was the highest-profile casualty of a race that also saw Olivier Gendebien upend his Ferrari Dino 246, injuring his chest and ribs. François Picard crashed his Formula 2 Cooper and sustained a fractured skull, while British privateer Tom Bridger was lucky to walk away from his wrecked Formula 2 Cooper. Part of the game, part of the risk.

Triumph and tragedy for Vanwall.

Above: **Tony Brooks smiles through the grime after his win in the 1958 Italian Grand Prix.**

Left: **Stuart Lewis-Evans in the pits at Casablanca, Morocco. The fast and talented Englishman was to crash in the race and later succumbed to the severe burns he recieved.**
Photos: Bernard Cahier

Stirling Moss in the shapely Vanwall dancing on the limit during the 1958 Morrocan Grand Prix. 'Stirl' won the race and set the fastest lap, but lost the championship to Hawthorn by a single point.

Photo: Bernard Cahier

FIA ANNOUNCES 1.5-LITRE LIMIT

There was certainly a sting in the tail of the 1958 World Championship and, after months of rumour and speculation, it was delivered on 29th October, 1958 within the lofty portals of the Royal Automobile Club in London's Pall Mall. The occasion was the presentation of awards to Mike Hawthorn and Tony Vandervell, but the president of the sport's governing body, the CSI, Auguste Perouse, threw a time bomb into the proceedings when he announced that a 1.5-litre F1, with a 500kg minimum weight limit, would supersede the 2.5-litre rules from the start of 1961. The British constructors were almost apoplectic with indignation.

Autosport responded with a suitably bold editorial. "The CSI can prattle about safety till they are blue in the face," boomed Gregor Grant. "The fact remains that all topflight drivers maintain the greater the power, the greater the safety."

He could have saved himself the effort. The new formula was a *fait accompli*. British race promoters wasted their time supporting a half-baked 3-litre 'Intercontinental Formula' for a couple more years, running various domestic events for this category, but it was real 'King Canute' stuff. Ferrari, meanwhile, settled down to develop a revised 1.5-litre version of the Dino V6 and, as time would demonstrate, the British teams were left behind. For the moment.

The Cooper now emerged as the car to beat. Jack Brabham's head-down, opposite-lock style of driving at the wheel of the four-cylinder Cooper-Climax would become an F1 trademark as the little team from Surbiton rose to humble the front-engined Ferrari Dino 246s and BRM P25s, which would be their prime opposition in 1959.

Throughout 1959, Brabham would be teamed with the young New Zealander, Bruce McLaren, and the bespectacled Masten Gregory from Kansas City. Brabham would win at Monaco and Aintree, while Stirling Moss, driving a Cooper-Climax for privateer Rob Walker, would triumph at Lisbon and Monza. For his part, McLaren would round off the season with his first F1 victory in the US Grand Prix at Sebring, where an exhausted Brabham pushed his out-of-fuel Cooper T51 home in fourth place to clinch the World Championship on a day when it could so easily have gone to Ferrari driver Tony Brooks, who had switched to the Italian team after Vanwall's belated withdrawal from F1.

Brooks, however, was bumped by team-mate Wolfgang von Trips on the run to the first corner and came in to check for damage at the end of the opening lap. Beneath his quiet exterior, Brooks had a very strong, unshakeable personal philosophy that was founded on an unobtrusive, but very real, set of Christian beliefs.

"Motor racing was always only part of my life," he explained. "I think I was blessed with a lot of natural

ability; I tried hard, but I never tried to the point that I might risk killing myself.

"I think that taking an uncalculated risk could lead to what amounts to suicide and I have a religious conviction that such risks are not acceptable. I learned from my accidents at Le Mans with an Aston Martin and at Silverstone with the BRM that I would never try and compensate for a mechanically deficient car.

"In my book, you should never drive to the point where you experience fear. I would drive to the very best of my ability, and persevere with a car if it was mechanically deficient in a non-dangerous way. I was fortunate enough that I could win races without going into that fear zone."

Part of that philosophy was shaped – or certainly endorsed – by his experience at Le Mans in 1957, when he rolled an Aston Martin after struggling with a troublesome gearchange. Lying under the upturned car was bad enough, but then along came a rival Ferrari, which crashed into the Aston, knocking it off Brooks. Under the circumstances, he was fortunate to have got away with relatively minor injuries; he could so easily have been killed. It certainly made him think.

Brooks had held on, waiting to see if Tony Vandervell would continue in 1959, and by the time the British industrialist decided to quit, the only available competitive seat was at Ferrari. It was a move that undoubtedly put Jean Behra's nose out of joint, but Tony was not the sort of character to indulge in personal rivalries.

Moss, meanwhile, judged that driving for Rob Walker's team was the best alternative available, following his two seasons with Vanwall. He had a close personal friendship with Rob, who was, and is, one of nature's true gentlemen and an outstanding sportsman-enthusiast.

Below: After Vanwall's withdrawal, Stirling threw in his lot with his longtime friend, Rob Walker, for whom he would score some of his greatest successes. Walker chief mechanic Alf Francis gets in on the act in the background of Bernard Cahier's shot.

Bottom: The 1959 season saw the Cooper works team come of age, Jack Brabham scoring his first GP win with a faultless drive at Monaco.
Photos: Bernard Cahier

Unfortunately, while Cooper was all too willing to sell Walker a car, it could not help with a gearbox, as it was at full stretch trying to make its ERSA-modified Citroën boxes sufficiently durable to handle the power of the 2.5-litre Climax four-cylinder engines over a full race distance.

As a result, Walker and his team had to turn to Italian transmission specialist Valerio Colotti to manufacture a gearbox for the car. It proved a real disaster, costing Moss sure victories in the Monaco and Dutch Grands Prix, and eventually prompting Rob to suggest that it might be better if he did not race the car until these problems were sorted out.

Moss's failure at Zandvoort had handed the BRM team its maiden Grand Prix victory, Jo Bonnier winning at the wheel of the much-improved P25, so a deal was cut for Stirling to drive a loaned BRM in the light green livery of the British Racing Partnership – an outfit run by his father, Alfred, and manager, Ken Gregory – in the French and British GPs.

Stirling spun off on melting tar at Reims, while an earlier clutch failure meant that he was unable to keep the engine running, but at Aintree he finished second to Jack Brabham's Cooper after a closely fought battle with Bruce McLaren.

Moss was impressed with the BRM P25. Ironically, BRP's BRM was totally destroyed when Stirling's one-time Mercedes team-mate, Hans Herrmann, suffered brake failure at Avus during the German Grand Prix. "A sad end to a car which was actually vastly better than its results might suggest," noted Moss.

For this race, Moss was back in the Walker Cooper-Climax, but again the gearbox gremlins intervened and he failed to finish. On this occasion, however, he hadn't expected to be a serious contender for victory. The Berlin race furnished Tony Brooks with his second Grand Prix win of the year in the elegant, revamped Fantuzzi-bodied Ferrari Dino 246.

Brooks's previous victory had come at Reims in sweltering conditions, where he calmly drove away from the pack; it was awesome. This was also the race where his volatile French team-mate, Jean Behra, finally fell out with the Ferrari management

"I didn't have any problem with Behra," said Brooks, "but we didn't communicate much, because I didn't speak French and his Italian was not very good – mine was quite competent – but there were never any nasty words.

"I don't know what Behra's problem was. Perhaps he thought he should have been appointed number-one driver. For my part, I just joined the team on the understanding that I was going to get a car as good as everybody else's. And at Ferrari, I did get a car which was always the equal of my team-mates', which is more than I can say for my time with Vanwall."

Carlo Chiti, Ferrari's chief engineer, felt that Behra was cut adrift emotionally by Ferrari, having joined the team believing he would be designated leader. At Reims, where he threw a punch at team manager Romolo Tavoni, he had got it into his mind that his Dino 246 was somehow mechanically deficient – and even reportedly made a protest to the sport's governing body to the effect that Ferrari had stitched him up, providing him with a chassis that had recently been shunted by Dan Gurney in testing at Monza.

"Jean was certainly not a very likeable charac-

ter," recounted Chiti with brutal frankness. "They called him 'the gypsy' because of his passionate temperament. He also had a particularly vulgar way of expressing himself.

"But the way he died led me, even so, to think deeply about it. We had completely abandoned that man to himself, with his brooding determination to win. We had obliged him to take refuge in his own desperation."

Behra, who had led at Monaco before blowing up his Dino's engine, worked himself up into a fury of frustration over his disappointment with the season, culminating in his knocking out cold Tavoni in a restaurant at Reims on the evening after he had trashed

another V6 engine.

As if that wasn't enough, he also had a major confrontation with a journalist in the same restaurant. "If you ever say that again, I'll punch you in the face," Behra threatened. He went to leave the restaurant, paused at the door and then back-tracked to the journalist's table.

"I've just thought about this," he said. "It's not worth waiting for the next time." With that, he punched the hapless scribe in the face.

Enzo Ferrari may have been privately quite amused that a member of the fourth estate should have been subjected to such summary justice. But thumping his team manager was another matter altogether. The episode cost Behra his place in the Maranello line-up, and the gallant Frenchman died soon afterwards when his

Continued on page 99

Opposite: Tony Brooks slides the elegant Fantuzzi-rebodied Ferrari Dino 246 on his way to victory in the 1959 French GP at Reims.

Below: The volcanic Frenchman Jean Behra, whose death shortly after he was fired by Ferrari came as a huge shock to the F1 fraternity, even at a time when fatal accidents were part and part and parcel of the business.

Photos: Bernard Cahier

Opposite: At long last, a victory for BRM. Joakim Bonnier takes the chequered flag at Zandvoort to win the 1959 Dutch Grand Prix in the 2.5-litre P25, bringing to an end a decade of disappointment.

Photo: Bernard Cahier

Left: **Refreshment stop for Harry Schell as Bernard Cahier provides some water for the BRM driver. Jo Bonnier, who had just retired from the race, looks on.**
Photo: Cahier archive

Opposite: **Tony Brooks in the winning Ferrari heads the Cooper of Masten Gregory and the Ferrari of Dan Gurney on the Avus banking during the 1959 German Grand Prix.**

Below: **Stirling Moss in the Walker Cooper harries the Ferraris of Tony Brooks and Jean Behra in the 1959 Dutch Grand Prix. Moss fought his way into the lead after a poor start, but the unreliable Colotti gearbox would let him down once more.**

Above: Jack Brabham on his way to victory in the 1959 British Grand Prix at Aintree.

Right: Brabham in the fourth-placed Cooper at Monte Carlo in 1958.

Photos: Bernard Cahier

CHARLES AND JOHN COOPER

A STRONG streak of technical and mechanical ingenuity ran through the post-war British motor racing scene like the lettering in a stick of Brighton rock. Nowhere was it more evident than in the achievements of Charles and John Cooper, the father-and-son partnership who rocked the F1 establishment to its core in the late 1950s.

The Coopers had built their first single-seat racer in 1946, when they produced a creation fashioned from a couple of Fiat Topolino saloons and propelled by a single-cylinder JAP engine. Thus they were in on the ground floor of the 500cc F3 category, which took off spectacularly as a nursery for future F1 stars such as Stirling Moss and Peter Collins. In the early 1950s, Coopers were everywhere on the F3 scene.

Charles and John provided a uniquely balanced partnership. The son's sometimes over-ambitious and effervescent enthusiasm was tempered by the Old Man's ingrained conservatism and reluctance to spend money unless absolutely necessary. Ultimately this conservatism would lead to the Cooper F1 team's downfall in the late 1960s, but those days were far ahead when Mike Hawthorn started out on his quest for stardom in the Cooper Bristol F2 car in 1952.

The Cooper Bristol indirectly shaped the company's path into F1 via the achievements of Australian Jack Brabham, who arrived in Britain at the end of 1954 after racing one of these now-ageing F2 cars in his native land. In the 1955 British Grand Prix at Aintree, Brabham debuted an aerodynamically-bodied, 2.2-litre Bristol-engine Cooper in the British GP. It marked the company's debut as an F1 constructor.

From the start of 1957, Cooper really got into the swing of things, pitching its F2 Climax-engine cars into the baffle for F1 supremacy. They lacked power, but displayed splendid agility. Their best result was Roy Salvadori's fifth place in the British Grand Prix at Aintree. But better would come in 1958 and beyond.

Above: **From little acorns. John and Charles Cooper with their 500cc special in 1946.**
Photo: **LAT Photographic**

Below left: **A welcome swig of bubbly for Jack Brabham after his victory in the 1959 British Grand Prix.**

Right: **No team uniform for John Cooper in 1959, just a BRDC lapel badge proudly worn on his rather careworn jacket!**
Photos: **Bernard Cahier**

Porsche sports car crashed on the Avus banking during a supporting event at the German GP meeting.

Moss won at Lisbon and Monza, successes that helped clinch Cooper's victory in the Constructors' World Championship, which meant that a British manufacturer had won this newly instigated award for the second year running.

Although his experience in 1958 meant that Moss wasn't terribly concerned about the significance of the World Championship as a whole, 'Stirl' could still take the title if he won the US race at Sebring and posted fastest lap into the bargain. Six laps in and the gearbox broke again. So that was that.

With the best five results counting, Brabham took the title with 31 points (net), with Tony Brooks second on 27 and Moss third on 25.5.

ENTER THE SENSATIONAL LOTUS

The 1960 season saw the first flowering of Colin Chapman's design talent in the form of the superb Lotus 18, the car that would take the baton from Cooper and progress the rear-engined F1 concept to fresh levels of technical sophistication.

Cooper attempted to match the wind-cheating profile of the Lotus with the 'lowline' T53 challenger, and this duly carried Jack Brabham to his second straight World Championship with wins in the Dutch, Belgian, French, British and Portuguese Grands Prix in commanding style. Nevertheless, the Lotus was the class of the field. Light, compact and – unfortunately – horrifyingly frail, the type 18 was fielded not only by the factory team, with Innes Ireland, Jim Clark and former motorcycle champion John Surtees doing the driving, but also by Rob Walker, who immediately had purchased a car for Stirling Moss.

Above: Endangered species. The front-engined Lotus 16 of Alan Stacey leads the BRM of Jo Bonnier at Aintree in 1959.

Right: Scarab arrived in 1960, but its beautifully crafted, front-engine machines were two years too late and had missed the rear-engine boat. Team patron Lance Reventlow, whose mother, Barbara Hutton, was heir to the Woolworth fortune, is seen here displaying a disreputably battered Bell helmet – and seat belts – in the Dutch GP at Zandvoort.

Above right: A beaming smile from the youthful Bruce McLaren, who took victory for Cooper in the 1960 Argentine Grand Prix.

Left: The sensational Lotus 18 was the template for the future. John Surtees drives past a post box and a lamp post barely protected by straw bales at the 1960 Portuguese Grand Prix held in Oporto.

Photos: Bernard Cahier

Right: Chris Bristow pushing too hard at the wheel of his Yeoman Credit Cooper shortly before meeting his death in the 1960 Belgian Grand Prix.

Below right: Innes Ireland at work with the Lotus 18 in the 1960 British Grand Prix. The Scot is using a visor rather than the traditional goggles.

Below: An interesting comparison at the French Grand Prix between Bruce McLaren's works T53 'lowline' Cooper and Olivier Gendebien's year-old T51 Yeoman Credit car.

Photos: Bernard Cahier

The Lotus 18 had hardly turned a wheel before making its F1 debut in the Argentine Grand Prix, yet Ireland enjoyed a symbolic lap at the head of the field before being overwhelmed by his opposition. He finished sixth. The second race of the season saw Moss win at Monaco, a race that also marked the debut of the front-engined American Scarabs, bankrolled by millionaire team owner Lance Reventlow.

The Scarabs were extremely well-built machines that, like the front-engined Aston Martins, which had been introduced the previous year, had missed the F1 boat in the biggest possible way. Ferrari also retained the front-engined Dino 246 for a final season before switching to a rear-engine configuration for the start of the 1.5-litre F1 in 1961.

At Monaco, Moss and the Rob Walker *équipe* gave Lotus its maiden Grand Prix victory, just as they had done for Cooper two years before in Buenos Aires. But while the rugged Cooper would enable Brabham to reel off that succession of World Championship winning victories throughout the summer, the Lotus squad would have an infinitely more stressful time.

Lotus always had a reputation for fragility, and this was underlined when Moss's car shed its left rear wheel midway through Spa's 140mph Burnenville corner during Saturday practice for the Belgian GP. The car crashed heavily, turning over and throwing Moss out on to the side of the circuit.

"Shunt. Nose, Back, Legs, Bruises. Bugger!" read the cryptic note in Moss's diary for 8th June, 1960. Yet he was the lucky one. Lotus privateer Michael Taylor was badly hurt when his Lotus 18's steering failed in the same session. Then in the race itself, works Lotus driver Alan Stacey was killed when he hit a bird on the Masta straight, and Yeoman Credit Cooper driver Chris Bristow crashed fatally at Burnen-

Above: **Lotus team-mates for 1960, Jim Clark (left) and the luckless Alan Stacey, who would be killed in a freak accident at Spa-Francorchamps.**

Top: **Stirling Moss displays his usual unflappable cool in the Walker team Lotus 18, winning at Monaco in 1960.**
Photos: Bernard Cahier

ville while embroiled in a lurid battle for second place with Willy Mairesse's Ferrari Dino 246.

Ferrari, meanwhile, was having a disappointing season. Cliff Allison finished second to McLaren's winning Cooper in Buenos Aires, but then crashed spectacularly during practice at Monaco, where he hit the chicane and was hurled from the car. With Brooks having moved to the Yeoman Credit Cooper outfit, this left the responsibility for team leadership on the shoulders of the relatively inexperienced Phil Hill, who at least managed to win the Italian Grand Prix at Monza.

Not that this amounted to a great deal, as the British constructors were reluctant to risk their cars on the combined banked track/road circuit on which the Italian round of the championship took place.

At an RAC Competitions Committee meeting on 13th July, 1960, it was reported that the main British constructors had advised the Italian Automobile Club of their unwillingness to participate in the Italian Grand Prix, "which is this year the Grand Prix of Europe, as it is to be run over the full circuit at Monza, i.e. the banked track and the road circuit combined. They would be prepared to enter an event on the road circuit only, as has been the case since 1957. So far, no reply has been received."

The Italians really could not have cared less. They had their beloved Ferraris and went ahead with their

With no garages available for the US Grand Prix at the track, the teams were obliged to rent space in the city of Riverside, some 10km away from the circuit. As none of the teams had transporters, the only way to get back and forth was by driving the cars on the open roads, much to the excitement of the local population – not to mention the police! Maurice Trintignant (left) drives his Scuderia Centro Sud Cooper among the freeway traffic, while John Surtees (below left) in his Lotus negotiates a street junction and traffic lights.

Right: Phil Hill with Tavoni after his win in the 1960 Italian Grand Prix.

Below: Nineteen-sixty was the last hurrah for the traditional front-engined car in Formula 1. Wolfgang von Trips grapples with his Ferrari Dino 246 in the season's opener at Buenos Aires.

Photos: Bernard Cahier

own race on their own terms. Hill, Richie Ginther and Mairesse duly delivered a grand slam 1-2-3 victory against makeweight opposition, Giulio Cabianca's Cooper-Ferrari finishing fourth, ahead of Wolfgang von Trips in the 1.5-litre Ferrari 156 prototype. Over two months after that Monza event, the final round of the title chase took place at California's Riverside circuit, where Moss's Walker Lotus won the US Grand Prix, ahead of Ireland's works car, the Coopers of McLaren and Brabham, Jo Bonnier's BRM and Phil Hill, driving a borrowed Cooper, as Ferrari did not make the trip. Jack Brabham was comfortably World Champion for the second time on 43 points, with McLaren second on 34 (net), ahead of Moss and Ireland.

THE 1.5-LITRE FORMULA

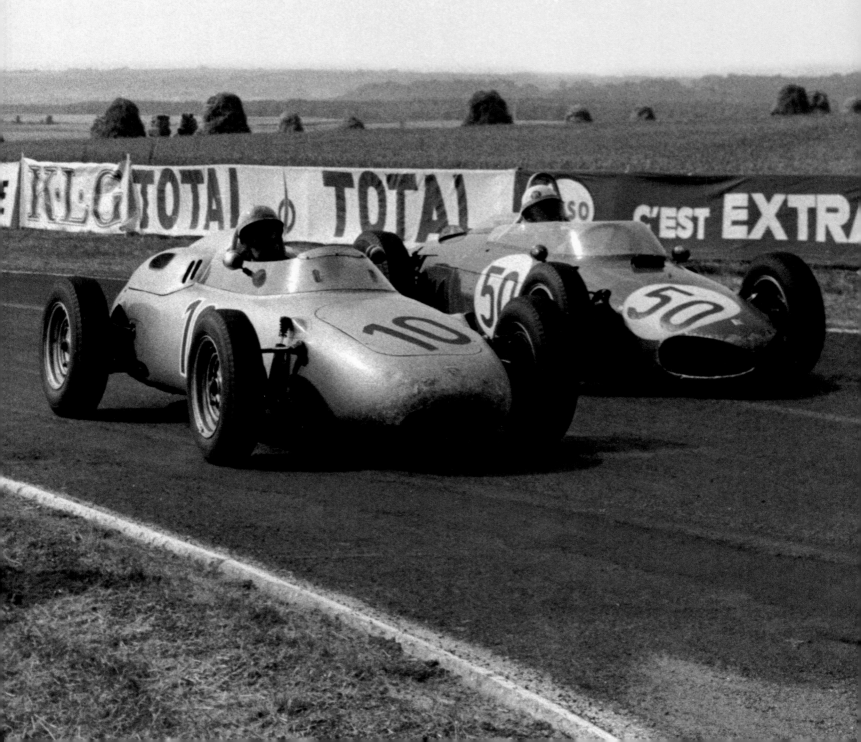

Photographers take their chances trackside in the braking zone for the Thillois hairpin during the 1961 French Grand Prix at Reims. Contesting the lead are Jo Bonnier's Porsche (10) and the Ferrari 156 of debutant Giancarlo Baghetti (50), just ahead of Jim Clark's Lotus 21 (8) and Dan Gurney's Porsche (12).

Photo: Bernard Cahier

WHILE the British teams griped and groaned over the introduction of the new 1.5-litre regulations, Ferrari's engineers got their heads down and pressed on with a suitable engine. Throughout the final three years of the 2.5-litre F1, the Italian team had continued developing a small-capacity version of its 65-degree V6 engine for F2 purposes; this unit formed the basis of the 1961 challenge.

One of these rear-engined Dino 156 prototypes had been used in the 1960 Italian Grand Prix, where Wolfgang von Trips had finished fifth. Preparation for the following season – and the new formula – continued on 2nd October, when von Trips took the same car to third place in the non-title Modena GP, behind Jo Bonnier's Porsche and Willy Mairesse's front-engined Dino 156.

Ferrari's chief engineer, Carlo Chiti, also produced a 120-degree version of the original 65-degree V6, this revised unit developing around 190bhp at 9500rpm. This was more than sufficient to eclipse the 1.5-litre four-cylinder engines from Coventry Climax and BRM that were used by the majority of the British opposition.

Both Climax and BRM were working flat out on V8 designs, but these would not see the light of day until midway through 1961, and would not race competitively until the start of the following year.

The Ferrari V6 engines were installed in space-frame chassis, which were clothed in distinctive bodywork, the main feature of which was the twin-nostril 'shark nose' treatment of the front end. Drive was by means of a five-speed transaxle positioned ahead of the rear axle line – a configuration supposedly adopted to allow sufficient room in the engine bay for a 2.9-litre engine to be installed just in case the Intercontinental Formula should get off the ground after all. Ferrari had all the bases covered.

The driver line-up included Californians Phil Hill and Richie Ginther, the German Count von Trips, and the Italian novice, Giancarlo Baghetti, whose semi-independent car was fielded under the auspices of a group of Italian racing teams keen to encourage home-grown talent. Later in the year, they would be joined by the brilliantly talented 19-year-old Mexican, Ricardo Rodriguez.

It was Baghetti, driving in his first F1 race, who gave the Ferrari 156 a victorious debut in the non-title Syracuse Grand Prix in Sicily. On this occasion, the Milanese driver had a relatively easy task in defeating what was essentially makeweight opposition. But things would not be so straightforward come the Monaco Grand Prix, the opening round of the World Championship battle.

On the famous street circuit, where inevitably chassis agility would even the balance against an engine power advantage, Stirling Moss and the Rob Walker Lotus 18 were in a class of their own. The team was using one of the later Mark 3 Climax FPF engines, which benefited from a strengthened bottom end and delivered performance across a wider torque range.

Moss duly qualified on pole. Shortly before the start, there was a very worrying moment when he discovered a cracked chassis tube on the Walker Lotus. No matter; his loyal mechanic, Alf Francis, cool as a cucumber, welded the offending tube on the starting grid, after wrapping the brimming fuel tanks with wet towels! Just in case, you understand.

Above: **Richie Ginther strains every sinew at the wheel of his Ferrari 156 as he rounds Station hairpin in his pursuit of Stirling Moss's Lotus 18/21 during the 1961 Monaco Grand Prix. In the background, Roy Salvadori vacates the cockpit of his Bowmaker Lola on the station steps.**

Opposite top: **Phil Hill, 1961 World Champion. Few more deep thinking and sensitive souls ever got behind the wheel of an F1 car than this modest American.**

Opposite, bottom: **Stirling Moss takes his Lotus 18 to victory in the 1961 Monaco Grand Prix.**
Photos: Bernard Cahier

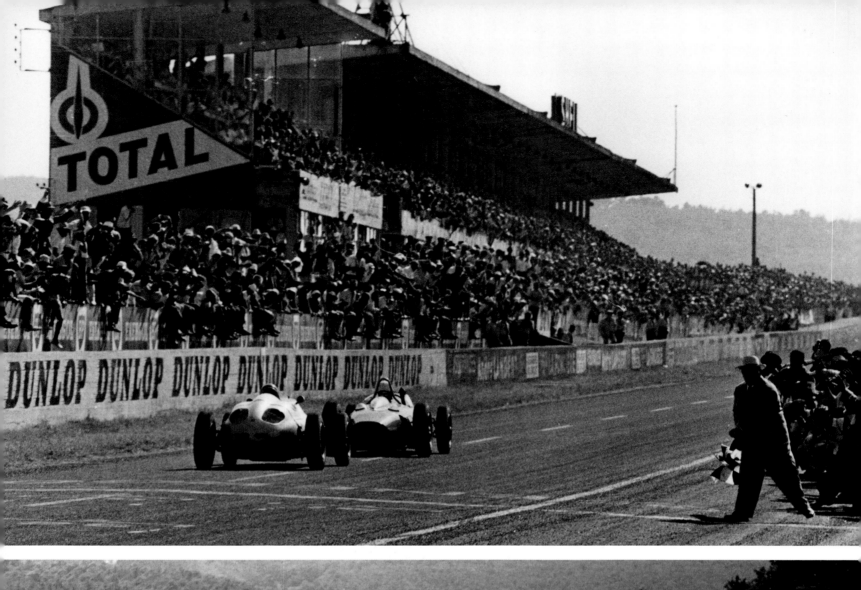

Despite giving away 35bhp to the Ferraris, Moss won brilliantly, taking the chequered flag ahead of Ginther. For the rest of his life, the wiry little Californian driver would rate it as the best personal performance of his racing career.

"My car and my effort were stronger than the opposition when I won in the Honda [at Mexico City in 1965], which was just plain faster than the opposition," he said, "but at Monaco, both Stirling and I were three seconds below the pole time in the race. Staggering, isn't it?

"I set the lap record very late [16 laps from the finish], but Stirling equalled it next time round. That son of a gun! If you did well against him, then you'd really done something special."

Phil Hill, who would finish third, ahead of von Trips, later likened chasing Moss's Lotus around Monaco to trying to race a greyhound around your living room with a carthorse.

On the same day, Baghetti had an easy afternoon winning the non-title Naples Grand Prix, but von Trips got Ferrari's World Championship juggernaut seriously rolling with victory in the Dutch Grand Prix at Zandvoort. Hill finished second and then led home a Maranello grand slam in the Belgian GP at Spa-Francorchamps, with von Trips, Ginther and Belgian sports car ace Olivier Gendebien – winner of that year's Le Mans classic – following along behind.

FIRST-TIME WINNER

Next up was the French GP at Reims-Gueux, traditionally a sweltering affair under a relentless sun. The 1961 fixture proved no exception, and Baghetti's FISA-entered 156 supplemented the works effort. Hill, who had learned a thing or two about psyching out his contemporaries, put in a stupendous lap to take pole – over a second faster than the frustrated von Trips.

Ginther led initially, but had an early spin, leaving von Trips and Hill to battle over the lead. Von Trips went out after 20 laps with a stone through the radiator, then Hill spun at Thillois and was clouted by Moss's Lotus. Phil stalled and couldn't restart. All this drama allowed Ginther through into the lead, but his chances were thwarted by fading oil pressure.

Baghetti now found himself embroiled in a frantic battle for the lead of his first World Championship Grand Prix with the two powerful four-cylinder Porsches driven by Dan Gurney and Jo Bonnier.

Two laps from the chequered flag, Bonnier dropped from the fray, leaving Gurney – himself a former Ferrari man – to try to get the better of the Prancing Horse. Going down the long straight into the final Thillois right-hander for the last time, Gurney slipstreamed past into the lead, staying there as the two cars scrabbled through the turn and made for the line.

In a perfectly judged move, Baghetti swung out of Gurney's slipstream and surged past to win by one-tenth of a second. The baby of the team had saved the day for Maranello. It was the pleasant Italian's only victory in an international motor race of major consequence.

Von Trips scored his second win of the season in the British Grand Prix at Aintree, an event that was marked by the sole World Championship outing of the technically innovative Ferguson P99 four-wheel-drive

Above: Wolfgang von Trips, garlanded and seemingly immersed in thought after winning the 1961 British Grand Prix at Aintree for Ferrari.

Opposite, top: Giancarlo Baghetti drives into the history books as the only man ever to win his maiden Grand Épreuve, the Italian's Ferrari 156 just pipping Dan Gurney's four-cylinder Porsche to the flag in the 1961 French Grand Prix.

Left: Phil Hill and Wolfgang von Trips contest the lead of the 1961 Belgian Grand Prix at Spa-Francorchamps.
Photos: Bernard Cahier

car. The machine had been developed primarily as a competition test bed for tractor magnate Harry Ferguson's four-wheel-drive systems. Ferguson Research, established with the technical know-how of former pre-war motorcycle ace Fred Dixon and Le Mans winner Tony Rolt, was at the cutting edge of four-wheel-drive technology well in advance of any real interest from the general motor industry.

Powered by a 1.5-litre Climax FPF engine, the Ferguson P99 was completed in the spring of 1961. It was a front-engined machine with its engine canted over in the space-frame chassis. A normal clutch took the drive to a bespoke Ferguson five-speed gearbox, which had been developed in conjunction with Colotti, the Italian gearbox specialist. From this point, transfer gears stepped the drive sideways towards the centre of the car and propshafts that passed it to the front and rear, the rear shaft running to the left of the driver's seat, where a small crown wheel and pinion was fit-

ted. At the point where the transfer gears stepped the drive out to the propshafts, there was a system of free-wheels and limited-slip differentials that made it virtually impossible to spin the wheels.

In addition, the Ferguson P99 was equipped with brake servos operated by hydraulic pressure from an engine-driven pump, incorporating the Dunlop developed 'Maxaret' braking system, which prevented any wheel from locking in wet conditions. Driver controlled, the Maxaret system could be switched on and off from the cockpit.

An agreement was reached for Rob Walker's team to enter the car, and the P99 made its debut in the British Empire Trophy race at Silverstone one week prior to the 1961 British GP at Aintree. Jack Fairman was at the wheel on that occasion, but Moss had the option of driving the P99 in the British Grand Prix. Instead he opted for his regular Lotus 18/21, which eventually retired with brake trouble.

At this point, Fairman was called in to hand over the Ferguson to Stirling. The Ferrari pit immediately advised its drivers of the change, warning them that they should not be tricked into thinking it was Fairman if they came across the Ferguson lapping unexpectedly fast.

However, race officials politely pointed out that Fairman had contravened the regulations by being push-started after a pit stop, but everyone involved was so delighted over the way the car was performing that it had been kept running to gain some useful test mileage. Unfortunately, under pressure from other teams, the Ferguson was called into the pits and withdrawn.

Moss was impressed beyond doubt by the Ferguson's capability in the wet and agreed to drive it in the non-championship Oulton Park Gold Cup meeting later that summer. In patchy wet conditions, he won at a canter from the works Coopers of Brabham and McLaren. The

Above: After yet another majestic performance, Stirling Moss takes the chequered flag in the 1961 German Grand Prix.

Above right: Jack Brabham in the new Climax V8-engined Cooper, which qualified second only to Phil Hill's Ferrari under sunny conditions.

Right: Prelude to disaster. Jim Clark trails the four works Ferrari 156s in the early stages of the 1961 Italian Grand Prix. The Scot would tangle with von Trips (fourth in the group) with catastrophic consequences.

Photos: Bernard Cahier

car was then withdrawn from front-line competition, although Peter Westbury would use it to great effect to win the 1964 British Hillclimb Championship.

The frenzied battle for engine power in the first year of the 1.5-litre F1 completely eclipsed the longer-term potential of the Ferguson concept, but the idea would resurface eight years later, in 1969, with a new crop of four-wheel-drive challengers. As we shall see, by then there were further complications to prevent them from realising their theoretical potential.

Back in the mainstream action, the 1961 German Grand Prix at the Nürburgring would go down in history as another fine against-the-odds victory for Moss in the outdated and uprated Walker team Lotus 18/21. Moss also chose to race on the Dunlop D12 'green spot' rain tyres, which his old pal, Innes Ireland, had used to such good effect to win the non-title Solitude Grand Prix in the works 21. These tyres gave terrific extra grip and, with rain showers forecast for the Nürburgring, Moss took the gamble of using them, even though, in his own words, Dunlop's racing manager, Vic Barlow, "had kittens" and told him that he would race on them at his own risk.

The 1961 German Grand Prix was a landmark, however, in that it saw the race debut of the splendid 63 x 60mm, 1495cc, two-valves-per-cylinder Coventry Climax V8, which developed 180bhp at 8500rpm, installed in Jack Brabham's works Cooper T58. He qualified second to Phil Hill's Ferrari, but slid off the road on the opening lap. However, it had shown F1 a glimpse of the future.

TRAGEDY AT MONZA

The World Championship was wide open between Phil Hill and Wolfgang von Trips as the Ferrari team arrived at Monza for the Italian Grand Prix. Von Trips took pole from 19-year-old Mexican new boy Ricardo Rodriguez – whose wealthy father had bankrolled his place in the Maranello squad – but, due to running high final drive ratios, the Ferraris were slow off the line. This allowed Jim Clark's Lotus 21 to get in among them on the opening lap.

Going down to Parabolica for the second time, von Trips was getting into his stride and had just overtaken Clark before the braking area when apparently he moved over on the Lotus before he had completely cleared its left front wheel. The two cars interlocked, and the Ferrari cartwheeled up the bank and along the spectator fence, killing 14 members of the public, before crashing back on to the edge of the circuit. Clark's Lotus spun to a halt, the Scot emerging unhurt, but von Trips had been hurled from his car and lay fatally injured at the trackside.

Phil Hill won the race in the sole Ferrari to make the finish, clinching the World Championship crown ahead of Dan Gurney's Porsche, Bruce McLaren's Cooper and the private Cooper of Jack Lewis. Hill took the title with 34 points to von Trips's 33, with Moss and Gurney sharing third place on 21 points apiece.

Ferrari did not attend the 1961 US Grand Prix, which Ireland won for Lotus just prior to his unceremonious sacking by Chapman. Gurney was second

and Tony Brooks third in the underpowered BRM-Climax, a performance that rounded off the career of the 29-year-old one-time Vanwall star, who opted to retire to concentrate on his expanding garage business back home in Surrey.

Although Brooks never had any regrets about his decision to quit, one is bound to wonder what would have happened in 1962 had he continued racing for BRM. Monza in 1961 saw the first appearance of the 90-degree BRM V8 engine, the 68.5 x 50.8mm, 1498cc unit developing 185bhp at 10,000rpm with an initial 13:1 compression ratio.

Subsequently the compression ratio was reduced to 10.5:1 in an effort to protect the pistons from the effects of detonation. A six-speed gearbox had been designed to complement the V8 when it was in-

stalled in the new BRM P56 chassis for the following season.

History, of course, relates that Graham Hill would drive the BRM to the 1962 Drivers' World Championship. Yet had it not been for that retirement decision, perhaps that title would have fallen to Tony Brooks, whom many regarded as a much superior driver to the mustachioed Hill.

Brooks eventually got to drive a BRM P56 some 35 years after Graham Hill's title success. The occasion was the impromptu Basildon Grand Prix, arranged by the enterprising Canon Lionel Webber around the ring roads of the Essex town in 1997.

"It was the first time that I had ever driven the V8 BRM," said Brooks, by then 65. "It made me think that I had retired a year too soon!"

END OF THE F1 ROAD FOR MOSS

There were several key elements to the 1962 F1 season: the arrival of the BRM V8 as a front-line challenger, the sensational debut of the monocoque Lotus 25 and the fading fortunes of the Ferrari team, which had been subjected to a wholesale defection of key staff to the ambitious new ATS operation.

However, all these were mere footnotes when compared with the accident at Goodwood on Easter Monday that marked the end of Stirling Moss's Grand Prix career. Driving a Lotus 18/21 'special', powered by a BRM V8 and entered by the UDT Laystall team operated by his father, Alfred, and manager, Ken Gregory, Moss was contesting the Glover Trophy race, in which he had lost time early on with a pit stop to rectify a sticking throttle.

He resumed well behind Graham Hill's leading BRM and, poised to unlap himself from the future World Champion, slammed off the road at St Mary's Corner and crashed head-on into an earth bank. It was a miracle that Moss survived at all. The flimsy Lotus space-frame collapsed around him and it seemed to take an age to remove him from the wreckage.

Moss was freed from the twisted shell of his car with deep facial wounds, his left cheekbone crushed, the eye socket displaced, and his left arm, nose, left knee and ankle broken. He was unconscious for a month and paralysed down his left side for six months. Thirty-seven years later, he acknowledges that probably he retired prematurely, even though he did not make his final decision to quit until the spring of 1963.

Moss effectively relinquished his role to Jimmy Clark, who would be armed with the superb monocoque Lotus 25 from the first Grand Prix of the season, the Dutch GP at Zandvoort. The aluminium 'bathtub' monocoque around which the 25 was built provided compactness allied to torsional rigidity, plus benefits in terms of driver protection, although these were very much a secondary consideration during the early 1960s.

Of course, in introducing the Lotus 25, Colin Chapman was performing a ruthless and lurid commercial juggling act. He had a good business selling F1 cars to private customers, and when it was announced that Innes Ireland was joining the UDT Laystall F1 team for 1962, Chapman confirmed that the customer Lotus 24s – one of which was also going to Rob Walker – would be 'virtually the same' as the factory 25s.

Rob Walker remembers John Cooper making it clear that he knew precisely what Chapman was up to in the pit lane at Zandvoort when he cast an appraising glance over the new monocoque Lotus. Having looked studiously into the cockpit, he said to Chapman, "Oh yes, I see what you mean; they're exactly the same – you just forgot to put the chassis in this one."

Chapman smiled weakly. Needless to say, the Lotus 24 wasn't in the same league as the factory cars, although, in fairness, none of the privateer drivers was in the same league as Jimmy Clark either.

Graham Hill had won the Dutch Grand Prix at the start of what would be a crucial year for BRM. From the outset, Sir Alfred Owen had made it clear that the team's future depended on it winning at least two Grands Prix that season. Although Jim Clark got into his stride with victories in the Belgian and British

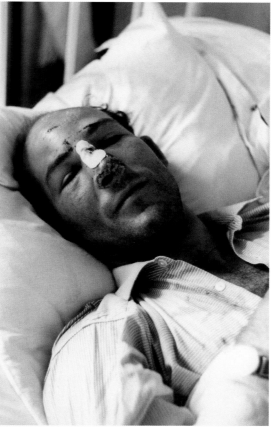

Left: Stirling Moss recovering in hospital from the crash at Goodwood that ended his career.

Opposite, top: Spirit of the Sixties. Jimmy Clark and the revolutionary monocoque Lotus 25 on the way to their first victory in the 1962 Belgian Grand Prix at Spa-Francorchamps.

Opposite, bottom: The popular Bruce McLaren accepts the plaudits after winning the 1962 Monaco Grand Prix in the works Cooper-Climax.

Below: Graham Hill ended BRM's long drought by deservedly taking the 1962 World Championship.

Photos: Bernard Cahier

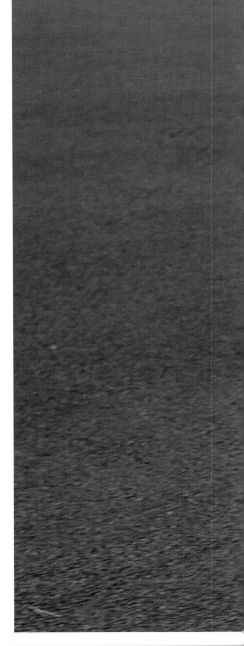

Grands Prix (held at Aintree for what would be the last time), Hill guaranteed the future of the BRM organisation by scoring a close win over John Surtees's Lola and Dan Gurney's Porsche in the German GP at the Nürburgring.

Hill would consolidate BRM's position when he won again at Monza and clinched the World Championship in the South African GP at East London with only two days of the old year still left. Clark's Lotus had seemed on course for the title until sidelined by an oil leak while leading comfortably, but BRM deserved its moment in the sun, as the transformation in its fortunes under the engineering direction of the talented Tony Rudd had been quite remarkable.

Hill won the championship with 42 points (net), ahead of Clark on 30 and McLaren on 27.

As for Lotus, Chapman's cars had proved the class of the field, but undeniably frail, experiencing some problems with their German-built ZE gearboxes, and there was plenty of evidence that the outfit concentrated primarily on Clark's car to the exclusion of the number-two driver, in this case the very talented Trevor Taylor.

For its part, Ferrari had an absolutely dreadful season in 1962. Phil Hill had signed on again with the *Commendatore* when he was on the crest of an emotional wave in the aftermath of that championship clincher at Monza the previous September, which had seen the tragic death of Wolfgang von Trips.

The team continued to rely on uprated versions of the Dino 156 Sharknose, but now the British V8s had parity of power, better chassis and superior drivers. Small wonder that Maranello had to play a supporting role given that Carlo Chiti and most of the engineering team had departed to ATS.

PORSCHE'S LONE F1 SUCCESS

Porsche, which had been competing in F1 with outdated four-cylinder cars, really raised the standard of its game in 1962 with the 66 x 54.66mm, 1494cc flat-eight-cylinder Porsche 804, which developed 185bhp at 9200rpm. Dan Gurney was the number-one driver, paired with Jo Bonnier, and he won the French Grand Prix at Rouen-les-Essarts.

It would be the sole World Championship Grand Prix victory to be won by the famous German car maker, which then withdrew from F1 at the end of the season.

The Porsche company's F1 involvement had been inspired by the success of the modified single-seater 1500 RSK sports car that Jean Behra had used to win the Formula 2 race at Reims in 1958. Porsche then built a four-cylinder rear-engined F2 car for the following year, and by 1961 was an established force in F1 racing, Dan Gurney taking a close second place to Baghetti's Ferrari in the French GP at Reims.

Ferry Porsche, the son of the company's founder, later wrote that he believed that the F1 programme was on the right road, but financial constraints meant that the relatively small German sports car maker could not continue to bankroll such a costly programme.

During 1962, Porsche was also involved in considerable investment when taking over car seat manufacturer Reutter. "After a thorough study of the situation and lengthy deliberation on the matter, I came to the conclusion that we could not actually afford Grand Prix racing at all," said Ferry Porsche. Therefore the company withdrew at the end of 1962 and would concentrate most of its future racing efforts on sports cars.

Above: Graham Hill heads for his first victory for BRM in the 1962 Dutch Grand Prix at Zandvoort, a major step on the road to his first World Championship crown.

Left: Dan Gurney speeds to victory wih the flat-eight-cylinder Porsche 804 in the 1962 French Grand Prix at Rouen-les-Essarts.

Right: Ricardo Rodriguez, the Mexican prodigy, showed star quality driving for Ferrari in 1962, only to be killed while practising in Rob Walker's Lotus 24 for the Mexican Grand Prix later in the year.

Photos: Bernard Cahier

Main photo: Tony Maggs (24) uses all of the track as he chases John Surtees's Lola during the 1962 French Grand Prix at Rouen.

Inset left: Phil Hill chases his young team-mate, Ricardo Rodriguez, around Spa-Francorchamps. The pair finished third and fourth respectively, just 100ths of a second apart after more than two hours of racing.

Photos: Bernard Cahier

Eric Broadley's Lola company was also struggling to make its F1 mark. Its cars, fielded by Bowmaker Racing under the management of the respected Reg Parnell, were driven by John Surtees and Roy Salvadori. Surtees would post the team's sole victory in a non-title race at Mallory Park.

Cooper's star would fade progressively, but McLaren did a grand job to beat Phil Hill's Ferrari into second place at Monte Carlo. It would be the marque's final Grand Prix win under the Cooper company's ownership, its former World Champion driver, Jack Brabham, having gone it alone to build his own Climax V8-engined F1 car, which made its debut in the 1962 German Grand Prix. When it came to marshalling the elements needed to achieve Grand Prix success, the trend towards the small specialist chassis manufacturer, using an engine produced by a separate organisation, was confirmed as the 1960s unfolded. Dynamic individualists like Colin Chapman spawned a new breed of team owner, who would be followed in the fullness of time by the likes of Ken Tyrrell, Frank Williams and Ron Dennis. More than 45 years after Jim Clark's first win for Lotus at Spa, the changing commercial circumstances of F1 brought the major motor manufacturers of the world into the Grand Prix arena.

That was never something Chapman could envisage in his early days. The Lotus boss was usually correct, but he certainly made an incorrect prediction about immediate future F1 form in response to a question as to what he was expecting from the BRM.

"I don't think they will offer any really serious opposition," said Chapman. "Personally, I think that any firm who tries to build an engine – its own engine – and a chassis is in difficulty from the start.

"Take Ferraris for instance. They have difficulties at the moment. They either get their engines working properly at the same time as they find faults in the chassis or when they eradicate the chassis faults, they find their engines need improving.

"Besides which, Ferraris never seem to have a chassis working as well as my own or Cooper's do. They are learning and they are copying, but, happily, people who copy are always just that little bit behind the original designer."

The success of the BRM in 1962 – and indeed for the remaining years of the 1.5-litre formula – may have been a minor embarrassment for Chapman when one considers these remarks. But in general terms, he was correct. The quick response times demanded by the F1 business were such that the sport's most senior category would continue to be ruled by the small specialist chassis constructors. For the foreseeable future, at least.

On the technical front, low-pressure fuel injection became *de rigueur* in 1963, with Lucas systems boosting both Coventry Climax and BRM power outputs to just above the 200bhp mark. Meanwhile, in Italy, Ferrari started along the road back to serious success with the recruitment of John Surtees as its lead driver, the former motorcycle ace having apparently found the sort of personal rapport with Enzo Ferrari that he

Continued on page 123

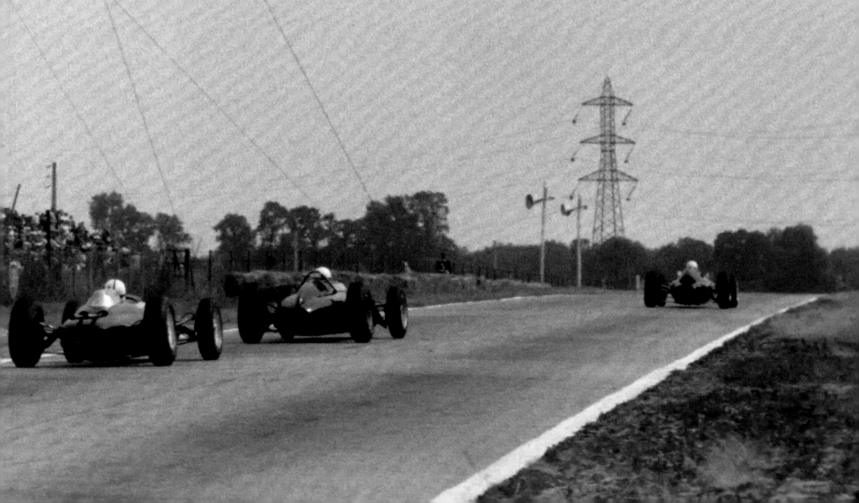

JIMMY CLARK AND COLIN CHAPMAN

JIM Clark, who died at the age of 32 when his Formula 2 Lotus 48 crashed at Hockenheim on 7th April, 1968, is still regarded by his many fans as the greatest racing driver the world has ever seen. For his fellow Scot, Jackie Stewart, this is also the inevitable verdict. It is a judgement that comes from a man who not only raced against Clark in F1 regularly from 1965 through to the first Grand Prix of 1968, but also won three World Championship titles to Clark's two. Stewart's assessment also underlines the reality – appreciated by the likes of Stirling Moss and Tony Brooks – that championships alone produce an incomplete picture of a racing driver's overall talent.

Clark's racing apprenticeship was played out against a backdrop of considerable anxiety on the part of his parents. His father and mother would have been happier if he had been content to channel his energies into the family farm, which nestled in the Scottish border countryside, close to the village of Chirnside At one point, Jim had to justify his involvement in the sport on the basis that he believed it was a hobby that he could make pay for itself.

"I suppose, in a way, if I had set out to be a Grand Prix driver and made it my life's ambition, then I might have felt a greater sense of achievement," he once said. "But, really, I tried to fight against it to a certain extent."

Clark began racing at club level before dominating the 1960 British Formula Junior Championship in tandem with his Team Lotus running mate, Trevor Taylor. That same season, driving occasionally in the works F1 Lotus 18, he finished fifth on his debut in the Dutch Grand Prix at Zandvoort.

Later that year, he was third in the Portuguese GP and, in 1961, armed with the uprated Lotus 21, he finished third at Reims, ahead of his team-mate, Innes Ireland. After also employing John Surtees and Alan Stacey – who was killed at Spa – in 1960, Colin Chapman concentrated on the Ireland/Clark combo for the following season, even though he realised that they were potentially oil and water.

Robert McGregor Innes Ireland was truly a one-off. Also brought up in the Scottish borders – but in his case in Kirkcudbright, on the opposite coast to Clark's home at Chirnside – he was the son of a veterinary surgeon. In his youth, he was apprenticed to Rolls-Royce in Glasgow and London, and later, during his National Service, he was commissioned in the King's Own Scottish Borderers and seconded to the Parachute Regiment.

Innes began racing in a vintage Bentley bequeathed to him by an elderly lady friend of his family, and hit the headlines in 1960 when his works Lotus 18 twice beat Stirling Moss's Rob Walker Cooper in races at Oulton Park and Goodwood. He was sufficiently shrewd to appreciate just how superior his machinery had been on those two occasions.

He never believed himself to be in Moss's class, but nevertheless posted Team Lotus's maiden World Championship victory in the 1961 US Grand Prix at Watkins Glen. Weeks later, he was fired by Chapman and replaced by Trevor Taylor.

It was a crushing blow to Ireland's morale, kindling a legacy of bitterness that took years to erase. In his own mind, he blamed Jimmy for the split with Chapman. Clark, easy-going in some ways, yet never privately doubting his own status and ability behind the wheel, felt that Ireland was wrong in blaming him.

Instead of thrashing out their differences and clearing the air, the two Scottish drivers remained at odds until Clark's death in 1968. They never made their peace, although Ireland went some way towards doing so in an emotional, yet dignified obituary on his compatriot published in *Autocar*, the magazine for which he was sports editor at that time.

Chapman and Clark became a legendary partnership. In 1962, driving the new Lotus 25 powered by a Climax V8 engine, the Scot began a run of domination that was only fleetingly interrupted by the advent of the 3-litre F1 regulations in 1966.

The Lotus founder produced a succession of highly competitive racing cars that were complemented by the tippy-toes driving genius of a man who – like Michael Schumacher more than a generation later – never bothered with detailed self-analysis. "I just get in and drive the car," said Schumacher in 1997. It was the same for Jimmy Clark.

His old friend, Jabby Crombac, said in 1999, "Jimmy was the quickest in the world, but he didn't know why. He was just ultimately competitive. The driving just came to him; he didn't have to try.

"One of his main assets was that he was ten-tenths from the start of every race. By the time the others were up to speed, Jimmy had gone."

The relationship between Clark and Chapman was complex and comfortable. It was founded on mutual trust, although the Lotus boss was probably the dominant partner. It's traditional to depict the pair as something approaching blood brothers, Chapman demonstrating an almost telepathic ability to interpret Clark's comments about the cars' behaviour to make specific changes to their set-up.

Despite this, he never let any sentimentality he might have felt towards Jimmy compromise his efforts to get the Scot's services at the cheapest possible price. Chapman always drove a hard bargain.

Clark's first World Championship victory was at Spa-Francorchamps in 1962, in the Belgian Grand Prix,

a race he would win for the following three years. His last came barely six years later, at Johannesburg's Kyalami circuit in the epochal Lotus 49.

He won just two World Championships, in 1963 and 1965, but missed the 1962 and 1964 titles by a hair's breadth. The combination of Clark and Lotus dominated that entire era. When Jimmy had a competitive car, the battle was for second place.

The satisfaction Clark derived from his motor racing was deeply personal. "It's not so much the racing, more the satisfaction of driving a car on the absolute limit and still being in control of it," he reflected. "That's the greatest feeling of fascination I get from this business."

Jim Clark was characterised as the sport's last great driver from the essentially amateur era, but that in no way lessened his professionalism and determination. His death almost literally coincided with the arrival of Lotus's Gold Leaf cigarette sponsorship, a deal that triggered a sea change in the financing of Grand Prix racing that would alter its face for ever.

"By the end of his life, Jimmy was becoming much more sophisticated and worldly-wise," Jackie Stewart told the author. "I honestly don't think he would have returned to the business of farming when he retired."

Nobody would ever know. Clark died at Hockenheim at the peak of his achievement. Author Eric Dymock, an old friend of Jimmy's, summed it up perfectly when he wrote that "motor racing almost died of a broken heart".

**Poetry in motion. Jim Clark and the
Lotus 25 winning the 1963 British
Grand Prix at Silverstone.**
Photo: Bernard Cahier

had previously enjoyed with Count Domenico Agusta during his days of two-wheeled competition.

There were also changes on the technical side at Maranello, Carlo Chiti's defection to ATS accelerating the career prospects of a talented young engineer, Mauro Forghieri, whose father, Reclus, had been a pre-war Scuderia Ferrari pattern maker who had worked on the cylinder heads for the first Alfa Romeo 158s.

"I had originally been to see Ferrari at the end of 1960," recalled Surtees, "but when I decided to join them at the end of 1962, I judged it had to be the finest time to go there. They were on the floor, but they also wanted to pick themselves up and have a bit of a go. Forghieri had come in, and I got on with him fine."

Fitted with a specially developed high-pressure Bosch fuel injection system, the initial 1963 Ferrari 156 developed a theoretical 200bhp at 10,000rpm. "The problem was that it wasn't safe to rev it where it developed its full power," said Surtees wistfully. "There was no comparison with the Climax or BRM V8s."

Yet there were no ifs or buts about the outcome of the 1963 World Championship. Jim Clark and Lotus fully realised the potential that clearly had been lurking the previous year. Armed with the elegant Lotus 25, the shy Scot won the Belgian, Dutch, French, British, Italian, Mexican and South African Grands Prix to clinch the title with 54 points net (counting the best six results – which were six wins!), ahead of Graham Hill and his BRM team-mate, Richie Ginther, on 29 points apiece.

Yet Surtees would put Ferrari back in the F1 winner's circle for the first time since Monza in 1961 when he took the latest 156 to victory in the German Grand Prix at the Nürburgring. Clark strained every sinew to keep up with a misfiring Lotus 25, which was running on only seven of its eight cylinders for much of the distance. It was Ferrari's sole win of the season, but it did much for the team's morale.

Back in Maranello, this success was greeted with considerable satisfaction. In particular, it served as a dramatic counterpoint to the efforts of ATS, the new Italian F1 operation founded by Count Giovanni Volpi de Misurata, industrialist Giorgio Billi and Jaime Orliz Patino, the millionaire heir to a Bolivian tin fortune.

Under the technical guidance of Carlo Chiti, ATS set up shop in opposition to Ferrari, designed and built its own V8 engine and signed up fellow Maranello refugees Phil Hill and Baghetti to drive. The whole project was an utter disaster. The money quickly ran out and ATS vanished, almost without trace, at the end of the season.

Elsewhere on the F1 grids, Cooper was in steady decline just as the new Brabham team began to emerge as a force to be reckoned with. After Porsche withdrew from F1 at the end of 1962, Dan Gurney signed to drive for Jack Brabham's new outfit and would stay there for three seasons. It was a partnership that would yield two Grand Prix victories, both in 1964, and confirm the lanky American as one of the few drivers capable of giving Clark a decent run for his money.

Yet Clark remained easily the man to beat into the 1964 season. Early that year, the Japanese Honda company decided on an F1 involvement and sent its chief engineer, Yoshio Nakamura, to Europe to make contact with the competing teams and find one that might be prepared to use its engine.

Nakamura was impressed with Brabham, but then Colin Chapman muscled in on the deal. A mock-up of Honda's transverse V12 engine duly arrived at the Lotus headquarters at Cheshunt, Hertfordshire, but no more was heard of the project. The ever-resourceful Chapman had been using the possible Honda connection to put pressure on Coventry Climax to continue development of its own V8. The ruse worked a treat. Honda, slightly irked that it had been used in such tawdry fashion, pressed on with the development of its own car.

FERRARI PICKS UP THE PACE

During the second half of the 1963 season, Ferrari produced a 64 x 57.8mm, 90-degree, 1487cc V8 engine, developed under the direction of Angelo Bellei, but although it was exhaustively tested, the new unit did not make its race debut until the following year's non-title Syracuse Grand Prix in Sicily. The power output was claimed to be in the order of 210bhp at 11,000rpm, which was enough to keep Maranello in play with the opposition from BRM and Coventry Climax. Predictably, Ferrari's customary preoccupation with its Le Mans sports car programme meant that the V8 was beset by reliability problems and didn't really get into its stride until the second half of the year.

Lotus, meanwhile, was determined to sustain its World Championship momentum. The type 25 reached its ultimate development in the shape of the type 33 derivative, which was a broadly similar concept, with a stiffer monocoque and suspension geometry specifically designed to cater for the new 13in, wide-track Dunlop tyres.

The Lotus 33 was powered by the latest flat-crank Mk 2A Climax V8, which developed 204bhp at 9800rpm, while the rival BRM delivered 208bhp at

11,000rpm. BRM also concentrated its efforts on the new monocoque P261 chassis, which first hit the headlines when Graham Hill drove it to his second straight Monaco Grand Prix victory.

On the driver front, Clark had a new partner in Peter Arundell, Colin Chapman having ditched the amiable Trevor Taylor, who – although very quick – seemed to have become dangerously accident prone during the 1962 and 1963 campaigns. This was unfortunately ironic, for Arundell's promising season as Lotus number two came to a premature end when he was involved in a horrifying crash in the Reims F2 race. It would take him 18 months to recover and, while Chapman kept his drive open for 1966, the pleasant Essex driver was never quite the same competitor again.

Taylor would join fellow displaced Lotus man Innes Ireland driving the superbly crafted, Tony Robinson-designed, BRM V8-engined cars produced by the British Racing Partnership. For his part, Ireland was absolutely determined to get his own back on Chapman and Clark, and there would be at least one occasion during the 1964 season when he made it extremely difficult for Clark to lap him, a strategy that merely served to heighten the tensions between them.

BRABHAM EMERGENT

By the beginning of the 1964 season, it was also clear that the Brabham F1 team was becoming a serious force to be reckoned with, particularly now that Dan Gurney was getting into his stride as its *de facto* number-one driver.

Jack Brabham was a shrewd operator. He knew that the initial promise displayed by the fine-handling works BT7s during the 1963 season had prompted a considerable degree of interest among the substantial body of privateers within F1 racing, most of whom

Above: **The Climax V8 engine that powered Jim Clark's championship winning Lotus 25.**

Left: **Dan Gurney tries to cool his overheating feet on the pit counter at Mexico City, 1963.**

Photos: Bernard Cahier

hitherto had relied on second-hand Lotus or Cooper machinery to take part.

By the end of the 1963 season, Cooper's level of competitiveness was fading fast, and independent teams were continually frustrated by Colin Chapman's policy of never allowing the customers to have equipment anywhere near as good as that available to the works drivers. Several private entrants had been more than slightly put out when Chapman sold them Lotus 24s at the start of 1962, having assured them that he was supplying them with up-to-the-minute machinery, and then equipped his works team with the new monocoque Lotus 25s, justifying this on the basis that these were the 1963 cars 'under development'.

Interestingly, if anything, Brabham took the opposite view and made sure that most of its 1964 customer BT11s were supplied to their purchasers before the works cars were built up. One of the converts to Brabham ownership in 1964 was none other than Rob Walker, who had experienced much sadness over the previous couple of seasons, Stirling Moss's Goodwood accident having been followed all too soon by the deaths of both Ricardo Rodriguez and former motorcycle ace Gary Hocking at the wheels of his Lotus 24-BRMs at the end of the 1962 season.

Unhappily, Walker's new Brabham-BRM, driven by Jo Bonnier, was burnt out in an unfortunate fire during practice for the 1964 Silverstone International Trophy race, an event that marked the Brabham marque's maiden F1 success after Jack lunged around the outside of Graham Hill's BRM on the final lap at Woodcote Corner.

Jack and his highly regarded chief designer, Ron Tauranac, gained much wry amusement from the fact that the space-frame Brabhams with their outboard front spring/dampers were fully competitive with the monocoque BRM and Lotus, both of which sported inboard front suspension neatly tucked away out of the airflow. Tauranac attributed at least part of the effectiveness of those early Brabham-Climaxes on fast circuits to the aerodynamic lessons learned from his links with no less a company than Jaguar.

"I knew Malcolm Sayer, who had done the aerodynamics of the Jaguar D-type, and we went to the MIRA wind tunnel under his auspices," Tauranac told the author. "From that we learned to run the nose of our cars as close to the track as possible in order to prevent too much air getting underneath and generating lift. I think this was the problem with the Lotus 24 which Jack had complained about at Spa in 1962."

Left: Jack Brabham's Climax-engine Brabham BT7 on its way to third place in the 1964 Belgian Grand Prix at Spa-Francorchamps, a race dominated by his team-mate, Dan Gurney.

Below: When the world was young. From left: Dan Gurney, Jim Clark, John Surtees and Phil Hill.

Bottom: Graham Hill in the elegant BRM P261, which carried him almost, but not quite, to the 1964 championship.
Photos: Bernard Cahier

Jack had briefly raced his own private Lotus while waiting for the first Brabham F1 chassis to be readied that year.

Graham Hill may have won in Monaco, but Gurney put the Brabham on pole at Zandvoort for the Dutch Grand Prix, only to retire with a broken steering wheel. Clark won that race commandingly for Lotus, but then Dan ran away with the Belgian GP at Spa-Francorchamps before experiencing a heartbreaking retirement in the closing moments of the race.

After only five laps around the daunting Belgian track, Gurney was 12s ahead of a battle between Clark, Hill and Bruce McLaren's Cooper for second place. John Surtees's Ferrari was an early retirement, and Gurney piled on lap record after lap record, finally leaving it at 3m 49.2s, a stunning average of 137.60mph. It would have been quick enough 30 years later, but this was being achieved by a tiny space-frame Brabham running on tyres that were narrower than one finds on the average modern high-performance road car.

Clark was experiencing quite severe overheating with the Lotus 33 and came in to top up with water on lap 28, only for Gurney suddenly to slow. On lap 30, Hill tore past into the lead as Gurney's Brabham hurtled into the pits, its driver crying, "Fuel, fuel!"

However, this wasn't the highly disciplined and organised world of Grand Prix racing of today. No fuel was immediately available and, rather than wait for the churns to be humped around from behind the pits, Gurney resumed the chase. He had almost ground to a halt on the previous lap as the Brabham spluttered low on fuel, but the mechanics were convinced he had sufficient to make it to the flag.

Into the last lap, therefore, the order was Hill, McLaren, Gurney and Clark, but Dan never made it to the finish, rolling to a halt with dry tanks at Stavelot. Hill ran out shortly afterwards, and McLaren was left to stagger on in the lead, his Cooper misfiring ominously with a flattening battery.

Just as it looked as though the Cooper might score an incredibly lucky outsider's victory, Clark came as if from nowhere and surged by Bruce within yards of the flag to take one of the most unlikely wins of his career. Ironically, his Lotus 33 then ran out of fuel on the slowing-down lap and he coasted to a halt alongside Gurney's silent Brabham. Neither knew the true outcome of the afternoon's events and they commiserated with each other until they were told that Jimmy had emerged the winner.

Gurney's big day finally came in the French Grand Prix at Rouen-les-Essarts. Two years after winning there for Porsche, the American scored the Brabham team's first World Championship victory. Clark hit trouble after leading initially, but Gurney had been the class of the field at Spa and certainly deserved this consolation prize.

Brands Hatch hosted the British Grand Prix for the first time in 1964, and Clark won his home race for the third year in a row, beating Graham Hill's BRM by just over a couple of seconds. John Surtees was third in the improving Ferrari 158 and would go on to score his second straight win in the German Grand Prix at the Nürburgring, the next round on the title schedule.

Surtees edged out Clark's Lotus 33 to take pole position, and while Jimmy led the opening lap, Surtees was soon through into the lead. Both Clark and Gurney hit trouble, allowing the Ferrari team leader to storm home first by over a minute from Graham Hill's misfiring BRM, Lorenzo Bandini in the earlier Ferrari 156 and Jo Siffert's private Brabham-BRM.

HONDA MAKES ITS F1 BID

After that earlier rebuff from Colin Chapman, Honda's new RA271 F1 challenger made its debut in the 1964 German Grand Prix. Its 58.1 x 47mm, 1498cc, four-overhead-camshaft V12 was mounted transversely in the chassis, and it was claimed that this latest F1 machine produced in excess of 200bhp on its debut outing. That may well have been the case, but the Honda engineers directed by Yoshio Nakamura certainly needed to polish their chassis engineering technology. The tale of how the team's driver, Ronnie Bucknum, came to drive the car on this occasion remains one of the strangest stories of post-war F1 history. An SCCA sports car driver from California, he was plucked from relative obscurity to debut the new Honda following the somewhat convoluted logic that, since the Japanese company did not have any F1 experience, it made sense to recruit a driver who was correspondingly raw to the challenge. Needless to say, the car ran right at the back of the pack.

Nürburgring 1964 was the start of a good run for Maranello. Later in August, the Zeltweg military aerodrome turned its runways over to racing cars as the venue for the first F1 Austrian Grand Prix. By the mid-1990s, the airfield would be crammed to bursting point with the executive jets owned by F1's new glitterati, but in 1964 F1 was a much more primitive affair.

Although the 3.2km, straw bale-lined perimeter road/runway track looked pretty crude, even by the fairly tolerant standards of the day, most people praised the initiative and enthusiasm of the organisers in having managed to stage a World Championship qualifying round at all. The race also marked the F1 debut of Austrian rising star Jochen Rindt, who drove Rob Walker's Brabham-BRM only a couple of months after stunning the British racing community with a dazzling win in the Whit Monday Formula 2 international at Crystal Palace at the wheel of his own Brabham-Ford.

Dan Gurney's Brabham led off the line, but John Surtees nipped ahead in the Ferrari 158 on the second lap, only for the Italian car's rear suspension to become one of the first casualties of the dramatically bumpy track surface a few laps later. Gurney looked set for an easy win – Clark having retired with a broken driveshaft – but a front suspension radius arm pulled out of the Brabham's chassis. All this drama and mechanical mayhem allowed Ferrari number two Lorenzo Bandini through to post the sole Grand Prix win of his career.

The Austrian race marked another twist in the downhill spiral in which Cooper seemed to have been locked for over a year since John Cooper had been involved in a road accident that had left him badly bashed about. For the 1964 season, it had been planned to run the very promising young American driver, Timmy Mayer, as Bruce McLaren's team-mate, but tragedy intervened early in the season when Mayer – whose elder brother, Teddy, would later become a director of

Opposite: **Men at work. Fine studies of Jim Clark (top) and John Surtees captured at the 1964 German Grand Prix meeting.**

Photos: Bernard Cahier

McLaren Racing – was killed during practice for one of the Tasman series races at Longford, Tasmania.

Mayer's place in the factory Cooper team was taken by 1961 World Champion Phil Hill, but the pleasant American was beginning to run out of enthusiasm for the business. Emotionally bruised by the ATS experience, he now found himself behind the wheel of another less-than-totally-competitive Grand Prix car. It just didn't work out.

At Zeltweg, he crashed heavily in practice, then again in the race with the team's spare car. On the second occasion, the Cooper burst into flames. In the aftermath, strong words were exchanged between Phil and John Cooper, and the American driver was fired, only to be reinstated in the team in time for his home race at Watkins Glen, the next race but one on the World Championship schedule. Sadly, while his son and the team were away in America, Charles Cooper died suddenly at his home in Surrey, at the age of 71.

After Bandini's win in Austria, Ferrari attempted to raise the tempo of its challenge for the Italian Grand Prix at Monza with the introduction of its new Mauro Forghieri-developed flat-12-cylinder engine. This 56 x 50.4mm, 1489cc unit was claimed to develop 220bhp at 11,500rpm, giving it quite a performance increment over its contemporary V8 rivals.

Bandini briefly tried the 1512 – as the flat-12-engined car was designated – in wet practice on the second day of the Monza meeting, but Surtees used the 158 to take pole position a full 0.8s ahead of Gurney's Brabham. In the event, Surtees would win commandingly after his key opposition failed, most notably Graham Hill's BRM, which lurched to a halt on the grid when its clutch thrust mechanism seized at the start.

Bandini finished third, behind Bruce McLaren's Cooper, just beating Richie Ginther's BRM to the line in a photo finish, while Ludovico Scarfiotti finished ninth in one of the earlier 156s.

Before the teams moved on to North America for the final two races of the season, Ferrari fell out with the Italian automobile federation over the disputed homologation of the 250LM sports car. In a fury, the Old Man announced that he would be relinquishing his entrant's licence and would not be fielding cars in his name on home soil again.

To underpin this latest outburst, Ferrari's works entries for the US and Mexican Grands Prix were turned out in the blue and white racing colours of the USA, being entered by loyal American importer Luigi Chinetti's North American Racing Team.

Clark, Graham Hill and Surtees all crossed the Atlantic knowing they could win the World Champi-

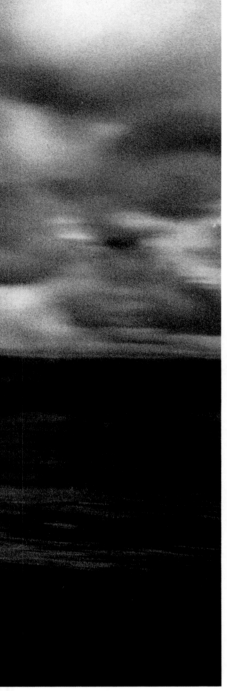

Below: The magnificent little Honda V12 engine transversely mounted in the RA271 chassis on its debut outing in the 1964 German Grand Prix at the Nürburgring.

Bottom: Will this work? Ad-hoc briefing in the Monza pit lane between Bucknum and his mechanics.
Photos: Bernard Cahier

onship. Jimmy was favourite; he qualified on pole at Watkins Glen and was just beginning to get the upper hand in a battle with Surtees when he dropped from contention with fuel injection problems.

Surtees's chances of victory were wiped out by a spin while lapping a slower car, so John had to settle for second, behind Graham Hill's winning BRM.

Hill looked likely to take the title, but in Mexico City Bandini pitched him into a spin as they jostled for position going into one of the slowest hairpins, and Graham had to make a pit stop to have his BRM's squashed exhaust tailpipes prised open after making smart contact with the guard rail.

"That won Surtees the World Championship," recalled Tim Parnell, son of Reg. "I suppose Lorenzo was embarrassed to a certain degree. He was typically Italian in that, having done something like that in the heat of battle, he would then be apologetic and *simpatico* in the aftermath. But he certainly robbed poor old Graham of that title."

John Surtees recalled the episode from his own perspective: "In the aftermath of the accident, a lot of people started gunning for Lorenzo, suggesting that he had driven recklessly in order to help me. Most of these critics were, of course, a good way from the incident and in no position to judge it for themselves.

"Lorenzo may have occasionally tended towards over-exuberance, but he never indulged in dirty tactics. He and Graham shook hands over the whole business very soon after the event and there was no lasting animosity between them."

Yet this was only part of the story on that sweltering afternoon. While all this drama had been going on way down the field, Jimmy Clark was again in complete control at the head of the pack. Unfortunately for the Scot, his car was losing oil in the closing stages, and what should have been a dominant, flag-to-flag, title clinching victory was snatched away on the final lap when the Lotus's Climax engine seized.

Gurney went through to win for Brabham, while Bandini dropped behind Surtees to give the one-time motorcycle champion his first and only F1 drivers' title, with 40 points to Hill's 39 and Clark's 32.

Continued on page 136

Left: **The Ferrari 1512 flat-12 engine, which appeared in practice for the 1964 Italian Grand Prix at Monza.**

Right: **The Angelo Bellai-developed 158 V8 engine revealed in the paddock at the 1964 Dutch Grand Prix.**
Photos: Bernard Cahier

Right: **A very young Chris Amon at the Nürburgring in 1964 with the Parnell Racing ex-works Lotus 25 powered by a BRM V8.**

Below: **The works BRM P261 at the 1964 Mexican Grand Prix.**
Photos: Bernard Cahier

GOODYEAR AND STEWART ARRIVE ON THE SCENE

The 1965 season was the last under the 1.5-litre regulations, and it was marked by two arrivals on the Grand Prix scene that would have enormous future significance for the sport. On the driver front, the appearance of the young Scot, Jackie Stewart, as Graham Hill's team-mate at BRM, would have huge ramifications on several fronts.

Stewart had won the 1964 British F3 Championship at the wheel of a Tyrrell team Cooper-BMC, and not only would he emerge as one of the finest F1 drivers of his era, but also he would play a major role in making Grand Prix racing a much safer sport.

The other significant development was the arrival of the US tyre company, Goodyear, to challenge the supremacy of Dunlop, which had dominated the sport since 1958.

Goodyear had returned to motor racing in the mid-1950s after a lay-off of more than 30 years, initially with sports cars and stock cars, and it was during this period that the Akron based company pioneered the semi-slick tread pattern. The company also made a preliminary, almost unnoticed, foray into F1, supplying tyres for Lance Reventlow's Scarab project, and then began to raise its commercial profile with a first foray to Indianapolis in 1963.

Goodyear tyres were next raced in Europe in 1964, when Frank Gardner competed at Pau in a John Willment entered Lotus 27. The company then graduated to Grand Prix racing with Honda, and for 1965 it also supplied the works Brabham team.

BRP FORCED TO CLOSE ITS DOORS

As Honda ramped up its F1 efforts, so Ken Gregory and Alfred Moss found themselves forced by commercial pressures to close the doors of the British Racing Partnership. This was one of the very first examples

of F1 teams acting as a cartel to squeeze out one of their own. BRP had been running its Tony Robinson-designed, BRM-engined cars since the start of 1963, but now it fell foul of the Paris Agreement, a cosy deal between BRM, Lotus, Cooper, Brabham and the Grand Prix organisers.

This amounted to a relatively simple predecessor of the present Concorde Agreement by which the commercial dimension of the sport is governed to the present day. In essence, the terms of the Paris Agreement were that each of the signatories would get £800 starting money per car in each Grand Prix – on top of which, the drivers concerned would get starting money of between £150 and £450 per race, depending on their points score from the previous year.

However, BRP was not a signatory of the Paris Agreement and found itself progressively squeezed throughout the 1964 season. Towards the end of the year, it applied for 'membership' of the agreement, and at the US Grand Prix at Watkins Glen Tony Robinson announced that the cars were ready for inspection at any time.

The outcome of this process was that BRP was not permitted to join the Paris Agreement, as it was decreed that the team did not make a sufficiently large proportion of its own car. Faced with a loss on the season of £7000 – a huge amount of money in 1964 for a private venture – the BRP operation was forced to close.

Innes Ireland never minced his words when it came to the subject of the British Racing Partnership. Perhaps he hadn't enjoyed the success he felt he deserved during his two years driving for Ken Gregory and Alfred Moss. Perhaps he was too much of an enthusiast in an increasingly intense, professional sport.

Yet nobody could deny the fact that Innes was a racer to the core of his soul. He also had a very well-defined sense of right and wrong. And the treatment meted out to the British Racing Partnership deeply offended the Scot's sense of propriety.

Above: "Don't laugh. One day you will be a Honda driver!" Ronnie Bucknum and Richie Ginther chat with John Surtees before the start of the 1965 Belgian Grand Prix. Dan Gurney looks on with interest.

Above right: Mauro Forghieri gets to grips with his Ferrari chassis at Silverstone.

Above far right: Enzo Ferrari at Monza in 1965.

Right: Graham Hill (7) takes an initial lead at the start of the 1965 Belgian Grand Prix. The race was won by Jim Clark (17), with newcomer Jackie Stewart (8) taking second place for BRM. Behind are Siffert (21), Ginther (10), Gurney (15) and Surtees (1).

Photos: Bernard Cahier

"How ludicrous it is that a large and properly organised outfit like BRP cannot afford to race," he wrote. "I feel it is an indication of how much 'sport' is left within the sport when there is so little concern that a fine team like BRP has had to go to the wall."

Innes was certainly becoming embittered and recounted in his excellent autobiography, *All Arms and Elbows* (Pelham Books, 1967), how he had once had a chat with another driver who began questioning him about the financial details of motor racing. Innes admitted, rather sniffily, that he hadn't a clue about these things.

Reading between the lines, it would be all too easy to conclude that the driver he was referring to was the commercially astute Jackie Stewart. Ireland had his enthusiasm for Jackie well under control for many years, but his feelings definitely mellowed towards the end of his life. By the time Innes died – far too young at 63 – in 1993, he had developed a grudging respect and admiration for his younger compatriot.

Meanwhile, for Stewart, the decision to join the BRM team in 1965 was not a difficult one. In fact, he recalls it as one of the best moves he ever made during his racing career.

"I was being courted heavily by Colin Chapman, and it was a very intoxicating thought to go and join Jim Clark, another Scot, whom I admired enormously," he said.

"I was very much in awe of his talent, but it wouldn't have worked for me, and I was certainly aware of that. I could [also] have gone to Cooper" – the berth alongside Bruce McLaren was eventually taken by Jochen Rindt – "but I chose BRM because it was a good team and I knew that I needed a team that wouldn't push me too hard too soon.

"They had Graham Hill as a number-one driver, and anybody who came along as number two was going to be just that. Nevertheless, I saw in Graham a talent not as great as Jim Clark's, in sheer driving skill, but also an enormous determination and a wealth of knowledge I could learn from.

"Funnily enough, I didn't think there was much I could learn from Jimmy because his natural talent was so great that sometimes I don't think he knew how he did it."

Stewart proved to be an outstandingly promising F1 novice. He finished sixth on his World Championship debut in the South African Grand Prix, beat reigning title holder Surtees into second place in the Silverstone International Trophy and then out-fumbled team-mate

Opposite: **Jackie Stewart and Graham Hill, BRM team-mates at Monza, 1965, where JYS would score the first of his 27 career victories.**

Below: **My turn next! Jackie Stewart congratulates Graham Hill after the Londoner had completed his Monaco Grand Prix hat trick in 1965.**
Photos: Bernard Cahier

Graham Hill to win the Italian Grand Prix at Monza. Clearly he was going to be quite a player.

Yet it was Clark who dominated the 1965 season with his trusty Lotus 33, clinching the World Championship as early as the German Grand Prix at the Nürburgring, a race that he utterly dominated. He wrapped up the title with three races remaining, despite the fact that he had not taken part in the Monaco Grand Prix, as he was away winning the Indianapolis 500. That left Graham Hill to score a hat trick of victories for BRM. "Wish Jimmy had been there to see it," remarked Hill laconically.

Both the Lotus and Brabham teams were supplied with uprated 32-valve versions of the Climax V8, now nudging the 215bhp mark at 10,800rpm, but somehow Dan Gurney's unit always seemed to be running into technical trouble. Clark's tended not to, of course, and it was more than enough to keep the brilliant Scot in play at the front of the pack, even though the rival BRM and Honda engines were reputedly developing more than 220bhp.

The Brabham team's 32-valver never worked properly after Jack himself blew it up during the Monaco Grand Prix. "It never ran well from that day onwards, even though Climax tried hard to repair it," said Gurney. "My best run with it was at Clermont Ferrand,

I suppose, when I set fastest race lap quite early on. Then the darn thing broke, as usual, and Jimmy went faster anyway…"

And on that day, Clark was using the Team Lotus spare type 25, fitted with an earlier-spec 16-valve Climax V8!

At the same time, Coventry-Climax was planning a last hurrah in the form of the FWMW flat-16, a complex 54.1 x 40.64mm, 1495cc unit that employed a central gear train to drive its eight overhead camshafts (four on each bank). In fact, the engine ran into all sorts of problems during dynamometer testing, most of them due to the use of its central power take-off, and although there were tentative plans for it to be raced at Monza, another major failure on the test bed a few days before it was due to be shipped consigned this novel engine to the F1 history books.

Although mechanical unreliability thwarted Dan Gurney's efforts through 1965, to the point where the Brabham number one was unable to add to the marque's victories of the previous year at Rouen and Mexico City, Honda really began to make its presence felt now that former BRM ace Richie Ginther had been signed to lead the team.

For the British Grand Prix at Silverstone, Ginther qualified third on the front row of the grid, just 0.5s

away from Clark's pole-position Lotus 33, and briefly led through the first corner before dropping back steadily, later to retire.

At Zandvoort, Ginther again made the front row with third-fastest time and led the opening lap, eventually scoring Honda's first World Championship point with a sixth-place finish.

Finally, on 24th October, the curtain rang down on the 1.5-litre F1 when Ginther romped away to win the Mexican Grand Prix. "I looked in my mirror at the end of the first lap and just didn't see a soul until I was clear past the end of the pits," he recalled. "I thought that I had dropped a gallon of oil and they had all spun out behind me."

Ginther maintained an iron grip on the race, aided by a combination of sticky Goodyear rubber and the Honda technicians' success in making the transverse V12 perform well at the Mexico City circuit's 7000ft altitude. He came home the winner by 2.7s from Gurney's similarly shod Brabham. With this victory, Honda had grasped a prize beyond the reach of Brabham and Ferrari, both of which had failed to win a Grand Prix during the course of the 1965 season. For its part, Maranello had concentrated on the development of its flat-12 engine, and this never really came right until the Italian Grand Prix at Monza, where revised cylinder heads enabled Surtees to really pile on the pressure.

He qualified the Ferrari 1512 on the front row of the grid alongside Clark's Lotus 33 and, although hydraulic problems with the clutch caused him to get away slowly and complete the opening lap down in 14th place, he clawed his way back up into the leading bunch. After he had contested the lead for a few laps, the clutch slipped out of business for good.

It was John Surtees's final outing at the wheel of a 1.5-litre F1 car, for he crashed his own Team Surtees Lola-Chevrolet sports car at Toronto's Mosport Park circuit only a few weeks afterwards. John was very seriously hurt, hovering between life and death for a few days before starting out on the road to recovery that would see him back behind the wheel of an F1 Ferrari the following season.

The final points tally at the end of the year confirmed that Clark had won the World Championship again, with 54 points to Graham Hill's 40 and Stewart's 33.

Now it was a question of planning for the future. In the Lotus line-up, Peter Arundell was poised to return and displace stand-in Mike Spence as Jim Clark's teammate for 1966, the first season of the new 3-litre F1. Bruce McLaren was off to start his own F1 operation, leaving Jochen Rindt to lead the once-famous Cooper team; Bandini would remain partnering Surtees at Ferrari; while Dan Gurney decided he would leave Jack Brabham to start his own All American Racers Grand Prix programme. Dan admitted that he was moving with more than a sliver of regret.

"I felt at home on the team and Jack had gradually come to rely on my driving as the strongest," he said. "However, I had the chance to do it with my own Eagle. That was too good a prospect to turn down, so I had to say goodbye with regrets.

"I always admired Jack and enjoyed working with him. We were a very small team, but we always seemed to be in the hunt. Jack was a very good engineer and a great man to fix things in the field, despite the fact that we might not have the proper tools or facilities.

"He was also tighter than a bull's ass in fly season. Those were the days!"

Above: Richie Ginther gave the Honda RA272 Honda a resounding victory in the last race of the 1·5 litre era

Left: The one and only Grand Prix win for Ginther, but the first of many for Goodyear, who were set to become a dominant force on the Grand Prix scene in the next two decades.

Far left: Jack Brabham – "tighter than a bull's ass in fly season" – with his driver, Dan Gurney, the pair enjoyed a tremendous working relationship, even if ultimate success evaded them during their three years together.

Photos: Bernard Cahier

Jim Clark in the groundbreaking Lotus 49 with its bespoke Cosworth DFV 3-litre V8 engine. Few other F1 cars in history can match the 49 for elegant and uncluttered simplicity.
Photo: Paul-Henri Cahier

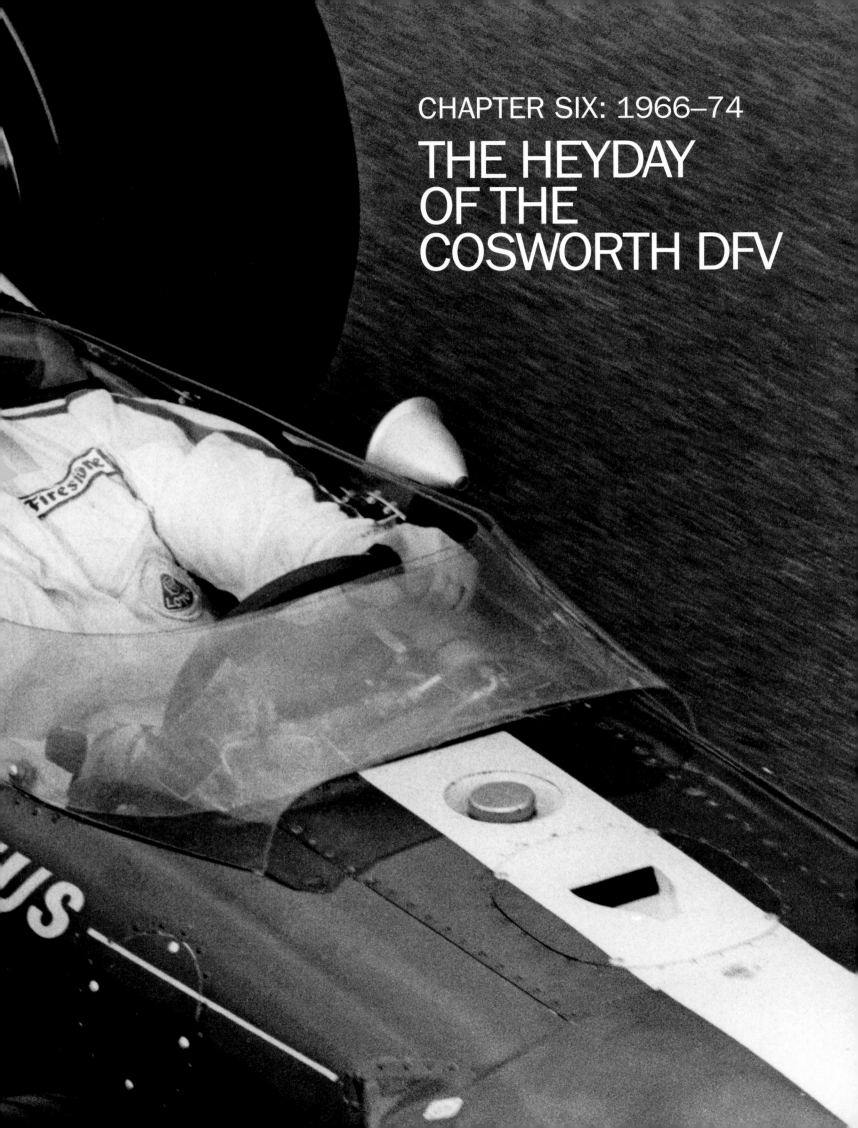

THE HEYDAY OF THE COSWORTH DFV

A wide technical diversity of engines was pressed into service during the first season of the 3-litre formula in 1966: (above) John Surtees in the Cooper T81 powered by the Maserati V12; (opposite top) the GM-derived Repco V8 that powered Jack Brabham to the 1966 title; (opposite, bottom) the distinctive tangle of exhausts on the Ferrari 312 V12 that carried Scarfiotti to victory at Monza.

Photos: Bernard Cahier

TOWARDS the end of 1963, the CSI announced technical regulations for the new Formula 1 that was scheduled to start on 1st January, 1966. At the time, there was a feeling inside motor racing that a move to more powerful cars would probably be appropriate when it came to the next change of rules, so it was decided that from the start of 1966, engines would be 3 litres unsupercharged or 1.5 litres supercharged.

The latter provision was implemented as a stop-gap measure to help those teams who wanted to continue in F1, but lacked access to a 3-litre engine. It was felt that supercharging the old 1.5-litre V8 BRM or Climax units might be a short-term solution. In reality, this was a somewhat fanciful proposal; Coventry Climax had announced its withdrawal from F1 at the end of the 1.5-litre era and nobody pursued this complicated option. However, it would come back to bite the Grand Prix world more than a decade later, as we shall see.

As far as Enzo Ferrari was concerned, the 3-litre rules were just fine by him, but the speed with which he produced the prototype of his first car for the new formula, the V12-powered 312, helped create a false impression as to the potential for Maranello domination in 1966. Nevertheless, he was first out of the box.

The first 312 was unveiled at Maranello in December 1965. Frankly, it looked a very large machine indeed. Its 60-degree, 77 x 53.5mm, 2989cc V12 engine was closely related to the 3.3-litre Le Mans engine, reputedly developing 360bhp. Subsequently this turned out to be rubbish. Similarly, it was claimed that the Ferrari 312 tipped the scales at 548kg, at a time when the minimum weight limit was set at 500kg. However, when it was scrutineered at Syracuse for its first race, it was found to weigh 604kg. Put simply, Ferrari was set for a fall.

Ranged against the Maranello brigade was what, in retrospect, one can only describe as a rag-bag of improvised machinery. At the start of 1965, John Cooper had sold out to the Chipstead Motor Group for around £200,000. This relieved John, who was still feeling the after-effects of that 1963 road accident, of the business worries of running the company while allowing him to retain hands-on involvement with the racing team.

Chipstead had been concerned at the costs involved in using the Climax engines during that final season under the 1.5-litre regulations and eventually struck a deal to use a 3-litre Maserati V12, which was an uprated version of the unit fitted to Jean Behra's Maserati 250F a decade earlier.

Maserati engineer Giulio Alfieri revised the engine with 70.4 x 64mm, 2989cc dimensions, and it developed around 340bhp at 9000rpm. The first Cooper-Maserati was tested at Goodwood in November 1965, and eventually the works team would be supplemented by customer T81 chassis supplied to Rob Walker (driven by Jo Siffert) plus owner-drivers Jo Bonnier and Guy Ligier.

The works Coopers would be driven by Jochen Rindt and Richie Ginther, the latter waiting for the new 3-litre Honda V12 to be race ready, although Denny Hulme briefly tried the car during an early test. In fact, Hulme would remain with the Brabham team, for whom he had driven in F1 on an intermittent basis over the previous 18 months or so.

Jack Brabham opted for what turned out to be the most successful route for the new formula. The Australian Repco company was developing a new V8, based on General Motors' abandoned linerless engine programme for a projected 3.5-litre Buick 'compact' saloon, with the intention of providing a Tasman-formula power unit to replace the elderly 2.5-litre Climax four-cylinder engines that had been the mainstay of the Antipodean category for many years.

However, designer Phil Irving concluded that the F85 Oldsmobile cylinder block, which was the basis of the Repco V8, could easily deal with the stresses and strains of running in 3-litre form. With just a month or so to go before the opening race of the new formula, the first type 620 Repco V8 was installed in the Brabham BT19 chassis, which had originally been earmarked for the stillborn flat-16 Climax engine. With a bore and stroke of 88.9 x 60.32mm, the 2995cc engine developed 315bhp at a relatively leisurely 7250rpm. And it was just the ticket

Some motor racing historians portray Jack Brabham as little more than a driver-cum-mechanic who got lucky. Such judgements are extremely wide of the mark. Objectively, when preparing for the 1966 F1, he and Ron Tauranac were the only people who stuck to what has always been the most basic tenet of racing

car design, namely that the machine should always be as light and agile as possible.

Colin Chapman can be excluded from this blanket criticism because, as we shall see, he had already taken steps to guarantee Team Lotus's future with the Cosworth Ford DFV programme. Yet that was only in its fledgling stage at the start of 1966, leaving Jim Clark to set about defending his World Championship with a 2-litre Climax V8-engined Lotus 33. Until, that is, the BRM H-16 engine was made available to Lotus on a customer basis. The H-16 was the brainchild of BRM engineer Tony Rudd, the man who had masterminded the British team's rise to consistent competitiveness during the halcyon days of the 1.5-litre formula. His idea was, effectively, to couple together two of the 1.5-litre V8s, but with their cylinder banks redesigned to create two horizontally opposed eight-cylinder units, allowing the crankshafts to be geared together. This 69 x 48.8mm, 2998cc engine reputedly gave 400bhp at 10,750rpm from the outset. Yet its supposed competitiveness was undermined by its weight and a level of technical complexity that made it hideously unreliable.

Nevertheless, the media greeted this new engine with customary deference. Writing in *Autosport*, John Bolster noted, "An extremely high standard of engineering will be called for to make the units fully interchangeable without upsetting the suspension adjustments, but fine engineering is right up BRM's street."

At the same time as developing the H-16, BRM commissioned a parallel V12 engine programme, which was carried out by former BRM chief engineer Peter Berthon, now working in conjunction with Harry Weslake's company at Rye in Sussex.

Installed in the works BRM P83s, the H-16 never delivered a seriously worthwhile result in 1966, although Jim Clark would drive an H-16-engined Lotus 43 to a lucky victory in the US Grand Prix at Watkins Glen. Ironically, on that occasion, Clark was using the BRM works team's spare engine, loaned to Team Lotus prior to the race after the Scot had suffered an earlier engine failure. To this day, F1 insiders believe that the key factor in this lone victory for the H-16 engine was Clark's extraordinary mechanical sensitivity.

Elsewhere on the F1 landscape, the trusty old Climax four-cylinder engines – enlarged to 2.7 litres – were used by privateers and Dan Gurney's AAR Eagles, whose bespoke V12 Weslake units would not be seriously race ready until 1967. On the tyre front, Firestone had joined the F1 party with deals for Lotus, Ferrari and McLaren; Brabham, Honda and Eagle were on Goodyear, while Cooper remained on Dunlop. BRM didn't have a tyre deal and used either Dunlop or Firestone products during the course of the year.

The opening race of the 1966 season was at Syracuse, where John Surtees won easily in the Ferrari 312. Then came the Silverstone International Trophy race – an

Left: Overweight, over-complex – and ultimately unsuccessful. The BRM H-16.
Photo: Bernard Cahier

Right: Jack Brabham made fun of himself in 1966 by appearing on the grid at Zandvoort wearing this false beard, but he went on to prove that life really did begin at 40 by winning the race!

Below: Jackie Stewart on his way to victory in the 1966 Monaco GP at the wheel of the 2-litre BRM V8.
Photos: Bernard Cahier

Right: Making do. Privateer Bob Anderson (34) wrings the maximum from his elderly Brabham Climax V8, now stretched to 2.7 litres, while Peter Arundell (8) has to settle for a 2-litre BRM engine in his Lotus 33 as they battle at Zandvoort.
Photos: Bernard Cahier

even more important curtain-raiser – where Surtees was thrashed by Jack's new Brabham-Repco.

The F1 fraternity seemed stunned, but the result came as no surprise to Surtees, who had been deeply concerned about the Ferrari 312's apparent lack of performance since he had driven it at Syracuse. It had also been two-and-a-half seconds slower around Modena than the compact Dino 246, which had originally been built for Surtees to contest the 1966 Tasman Championship, but had not been used following his accident in Canada.

"Everybody was saying, 'Poor old Jack Brabham has only got 290/300bhp from his Repco engine,' and this bloody Ferrari V12, which weighed God knows how much, was really only giving about 270bhp," Surtees noted years later.

Surtees led at Monaco until eventually being sidelined with transmission failure. Jackie Stewart won in the 2-litre Tasman BRM P261, which the team was using while the H-16 was being made race ready, and Lorenzo Bandini finished second in the little Dino 246.

That year's Monaco Grand Prix also marked the debut of Bruce McLaren as a driver/constructor. In 1965, he had decided to go it alone and had signed a

promising young designer called Robin Herd to develop his new team's first F1 car. The resultant McLaren M2A was a fascinating machine, albeit somewhat over-complex. Herd took the ambitious step of building the chassis from a composite laminate of aluminium sheet bonded to a sandwich filling of balsawood. The material was known as Mallite and had been developed originally for internal panelling in the aviation industry. Light and torsionally rigid, it was also quite complicated to repair in the event of an accident.

The McLaren M2A was powered initially by a 4.5-litre Oldsmobile V8 prepared by engine specialist Traco Engineering and was employed as a development vehicle for Firestone's F1 tyres. Then the car was fitted with a pushrod Ford Indianapolis V8 engine, which had been reduced from 4.2 to 3 litres at Traco's Californian workshops. This was something of a stop-gap, hardly providing McLaren with a realistic long-term answer to his needs for a seriously competitive F1 power unit.

The Ford V8 engine transmitted its reputed 300bhp power output through a rather basic four-speed ZF gearbox, and it didn't take long for Bruce to conclude that a lot more development work would be required if his F1 effort was to be taken as seriously as he planned.

Above: A motley collection of largely interim cars at the start of the 1966 French Grand Prix at Reims, the final occcasion this race would take place on the classic road circuit in champagne country. Lorenzo Bandini's Ferrari 312 (left) just gets the jump off the line ahead of John Surtees's Cooper-Maserati, Mike Parkes's Ferrari 312, Jo Siffert's Rob Walker Cooper-Maserati, Jack Brabham's Brabham-Repco, and the factory Cooper-Maseratis of Chris Amon and Jochen Rindt.
Photo: Bernard Cahier

The McLaren-Ford F1 debut ended when an oil-pipe union came undone in the nose section, dumping lubricant all over Bruce's feet and the track surface. He switched off before the engine broke.

The Ford V8 was withdrawn for further development, leaving McLaren to find a replacement engine. He turned to Count Volpi's Serenissima company, which had available a sports car-based 3-litre V8 that had been produced by Alberto Massimino, the man who'd designed some of the very earliest Ferraris.

Unfortunately the Serenissima V8 produced only about 260bhp, but it was better than nothing and was duly installed for the Belgian Grand Prix at Spa-Francorchamps. The first experience of the Italian engine proved to be substantially worse than the Ford outing at Monaco. Once coaxed into firing on all cylinders, it ran its main bearings inside a lap and had to be withdrawn from the race.

The McLaren-Serenissima made its next F1 appearance in the British Grand Prix at Brands Hatch, where Bruce ran in the top six during the early stages, finally finishing sixth to score the marque's first World Championship point.

Then Surtees took a brilliant win at the Belgian Grand Prix at Spa-Francorchamps. But this wasn't good enough for Ferrari's Machiavellian team manager, Eugenio Dragoni, who felt that the British driver should not have spent so much time behind Rindt's Cooper-Maserati.

Yet the 1966 Belgian Grand Prix would be best remembered for a first-lap cloudburst that saw the field decimated by a succession of accidents within a mile or so of the start. Cars skated off the track in all directions, but by far the most serious accident involved the

BRM driven by Jackie Stewart, then one of the sport's most promising young rising stars.

"I must have been doing around 165mph when the car aquaplaned and I lost control," said Stewart. "We just ran into a wall of water in the way it can rain only in southern Belgium.

"First I hit a telegraph pole, then a woodcutter's cottage, and I finished up in the outside basement of a farm building. The car ended up shaped like a banana and I was still trapped inside it.

"The fuel tank had totally ruptured inwardly and the monocoque literally filled up with fuel. It was sloshing around in the cockpit. The instrument panel was smashed, ripped off and found 200 metres from the car, but the electric fuel pump was still working away. The steering wheel wouldn't come off and I couldn't get out."

Eventually Stewart was helped from the wrecked car by fellow-BRM drivers Graham Hill and Bob Bondurant. He sustained four broken ribs, a broken shoulder and pelvic injuries in what was the worst accident of his professional career. It also prompted the Scot to recalibrate his approach to the sport. Racing drivers, he reasoned, should be paid to demonstrate their skill, not simply their bravery in what now seem prehistoric conditions.

Although it may not have been appreciated at the time, this was a seminal moment in the history of Grand Prix motor racing. For his part, Denny Hulme recalled, "I think it put me off motor racing in the rain for the rest of my life."

Then Brabham got into his stride with the lightweight Repco-engined car, winning the French, Dutch, British and German Grands Prix in splendid style.

Surtees, meanwhile, had a terminal breach with Enzo Ferrari after Dragoni had effectively tried to demote him to 'second driver' status for the Le Mans 24-hour sports car classic.

Surtees went straight to Maranello for a face-to-face meeting with Enzo Ferrari, as a result of which he left the team with immediate effect. Cooper promptly signed him up for the balance of the season, a partnership that yielded victory in the Mexican Grand Prix.

Meanwhile, Ferrari's fortunes slumped dramatically. Dragoni's somewhat naïve contention that his team's cars were so superior that he could employ second-rate drivers and win anyway was so absurdly wide of the mark that one could hardly credit it. However, after a summer of acute embarrassment at the hands of its rivals, Maranello produced a revised three-valve (two inlet, one exhaust) cylinder head that gave around 370bhp in time for the Italian Grand Prix at Monza. That was sufficient for Ludovico Scarlotti and Mike Parkes to finish in 1-2 formation, a morale-boosting performance for the Italian squad on its home circuit.

Clark qualified the Lotus 43-BRM on the front row at Monza, running quickly, but fruitlessly, after an early delay. Then he scored that fortuitous lone victory for the H-16 engine in the United States Grand Prix at Watkins Glen. In the same race, the Indy-based Ford V8 powered McLaren to a fifth-place finish, but then it failed again in Mexico City. It marked the end of that particular project, but Ford's name would soon be writ large in the Formula 1 business. The Cosworth DFV was coming

A NEW ENGINE FOR A NEW ERA

The Cosworth Ford DFV V8 F1 engine, introduced in the middle of the 1967 season, was not only the best power unit in the business, but also it would be responsible for an expansion of interest in the sport that gave added momentum throughout the following decade and beyond.

Designed by the brilliant Keith Duckworth as part of a £100,000 package funded by the Ford Motor Company, it was the bargain of the post-war F1 age. For its investment, Ford became instantly recognised as the sport's benefactor. From the start of 1969, there would be an off-the-shelf, commercially available F1 engine for anybody with £7,500 to spend.

The new engine's design reflected Duckworth's personal philosophy. Apart from being an intuitive engineer, he was a firm believer that race engine designs should be as simple and uncomplicated as possible.

Duckworth had worked from 1957 to 1958 as a transmission development engineer with Lotus before establishing his own business. The very first Ford design to which Cosworth contributed any technical input was the 1963 Cortina GT, which used an inlet manifold and camshaft design that emerged from the Edmonton based specialist.

Yet even by this stage, Cosworth had used Ford engines as the basis of its racing units, most notably in the 1.1-litre Formula Junior category, which came to an end in 1963. The engines were then reworked for the new 1-litre Formula 3, which took over as the

Below: **The sensational Cosworth DFV made a winning debut at Zandvoort in 1967.**

Photos: **Bernard Cahier**

training ground for future Grand Prix stars; the MAE (modified Anglia engine) was developed into a winning power unit that would be successful right through to the end of the 1970 season, when the formula was superseded.

Duckworth was one of the very first designers to appreciate that, although an engine may be sufficiently powerful to fulfil its intended purpose, its potential can be fully harnessed only if it can be integrated with the chassis. This was also one of Lotus founder Colin Chapman's abiding principles, so it came as no surprise when the DFV-engined Lotus 49 became such a spectacular trendsetter.

The spark that produced the partnership between Ford and Cosworth was initially kindled by Walter Hayes, a former Fleet Street journalist who had joined Ford in 1962 at a time of great expansion of the company's ambitions. It was believed, correctly as it turned out, that the new Cortina saloon would transform Ford's image.

In his new role as director of public affairs, Hayes immediately decided that in the Cortina Ford had the ideal vehicle with which to enter motor racing. He knew very well that Cosworth had amassed much experience developing those production Ford engines for racing purposes, so when Coventry Climax withdrew from F1 at the end of 1965, it seemed an opportune moment for Ford to fill the breach with a totally new Grand Prix engine.

The DFV package also included the development of a four-cylinder Formula 2 engine, which became the highly successful 1.6-litre EVA that dominated motor racing's second-division single-seater class from 1967 to 1971.

HILL AND CLARK: F1'S FIRST SUPER-TEAM

With the Ford Cosworth DFV in the pipeline for Team Lotus and the all-new type 49 under construction as the first absolutely bespoke engine/chassis combination of the 3-litre formula, Ford bankrolled Graham Hill's switch to the Lotus team as Jim Clark's running mate for the 1967 season.

This was F1's first 'super-team' of the post-war era, pre-dating the great Prost/Senna partnership at McLaren by 21 years. Hill once said he had become so identified with BRM over the previous seven seasons that he was worried he would be "sprayed dark green and stood in the corner of the workshop" if he stayed much longer. He was paid handsomely for the switch, a move that also had the effect of dramatically boosting Clark's salary to a commensurate level – probably around £30,000.

Lotus began the 1967 season racing the Lotus-BRM H-16s, but after the South African Grand Prix – won by the Cooper-Maserati of Pedro Rodriguez (the older brother of the late Ricardo Rodriguez) ahead of local hero John Love's Cooper-Climax 4 – Chapman decided that the BRM rebuilding fees were too expensive, with the result that the team reverted to using the old 2-litre-engined type 33s until the 49s were ready to race.

Elsewhere on the F1 scene, Brabham and Hulme remained together in the Brabham-Repco squad; Rindt was joined by Rodriguez at Cooper – where a newly recruited 19-year-old mechanic by the name of Ron

Dennis was just starting his racing career; and John Surtees moved to Honda. Richie Ginther joined Dan Gurney briefly in the Eagle F1 operation, now using its new Gurney-Weslake V12 engine, and in the Ferrari camp the promising young New Zealander, Chris Amon, joined Lorenzo Bandini. "In 1967, Ferrari paid me nothing, just a share of the prize money," said Chris, "which was fine by me."

BRM continued with its P83 H-16 development programme, with Jackie Stewart now partnered by Mike Spence, while the V12 BRM unit was earmarked for McLaren, who made do with a 2-litre Tasman BRM V8 installed in an uprated M4A Formula 2 chassis until the new engine was ready mid-season.

Ferrari did not attend the South African Grand Prix, but Bandini finished a strong second to Dan Gurney's victorious Eagle-Weslake in the Brands Hatch Race of Champions. Then came the Monaco Grand Prix, where the popular Italian driver made a fatal error while chasing Denny Hulme's winning Brabham-Repco.

On lap 82, as Bandini took the chicane on to the harbour front, his Ferrari 312 clipped the inside wall with its right-hand wheels. It ran wide to the left, climbing up the straw bales and slamming into a lamp post. The car turned over on to the track and erupted into a horrifying pillar of flame. The Italian succumbed to terrible burns three days later.

Certain people believed that Bandini was under some stress just prior to the 1967 Monaco race. According to Ferrari, Lorenzo wanted to take things

Above: John Surtees in the Honda chases Lorenzo Bandini's Ferrari through the waterfront chicane during the early stages of the 1967 Monaco GP, the point on the circuit where later the Italian would crash with fatal consequences.

Opposite top: Jim Clark closed out the 1967 season with a dominant victory in the Mexican Grand Prix. Four wins were still not enough, however, for him to claim the title.

Opposite bottom: Denny Hulme, seen here winning his first Grand Épreuve at Monaco, would add the German GP to his victory tally on his way to the World Championship.

Photos: Bernard Cahier

steadily at Monaco and didn't want Scarfiotti to be at the race. If Ferrari's analysis of the situation is to be believed, Bandini was envious of Scarfiotti's patrician status – he was a second cousin of Fiat patriarch Gianni Agnelli, which contrasted so dramatically with his own humble background.

Enzo Ferrari recalled "the Bandini who looked up to Surtees's insufferable pretensions and later the Bandini who begged for tranquility" before that fateful 1967 Monaco race. He claimed that he had accommodated Bandini's worries by including Chris Amon in the team for that race, although on the face of it this seems demonstrable nonsense on the part of the Old Man, who had signed the young New Zealander simply because he was regarded as a much better driver than Scarfiotti.

If Bandini was worried, he certainly didn't show it to Amon, who recalled the two of them stopping on their way to the principality after a quiet lunch together up in the mountains on the Wednesday before the race. Lorenzo just wanted to savour the view and reflect on things. Chris would later allow himself to wonder whether this was some sort of premonition.

The New Zealander, who shared the winning Fer-rari 330P4 sports car with Bandini at both the Daytona 24 Hours and the Monza 1000km just before his death, remembered his old team-mate with affection.

"I have to confess that I was a little wary about him when I first joined the team," he said. "I suppose his reputation had rather gone before him from the occasion when he knocked Graham [Hill] off in Mexico back at the end of 1964, so I suppose I thought he might turn out to be a little aggressive towards me.

"But he was utterly charming. He was so pleasant and really helpful when it came to sorting out problems with the car. He really was one of the nicest guys I ever came across, and the greatest tragedy of the whole affair is that he was just beginning to emerge from behind the shadow of John Surtees. He really was maturing into a first-class number one in his own right."

The Cosworth Ford DFV, installed in the beautiful Lotus 49 chassis, made its debut in the third round of the World Championship, the Dutch Grand Prix at Zandvoort. At a stroke, it rendered obsolete every other Formula 1 car on the starting grid.

The 90-degree, 85.7 x 64.8mm, 2993cc V8 devel-

Continued on page 160

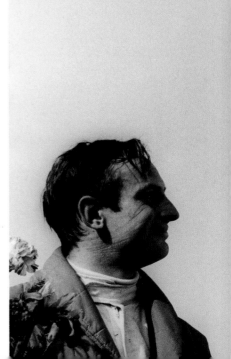

Left: The Weslake V12 that powered Dan Gurney's Eagle to victory in the 1967 Belgian GP.

Far left: The Eagle flies on Sunday. Dan Gurney scored his only victory as a constructor in the 1967 Belgian Grand Prix at Spa.
Photos: Bernard Cahier

Above: Lorenzo Bandini was one of the most popular F1 drivers of his era and was sorely missed after the Monaco tragedy.

Left: Dan Gurney on the rostrum after winning at Spa. He is accompanied by a similarly exuberant Jackie Stewart, whose BRM H-16 lasted the distance to take second, and Ferrari's third-placed Chris Amon.
Photos: Bernard Cahier

Inset right: **Man and machine. John Surtees with his Honda RA273 at the 1967 German Grand Prix. He would finish fourth in this car, which was replaced for the next race at Monza by the Lola-developed RA300.**
Photo: Bernard Cahier

Main photo: Four different machines on the front row for the 1967 German Grand Prix. Jim Clark smokes the tyres on his Lotus 49 as he gets the drop on the Brabham-Repco of Denny Hulme. Jackie Stewart in the BRM H-16 and Dan Gurney in the Eagle are just a split second behind them.

Inset left: Brabham brakes hard for Parabolica on a freshly laid oil slick as Surtees in the Honda prepares to pounce on the sprint to the line during the last lap of the 1967 Italian GP.

Photos: Bernard Cahier

Above: **Everything seems okay after a track inspection at Monza for (left to right) Jack Brabham, Denny Hulme, Chris Irwin, Ludovico Scarfiotti and Bruce McLaren.**

Photos: Bernard Cahier

oped 400bhp at 9000rpm. It wasn't the most powerful engine in F1 at that time, but it was the only one to be so beautifully integrated with its chassis. It had been designed to be used as a stressed member, acting as a load-bearing part of the chassis rather than simply sitting within a supporting structure. The Lotus 49 was light, compact and elegant. It was also brittle, only averagely reliable and delivered its power quite abruptly. Nevertheless, it was the class of the field.

Graham Hill led the opening stages of the Dutch Grand Prix, retiring only after a timing gear broke, and Clark took over to score the new car's maiden victory on its debut outing.

That was effectively the whole story of the 1967 season. Ferrari struggled with lack of power, Gurney's Eagle Weslake scored a glorious victory in the Belgian Grand Prix, and the Brabhams and Cooper-Maseratis were consigned to the supporting cast.

John Surtees's Honda – the heaviest car by far on the grid at 1500lb (680kg) – posted a terrific last-lap win at Monza in a wheel-to-wheel sprint to the line with Jack Brabham's Brabham BT24. But neither of them would have been in with a chance had not Clark's Lotus 49 spluttered, low on fuel, in the closing moments of the race. Jimmy, lest it be forgotten, had earlier made up a

full lap on the entire field after an early stop to change a punctured tyre.

The writing was very clearly on the wall: anybody without a Cosworth DFV was wasting his time in front-line F1. Cosworth initially built the DFV for Ford to supply on an exclusive basis to Team Lotus. However, when it became clear that the V8 would effectively make all other F1 units uncompetitive, Walter Hayes had a word with Colin Chapman, who most generously agreed to relinquish his exclusivity agreement in the wider interests of the sport.

Jim Clark was not happy about this. "I'm not terribly keen," he admitted, "particularly as we haven't really scored when we should have done.

"One way and another, the car hasn't quite lived up to its original promise, though it's difficult to pin the blame anywhere because the things that have gone wrong with my car have been different every time.

"At Spa, a plug popped out. At Le Mans, the final drive housing wasn't stiff enough. At the Nürburgring, I got a puncture, at Mosport, I got water in the electrics, and at Monza, I ran out of fuel.

"It was just like 1962. The car didn't quite come up to expectations there either, and all because of a lot of stupid little faults."

Above: Raw power. Pedro Rodriguez takes on the challenge of the Spa-Francorchamps circuit in his Cooper-Maserati.

Left: Denny Hulme and Jim Clark before the 1967 Mexican Grand Prix.
Photos: Bernard Cahier

Jimmy also confirmed that the DFV's power came in with a rush at around 6300rpm and, while it wasn't ideal allowing the revs to drop to that level in the first place, with the fixed-ratio ZF gearbox fitted to the Lotus 49, this wasn't always easy to avoid.

He also conceded that it might have been an advantage to 'soften' the DFV's power curve, "but as the season [has] progressed, we have learned to cope with the power and it was nothing like as bad as I had expected in the wet at Mosport.

"I must admit that before the start of that race, I was convinced that I was going to be dropping right to the back of the field, but it was possible with very judicious throttle control to get the car through this period.

"I'm not saying it wasn't difficult to drive – it was very difficult when the track started to dry out and there were still some wet patches – but this wasn't so much to do with the engine as with the tyres and chassis."

Once the DFV became available for other teams, Bruce McLaren put his money down immediately. The BRM V12 may have allowed his McLaren M5A to lead in the rain at Mosport Park, but those were freak conditions.

Yet at the end of the day, it was Denny Hulme who won the World Championship with two wins and a consistent string of results to Clark's four victories. The New Zealander wound up with 51 points to Brabham's 46 (net), while Clark was third on 41. Hulme would now move to McLaren where he, too, would benefit from the Cosworth DFV's power.

The 1968 season saw the arrival of commercial sponsorship in the form of major backing for the factory Lotus team from the Player's Gold Leaf cigarette brand. It was estimated as being in the order of £60,000 for the season, and this included identification on the Formula 2 and sports cars in addition to the factory Lotus 49s.

Yet the 1968 season would not be remembered for the first steps towards the big-money era that would see Grand Prix racing attain a position of unimaginable international status and wealth over the following generation. Instead, it would be remembered as the season that cost the lives of Jimmy Clark, Ludovico Scarfiotti, Mike Spence and Jo Schlesser.

Clark would be killed in a minor-league F2 race at Hockenheim on 7th April. It was such a momentous event that it forced everybody to recalibrate their attitude towards the sport. If it could happen to Jimmy, nobody was safe.

Then Mike Spence – ironically replacing the late Jim Clark – was killed testing a Lotus turbine car at Indianapolis. Scarfiotti perished when he crashed his Porsche at a mountain climb event, and Schlesser, a veteran 40-year-old making his F1 debut in front of his home crowd at Rouen-les-Essarts, died horrendously when the air-cooled Honda RA302 crashed on the third lap of the French Grand Prix and burst into flames. The implications and consequences of this human mayhem and misery are dealt with in more detail within the accompanying essay on safety in F1.

After Clark's death, Graham Hill pulled the Lotus team together to win the World Championship, yet the Lotus 49 was no longer in a class of its own. Ken Tyrrell had started his own Grand Prix team, using French Matra chassis and Cosworth Ford DFV engines, with

Jackie Stewart doing the driving. Jackie very nearly won the championship in his first year with the team, but in the end Hill took the crown by a comfortable margin with 48 points to Stewart's 36.

The 1968 season was also highlighted by a superb British Grand Prix victory at Brands Hatch for Jo Siffert, now driving an elegant dark-blue Lotus 49B for Rob Walker's privateer team. It was one of the most emotionally satisfying days for F1 in a season otherwise blighted by disaster, for it represented a memorable comeback for the famous private team after a disastrous outing in the Race of Champions at the same circuit earlier in the year.

Rob had purchased a Lotus 49 for Siffert to drive in that early-season race, but he had crashed heavily in testing. The wreckage was taken back to Walker's Dorking race headquarters, only for a stray spark to ignite petrol vapour as mechanics were stripping down the wreckage. Within seconds, the race shop was ablaze and, while the workforce escaped unhurt, all Rob's priceless archives and memorabilia were destroyed in the inferno that followed. Yet Rob would be back in business; the Walker team's brand-new Lotus 49B was delivered only days before the British Grand Prix.

McLaren also enjoyed the benefits of Cosworth

Above: **Graham Hill, who pulled together the Lotus team following the death of Clark in 1968. He would go on to take his second World Championship that year.**

Opposite, top: **Jo Siffert heads for victory in the 1968 British Grand Prix at Brands Hatch in the dark blue Rob Walker Lotus 49B.**

Opposite, bottom: **It was an emotional occasion and the last GP win for a genuine privateer with a customer car. Rob Walker (second left) enjoys the victory parade on the back of a flatbed truck. To his right are Siffert, team patron Jack Durlacher and third-placed Jacky Ickx.**
Photos: Bernard Cahier

Right: An inspired Richard Attwood took second place and set the fastest lap for BRM at the 1968 Monaco Grand Prix.

Below: All smiles at Monza for Bruce McLaren after his driver, Denny Hulme, took victory for McLaren. Johnny Servoz-Gavin looks suitably pleased with a career-best second in his Matra.

Photo: Bernard Cahier

DFV use. Bruce McLaren scored his first Grand Prix victory since Monaco 1962 when his M7A inherited a win at Spa-Francorchamps after Stewart's Matra MS10 ran out of fuel in the closing stages. Later in the season, Denny Hulme would take wins in both Italy and Canada.

Brabham, meanwhile, had faded dramatically. After winning two back-to-back championships, the team had high hopes for 1968, with Jochen Rindt joining from Cooper as a replacement for Hulme and a new four-cam Repco type 860 engine installed in the latest semi-monocoque BT26 chassis. But the whole season turned into an absolute fiasco.

By the end of 1968, it had become abundantly clear that the Repco F1 engine programme's salvation would depend on an almost unimaginable turn-around in technical reliability. It was a forlorn hope. There was no way in which the 12,000-mile supply route between England and Australia could survive another season like this. Formula 1 was changing.

Brabham made what was tipped as a short-term, stop-gap switch to Cosworth DFVs for 1969, but everybody knew it was the death knell for the Australian V8s.

"I think, given time, we could have sorted out the mechanical problems on the Repco 860," said John Judd, the Brabham engineer responsible for liaising with the Australian company, who became a respected F1 engine designer in his own right. "But the DFV was a good package which could be used as a stressed member, and our engine couldn't. At the end of the day, the Cosworth DFV was far ahead in terms of design. So many things they did for the first time. And did them right!"

Above: On the buses. Surtees, Hill and Stewart take a slower run around the Monte Carlo circuit.

Opposite: Graham Hill takes his Lotus 49B to victory past the crumpled car of team-mate Jackie Oliver.
Photos: Bernard Cahier

SAFETY AND SECURITY:
THE BIGGEST LEAP FORWARD OF ALL

THE fatal accidents that befell Roland Ratzenberger and Ayrton Senna during the 1994 San Marino Grand Prix meeting catapulted the issue of motor racing safety into the headlines around the globe, focusing the spotlight on what had become the most media-intensive sporting activity in the world.

Twenty-six years had passed since Jim Clark's death at Hockenheim had grabbed the newspaper headlines in the same way as Senna's. Yet the world – and the public's attitude towards motor racing – had changed dramatically during the intervening generation.

Essentially, Clark lived, raced and died at a time when the prevailing attitude could be summed up rather frivolously as "you pays your money and you takes your choice". When his Lotus 48 smashed into the unprotected trees at Hockenheim on 7th April, 1968, only 29 years had passed since Dick Seaman's Mercedes-Benz had been wrapped around a tree at Spa-Francorchamps on the eve of the Second World War.

Racing drivers crashed and died – it was as simple as that. The philosophy endured through the immediate postwar years and into the 1950s. The three Grand Prix regulars who lost their lives in 1958, for example, Peter Collins at the Nürburgring, Luigi Musso at Reims and Stuart Lewis-Evans, after an excruciating struggle against burns sustained when his Vanwall crashed in the Moroccan Grand Prix at Casablanca, were all victims as much of their time as of the physical injuries they sustained.

Consider Lewis-Evans's plight. Today an injured driver can expect to receive state-of-the-art medical attention at any circuit in the world. More than that, the provision of such facilities is a fundamental prerequisite of a track being permitted to hold a Grand Prix in the first place.

Yet for Lewis-Evans, who was informally managed by 27-year-old Bernie Ecclestone at that time, the situation was very different. A 1990s-style flameproof driving suit would probably have enabled the young driver from Kent to have survived the inferno that erupted after his Vanwall slid into a tree following an engine seizure. But Lewis-Evans was wearing nothing so sophisticated.

There were no medical facilities on hand to deal with the burns he sustained, and he faced a painful flight on a stretcher in Vanwall boss Tony Vandervell's chartered Viscount airliner back to Britain. There he was taken to the East Grinstead burns unit, which had been established by eminent surgeon Sir Archibald McIndoe to treat the horrific burns suffered by wartime fighter pilots. There was a cruel irony here. Racing drivers were just that in the 1950s: fighter pilots contesting what amounted to an undeclared war.

"When they took Stuart to the hospital at Casablanca, they just sat him in a chair with a blanket around him," said Ecclestone. "It wasn't because they were particularly neglecting him; that was just how things were there.

"It seems difficult to imagine, looking back from today's perspective, but you got used to people being killed. It was just part of the sport. One expected it."

Notwithstanding the tragedies at Imola in 1994, today's F1 stars have to be pretty unlucky to be killed at the wheel. A stark statement, perhaps, and arguably tempting fate.

"When I raced, the batting average was that you had a three out of five chance that you were going to die in a racing car if you survived five years," said Jackie Stewart.

The Scot's attitude towards F1 safety had been shaped in 1966, when he had crashed heavily on the opening lap of the Belgian GP at Spa-Francorchamps. He had been driving a 2-litre Tasman BRM in this first season of the 3-litre F1 regulations. These were relatively sophisticated cars by, let's say, pre-war standards, yet the Belgian track was virtually unchanged since Dick Seaman's fatal accident in 1939. It was the equivalent of trying to operate a Boeing 747 from a grass airstrip.

By the time Jackie returned to the cockpit for the British Grand Prix at Brands Hatch, his car had been fitted with a spanner taped to the steering wheel, the better to facilitate his escape if he were to experience another major accident. Later in the season, his car would also be fitted with seat belts at his request.

"This was not because of the Spa accident," he explained, "but because I'd driven a Lola in the Indianapolis 500 the previous week and it was fitted with belts. Admittedly they were a bit basic, but it struck me they made a lot of sense. If anybody at the BRM team thought this was a little eccentric, they suffered in silence. As far as I was concerned, they were very receptive to my request."

Yet many people did regard Stewart's request as distinctly odd. An amazing number of drivers still clung to the notion that being flung out of a car was probably the best way to survive a major accident. This was at best questionable, at worst nonsense, of course, as Ferrari driver Michael Parkes would demonstrate when he was tipped out of his Ferrari on the second lap of the following year's Belgian Grand Prix.

The English driver suffered severe multiple leg fractures, which effectively ended his front-line motor racing career. Ironically, he went off on oil dropped by Jackie Stewart's BRM H-16, a real gusher on four wheels if ever there was one.

However, seat belts would not have helped Lorenzo Bandini when, on 7th May, 1967, he suffered burns that were to prove fatal after upending his Ferrari 312 in the Monaco Grand Prix. The darling of the Italian motor racing community, Bandini was perhaps poised on the verge of greatness when a momentary lapse of concentration cost him his life.

The Italian had been chasing Denny Hulme's winning Brabham in the closing stages of the race when his car clipped the chicane, bounced on to the straw bales on the opposite side of the track and hurtled into an unprotected lamp post. The car cartwheeled on to the track and instantly exploded into a fireball.

Eventually extricated from the wreckage, Bandini was fatally injured. He died from his burns, and from serious internal injuries, three days later, shortly before his heavily pregnant wife, Margherita, suffered a miscarriage in the same hospital. It was one of F1's most gruesome episodes, and it helped kick-start the sport into directing its thoughts towards improved safety standards.

Back in the pits, Stewart watched the smoke rise above the chicane with a sense of foreboding. He had also led in the opening stages until his BRM had broken its transmission.

"I was far enough away from the accident not to realise that the driver was still in the car for 90 per cent of the fire," he said. "I just saw the intensity, the smoke, the turmoil of it all. I just thought, 'Oh no, this is a big one.'

"But keep in mind that the real frequency of fatal accidents seemed to come the following year, 1968, when they were dropping like flies with the deaths of Jim Clark, Ludovico Scarfiotti, Jo Schlesser and Mike Spence. Putting it harshly, the Bandini accident represented the reality of the business at the time. No more than that.

"The racing driver is a peculiar animal with regard to observing accidents, dealing with them and despatching the issues from his mind. [Drivers] are incredibly capable of doing that."

Jim Clark's death was front-page news in most European newspapers. Scarfiotti was killed at the Rossfeld hillclimb in Germany, thrown from his Porsche. Schlesser died when his Honda became an inferno after crashing in the French Grand Prix at Rouen-les-Essarts. Spence hit the wall at Indianapolis and a wayward wheel smashed his skull.

A year later, Lucien Bianchi, although carried from his wrecked Alfa sports car alive, wide-eyed and shaking, succumbed to burns, internal injuries and massive shock after slamming into a telegraph pole during testing for the Le Mans sports car race.

Yet somehow the Bandini tragedy was different The aforementioned accidents took place almost anonymously. In a way, without reels of gruesome cine film recording these painful episodes, the reality of death was easier to confront.

Bandini's accident briefly pulled aside the curtain protecting violent sports from media intrusion. The paying public got a taste of what they would see played out, live, on prime-time television at Imola a quarter of a century later.

The Bandini crash – and the events that followed in 1968 – further strengthened Stewart's resolve to step up his personal campaign for better safety. Racing drivers, he reasoned, should be paid to demonstrate their skill, not simply their bravery in what now seem prehistoric conditions.

"The Monaco disaster was yet another nail in the coffin of the traditionalists who didn't think they needed safety," said Stewart, "and there wasn't a more graphic example of their inadequacies and inabilities to change things fast enough."

Yet those traditionalists went for his jugular. In particular, Denis Jenkinson, the respected Continental correspondent of *Motor Sport* magazine, derided Jackie and his colleagues as the "milk and water" brigade.

On 13th June, 1972, Stewart felt moved to reply to Jenks's latest invective in a letter to the magazine. "What Denis Jenkinson thinks or says concerns me little," he wrote. "To me he is a fence-sitter, doing little or nothing to secure a future for our sport.

"All Mr Jenkinson seems to do is lament the past and the drivers who have served their time in it. Few of them, however, are alive to read his writings."

Nor were the drivers the only ones at risk. It is almost too frightening to consider what the consequences might have been at Barcelona's Montjuich Park circuit had there not been at least a single-height guard rail to restrain the Lotus 49Bs of Graham Hill and Jochen Rindt from plunging into the crowd following the failure of their strut-mounted rear wings in the 1969 Spanish Grand Prix.

Thanks to Stewart and many others who subsequently picked up the torch to campaign for improved safety after his retirement in 1973, today's F1 drivers enjoy levels of personal security that seemed unimaginable 35 years ago. Between 1978 and 2005, their medical requirements were dealt with by Professor Sid Watkins, one of the world's most eminent neurosurgeons, who was employed as the FIA medical delegate. Following his retirement, the role was taken on by his deputy, Dr Gary Hartstein, another highly regarded medical man. Back in 1969, Stewart was regarded as almost eccentric when he hired his own doctor to accompany him to every race.

"Prof Watkins has made such a terrific contribution to all this because he hasn't been a team owner, he hasn't been a driver or even been part of a national governing body," Stewart said. "That neutrality has helped him considerably, but still to this day I feel that the drivers do not have enough authority and enough say in what goes on.

"By the same token, the drivers can be incredibly lethargic about safety. They don't want to sacrifice the time to make the improvements required. But if they did that, they would be able to sleep more comfortably.

"I'm clearly not a believer in the syndrome which suggests that motor racing should be dangerous. It will never be safe, but there is absolutely no reason for the competitors to be exposed to unnecessary hazards. It wouldn't happen in any other business."

Yet the carnage would continue. In 1970, Piers Courage died when his Frank Williams entered de Tomaso crashed and burned in the Dutch Grand Prix at Zandvoort. Then Jochen Rindt, the World Champion-presumptive, died horrendously at Monza during practice for the Italian Grand Prix.

In 1973, Roger Williamson's March suffered a tyre failure during the Dutch Grand Prix at Zandvoort, somersaulting to a halt upside down and then bursting into flames. Despite the brave efforts of his rival, David Purley, Williamson was asphyxiated.

Then, at Watkins Glen, Jackie Stewart's Tyrrell team-mate, François Cevert, was killed when he slammed into a guard rail during practice.

Surtees driver Helmuth Koinigg was decapitated at Watkins Glen the following year, when his Surtees slid beneath inadequately secured guard rails. In 1978, Ronnie Peterson died from injuries sustained when his Lotus 78 crashed while accelerating away from the start line at Monza during the Italian Grand Prix.

Four years later, the F1 fraternity was numbed by the death of Gilles Villeneuve when his Ferrari 126C2 somersaulted over the back of Jochen Mass's March during qualifying for the Belgian Grand Prix at Zolder. Only

weeks later, Osella F1 team novice Riccardo Paletti was fatally injured when he slammed into the back of Didier Pironi's stalled pole-position Ferrari on the start line at Montreal.

Two years after that, Elio de Angelis, the charming and courteous Roman, died after crashing his Brabham BT55-BMW during a test session at the Paul Ricard circuit near Bandol. Yet by this point, safety had improved dramatically. After de Angelis's sad loss, another eight years would pass before the double May Day disasters at Imola.

The accidents to Ratzenberger and Senna further accelerated safety moves, but nothing could ever entirely eliminate the danger element. On Sunday, 10th March, 1996, television viewers around the world could have been forgiven for thinking that this was the day 35-year-old Martin Brundle's luck had finally run out.

On the opening lap of the Australian GP at Melbourne, the King's Lynn driver's Jordan-Peugeot somersaulted off the track at around 180mph after being launched over the back of a rival's car. Yet the only injury he sustained was a badly bruised foot – incurred as he jogged energetically back to the pits to take over the Jordan team's spare car in time to drive in the restarted race.

However, it was not by chance alone that Brundle emerged unscathed. Obviously luck plays a part in the outcome of any accident, whether on road or race track, but for the past couple of decades or more, Grand Prix car design has been tailored to offer the occupants of these precision-built high-speed projectiles the best possible chance of survival in the event of a catastrophic accident

"Performance and safety are prob-

ably the two most important concerns in your mind when you sit down to design a car," said Gary Anderson, the Jordan F1 team's technical director at the time, after Brundle's escape. "You want your driver to be as quick as possible, and as safe as possible.

"Motor racing does have inherent dangers, as was demonstrated in Australia. The difference between Martin hurting himself in that accident, and not hurting himself, is partly down to luck. You never know where bits of the car are going to end up, or whether another driver is going to hit you in that situation.

"You can, however, devise regulations to ensure that the drivers are safe in as many situations as possible, hence the regulation concerning cockpits [designed to provide added lateral protection against head and neck injuries in the event of a side impact, which was brought in for the 1996 season]. As far as our cockpit sides are concerned, safety was the first thing we looked at because that, after all, is the reason that the latest regulations were introduced in the first place."

There would be many more close shaves over the years that followed. Grand Prix racing, said the critics, was going soft. Yet that wasn't the case. It was simply running slightly ahead of public opinion. The concept of willingly risking one's life in a reckless fashion was no longer really acceptable. So the sport worked hard to keep a safety net beneath its high-wire exponents for as much of the time as conceivably possible.

As the end of the millennium approached, Grand Prix racing had become big business. And multi-national sponsors were not accustomed to losing their biggest investments – that's to say, the drivers – in avoidable accidents.

One only has to consider the furore surrounding Michael Schumacher's fractured right leg, sustained in the 1999 British Grand Prix at Silverstone, to get the point. To judge by the reactions of some people in the F1 paddock, one could have been excused for thinking that this was a disaster of monumental proportions.

The only man with a realistic perspective on the whole business was Schumacher himself. "Hello, Sid, it's just my leg; it's not a big problem," he said when Prof Watkins arrived at the side of his shattered Ferrari. Within three months, he was back again on the Grand Prix starting grid.

FERRARI OPENS THE AEROFOIL ERA

At the 1968 Belgian Grand Prix, Ferrari arrived with fixed aerofoils above the gearboxes of its 312s for Chris Amon and new star Jacky Ickx, who had been recruited at the start of the season.

"People reckoned that I'd copied the Chaparral [sports car] concept," said chief designer Mauro Forghieri, "but that wasn't really the case. I'd got my inspiration from the ideas tried by Swiss engineer Michael May, who'd tried an aerofoil on a Porsche sports car more than ten years earlier. May had worked informally as a fuel injection consultant to Ferrari for some years [most notably on the 1963 1.5-litre V6], so there was already a line of communication."

Amon reckoned he should have won that race easily, but Surtees's Honda kicked up a stone that holed the Ferrari's radiator. It was the story of the brilliant New Zealander's career. "That Honda was a bloody nuisance, actually, both in 1967 and 1968," he recalled. "It was very quick in a straight line, but always got in the way on the corners."

On the basis that bigger is better, Colin Chapman soon eclipsed the modest wings on the Ferraris. For the French Grand Prix at Rouen-les-Essarts, the works Lotus 49Bs of Graham Hill and Jackie Oliver appeared with tall, strutted rear aerofoils working directly on the rear suspension uprights.

Chapman and his colleagues had calculated that these appendages developed 400lb of downforce at 150mph, but Oliver demonstrated the dangers of loss of such downforce when he pulled into the slipstream of a rival car during practice. Approaching the pits, he spun into a very substantial gatepost that split the car in two and catapulted its hapless driver out on to the road, standing upright and without a scratch.

"I thought I'd arrived in heaven," he recalled.

Throughout the 1968 season, the development of movable aerofoils continued apace. In time for the Italian Grand Prix, Forghieri had equipped the Ferrari 312s with a very sophisticated system activated by engine oil pressure and braking effort. The principle was that the wing angle was steeply inclined in first, second and third gears, and when the drivers applied the brakes in fourth and fifth. It feathered in fourth and fifth when the driver was on the throttle.

All this seemed a little too complex to Amon, who preferred to use the manual override system in the cockpit. Lotus, meanwhile, had a feathering wing, operated by a fourth pedal in the footwell, which was ready in time for the 1968 Mexican Grand Prix. The unfettered development of these high aerofoils continued into 1969, several teams supplementing them with similar structures mounted on the front suspension.

This latest spiral in Formula 1 technology came to an abrupt end after massive accidents caused by wing failures befell both Graham Hill and Jochen Rindt during the Spanish Grand Prix at Barcelona's Montjuich Park. Rindt, who had joined Lotus from the Brabham team at the start of the season, was seriously unnerved by this episode, which left him with a hairline fracture of the skull. From then on, he never shied away from expressing his concerns to Colin Chapman over the possible frailty of Lotus equipment.

Rindt wrote, "I have been racing in F1 for five years

and I have made one mistake (I rammed Chris Amon at Clermont-Ferrand) and I had one accident at Zandvoort due to gear selection failure. Otherwise I stayed out of trouble. This situation changed rapidly since I joined your team.

"Honestly, your cars are so quick that we would still be competitive with a few extra pounds used to make the weakest parts stronger. Please give my suggestions some thought. I can only drive a car in which I have some confidence and I feel the point of no confidence is quite near."

Meanwhile, faced with mounting concern over these aerodynamic developments, motor racing's governing body, the CSI, made a move on the issue after first practice for the Monaco Grand Prix.

After a lengthy debate on the subject, the CSI decided on an immediate ban on these wings, although the use of small fins mounted on the front suspension was permitted as long as they did not project beyond the inside edge of the wheel or above the highest part of the bodywork at that point.

Several of the constructors were quite happy with this ruling, but Ken Tyrrell protested strongly, saying that the Matra MS80 had been designed around these wings and could well be dangerous without them. He also pointed out that the CSI had broken its undertaking that the rules would not be changed without adequate notice, but in turn he was reminded that changes could always be made in the interests of safety. As a result of the ban, all the first day's practice times were invalidated.

Thereafter, the F1 teams would develop a generation of lower rear wings mounted on the engine covers, working in conjunction with nose wings. It was the start of an aerodynamic programme that is still recognisably the same some 40 years later.

Above: **Ludicrous by today's standards – Jack Brabham finds downforce in the monstrously ugly double-winged BT26 at Mexico in 1968.**
Photo: Bernard Cahier

Opposite, top: **Jacky Ickx took his first Grand Prix win in the 1968 French Grand Prix. The aerofoil was modest by the standards of the Lotus.**
Photo: Paul-Henri Cahier

Opposite, bottom: **Graham Hill helps to extricate team-mate Jochen Rindt from the wreckage of his Lotus 49 after the Austrian's rear aerofoil had collapsed during practice for the 1969 Spanish Grand Prix. Rindt was lucky to escape with a hairline skull fracture. High strut-mounted aerofoils were banned forthwith.**
Photos: Bernard Cahier

Above: Jackie Stewart in the superb Bernard Boyer-designed Matra MS80, fielded by Ken Tyrrell's team, which gave him the means to take the World Championship by storm.

Right: After the failure of four-wheel-drive in 1969, Lotus pursued the idea with its Type 56 turbo car. Reine Wisell whistles his Pratt & Whitney engined car around Silverstone to no great effect during the 1971 British Grand Prix.

Photos: Bernard Cahier

STEWART TAKES A TITLE FOR TYRRELL AND MATRA

The partnership between Ken Tyrrell and Jackie Stewart was based on mutual respect and genuine affection. It lacked, perhaps, some of the mystique that has retrospectively been credited to the relationship between Colin Chapman and Jim Clark, but arguably it was even stronger.

After two years of wrestling with the BRM H-16, Stewart was ready for a change by the end of the 1967 season. Tyrrell made an approach and Jackie accepted, privately wondering whether or not Ken could raise the £10,000 retainer he was asking for.

It wasn't a new partnership. Tyrrell had first seen Jackie testing a Cooper F3 car in 1963 at Goodwood. "Within three laps, he was going faster than Bruce McLaren in the same car, and by the end of the day, I was convinced that he was going to be a great driver," said Ken.

"I offered him £3000 to sign with me, on condition that I took ten per cent of his earnings for the next five years. But he declined. Pity, that."

Nevertheless, Jackie won the British F3 Championship for Tyrrell with a Cooper the following season and stayed on the Tyrrell F2 team long enough to have

his first taste of the French Matra chassis in the second division category. By the time the F1 offer came, Stewart was convinced of their potential.

Tyrrell's cars were prepared in an unprepossessing wooden hut in the family timber yard, which drew the memorable remark "What a dump!" from Ford's Walter Hayes on first acquaintanceship.

"Nobody bothers us, and we can get on and do the job properly," said Tyrrell mechanic Roger Hill by way of defence.

For the 1969 season, the Matra MS10 was replaced by a new chassis, the Bernard Boyer-designed monocoque MS80. Jackie used the MS10 to open the season with a win in South Africa, then won the Spanish, Dutch, French, British and Italian races, clinching his first World Championship at Monza after pipping Jochen Rindt's Lotus 49B into second. Brabham's Jacky lckx was runner-up in the points table with two wins.

Ferrari was now fading fast as a competitive F1 force, the company being so overwhelmed by the cost of its Grand Prix and sports car racing programmes that Enzo Ferrari had to seek the help of Fiat patriarch Gianni Agnelli to keep the show seriously on the road. He succeeded, but his problems meant that every race of the 1969 F1 season was won by a Cosworth DFV-engined car.

That said, increasing the DFV's operational rev limit to around 10,000rpm might have produced another 30bhp, but the engines remained brittle. Camshaft failures were quite frequent, as were valve spring breakages and lubrication problems. Despite all this, the DFV was unquestionably the engine to have.

In 1969, Frank Williams also made his first appearance on the F1 stage, running a car for old Etonian Piers Courage. The ever enterprising Williams had managed to pull a flanker on Jack Brabham by acquiring an ex-works Brabham BT24 chassis at the end of 1968. The plan was to race it in the Tasman Championship, a lucrative series of races in Australia and New Zealand that was really a winter Grand Prix series by another name, but Frank eventually decided to make the logical progression and contest the 1969 F1 World Championship with Piers driving the car.

Much to the annoyance of Jack Brabham, whose works cars ran on Goodyear tyres, the Williams Brabham was contracted to race on Dunlops. Piers really came of age that season, second places in the Monaco and United States Grands Prix testifying to his growing ability.

4WD FORMULA FOR FAILURE

The 1969 Formula 1 season was highlighted by a spate of four-wheel-drive cars from Lotus, Matra, McLaren and Cosworth. Yet the concept proved a frustrating blind alley for all concerned.

McLaren engineer Robin Herd left his post with the team to design the Cosworth 4WD challenger, which was never raced. The basis of his new design was a pair of sponsons between the wheels on each side, joined by a stressed-steel floor, the whole chassis achieving its rigidity from the engine and box-like structures front and rear.

The side sponsons carried the fuel, and the front and rear boxes the suspension and differentials. The Cosworth DFV engine was turned through 180 degrees so that the clutch faced forward. From there, a Cosworth gearbox containing Hewland gears side-stepped power to an angled bevel differential mounted on the right, which distributed the torque between the front and rear wheels.

"It was possibly rather shallow thinking," said Herd. "If we'd all thought a little bit longer, then we would probably have realised that, with the trends going the way they were, four-wheel drive wasn't going to be practical."

In the case of the Lotus 63, the car's Cosworth DFV engine had again been turned through 180 degrees, with a five-speed Lotus/ZF gearbox stepping the drive to the left-hand side of the chassis, a design legacy of the Indianapolis 4WD turbine Lotuses, which were built with a weight bias to that side.

The Matra M584 4WD machine was built around a space-frame chassis for reasons of maintenance and economy. Its five-speed gearbox, central differential, control unit and stepped take-off drive were all Ferguson components loaned to Matra for the project.

Designed by the late Jo Marquart, the four-wheel-drive McLaren M9A appeared at Silverstone for the British Grand Prix with Derek Bell in the cockpit. It had already undergone tests in the hands of Bruce McLaren and Denny Hulme, but, despite a barrage of encouraging reports in the media, by the time the team arrived at Silverstone, it was clear that they were barking up the wrong tree.

Bruce himself coined perhaps the most apt description of the sensation of four-wheel drive: handling the M9A was like "trying to write your signature with somebody jogging your elbow"; after those preliminary trials, he looked glum and said, "Why bother?" to his team.

That pretty well summed up the general feeling towards this generation of four-wheel-drive racers. The only World Championship point ever scored by a

4WD car came at Mosport Park, where Johnny Servoz-Gavin finished sixth in the Canadian Grand Prix, driving the Matra M584.

As for the rest, the development of aerofoils, even in their newly truncated form, meant that two-wheel-drive cars were quicker as well as less complex than their four-wheel-drive counterparts. It was the end of the road.

Well, not quite. Two years later, Lotus brought out its four-wheel-drive Lotus 56B turbine car for several events. Much trouble was experienced in reducing the turbine's throttle lag, but during the soaking wet 1971 Dutch Grand Prix at Zandvoort, the smooth characteristics of the turbine motor, allied to four-wheel-drive, opened the door just a fraction for a possible renaissance.

F1 novice David Walker was picking off seasoned runners with no trouble at all in the early stages of the race, until he overdid things and crashed at the end of the main straight.

Colin Chapman reflected some years later, "That was the one race that should, and could, have been won by four-wheel drive."

FERRARI RESCUED BY FIAT

As we have seen, by the start of the 1969 season, Ferrari finances were becoming pretty stretched. The *Commendatore* was finding it extremely difficult to pay for programmes for Formula 1, Formula 2, sports cars, Can-Am and hill-climbing from budgets culled exclusively from traditional motor industry sources.

Firestone and Shell were both putting a lot of money into the Italian team, but this was not in the same league as that which would soon be provided by the tobacco barons. In any case, Ferrari was involved in a far more ambitious overall racing programme than any rival team, and it was quite clear that, at the start of 1969, the Prancing Horse had its back to the financial wall.

The company's long-term salvation and security were finally achieved on 18th June, 1969, when Enzo Ferrari forged a deal with Fiat overlord Gianni Agnelli to guarantee the marque's future. The racing cars were to remain under Ferrari's personal guidance and control for the rest of his life – he would live another 19 years to the age of 89 – while the road cars would fall more directly under the control of Fiat.

Thus Fiat became a 50-per-cent shareholder in the Ferrari organisation, and its nominee, Giuseppe Dondo, became managing director, while another Fiat appointee, Francesco Bellicardi, also joined the board. Bellicardi had previously been a director of the Bologna based Weber carburettor company and was a long-standing friend of Enzo Ferrari

The arrangement with Fiat was concluded *in vitalizio*, which meant that the company effectively paid Ferrari an annuity over the remainder of his life for the privilege of using his property and facilities. On Enzo Ferrari's death in 1988, the whole manufacturing facility was ceded to Fiat. It certainly paid its dues for a long time!

The Fiat/Ferrari alliance was agreed some six years after Henry Ford II had made a bid to purchase Ferrari. The *Commendatore* backed out of that deal at the last minute, which resulted in Ford building its own cars to take on Ferrari at Le Mans.

Gianni Agnelli, at 49 more than 20 years Ferrari's junior, was an altogether more sensitive visionary. He handled Enzo Ferrari with the respect and caution that the Old Man rightfully believed was his due, and was quick to understand that Ferrari was not only a valuable public relations tool for Fiat, but also a standard-bearer for his country as a whole.

Above: Even in 1970, paddock facilities were still rudimentary to say the least. The works March and BRM teams work on the grass below the track at Clermont-Ferrand.

Far left: Jean-Pierre Beltoise kicks up the dust in his Matra at the 1970 Spanish Grand Prix.

Left: Henri Pescarolo takes a career-best third place in his Matra V12 at the 1970 Monaco Grand Prix.

Photos: Bernard Cahier

Above: New kids on the block. Robin Herd and Max Mosley, who took on the might of Formula 1 with their March team in 1970.

Opposite: Chris Amon leads Jack Brabham, Jacky Ickx, Jean-Pierre Beltoise and Denny Hulme around the old Station hairpin. The temporary grandstand hides the vacant lot that would soon become the Loews Hotel.

Photos: Bernard Cahier

MARCH MAKES ITS F1 BOW

In many ways, the car of the 1970 Grand Prix season was the Robin Herd-designed March 701, produced by the newly established Bicester based constructor that had committed itself to building machinery for F2 and F3 in addition to the sport's most senior category.

March Engineering was an ambitious new company. One of its founders was Max Mosley, the son of former British fascist leader Sir Oswald Mosley, who had been a keen amateur racer in his own right A highly qualified barrister, Max had gained a reputation for being shrewd and far-thinking, perhaps even a touch ruthless. Twenty-three years later, he would be elected president of the FIA.

Max's fellow directors were Robin Herd, former racer Alan Rees, who'd run top F2 team Winkelmann Racing for much of the 1960s, and Graham Coaker. Initially they tried to coax Jochen Rindt to join their team. "That's just something you've knocked up together in Graham's shack," said Rindt, scornfully, in his richly Austrian-accented English. Mosley was so amused that he registered 'Gremshek Engineering' as a company name. But they didn't get Rindt's services; he stayed with Lotus.

The March 701 was a very basic, Cosworth DFV-engined 'kit car', two of which would be fielded by the STP backed works team for Chris Amon and Jo Siffert, and two others – amazingly – would be driven by Jackie Stewart and Johnny Servoz-Gavin under the Elf Tyrrell banner.

Ken Tyrrell had finished the 1969 season with a World Championship title – and a major problem on his hands. Matra would no longer supply chassis for his team to use with Ford engines. Jackie Stewart tried the French constructor's Matra V12-engined car at Albi, in south-west France, late in 1969, but couldn't convince himself. Sure enough, the chassis was fine,

but the engine felt strangulated alongside the Cosworth DFV.

Thus Tyrrell had no alternative but to look around for another car. March was the only option, so he purchased three of the 701s. Mosley wanted to charge Tyrrell £6000 per chassis, a reasonable price, he reckoned, since they had cost about half that to build.

"I told them they would soon be out of business if they didn't price the cars higher than that," said Ford's Walter Hayes. So March increased its price and Ford ended up paying £9000 each for the two Tyrrell race cars. That was 'nickels and dimes' if it was what had to be done to keep Jackie Stewart on the Ford books, although Mosley recalls making Tyrrell squeal like hell by billing him direct for another £9000 for the team's spare chassis.

"But since Ken couldn't really tell me that Ford had already agreed to buy the cars, but only two of them, he couldn't do much more than grizzle," laughed Max. "But Walter's advice made the difference between staying in business and going under. At the end of the year, we finished up with a nominal profit of £2000. If we'd sold the seven customer 701s we produced for £6000 each, we'd have lost over £20,000, and that would have been that."

But Ken Tyrrell wasn't happy. Right up to the start of the season, he'd been hoping that Matra might relent and build his team a car to take the Ford engine. He also toyed with the possibility of doing a deal with either Brabham or McLaren, but both those teams had Goodyear tyre contracts, and Ken's cars ran on Dunlops. There was no choice but the March.

But Tyrrell quickly concluded that this could only be a stop-gap. "Here we were with the reigning World Champion signed up, yet our racing future was to depend on what we could buy from other manufacturers. Until that time, I'd had no ambition to build my own car. I'd been happy running a semi-works team, bearing the cost of engines and transmissions and their breakages, while Matra took care of the chassis. The cost of rebuilding a wrecked chassis could have been enormous and it was a responsibility I didn't want. Now I had no choice."

Even as the first March 701s were being unveiled to the media at Silverstone in February 1970, the first Tyrrell was being designed. The man recruited for the task was former Ferguson engineer Derek Gardner, and he began work in a converted bedroom at his home in Leamington Spa. The first Tyrrell chassis, Ken had told him, must be ready for the Oulton Park Gold Cup race on 22nd August. It was a tall order.

March also provided a 701 for its personal protégé, Ronnie Peterson, the dynamic young Swede who'd so memorably won the previous year's Monaco F3 supporting race. Mosley and Herd did a deal for Ronnie to run his March 701 under the Antique Automobiles banner, this being the historic car sales company owned by the enthusiastic Colin Crabbe.

The other March 701s, meanwhile, were having a half-way decent run. Amon's Firestone-shod factory car won the Silverstone International Trophy, while Stewart scored lucky wins in the Race of Champions at Brands Hatch and the Spanish Grand Prix.

Yet the March 701 was effectively living on borrowed time. It was struggling to look good against its opposition, which included the Brabham BT33 and

the promising new BRM P153. And this was before Colin Chapman's new challenger seriously got into its stride.

BRM, meanwhile, had undergone a major administrative shake-out the previous season. The P139 had proved uncompetitive in the hands of John Surtees, and the team's chief engineer, Tony Rudd, decided he could take no more of the high level of management interference from Louis and Jean Stanley, respectively brother-in-law and sister of Sir Alfred Owen, who were taking an increasingly larger hand in running the team.

After 19 years with the organisation, Rudd went off to become director of power-train engineering for Colin Chapman's road car company, and BRM designs were now entrusted to a young engineer named Tony Southgate. With the 73.6 x 57.22mm, 2998cc P142 V12 engine now developing 435bhp at a maximum of 11,000rpm, it was almost on a par with the Ford Cosworth DFV.

The BRM V12 was slightly heavier, of course, but Pedro Rodriguez drove the latest P153 chassis brilliantly around Spa-Francorchamps to beat Chris Amon's March and win the Belgian Grand Prix.

In the Brabham camp, 'Black Jack' had not originally intended to drive the new monocoque BT33 in 1970. He made it quite clear that he would have retired if he could have persuaded Jochen Rindt to return to the team.

Eventually, Bernie Ecclestone – Jochen's business manager – got in touch with Goodyear to see if there was any way a half-way serious financial deal could be put together to get Rindt back in a Brabham. But Chapman eventually trumped these negotiations with an offer of more money and a supplementary F2 programme. So Jochen stayed with Lotus.

Leo Mehl, then Goodyear's racing manager, recalled the negotiations. "Jack was very interested in doing this deal because he would have liked to retire," he said. "I had been quite a good friend of Jochen's and was very keen about the proposal, although I feared money would be the big problem.

"Jochen, Jack and I had talked about the deal, but nobody had really mentioned any hard figures. But Colin Chapman came up to me with a very serious look at one of the races and whispered, 'I don't care how much you are going to offer him because it won't be enough…' I was young and innocent, and Colin was old and forceful, so I never pursued the matter any further with my management."

Brabham won the opening race of the season at Kyalami, at the wheel of the BT33. He would have won the British Grand Prix at Brands Hatch had his car not run short of fuel in the closing moments of the race. Legend has it that chief mechanic Ron Dennis forgot to put in the final churn, but Ron Tauranac was not so sure.

"It's possible all the fuel didn't go in," he mused, "but the people concerned were very reliable, and marked off their churns and so on. We could have used more fuel; this is possible because the car did appear to be running rich during the race, but the other possibility is that we had a leak. We did find a suspect bag which was wet when we pulled it out of its carrier after the race, although we haven't got any proof that it leaked."

As for Lotus, the team began the 1970 campaign with the outdated Lotus 49, now in its fourth season of racing, which had been updated to use the latest 13in front wheels. But the car was entering the sunset of its competitive life and Colin Chapman knew it.

The charismatic Lotus boss had originally laid

plans for the radical type 72 after the 1969 Lotus 63 had sadly been numbered among that season's crop of four-wheel-drive failures. Thus the classic Lotus 49 had been doing yeoman service ever since its debut at Zandvoort in mid-1967, but now Chapman decided it was time to take another giant step forward.

Developed in conjunction with Firestone, the Lotus 72 was designed to have low unsprung weight and pitch-free ride characteristics that would allow it to get the best out of the softest rubber compound available.

To ensure the optimum performance as its fuel load was consumed, Chapman and his chief designer, Maurice Phillippe, decided to employ rising-rate suspension by means of torsion bars, the car's wedge profile guaranteeing its aerodynamic efficiency, and the side-mounted radiators preventing the driver's feet from becoming uncomfortably roasted.

From the outset, the car was hampered by problems with its inboard front brakes. Practising at Jarama, Rindt suffered a failure that left him with braking on only three wheels, which pitched him into an abrupt spin. He walked back to the pits and told Chapman he wasn't ever going to get into "that bloody car" again.

As Rob Walker later recalled, he asked Graham Hill what would happen now. Hill, an experienced Lotus campaigner who was driving Walker's private Lotus 49C, replied, "Colin will put his arm round Rindt's shoulder and lead him away for a friendly little chat, and Jochen will eventually get back into the car." That was precisely what happened.

After a disappointing debut in Spain, Rindt reverted to the works Lotus 49C, with which he scored a stupendous last-corner victory at Monaco. He used the old car again for the Belgian GP before a reworked Lotus 72 broke cover for the Dutch GP at Zandvoort. A suspension redesign, in Rindt's view, had given the car a "better feel" – its anti-squat characteristics had

been reduced – and he trampled the opposition underfoot to score his second win of the season, a success scarred by the death of his friend, Piers Courage, when he crashed the Frank Williams de Tomaso. This tragedy marked the beginning of the end for Rindt's enthusiasm for F1 racing. At Clermont-Ferrand, the venue for the 1970 French GP, he was still regarding the 72 with a justifiable degree of paranoia. Chapman fumed, "What am I going to do with this bloke? He has lightning reflexes, is bloody quick, but keeps telling me how to design my cars."

Jackie Stewart was possibly Rindt's closest friend for much of his racing career. "Colin's approach was just a little too slapdash for me," he admitted, "and that's why I never drove for him. By the time of his death, I think Jochen was certainly talking in terms of retirement. He told me, 'I can't get on with his car. It's going to break,' but he just had to drive it because it was so fast."

Herbie Blash, Jochen's mechanic on the Lotus 72 and today FIA Grand Prix race director, vividly remembered that Jochen was becoming increasingly preoccupied over Chapman's obsession with saving weight and bulk at any cost. Despite this, Rindt would win in France, then again at Brands Hatch and Hockenheim. He retired from the first Austrian GP to be held at the Österreichring, yet seemed poised to clinch the World Championship at the Italian Grand Prix.

Yet Rindt's alarming prophecy for the Lotus 72 would be fulfilled. On Saturday, 5th September, 1970, he went out to practise at Monza in preparation for the Italian race. At Chapman's insistence, he was running the car without nose wings or aerofoils in an attempt to match the straight-line speed of the powerful Ferrari 312B1 flat-12s.

John Miles, Rindt's Lotus team-mate, was told that he had to do the same, but reported to Chapman that the car felt "horrifyingly unstable" in this configuration. Going into Parabolica, Rindt had just overtaken Denny Hulme's McLaren M14A when his car began weaving under heavy braking and speared left into the inadequately secured guard rail.

Rindt succumbed to neck injuries sustained when he submarined deep into the cockpit. It would take another seven years of investigations before it was decided that a front brake-shaft failure had caused his loss of control, but the unsecured barrier was cited as the cause of his death.

By this stage, Rindt's championship points lead was almost unassailable. Ferrari team leader Jacky Ickx would have to win all three of the remaining races to take the title. He managed to win two, but when Emerson Fittipaldi took the Lotus 72 to victory at Watkins Glen in only his fourth Grand Prix outing, Jochen became the sport's only posthumous title holder with 45 points to Ickx's 40.

Above: **Rindt and Chapman had an uneasy relationship**

Above left: **Sombre and desolate after hearing of the death of his great friend Piers Courage, Jochen Rindt looks straight into Bernard Cahier's lens from the victory rostrum at Zandvoort in 1970.**

Left: **Rindt on his way to his first victory in the Lotus 72 at the 1970 Dutch Grand Prix.**
Photos: Bernard Cahier

Above: The promising Ignazio Giunti was promoted from Ferrari's sports car squad and given a chance to shine in F1.

Top: Jacky Ickx leads Clay Regazzoni to a 1-2 finish in Austria, 1970.

Opposite: Contrasting views of Monza during the 1970 Italian Grand Prix. Top: Jacky Ickx (2) leads Pedro Rodriguez away at the start, while the winning car of Clay Regazzoni is about to be engulfed by the *tifosi* on the slow-down lap.

Photos: Bernard Cahier

FERRARI STARTS TO FIGHT BACK

Meanwhile, Ferrari was on its way back. By the end of the 1969 season, the Italian team could reflect on just a single Grand Prix victory over the previous three years, Jacky Ickx having taken a superb win in the rain at Rouen-les-Essarts during the summer of 1968.

For his part, Chris Amon had endured enough. It wasn't a question of whether or not Ferrari regained its competitive edge, it was simply that he was running out of patience. Even though he had tested the new 312B1, powered by its sensational 180-degree, 12-cylinder engine, he wasn't about to be seduced into staying.

"For three years, I had been driving cars with super chassis that handled well, but couldn't hold a candle to their rivals when it came to power. Then, suddenly, here was the 312B1 with its flat-12 engine.

"The moment I tested it for the first time, I knew this was a completely different proposition. But three times I drove it at Modena, and three times it blew apart, always something drastic like breaking its crankshaft. I thought, 'God, I can't stand another season of this.'"

In his view, Mauro Forghieri had produced a gem. But despite his faith in Ferrari's extrovert and volatile chief engineer, Amon decided to leave the team. It is a decision he regrets to this day.

Forghieri and his colleagues had created a remarkably compact power unit of 78.55 x 51.55mm, producing a total capacity of 2991.01cc. Its four chain-operated overhead camshafts ran on needle rollers, operating 48 valves, and the crankshaft turned on four main bearings. Its reputed 460+bhp at an 11,700rpm maximum was judged to be more than enough to deal with the car's Cosworth DFV propelled rivals, even though the Ferrari was clearly thirstier and needed more fuel. Some of that fuel was contained within a rearward extending pontoon, under which the flat-12 engine was neatly slung. It was a cleverly executed package.

"I decided on the 180-degree engine configuration for two reasons," recalled Forghieri. "There was a slight weight saving as compared with the earlier V12s, and the centre of gravity would be significantly lower in the chassis. There was the added benefit of a smooth upper surface to the rear bodywork, and we decided to hang the 'boxer' from beneath a rearward extension of the monocoque, which could also be used to carry extra fuel."

The crankshaft was machined from a special alloy billet imported from the USA. "To cure those early crankshaft failures," said Forghieri, "we had a specially developed coupling between the crankshaft and flywheel, the purpose being to transfer flexing stresses along the length of the crankshaft."

Forghieri had developed the engine during a spell in 1969 when he had been 'banished' to Maranello's special projects department. "I began to think of the 'boxer' configuration at the end of 1968 after a year of pole positions, leading races and disappointing retirements with Chris Amon," he said.

Despite the advent of the Lotus 72, the Ferrari 312B1 acquitted itself magnificently throughout its first full season. New signing Clay Regazzoni was able to lead a Grand Prix for the first time at Hockenheim, where Ickx battled with Rindt for the entire distance, just finding himself out-fumbled on the final lap. In fairness, Rindt commented, "A monkey could have won in my car today." As we have seen, Jochen failed to finish his home race at the Österreichring, where Ickx and Regazzoni put on a convincing demonstration run to finish in 1-2 formation. Then Rindt was killed at Monza, where Regazzoni took victory – his first – and Ickx retired with a broken clutch. It was a dark weekend for the international motor racing fraternity, but there remained the tantalising prospect that Ickx, after all, just might beat his dead rival for the World Championship crown. Ickx finished the Italian GP weekend with a total of 19 points, way behind the total of 45 that Rindt had accumulated prior to his death.

The mathematics were simple. If Ickx could win the three remaining races – in Canada, the USA and Mexico – he would pick up another 27 points and take

the title by a single point. On the face of it, this seemed like a long shot, but he almost did it. He kept the battle open by winning the Canadian race at St Jovite, near Montreal, but a fuel line sprung a leak at Watkins Glen two weeks later and he could only scramble home fourth.

This confirmed Rindt as World Champion, but it was a close-run thing, as Ickx went on to round off the season with a victory in Mexico City. Thus he had won a total of four Grands Prix during the course of the season, only one short of Rindt's total, but the Belgian driver acknowledged that it was only right that his Austrian rival should have emerged from the season as champion.

DE TOMASO VENTURE ENDS IN TRAGEDY

During the course of the 1969 season, Frank Williams had made the acquaintance of Alessandro de Tomaso, the dynamic and successful Argentine businessman whose marriage to the wealthy American, Isabelle Haskell, had spawned an ambitious business partnership. At the time, the couple were already manufacturing Ford-engined high-performance road cars – the Mangusta and the Pantera were two of their best-known products – in a bid to challenge Ferrari and Lamborghini in this prestige sector of the market.

De Tomaso had already produced a Formula 2 car that showed a degree of promise, designed by Gianpaolo Dallara, who would go on to become a leading F3 chassis maker in his own right some 25 years later. For 1970, de Tomaso proposed that his company should build a new Grand Prix car that Frank would prepare and enter for Piers Courage to drive.

Williams's contribution to the equation would be to furnish the engines, driver and organisational expertise, such as it was. Courage duly agreed to drive the Cosworth DFV-engined de Tomaso 505, turning down a £30,000 offer to join Jacky Ickx at Ferrari. Instead he stayed with Frank on a nominal £3000 retainer, topped up with a fee of £22,500 from the Autodelta Alfa Romeo sports car team.

But the de Tomaso 505 was far from the taut, easy-handling Brabham BT24 that Piers had driven the previous year. Courage struggled from the outset, Frank even asking Jackie Stewart if he would do a few laps in the car in practice for the Silverstone International Trophy meeting, just to provide an objective third-party view as to precisely what he'd got Piers involved with.

Gradually the team's efforts improved the de Tomaso, but on 21st June, 1970, Piers crashed while running midfield in the Dutch Grand Prix at Zandvoort. The car caught fire and its driver perished in the ensuing inferno. With this disaster coming barely three weeks after the universally popular Bruce McLaren had been killed testing one of his own Can-Am sports cars at Goodwood, the F1 fraternity began to wonder just how much more tragedy it could bear.

TYRRELL READY TO RACE

The Tyrrell 001-Ford was easily the best-kept secret in motor racing in 1970. It was formally unveiled at Ford's London showrooms in Regent Street on Monday, 17th August, when the press members saw a car that bore something of an inspirational resemblance to the previous year's Matra MS80.

Ken Tyrrell reckoned that first chassis had cost £22,500 to build – about two-and-a half March 701s in other words. It was the bargain of the age.

Derek Gardner had concentrated on producing the best possible aerodynamic profile, good weight distribution and the lowest permissible weight. The first monocoque was manufactured by Morris Gomm's specialist sheet metal works at Old Woking, a few miles from the Tyrrell headquarters, and the car was topped off with distinctive bodywork that included a full-width, flat nose wing.

Stewart instantly recognised that here was a car in which he could achieve things. Its outing in the Gold Cup race was blighted by teething troubles, including a jammed throttle and an oil pick-up problem that caused the engine to blow up. But Jackie came away from the weekend with a new Oulton Park lap record and the feeling that the car was as sharp and responsive as the March 701 was dull and ponderous.

Although Stewart raced the March 701 to an emotionally draining second place at Monza the day after his close friend, Jochen Rindt, had died, for the re-

Left: An interesting shot of Jackie Stewart snuggly fitted into his Tyrrell 003 chassis.

Below: Piers Courage, who turned down the opportunity to drive for Ferrari in 1970 and who would perish after crashing his de Tomaso at Zandvoort in 1970.

Photos: Bernard Cahier

maining three Grands Prix of the season – in Canada, the USA and Mexico – he would drive the Tyrrell. It never finished, but it did convince him that he could challenge for the World Championship in 1971.

Stewart also had the last word on the March 701. He played golf with Robin Herd shortly before practice at the Canadian Grand Prix. Robin suggested that if Jackie won the game, he should drive the Tyrrell. If he did not, he should drive the March.

With three holes to play, Herd was one up and, with practice starting shortly, he suggested that they call it a day there and then. Stewart fixed him with a horrified expression. "Robin," he said, "never has anyone had such an incentive not to lose a golf match." They played it out. Jackie finished one up and raced the Tyrrell.

Partnered by his talented young team-mate, François Cevert, who had replaced Servoz-Gavin in the middle of the 1970 season, Jackie posted the first Tyrrell victory in 1971 at Barcelona's Montjuich Park circuit, then followed that up with his second Monaco victory. But this was something very special, even by his standards.

Despite suffering from a badly upset stomach, Stewart qualified his Tyrrell-Ford on pole position, only to find that the brake balance bar was broken as he took his place on the grid, leaving him with braking on the front wheels only. Unconcerned, he led from start to finish, only to be sick on the winner's rostrum. With a touch of false modesty, he played down the magnitude of that achievement. "Although you might not think so, Monaco is not particularly hard on brakes because you are never slowing from really high speed," he said.

"But it was a good race. To do it with only two-wheel braking was quite something. It's also worth remembering that we had manual gearboxes in those days, and that meant a maximum of 2800 gearchanges during the course of the race with the six-speed box we had on the old BRM. You always ended the race with your gearchange hand badly blistered."

Thereafter, Stewart sped remorselessly towards his second World Championship, adding victories in the French, British, German and Canadian Grands Prix to his tally. To round off the season, Cevert won the US Grand Prix at Watkins Glen, where Stewart had tyre troubles, scooping the $50,000 first prize for Ken Tyrrell's team.

Tyrrell had run the 1971 season on Goodyear tyres after Dunlop's withdrawal from F1 at the end of the previous year and, with the advent of this new partnership, Jackie began to gain a reputation for tyre testing and development that stayed with him. F1 was becoming increasingly scientific.

Elsewhere in the field, Jack Brabham had finally retired at the end of 1970 and sold his shareholding in the Brabham team to long-time partner Ron Tauranac. But Ron was also losing interest and, after a rather indifferent 1971 season, finally would sell out to Bernie Ecclestone.

"There was a change of emphasis," said Tauranac. "In the old days, I would stay at the circuit with Jack and the mechanics, and we used to work on the cars, knock ideas about and discuss things. Then we'd knock off and go back to the hotel and eat, perhaps a little bit before the mechanics, but still not very early.

"Then Jack retired and things were different. The fun had gone out of it and, by 1971, we were having a rather fraught time. As far as Graham Hill [who had joined the team that season] was concerned, I think whatever talent he may previously have had as a driver had drifted away and only his determination was left.

"I was no good at getting sponsorship, and although Goodyear was paying the lion's share of the budget in 1971, it was still a £100,000 gamble every year, and I was in no position to take that on, particularly as I was still paying back Jack the money he lent me to buy his shares. So I started talking to Bernie Ecclestone and eventually sold it to him."

Ecclestone remembered, "Ron had initially spoken to me as early as the 1971 Monaco Grand Prix about the prospect of getting involved with him in the Brabham team, but negotiations were not completed until later that year. Ron initially asked me if I could give him some help on the business side, but later he said, 'I think I want to sell. Do you want to buy half?' I told

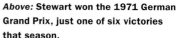

Above: **Stewart won the 1971 German Grand Prix, just one of six victories that season.**

Left: **The Scot wreathed in laurels after winning the 1971 French Grand Prix at the Paul Ricard Circuit.**

Right: **Ron Tauranac took over the Brabham team for 1971, but did not enjoy the experience. Here he confers with driver Tim Schenken.**

Far right: **Ronnie Peterson emerged as front-runner in 1971 with the March 711. Four second places (including this one at Monaco) helped him to the runner-up position in the championship, behind Jackie Stewart.**
Photos: Bernard Cahier

him that I didn't particularly want to buy half, but if he wanted to sell, then I would be prepared to buy the whole business. Which is what I eventually did."

The original idea was that Tauranac should stay on in a consultancy role, but Bernie found that it just didn't work out. "Ultimately you couldn't really employ anybody who had once owned the company," he reflected. "It wasn't good for him and it wasn't good for me."

In his new role as a team owner, Ecclestone would soon emerge as a leading light in the Formula 1 Constructors' Association (FOCA). Grand Prix racing reached a crucial fork in the road at around this time and, together with March's Max Mosley, the Brabham boss would be instrumental in guiding it in the direction of commercialisation. It didn't take long for Max and Bernie to form a shrewd, if informal, alliance within FOCA. In due course, Ecclestone would be elected the organisation's president, handling all the time consuming negotiations with race promoters. He could see that the commercial potential of Grand Prix racing was dramatically under-exploited. He would rectify that state of affairs over the next 25 years.

Meanwhile, motor racing was still enduring more than its fair share of tragedy. BRM's season was overshadowed by the death of Pedro Rodriguez, who lost his life when he unwisely used a weekend off from F1 to drive a private Ferrari 512M in what amounted to a German club race at the Norisring. Jo Siffert restored morale by giving the BRM P160 a fine victory in the Austrian Grand Prix, which was followed by a similar split-second triumph for Peter Gethin at Monza, but then Siffert, too, was killed at Brands Hatch in an end-of-season non-title F1 outing.

Ferrari, in the meantime, was dropping off the pace. The multi-talented Mario Andretti – who had original-

ly made his F1 debut at Watkins Glen in 1968, where he had qualified a works Lotus 49B on pole position – romped away with the South African Grand Prix at Kyalami. He was driving the elegant Ferrari 312B1, but this was soon superseded by the tricky-to-drive B2, in which Jacky Ickx could manage only a single win in a rain soaked Dutch Grand Prix, where his Firestone wet-weather tyres gave him a significant advantage. Jackie Stewart's Goodyear-shod Tyrrell was lapped in the same race.

At the same time, March was thriving with its very distinctive, Frank Costin-styled 711, with which Ronnie Peterson would score four second places to end the year as World Championship runner-up behind Jackie Stewart. The Scot scored 62 points, while Peterson gained 33 and François Cevert 26.

This was certainly the era of the F1 Cosworth 'kit car', which would continue through to the end of the 1970s, when another major sea change saw a crucial shift of emphasis within the Grand Prix business.

The original Tyrrell F1 design had been regarded by Derek Gardner as an essentially short-term solution, so during 1971 he completed the preliminary outline of a second-generation concept that finally saw action the following year as the lower and shorter 005/006 range, which had originally been designed to use inboard front brakes as a means of further reducing unsprung weight.

Unfortunately, in 1972, Jackie Stewart's high-pressure lifestyle finally caught up with him, and a duodenal ulcer was diagnosed. This forced him to miss the Belgian Grand Prix, and it would not be until the Austrian race that he finally gave the Tyrrell 005 its race debut, the car now fitted with outboard brakes after the original inboard configuration had produced quite severe vibration problems.

LAST WIN FOR BRM

The 1972 season also saw BRM relinquish its Yardley sponsorship in favour of the Marlboro cigarette brand, just as the Lotus 72s were repackaged in the distinctive black and gold colours of the John Player Special cigarettes. In pouring rain, Jean-Pierre Beltoise took the BRM P160 to an impressive win at Monaco. It would be the last Grand Prix victory for the famous British team, which by now seemed preoccupied with its somewhat shaky historic status rather than pressing on with imaginative ideas for the future.

Chris Amon had moved to Matra at the start of 1971, but although the French team decided to concentrate on running just a single car for the New Zealander the following year, his atrocious luck never deserted him. He ran away with the 1972 French Grand Prix at Clermont-Ferrand, only to sustain a punctured tyre and drop to third. Jackie Stewart won the race, the Scot making a return to the cockpit after missing the Belgian Grand Prix.

For its part, Lotus was now recovering from the aftershocks caused by Jochen Rindt's death. After finding his feet in 1971, Emerson Fittipaldi drove into the history books as the sport's youngest World Champion

Left and below: Day of days for Jean-Pierre Beltoise as he celebrates his win in the 1972 Monaco Grand Prix. No one could live with the BRM driver, who conquered the wet conditions to win the race by nearly 40 seconds.

Opposite: The ever-unlucky Chris Amon was totally dominant in the 1972 French Grand Prix at Clermont Ferrand, only to sustain a puncture that dropped his Matra to third.

Opposite, inset: A promising career was tragically cut short for Helmut Marko at the same race. The young Austrian was to lose the sight of an eye after a stone thrown up from another car pierced his visor.
Photos: Bernard Cahier

Above: **Denny Hulme plays the fool for Cahier's camera after his win in the 1973 Swedish Grand Prix.**

Top: **Emerson Fittipaldi won five Grands Prix in the 1972 season, including the Belgian Grand Prix (shown) held at the rather bland Nivelles track.**

Photos: Bernard Cahier

at the age of 25. The dynamic young Brazilian won the Spanish, Belgian, British, Austrian and Italian Grands Prix to clinch the title with 61 points to Stewart's 45, with McLaren driver Denny Hulme on 39.

Fittipaldi would put Brazil firmly on the international racing map. The son of a respected motor sport journalist and broadcaster, Wilson Fittipaldi, Emerson was born in São Paulo on 12th December, 1946. He and his elder brother, Wilson Jnr, raced motorcycles and karts in their early teens, and Emerson won the 1967 Brazilian Formula Vee championship before moving to Britain to race in Formula Ford two years later.

His progress through Formula Ford, F3 and F2 would prove meteoric. Offered his Grand Prix debut by Lotus in the 1970 British Grand Prix at the wheel of an outdated type 49C, he kept out of trouble to finish eighth. Then he finished fourth at Hockenheim and finally was propelled into the team leadership after Rindt's tragic death at Monza.

Eighteen months later, he was ready for the 'big time', and watching him reel off five confident victories that season was to see at work an unflustered natural talent that many were tempted to compare with Jim Clark's.

By the start of 1972, there would be no fewer than three Brazilians contesting the World Championship, Wilson Fittipaldi having secured a place in Bernie Ecclestone's resurgent Brabham team, while Carlos Pace was signed up by Frank Williams and later would join Team Surtees.

At the beginning of the 1973 season, Jackie Stewart confided to Ken Tyrrell that he was going to retire at the end of the year, but nevertheless he embarked on that final season with some gusto. Again using the 005/006 series cars, the monocoques of which were clad with the now-mandatory deformable structures

Left: American Peter Revson was a race winner with McLaren, but sponsorship changes connected with the arrival of Emerson Fittipaldi forced him out. He joined the Shadow team, but was killed while testing in the early part of the 1974 season.

Below: Argentine Grand Prix, Buenos Aires. Jackie Stewart seems happy enough with third place to Emerson Fittipaldi after the opening race of the 1973 season.

Photos: Bernard Cahier

KEN TYRRELL: THE GREAT SURVIVOR

EXCEPT for a few months after he had sold his family's F1 team to British American Racing at the end of 1997, Ken Tyrrell had never worked for anybody but himself since he had been demobbed from the RAF with a £30 gratuity in 1946. He had been retained by the new owner, but acting out the role of a hired hand in the company he'd founded was always going to be a non-starter, said the pundits. Sure enough, it did not take long for Ken and his son, Bob – the company's business development director – to clear their desks at the Ockham headquarters of the Tyrrell Racing Organisation.

"Originally, I didn't follow motor racing, but in 1951 the local football team, for which I used to play, got a coach trip together to go to Silverstone," he recalled, "but it could just as easily have been a trip to the seaside at Brighton or Bognor.

"The supporting race was for 500cc F3 cars, and one of the competitors was a guy called Alan Brown, who I saw from the programme came from Guildford, where I lived at that time. So when I got home, I went round and knocked on Alan Brown's door and said, 'I saw you racing at Silverstone, sir, could I see your car?'

"Well, he kept his car in a large garage in the garden of a nursery which his mother ran. So he showed me round the car, told me a little bit about it, and at the end of the year I bought it from him."

Ken raced through much of the 1950s, eventually going into partnership with Alan Brown and Cecil Libowitz in 1958 to run a pair of Cooper F2 cars on an international basis. "When eventually I discovered I could only finish fifth, sixth or seventh at this level, it didn't satisfy me," he recalled. "Then on one occasion I loaned the car to Michael Taylor at Aintree, and he drove much better than I did. So I decided that team management was my particular slot."

Ken remained self-effacing when it came to his reputation as a talent spotter. "It's not really true, you see," he grinned broadly. "It sounds all right when you read it in print, but it's not really like that.

"If you go back to 1960, when I started running my own Formula Junior team with loaned Cooper chassis and BMC engines, I had John Surtees and Henry Taylor, and we won races all over Europe. But most of the people we were racing against were owner/drivers competing for fun, while I was free to sign up whoever I thought was the best driver."

Jackie Stewart's relationship with Tyrrell was heaven-sent. Ken recalled that they fell out only once. "It was at an Oulton Park Gold Cup when Jackie was complaining bitterly about the March 701," he recounted, "and I do remember we had a few words. But we never fell out over money!

"He drove for me in F3, F2 and then F1, but the only year we had a written contract was the first year."

Jackie won three World Championships for Ken, the first in the Tyrrell entered Matra in 1969, the second and third with Ken's own cars in 1971 and 1973. Tyrrell had hoped to sustain the momentum of that great partnership into 1974, promoting Jackie's teammate, François Cevert, to the team leadership after Stewart's retirement. Sadly, Cevert was killed practising for the 1973 US Grand Prix at Watkins Glen and the link was broken.

"François absolutely worshipped Jackie as his idol," recalled Ken. "I remember Jackie's last F1 win, in the '73 German GP at the Nürburgring, where they finished in 1-2 formation. At the end of the race, he stepped out of the car and said, 'François could have passed me any time he liked. He was flat quicker than I was.'

"But the point was that François stayed in his wheel tracks because he still felt he had a lot to learn from Jackie. And, of course, he knew that Jackie was retiring at the end of the year, and that his time would come."

Jackie Stewart was the only rival F1 team chief who could be bothered to issue a press statement paying tribute to Ken Tyrrell on his departure from the Grand Prix scene. It was strange perhaps – even untypical – that neither Ron Dennis nor Frank Williams, both of whom had stood shoulder-to-shoulder with Ken in refusing to sign the 1997 Concorde Agreement, should take the same opportunity.

Ken's exit left Dennis and Williams as the sole remaining representatives of the F1 Old Guard. "Yes," said Tyrrell with great satisfaction in 1997, "and isn't it wonderful that they are both at the top of the tree?"

Despite Ken's protestations that he was no talent spotter, plenty of fine drivers served their apprenticeship under the Tyrrell banner. They included François Cevert, Patrick Depailler, Jody Scheckter, Didier Pironi, Michele Alboreto, Martin Brundle, Stefan Bellof, Jean Alesi and Mika Salo.

"Ken Tyrrell has shaped my personality in racing, and he's given me the knowledge and experience which have made me what I am today," said Jackie Stewart on his retirement from driving in 1973.

Twenty-five years later, Jackie would write, "He has been an immense contributor to motor racing, introducing and nurturing more drivers than anyone else in the sport."

As usual, Stewart was right on target.

Left: **Ken Tyrrell as expressive as ever.**

Below: **Jackie with his protégé, François Cevert. The Frenchman was poised to step up as the number-one Tyrrell driver before his tragic accident in practice for the 1973 US Grand Prix at Watkins Glen.**

Photos: Bernard Cahier

from the Spanish Grand Prix onwards, the jaunty Scot won the South African, Belgian, Monaco, Dutch and German Grands Prix on the way to his third and last World Championship.

Tragically, his team-mate, François Cevert, was killed at Watkins Glen practising for the United States Grand Prix; as a mark of respect, Tyrrell withdrew his two other entries for Stewart and Chris Amon. With Jackie's retirement, a great partnership had come to an end and the Tyrrell team would never again scale such peaks of achievement.

Meanwhile, Emerson Fittipaldi had grown restless after Colin Chapman had brought the brilliant Swede, Ronnie Peterson, into the Team Lotus fold for 1973. The pair scored a total of seven victories that season, but the wins were split between them in a tactically questionable manner, which allowed Stewart to take the drivers' championship; the frustrated Brazilian decided to switch to the McLaren team for the 1974 and 1975 seasons.

McLAREN'S M23 PICKS UP THE WINNING PACE

Fittipaldi would win a second World Championship in 1974 at the wheel of the McLaren M23, another outstanding machine from the mid-1970s crop. It had made its debut in the 1973 South African Grand Prix

at Kyalami, where Denny Hulme had gained the sole pole position of his Grand Prix career.

The car had won a total of 14 World Championship Grands Prix by the time it made its last appearance in 1978, although during the last two seasons of its career, it was displaced as a front-line challenger and was mostly seen in the hands of privateers, having had its last outing for the factory with Gilles Villeneuve in the cockpit in the 1977 British GP at Silverstone.

The M23 was Gordon Coppuck's first complete Formula 1 design. It was also one of the first F1 cars to be tailor-made to the new technical regulations, introduced for 1973, which required deformable structures along the sides of the chassis to provide added protection to the fuel tanks in the event of a lateral impact.

The new McLaren inherited the rising-rate front suspension of the earlier M19, while the rear suspension was conventional, with outboard spring/dampers, adjustable top links, reversed lower wishbones and twin radius rods. The car had a central fuel cell behind the driver's seat, and the Cosworth Ford DFV V8 engine transmitted its power through a Hewland FG400 transaxle.

During its first season, the M23 won three Grands Prix, the first being Hulme's victory in the Swedish Grand Prix at Anderstorp, where he snatched the lead from Ronnie Peterson's Lotus 72 in the closing stages. Peter Revson then went on to win at Silverstone and

Canada's Mosport Park track, while Hulme started
the 1974 season with a lucky win in Buenos Aires
after Carlos Reutemann's Brabham BT44 had run out
of fuel.

For 1974, the M23s were revamped with revised
weight distribution, achieved by means of a 3in spacer
between the engine and the gearbox, which length-
ened the wheelbase. The rear track was also wider, but
new team leader Emerson Fittipaldi was not totally
convinced about these changes and experimented with
different wheelbase lengths as he worked his way to
that year's title.

The Brazilian won only three of the season's 15 races, but impressive consistency allied to the outstanding
reliability of his Marlboro liveried McLaren enabled
him to hold off the challenges of Ferrari's Clay Regazzoni and two drivers who scored their first Grand Prix
victories during the course of the year, Jody Scheckter of Tyrrell and Regazzoni's Ferrari team-mate,
Niki Lauda.

For the start of the 1975 season, Fittipaldi appeared
in a car with heavily revised front suspension, Gordon Coppuck having taken a leaf out of Brabham's
book by adopting a fabricated top rocker arm config-

uration with pull-rod activation of the now semi-in-
board spring/damper unit. Later this was modified to
move the spring/dampers totally inboard again, and a
variety of secondary suspension modifications were
incorporated progressively over the balance of the
season, in which Fittipaldi took second place in the
championship.

For 1976, Fittipaldi switched to the Brazilian Co-
persucar team, which had been established the previous year by his elder brother, Wilson. That brought
the extrovert, public-school educated James Hunt
into the McLaren line-up as number-one driver, the
Englishman successfully exploiting the M23's continuing development potential to beat Lauda to that year's
World Championship.

Into 1977, there was still precious little indication
that the McLaren M23 was at the end of its competitive life. The new M26, introduced mid-season
in 1976, was proving difficult to sort out, and it was
not until after Monaco that Hunt abandoned the
M23 and switched to the new car. His final race win
with the M23 came in the Race of Champions at
Brands Hatch, the non-title curtain-raiser to the
European season.

Below: Moody brilliance. Carlos Reutemann brooding in the cockpit of his Brabham BT44.

Bottom: Niki Lauda's switch to Ferrari for the 1974 season was well timed. He took his maiden victory at Jarama (shown) and when the Forghieri-designed 312T arrived in 1975, he became virtually unbeatable.
Photos: Bernard Cahier

THE LOTUS 72: THE MOST ENDURING CAR OF ALL TIME?

O N 9th April, 1970, a pair of Lotus 72s were rolled out to make their F1 competition debuts in the Spanish Grand Prix at Madrid's Jarama circuit. Strikingly elegant and purposeful in the distinctive red, white and gold livery of Gold Leaf Team Lotus, and distinguished by their sleek needle noses and hip-mounted water radiators, they were driven on that occasion by Jochen Rindt and John Miles.

Over five years later, on 5th October, 1975, Ronnie Peterson and Brian Henton finished fifth and twelfth respectively in the US Grand Prix at Watkins Glen on the 72's last competition outing. These facts surely endorse this remarkable car's claim to be the most enduring F1 design of all time, for, although one must acknowledge that Maserati's remarkable 250F raced across the seven years of the 2.5-litre F1, from 1954 to 1960, for the last three seasons of its life, it was competing in the hands of privateers.

By contrast, the Lotus 72 was the factory team's front-line challenger in its first race and its last. That said, it was not meant to be in service for that length of time. It started out with Jochen Rindt regarding it as a death-trap – an unfortunately prophetic judgement, as things turned out – developed into one of the most formidable winning machines of its generation, and then suffered a gradual decline into a depressing old age.

After that promising, but bruising, first season, Team Lotus marked time in 1971. Emerson Fittipaldi was obviously a man of the future, but the after-effects of a mid-season road ac-cident left him distinctly below par for much of the year.

Not until 1972 was the young Brazilian able to exploit the 72's terrific potential. With his car now wearing the glossy black and gold John Player Special livery, Emerson stormed to victory in the Spanish, Belgian, British, Austrian and Italian GPs to become the sport's youngest ever World Champion until this distinction was taken by Fernando Alonso (2005) and then Lewis Hamilton (2007).

In 1973, Chapman decided to create a super-team by signing up the dynamic Ronnie Peterson as Fittipaldi's partner. Lotus switched from Firestone to Goodyear tyres, but the 72s were still the class of the field in the opening races of the year. Chapman now briefed his designer, Ralph Bellamy, to start work on a replacement chassis, the Lotus 76, which the chief decreed should be a Lotus 72, "but 100 pounds lighter".

At the start of the 1973 season, insiders began speculating as to what might happen when Peterson got his hands on a Lotus 72. Perhaps, they mused, he might learn to drive smoothly and tidily, a lesson the car had, in the last few months of his life, taught Jochen Rindt.

Those who watched Ronnie grappling with an intermittently sticking throttle, yowling through Woodcote on his way to second place in the 1973 British GP at Silverstone, might have thought otherwise. But Ronnie won four Grands Prix that season in brilliantly disciplined fashion.

With Emerson bagging another three, it was good enough to retain the constructors' title for Lotus, but dividing the wins allowed Jackie Stewart to take his third drivers' crown.

Fittipaldi, piqued that his position at Lotus had been undermined by Peterson's arrival, switched to McLaren in 1974 and duly won his second World Championship. Meanwhile, Lotus had a dreadful time with the new 76, which incorporated provision for left-foot braking, an accessory that neither Ronnie nor team-mate Jacky Ickx could make much sense of.

The new car also rather defeated the point by winding up heavier than the 72, broke with alarming frequency and ate its tyres. Small wonder that Peterson suggested rolling out the old 72, which then he used to win the Monaco, French and Italian GPs, although by the end of the year, the cars were suffering from near-terminal understeer on the latest generation of Goodyear rubber.

Ferrari, Brabham, Tyrrell and McLaren took the lion's share of Goodyear's development effort in 1975, leaving the Lotus 72s struggling to keep pace. Experiments with varied wheelbase and suspension configurations reflected a team in disarray, but good old Ronnie barnstormed his way through from 14th to run as high as fourth in the closing stages of the car's final race at Watkins Glen.

Only when the Swede locked up a brake two laps from home did James Hunt's Hesketh 308C nip ahead of the gallant old Lotus, which, fighting a desperate rearguard action, at least drove into the history books with all guns blazing right up to its final chequered flag.

Below left: Resplendent in Gold Leaf livery, John Miles's Lotus 72 stands in the Spa pits at the 1970 Belgian Grand Prix. Colin Chapman sits on the pit counter while the blue-shirted Rob Walker, Peter Warr and John Miles (hidden by Warr) are in discussion.
Photo: Bernard Cahier

Left: Emerson Fittipaldi in the 1973 Monaco Grand Prix. The arrival of Ronnie Peterson precipitated his switch to McLaren for 1974.

Below: Ronnie Peterson beating Fittipaldi at Monza in 1974 with the 72E. It would be the last Grand Prix win for the car, which had seen five seasons' service.

Photos: Bernard Cahier

Niki Lauda at the wheel of the Ferrari 312T2 *trasversale* that carried him to the second of his three World Championships in 1977. He is seen here on his way to victory in that year's Dutch Grand Prix at Zandvoort, one of three wins he scored that season.
Photo: Bernard Cahier

FERRARI'S flat-12 engine powered two World Champions during the second half of the 1970s: Niki Lauda in 1975 and 1977, and Jody Scheckter in 1979. However, although James Hunt's championship victory in 1976 with the McLaren M23 owed much to Lauda's near-fatal crash in Germany, Mario Andretti's success in 1978 for Lotus proved that technical innovation – specifically the development of ground-effect aerodynamics – could allow the British teams to remain competitive, despite their continued reliance on the Cosworth V8. Meanwhile, Renault took advantage of a legal loophole to introduce a 1.5-litre turbocharged engine, which established a trend that others would soon be obliged to follow.

From the moment Lauda first tried the Ferrari 312T– 'T' for *trasversale*, signifying that the car was equipped with a transverse gearbox – it was clear to the 25-year-old Austrian driver that here was a machine in which he could gain victory the 1975 World Championship.

So it proved. The brilliant 3-litre 180-degree flat-12 had been the cornerstone of Ferrari's technical armoury since the start of 1970, but the addition of that transverse gearbox to the package helped make the 312T one of the most consistent, neutral handling F1 cars of its generation. It was also superbly rugged and reliable, while its engine was powerful enough to keep Ferrari in play as a leading light right through to the end of 1979.

The Ferrari 312T was the making of Lauda's reputation. Together with its derivative, the 312T2, it won a Constructors' Championship hat trick between 1975 and 1977, during which time the design scored 16 Grand Prix victories.

But just how good was the 312T family set against its opposition?

Lauda joined the Ferrari team at the start of 1974 and won two Grands Prix that season with the Mauro Forghieri-designed 3121B3. This had a conventional, longitudinal gearbox and, Lauda remembers, was always prone to a touch of understeer. But Niki admitted that when Forghieri took the wraps off the new 312T immediately after the 1974 United States GP, he was a worried man.

Forghieri's intention had been to pursue the lowest possible polar moment of inertia by packaging as much of the car as possible between the front and rear wheels. The new transmission cluster was positioned across the car, ahead of the rear axle line, the shafts lying at right angles to the centre-line of the car and the drive being taken via bevel gears on the input side of the gearbox.

"When I was first shown the drawings of the 312T, I felt indifferent about the whole project," recalled Lauda. "I didn't really appreciate the advantages that it would offer, because it seemed such a very big change from a chassis about which we knew everything.

"Then, when I got to drive it at Fiorano, I quickly appreciated that it was a much more competitive proposition. The problem with the B3 had been its inclination towards understeer; no matter how you tried to tune the chassis, it always understeered very slightly. We had also used up all its potential, so we had to switch to the new car. There was no choice."

However, Lauda firmly believed that the 312T offered only a slight power advantage over the rival Cosworth Ford DFV-equipped machines from McLaren, Lotus, Shadow and Tyrrell. What it did provide was

totally neutral handling and a wide torque curve from the superbly flexible flat-12 engine. Driveability was the key.

In 1975, Niki won five Grands Prix to take his first World Championship crown. At the start of the following year, he won the Brazilian and Argentine races with the 312T, then his team-mate, Clay Regazzoni, triumphed at Long Beach. Not long afterwards, Lauda scored further victories in Belgium and Monaco with the evolutionary 312T2. Then came a spate of engine failures caused by a machining error that produced infinitesimal cracks at the point where a flange taking the drive to the ignition was pressed into the end of the crankshaft.

However, in 1976, Lauda faced strong opposition from James Hunt, an old sparring partner and rival from his F3 days. Hunt had driven Lord Hesketh's Harvey Postlethwaite-designed type 308 to victory in the 1975 Dutch Grand Prix, beating Lauda in the process, and was the logical choice for the McLaren team when it became clear that Emerson Fittipaldi was leaving at the end of that year.

In Holland, the race had started in the wet, and James had timed his switch to slicks perfectly, vaulting ahead of Lauda, who was unable to get back in front.

"James drove beautifully," remembered Lauda, "and there was understandably a great deal of excitement among the British press about his achievement, although, if I am honest, I would have to say that I took things a little easier than I might have done, as my main priority that day was to keep scoring points

to add to my World Championship tally. Nevertheless, James's success took him through a psychological barrier, which was bad for me."

No sooner did McLaren director Teddy Mayer hear that Fittipaldi was yesterday's news than he put a call through to Hunt, recently made redundant after Hesketh Racing had closed its doors as a front-line F1 operation. Hunt had been in the throes of negotiating with Lotus boss Colin Chapman, but both parties were making heavy weather of the talks.

Chapman still clung to the belief that people ought to be honoured to drive for Lotus and that it was better to invest money in the car's technology than in the driver's retainer. James replied that this was all very well, but he was a professional racer, and Lotus was poised on the outer rim of competitiveness. The bottom line was: he needed paying.

Mayer immediately told him to stop talking to anybody until they had had time to talk seriously together. The net result was that Teddy got James's signature on a 1976 contract for a reputed £40,000. This was chicken feed, even by the standards of the time, and for McLaren it would prove to be one of F1's all-time bargains.

James was partnered by Jochen Mass, the pleasant German driver who had been drafted into the McLaren squad in the middle of 1974 after Mike Hailwood had suffered severe ankle injuries when he crashed heavily during the German Grand Prix at the Nürburgring. Mass privately believed that he might be in a position to assert an advantage over his incoming rival, but Hunt quickly showed who was boss by qualifying in pole position for his first race in the M23, the Brazilian GP at Interlagos.

Lauda may have won the World Championship in 1975, but it soon became clear that he would have his work cut out if he was going to retain it in 1976.

"From the moment he got into the McLaren M23, James was predictably quick," said Niki. "The 1976 season has now gone down in motor racing history as one of the most remarkable of all time, but I have to confess I still felt very confident about the Ferrari's performance in the opening races of the year.

"Then both James and I began to encounter our troubles. I damaged a rib when a tractor rolled over on top of me while I was in the garden of my new home at Hof, near Salzburg. Then James won the Spanish Grand Prix for McLaren, beating me in the process, only to be disqualified when his car was found to have a fractionally too wide rear track."

The McLaren team seriously believed it had got the raw end of the deal in that race at Jarama. It felt that Ferrari somehow represented 'The Establishment' and that the sport's governing body was showing a degree of partiality towards the famous Italian team. It was a theme that would emerge regularly over the years.

Eventually James's race win in Spain was reinstated, which left Ferrari, on this occasion, feeling a bit miffed. Personal tensions began to build between Hunt and Lauda, although they were on a pretty mild level compared with some of the internecine strife between rivals that would follow over the ensuing decades. "We were rivals, but we respected each other totally, whatever the circumstances," said Niki.

Then Hunt won the French Grand Prix at Paul Ricard after both Ferraris had encountered engine problems. More controversy followed in the British Grand Prix at Brands Hatch. Lauda and his teammate, Regazzoni, touched wheels while accelerating away from the start into Paddock Bend, causing the

Swiss driver to spin, and then James's McLaren was pitched on to two wheels when it rode over Regazzoni's right rear wheel.

The race was red-flagged to a halt and eventually Hunt made the restart in his repaired race car, although initially McLaren had wheeled out its spare car, which was clearly against the rules. Technically he shouldn't have been allowed to take the restart at all, but it seemed to many onlookers that the race officials were so overwhelmed by the fans' vocal support for James that they relented.

"I suppose I was cast in the role of the villain in their eyes, although I have to confess this didn't really bother me in the slightest," said Lauda. "Having said that, in the later years of my career, particularly when I returned after my break to drive a McLaren, I tended to find the British fans extremely hospitable towards me, especially after I won at Brands Hatch in 1982 and '84."

Hunt's McLaren M23 stalked Lauda relentlessly after the British Grand Prix had been restarted and eventually sliced past into the lead with a bold move going into the Druids hairpin. He would be disqualified from that win later in the season, however, by which time Lauda was fighting back to health after his Ferrari had been transformed into a fireball when he crashed in the German Grand Prix at the Nürburgring.

Lauda clung between life and death for several days, and while his old friend was enormously concerned about his condition, his absence gave Hunt a golden opportunity to close the points gap on the Austrian. He won the restarted German GP – before the extent of Niki's injuries was fully appreciated – finished fourth in Austria and scored another

victory in Holland, by which time it was clear that Lauda was well on the road to staging a remarkable recovery.

"By the time I got back in the cockpit for the Italian Grand Prix at Monza, I was only two points ahead of James at the head of the World Championship table," Niki would recall. "I finished fourth there and James didn't score, so now I was five points ahead with three races to go. Then James got disqualified from the British Grand Prix, promoting me to the win, and went into the Canadian Grand Prix 17 points behind.

"People have often asked me whether I felt sympathy for James on this, and I suppose I would have to say, 'No', even though there was quite a bit of tension between the McLaren and Ferrari teams. We were locked in pretty fierce competition for that championship; we were both professionals and didn't allow our personal friendship to get in the way of that rivalry. But I would say that James drove the last few races of 1976, and the first of 1977, about as well as at any other time in his career."

At the same time, McLaren had really piled on the development of the M23, which, although not quite as powerful as the Ferrari, was certainly a tried and tested car with a well-proven competition record behind it. Lauda paid the price for Ferrari's lack of progress with a distant eighth in the Canadian Grand Prix and then third place in the US GP, both races being won by Hunt.

Then came the electrifying finale to a quite remarkable season. In the Japanese Grand Prix at Mount Fuji, Lauda pulled out of the race on the second lap,

Above: James Hunt's McLaren M23 momentarily airborne as he heads to victory in the 1976 German GP, the final such race to be held on the old epic 14-mile Nürburgring.

Above left: The Ferrari flat-12 engine that began winning races in 1970 and was still winning in 1979.

Left: Niki Lauda and his wife, Marlene, at Monza during his comeback following his fiery accident at the Nürburgring.

Far left: Roger Penske with driver John Watson. The Penske team took a single victory in Austria 1976, but quit F1 at season's end.

Photos: Bernard Cahier

convinced that driving in the prevailing conditions of torrential rain was absolute lunacy.

Some people said that Niki had taken a calculated gamble that James wouldn't finish the race, but that was unfair. Lauda had nothing to prove after that incredible return to the cockpit. For his part, Hunt looked as though he had the race in the bag, only to be sent scurrying into the pits to change a deflated tyre. He resumed the chase, throwing caution to the wind, and stormed back to third place – enough to give him the World Championship crown by a single point ahead of Lauda.

There was still an element of sportsmanship to the Grand Prix business in those days. Hunt made some very public remarks that were supportive of Lauda in the weeks immediately after the Japanese Grand Prix, at a time when the Austrian was being put through the mill by an unforgiving Italian press after being seen to throw in the towel and lose the title at the final gasp.

Unfortunately, Ferrari's chassis development pro-gramme had been allowed to drift during the weeks Niki was in hospital. For 1977, the Austrian turned things around and bounced back to take his second title. Yet there was a gradual, almost imperceptible, de-terioration in the Ferrari 312T2's performance in 1977, which served as a reminder that F1 cars are complex technical packages.

The Italian team was also slightly irked that Good-year's latest tyres seemed better suited to the rival McLaren M26, a state of affairs that resulted in Ferrari

switching to Michelin radials from the start of 1978.

That incredible flat-12 reliability continued to un-derpin Lauda's 1977 efforts. In the South African GP, his 312T2 ran over debris from the tragic accident that claimed the life of Shadow driver Tom Pryce, the flat-12 losing all its water and most of its oil as a result. But the car still finished, cockpit warning lights flickering, to post yet another victory.

TYRRELL PRODUCES AN F1 NOVELTY

For the 1976 season, the Tyrrell team produced one of the most surprising single technical developments of the decade. Chief designer Derek Gardner came up with the sensational six-wheeler Tyrrell P34, which some cynics believed was a practical joke when it was first unveiled prior to the start of the season.

The Tyrrell P34 featured four 10in-diameter steered front wheels, which were intended to offer reduced aerodynamic resistance and much improved turn-in. It was quite an impressive one-off development, which had its big day at Anderstorp in 1976, when Jody Scheckter and Patrick Depailler finished first and second in the Swedish Grand Prix.

The team persisted with the six-wheeler concept into 1977, when Depailler was partnered by Ronnie Peterson, but the car gained added weight and, if any-thing, lost its competitive edge. By 1978, this novel ex-ercise had been shelved, and in its place the team raced the more conventional four-wheeled Tyrrell 008, with which Depailler scored a superb victory at Monaco.

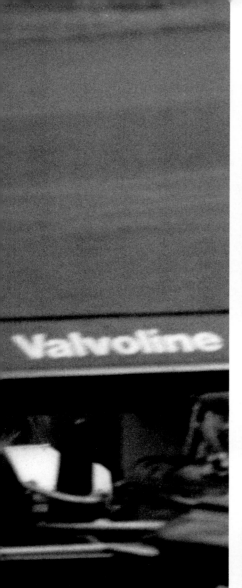

BRITAIN'S LOST F1 GENERATION

ETWEEN Jackie Stewart's victory in the 1973 German Grand Prix and Nigel Mansell's maiden F1 win in the Grand Prix of Europe at Brands Hatch two years later, only two British-born drivers won races at international motor racing's most exalted level.

Yet the achievements of James Hunt, who won the 1976 World Championship, and Ulsterman John Watson might well have been supplemented by those of Roger Williamson, Tony Brise and Tom Pryce had not fate and ill-fortune taken the trio to early deaths between 1973 and 1977.

Williamson was a tough, hard driving protégé of Donington Park circuit owner Tom Wheatcroft. He had originally starred at the wheel of a club racing Ford Anglia prepared with the help of his father, before moving into Formula 3 and then Formula 2 with distinction. Shortly before he died, Williamson won the prestigious F2 Monza Lottery race in a March-BMW fielded by Wheatcroft Racing. Then Tom did a deal for him to race a works 731 in the 1973 British Grand Prix.

Roger crashed out of that race, a peripheral victim of the huge first-lap accident triggered by Jody Scheckter. A fortnight later he went to Zandvoort for

the Dutch Grand Prix in the same car, settling down to run in close company with the similar privately entered March 731 driven by his old sparring partner, David Purley.

In the early stages of the race, the two Marches circulated in 13th and 14th places. Then came tragedy. Midway around the eighth lap, both Purley and Williamson were missing. Way across the sand dunes an ominous pall of smoke began to rise. The old hands, who had seen all this just three years earlier when Piers Courage died, shuddered.

Williamson had gone off the road on a long fifth-gear right-hander and slammed into the guard rail. Unfortunately, the rail, mounted directly into the sand, distorted to form a launching ramp. The works March was flipped into the air, flew for about 80 yards and then crashed back down on to the track. Upside down, it caught fire.

The Williamson debacle was one of the most disreputable episodes Formula 1 has ever delivered for public consumption. As Purley wrestled in vain to right the upturned March, the rest of the field passed the spot time and time again. Nobody else stopped to help. The late Mike Hailwood later confided to me that he felt "sick with guilt" that nobody else had given the selfless Purley a hand.

Purley, a former paratroop officer who had seen service in Aden and who seemed totally without fear, was rightly awarded the George Medal for his selfless bravery.

Williamson had raced against Tony Brise, the overwhelmingly talented then 21-year-old son of John Brise, a well-known 500cc F3 racer from the mid-1950s, who dominated the British F3 and Formula Atlantic series before moving into Formula 1 with Frank Williams's team at the 1975 Spanish Grand Prix.

Brise had the confidence and audacity of youth, but beneath a thin veneer of arrogance was a huge natural talent. Graham Hill recognised this and

signed him to drive for his Embassy Hill F1 team, from which the veteran twice former World Champion stood down in the middle of that season. From now on, Graham vowed, he would tutor Brise to become a future Grand Prix winner.

On 29th November, 1975, those dreams were ended with brutal finality. Flying back from a test session at the Paul Ricard circuit in the south of France, six members of the Hill team – including Graham and Tony Brise – were killed when Graham's Piper Aztec aeroplane crashed on Arkley golf course while attempting to land at Elstree, north of London.

The third member of this ill-starred trio, Tom Pryce, was the gentle, reticent son of a Welsh policeman. He won a Lola Formula Ford car in 1970 through a competition in the *Daily Express* newspaper and soon became an accomplished Formula 3 contender.

At the start of 1974, he made a false start in F1 by accepting a deal to drive the Token-Ford special, which was financed by shipbroker Tony Vlassopulo and Lloyd's underwriter Ken Grob, but the Monaco Grand Prix organisers declined their entry and instead Pryce drove a March 743 in the supporting Formula 3 race, winning easily.

Soon afterwards, he was signed to drive for the Shadow F1 team, showing tremendous skill and flair. In 1975, he won the Race of Champions at Brands Hatch and started the British Grand Prix at Silverstone from pole position in the promising DN5 challenger.

His best Grand Prix placings were third in the 1975 Austrian and 1976 Brazilian races. He was killed when he hit a marshal crossing the track in the 1977 South African Grand Prix at Kyalami in one of the most bizarre motor racing accidents ever seen.

By cruel coincidence, the mild-mannered boy from the Welsh hills died literally yards from the point where Shadow driver Peter Revson had been fatally injured during a testing crash three years earlier. Effectively, Tom had taken his place in the team.

LOTUS GETS IN ON THE ACT

If it hadn't been for the success demonstrated by Colin Chapman and his team in reversing the declining fortunes of Lotus, Ferrari would have ruled pretty well unchallenged from 1975 to the middle of 1979. Instead, at the start of the 1977 season, the British team restored its reputation for technical ingenuity and imaginative thinking by producing probably the most outstanding single leap forward in F1 car performance ever seen.

By the close of 1975, Lotus was on its knees. The type 72 was at the end of its career, and its planned replacement, the type 76, had proved to be a disaster. Chapman's design group now set about consolidating its position with a series of technical deliberations that would catapult Britain's most famous F1 team back into the limelight with dramatic effect.

During 1975, Chapman had produced a 27-page concept document in which he sought to reappraise the team's whole approach to Grand Prix car design. Then he handed it to his newly established research and development department and told it to come up with the answers. This group was under the control of Tony Rudd at Ketteringham Hall, a country house situated in tranquil surroundings a couple of miles from the main Lotus factory.

For 1976, the team produced the 'all adjustable' Lotus 77, which offered a theoretically unlimited number of wheelbase, track and weight distribution combinations. Yet all this project did was to publicly announce just how much at sea Lotus had become. By touting the car as all-adjustable, Chapman gave the impression that most of its development would take place during the course of the racing season. Which is precisely what happened.

If one compared the Lotus 77 as it appeared at the start of 1976 with the end-product that carried Mario Andretti to victory in the final race at Mount Fuji, it was clear that there had been much progress. The first race of the season saw an ungainly creation taking to the tracks, its front brake discs and calipers being mounted awkwardly in the airstream between the wheels and the monocoque. Driven by Andretti and Ronnie Peterson, the two cars managed to collide with each other during the Brazilian Grand Prix.

Peterson left soon afterwards to rejoin March, which, he hoped, would provide him with a simple and straightforward car. After a brief return to the American Parnelli outfit, Andretti would commit himself to Lotus and prosper with the team.

Lotus and Andretti had originally been thrown together in 1968, when, after an abortive outing at Monza, Chapman had invited the talented and versatile American to take the wheel of a Lotus 49B for the United States Grand Prix at Watkins Glen. He qualified on pole and led initially, but then Jackie Stewart's Matra went by, leaving Andretti eventually to retire while running second. In 1969, he was signed to drive for Lotus on a restricted basis, when his USAC commitments permitted, but failed to finish any of the three Grands Prix he started.

Unquestionably, Andretti was Formula 1 material, yet, while he loved the world of European open-wheelers, there was never any way he would abandon Indy Car racing.

"In the early Seventies, I was really torn between staying in Indy Car racing and concentrating on Formula 1," he later remembered. "I recall saying to Peter Revson [the American McLaren F1 driver] that I really envied the hell out of him. He was doing just a couple of 500-milers in the States each year, and spending the rest of his time in F1. It was exactly the programme I wanted.

"There isn't much security in this business, but my Firestone tyre contract represented a lot of that for me. I dropped Formula 1 pretty much in 1973 and '74. I had run for Ferrari the two previous years, but they quit Firestone at the end of '72, like Lotus did. They didn't really need me in F1 because they had their own guys in Europe."

Yet Andretti was a popular addition to the F1 scene on a personal level. He has great charisma. When he walks into a room, you are conscious that here is somebody special. He is civil and articulate. The man has always radiated star quality, underpinned by a firm sense of values.

In the early 1970s, Andretti freelanced for the Ferrari F1 team, and he eventually found his way back to Team Lotus by a somewhat convoluted route. He had returned to Formula 1 with the new Parnelli team

Opposite top: **Roger Williamson, who perished at Zandvoort in 1973.**
Photo: **Autocourse archive**

Opposite, bottom left: **Tom Pryce, the victim of a freak accident at Kyalami.**
Photo: **Bernard Cahier**

Opposite, bottom right: **Tony Brise, who was killed in the plane that was piloted by Graham Hill.**
Photo: **Autocourse archive**

Below: **Mario Andretti after his win in the 1977 Us Grand Prix West at Long Beach.**
Photo: **Bernard Cahier**

Above: **A quiet moment for Mario Andretti with the Lotus 78 during practice for the 1977 Japanese GP at the Mount Fuji circuit.**

Opposite: **Brilliant rising star Gunnar Nilsson won the 1977 rain soaked Belgian GP at Zolder, but succumbed to cancer at the end of 1978, just before his 30th birthday.**

Photos: Bernard Cahier

towards the end of 1974 and missed only a couple of Grands Prix the following year. Three races into the 1976 season, however, both he and Chapman were battling against the tide. So they cut a deal.

"Let's see if we can help each other, we decided," said Mario. "And I guess it worked out."

The next six seasons would see him lead a hectic life as he divided his time between his two loves, jetting back and forth across the Atlantic sometimes as often as a couple of times each week at the height of the season.

Chapman had effectively decided to start at technical 'base camp', to evolve a whole new concept of F1 car design. Many of the aerodynamic developments were tried on the Lotus 77, and Mario ended the 1976 season with that victory in the Japanese Grand Prix at Fuji, the race where James Hunt clinched his World Championship.

Lessons learned with the Lotus 77 proved crucial to the successful evolution of the superb Lotus 78. Up to this point, aerodynamic downforce had been achieved largely by the effect of front and rear aerofoils. Now Chapman proposed to use the chassis itself as a means

of generating downforce, the dramatic side pods on the type 78 featuring inverted aerofoil profiles. The airflow under the car was accelerated beneath them, thereby producing an area of low pressure that literally sucked the car to the track.

Throughout the first part of 1977, Lotus did a good job of concealing the true secret behind the car's advantage, attributing its outstanding performance to a preferential tank draining system and a rather special differential. The opposition seemed only too ready to accept this explanation, much to Lotus's satisfaction.

Andretti's sympathetic driving style was also a major factor in the equation. He won at Long Beach, Jarama, Dijon-Prenois and Monza, while his team-mate, Gunnar Nilsson, triumphed in the rain soaked Belgian Grand Prix at Zolder after Mario's impetuosity caused him to collide with John Watson's Brabham and spin out on the opening lap.

There were minor problems to be surmounted with the Lotus 78, of course. It had an aerodynamically cluttered rear end, with the airflow spilling out from beneath the two side pods into a tangle of outboard-mounted rear suspension components. In addition,

its centre of pressure – the point at which maximum downforce was generated – proved to be slightly too far forward, providing better grip at the front than at the rear. This was balanced by using slightly more down-force from the conventional rear wing than might have been ideal, the resultant drag taking the edge off the car's straight-line speed.

Nevertheless, Mario should have won the 1977 World Championship, but a spate of engine failures thwarted his ambitions. He had agreed to stay with Lotus for 1978, but then Ferrari appeared on the scene and offered to double whatever Chapman had proposed in an attempt to recruit the American as Niki Lauda's successor. Andretti was absolutely straight with Chapman, who proved sufficiently shrewd to match Ferrari's offer without complaint. Neither really wanted to fracture their partnership, but Colin could see his driver's viewpoint.

There was another side to this, of course. To partly fund Andretti's pay rise, Chapman re-signed Ronnie Peterson as his second driver for 1978. The blond Swede was recognised as one of the very quickest men in the F1 business, but his career had been in the dol-

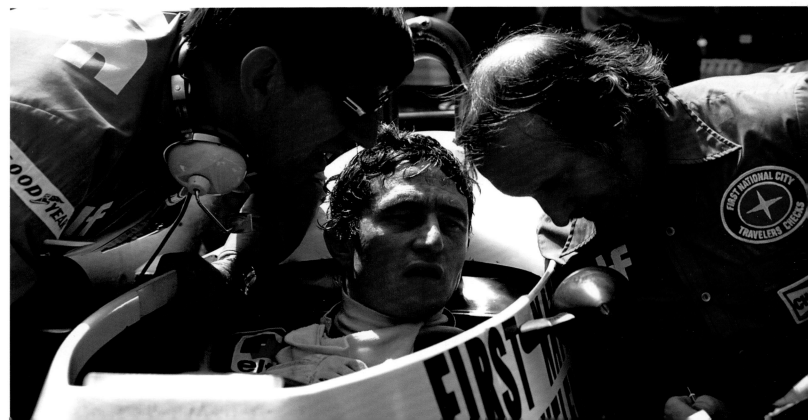

drums for several seasons and he jumped at the chance to revive it. Peterson also came virtually for nothing: his salary was paid by sponsorship from well-known racing philanthropist Count 'Gughi' Zanon and commercial backer Polar Caravans.

Peterson replaced Gunnar Nilsson, who had signed for Arrows, yet before the start of the season, the younger Swede was stricken with what proved to be terminal cancer and he did not survive 1978.

For this new season, Chapman took the 'ground effect' concept one stage further, producing the sensational Lotus 79. It was the car that prompted that immortal quote from Andretti: "If it hugged the road any closer, it would be a white line."

With inboard suspension front and rear, springs and dampers well out of the airstream, and a single central fuel cell that also kept the side pod area uncluttered, the new car was certainly a classic and clean concept by any standards.

Mario won the Belgian, Spanish, French, German and Dutch Grands Prix with the Lotus 79, in addition to the season-opener in Argentina, which he had bagged using the earlier type 78. Peterson proved to be every bit as quick as his team-mate, but was stuck by his deal to play second fiddle. "The Lotus 79 is the car it is largely because of the development effort put in by

Mario," said the Swede. The two men quickly became close friends.

Although Mario benefited on paper from the contractual stipulation that Peterson had to defer to him out on the circuit, the American driver had too much self-respect simply to cruise around at the front of the field, secure in the knowledge that his position guaranteed him precedence.

"I didn't want Ronnie to feel he was letting me win races," said Mario, "so I ran as hard as I possibly could, and he worked really hard to keep up in many places, of that I'm sure.

"Take the French Grand Prix at Paul Ricard as an example. I know a lot of people believed we were just cruising round ahead of Hunt, but that McLaren was chasing Ronnie really hard, and I, in turn, was having to run my engine up against the rev-limiter to stay ahead of him on the straight. Hell, that was one flat-out motor race, whatever it looked like from the outside."

Yet the season's domination ended on a tragic note. A multiple pile-up at the start of the Italian Grand Prix left Peterson with broken legs. Despite initial assurances that he would make a complete recovery, he died in the small hours of the following morning. Mario was bereft. He had lost one of his soul mates.

Above: **First lap of the 1978 Dutch GP at Zandvoort: the Lotus 79s of Mario Andretti and Ronnie Peterson lead through Tarzan, ahead of Niki Lauda's Brabham-Alfa BT46 and the Ferrari 312T3 of Carlos Reutemann.**
Photo: Bernard Cahier

Opposite, top: **Ronnie Peterson at Monza on the weekend he was fatally injured in the 1978 Italian GP.**
Photo: Paul-Henri Cahier

Opposite: **Ken Tyrrell and Maurice Phillipe confer with Patrick Depailler at the 1978 Monaco Grand Prix. The French driver's first (and only) Grand Prix victory at this race was enormously popular.**
Photo: Bernard Cahier

Right: The business end of the Brabham BT46B fan car.
Photo: Bernard Cahier

Below: Brabham designer Gordon Murray seems to be discussing handling with driver Carlos Pace.
Photos: Paul-Henri Cahier

BRABHAM THRIVES THROUGHOUT THE DECADE

Throughout the 1970s, the Brabham team continued to thrive under Bernie Ecclestone's control. By 1973, the young South African designer, Gordon Murray, was in firm charge on the technical side, and for 1974 he developed the BT44 'pyramid monocoque' cars that would win races over two seasons in the hands of Carlos Reutemann and Carlos Pace.

Bernie could be a difficult employer, insisting that the race shop at the Brabham factory be kept as tidy as possible. Sometimes he would pick up a broom and do a bit of sweeping himself, but more often somebody would be in deep trouble if they did not get the job done to his high standards.

He was also the master of the shrewd one-liner. When the author asked him many years ago why he didn't change the name of the team, he shot back, "Look, if you and I went into business and bought Marks and Spencer, we wouldn't rename it Ecclestone and Henry, would we? Brabham is a good name with a good reputation."

On the other hand, he was astute enough to realise that Murray was an unusually talented designer, and he was always prepared to spend money to make the

Brabham cars go faster. In that respect, Bernie was extremely pragmatic: the better the cars went, the more success they would achieve and the richer he would become on the back of that success.

Today's F1 television coverage has achieved global levels of exposure that would have seemed remarkable, perhaps even unbelievable, two decades ago. Did he really anticipate the potential of this hidden F1 asset when he bought the Brabham team in 1971?

"No, definitely not," he explained many years later. "I wasn't thinking in those terms at all when I bought Brabham. It was only when I began to get fully involved in the whole scene that I appreciated just how fragmented the television coverage had been. Some people covered a few races, some people none at all. My initial motivation was to get the whole business grouped together in an effort to get some decent overall coverage."

By the start of 1976, the Brabham team had subtly changed its emphasis. No longer did Ecclestone pay for customer Cosworth DFV engines, but instead had forged a deal with Alfa Romeo to use its powerful, but heavy flat-12. Alfa also paid handsomely for the privilege of supplying Brabham. The following year, Ecclestone replaced the team's title sponsor, Martini, with the Italian dairy company, Parmalat. It would remain on the flanks of the Brabhams for almost ten years.

At the end of 1977, Lauda quit Ferrari and joined Ecclestone's Brabham-Alfa squad. The 77 x 53.6mm, 2995cc Alfa flat-12 may have developed 510bhp at 12,000rpm, but it needed every ounce of that power to compete with the Cosworth V8s, given the aerodynamic and fuel consumption penalties it imposed on the Brabham chassis.

Lauda was fascinated by the prospect of working with Gordon Murray, and the high-tech BT46 with its 'surface cooling' radiators looked precisely the sort of project to attract his attention. Unfortunately, it just didn't work, so Murray had to go back to the drawing board in an effort to uprate the car's performance.

There was no question of building a conventional ground-effect car because the Alfa flat-12 was simply too wide to permit the necessary aerodynamic tunnels down each side of the chassis. Instead, Murray and his colleague, David North, came up with an altogether more radical concept.

After rejecting the idea of a conventional water radiator, fed by ducting, atop the engine, Murray finalised an arrangement that employed a large water radiator mounted horizontally on top of the engine, but with the whole engine/gearbox assembly sealed off from the outside air by means of flexible skirts and a large, gearbox-driven extractor fan to suck out all the air from beneath the engine/gearbox bay.

The Brabham designer was killing two birds with one stone, much to the orchestrated disapproval of the team's rivals. The cars, driven by Lauda and his teammate, John Watson, made their debut in the Swedish Grand Prix at Anderstorp, where they practised – at Ecclestone's insistence – carrying full fuel loads in an effort to throw the opposition off the scent as far as their race potential was concerned.

Despite this, the Brabham 'fan cars' were visibly quicker off the corners than their rivals, many of whom complained bitterly about all the debris that they were allegedly sucking up off the circuit and shooting out

behind them. In addition, the Brabhams were being challenged under the provision in the F1 rules that stated firmly that "aerodynamic devices – that is, any part of the car whose primary function is to influence aerodynamic performance – must comply with the rules relating to coachwork and must be firmly fixed while the car is in motion."

A total of five teams objected on the basis that the primary function was surely to generate downforce. Not so, replied Murray, who made the point that, if the fan was disconnected, the car would overheat. The long and short of it was that Lauda won the race brilliantly, overtaking Andretti's Lotus 79 with ease.

"I tell you, it was the easiest win I ever had," said Niki. "You could do anything with that car. I was pressing Mario really hard when one of the Tyrrells, [Didier] Pironi, I think, dropped oil all over the racing line and the track became very slippery.

"Mario's Lotus was sliding all over the place and my Brabham was just sitting there, like it was on rails. Then Andretti made a small mistake coming through a corner, I pulled over to the inside and just nailed him coming out. No problem at all."

Lotus and Tyrrell immediately protested the Brabham BT46B after its win, but the race stewards eventually decided not to adjudicate on the matter and

the whole affair was referred to the CSI, the sport's governing body, which decreed that fans were banned from that point onwards. The thing to note here is that the Brabham fan car was never declared illegal at the time it raced, nor was it disqualified from that Anderstorp victory.

Despite this moment in the sun for the Brabham-Alfa, it was the Ferrari flat-12 that posed the main threat to Lotus in 1978, with Carlos Reutemann and Gilles Villeneuve notching up five more victories. Then, in 1979, Jody Scheckter won the World Championship with the latest 312T4 design, winning three races, a tally matched by Villeneuve. But that was effectively the end of the story.

In designing the new car, Forghieri and his colleagues had made great efforts to incorporate the ground-effect aerodynamics pioneered by Lotus, but the width of the flat-12 inevitably hampered their attempts to harness the airflow beneath the car. Reliability and consistency would play crucial roles in Ferrari's championship victory.

In contrast to the partnership between Andretti and Peterson, the personal relationship between Scheckter and Villeneuve in 1979 looked likely to be intensely competitive from the outset. Villeneuve had been a member of the Ferrari squad for a year – and had

Above: **Lauda jumped ship from Ferrari for 1978 to work with Gordon Murray at Brabham.**
Photo: **Bernard Cahier**

already won a race for the team – by the time Scheckter joined at the start of 1979.

The highly experienced South African had been one of F1's most spectacular new stars in the early years of the decade, producing some wild performances at the wheel of a McLaren M23 – most notably his contribution to the first-lap multiple pile-up that resulted in the 1973 British Grand Prix being flagged to a halt.

Nevertheless, Jody quickly settled down when he joined Tyrrell in 1974, and then he switched to the newly refurbished Walter Wolf Racing outfit in 1977, winning three Grands Prix and finishing second in the World Championship. During the summer of 1978, he was given the opportunity to test the new Wolf WR5 ground-effect challenger at Ferrari's Fiorano test track. The Italian team monitored his progress and decided that he looked a likely lad.

It said much for Scheckter's maturity that he did not become downcast when Villeneuve won the Long Beach and South African Grands Prix early in 1979. "I knew just how quick Gilles was," he said, "and although in terms of sheer speed, he was faster than me, I could recognise he was still prone to making youthful errors, just as I'd done in my early years."

As it turned out, the two men had a well-matched season, winning those three races apiece. Yet Gilles faced the ultimate test of character when he found himself running second to Jody at Monza, knowing that all he needed to do to keep alive his chances of becoming World Champion was to overtake his team-

mate. Yet his deeply principled nature meant that he adhered to Ferrari's team orders and did not make an attempt to pass.

"I must admit that I just kept hoping that Jody's car would break down," Villeneuve said. It was a remark that reflected his underlying self-confidence and assurance.

Away from the circuits, Jody and Gilles were both Monaco residents, sharing each other's social lives to a degree without ever living in each other's pockets. Scheckter quickly learned that Villeneuve was a madman when it came to road driving and always said, "I'll drive," when Ferrari secretary Brenda Vernor telephoned to tell the duo they were needed for testing at Fiorano.

Subsequently, Villeneuve acquired a helicopter, but Jody refused to ride with him after one nerve-racking flight, during which a warning light flickered ominously on the instrument panel for the entire journey. Jody staggered away from the machine, calling Gilles a "mad bastard". Which he certainly was.

They raced together again in 1980, but that season's Ferrari 312T5 was a hopeless waste of time, and Jody retired from driving at the end of the season. A revised version of the championship winning 312T4, the car was completely outclassed by the latest ground-effect designs from Williams, Brabham and Renault. Add to that a succession of engine failures, and Maranello was relegated from champ to chump in a single season.

It was time to move on to the F1 turbo era.

CHAPTER EIGHT: 1979–82
THE TURBO WARS

THE first turbocharged Renault V6 took to the tracks at the 1977 British Grand Prix. It was not taken seriously. Most people regarded turbocharging as an unnecessarily complex means of exploiting a rule that had remained on the F1 statute book for more than a decade simply because nobody had bothered to delete it.

Jean-Pierre Jabouille struggled around at the back of the field in this dumpy new French contender before dropping out ignominiously in an expensive-looking cloud of smoke. Yet the turbos would not go away. Although two years would pass before Renault posted the first victory of this latest forced-induction era, the 1977 British Grand Prix represented a turning-point for the sport after which there would be no going back.

This 'equivalency' formula would eventually cause a great deal of debate and consternation. In truth, as many F1 engine designers would later point out, it was virtually impossible to accurately frame such comparisons between the performance of naturally aspirated and forced-induction engines.

Between 1948 and 1951, the F1 rules were governed by regulations that provided for 1.5-litre supercharged or 4.5-litre non-supercharged engines. In reality, such notional equivalency had simply been plucked from the sky. There was no totally reliable method of predicting which would produce the most power, let alone which equation of relative cylinder capacity would provide some semblance of parity between the two types of engine.

So it was with the 1.5-litre supercharged/3-litre naturally aspirated rules introduced in 1966. In any event, there would be no shortage of 3-litre F1 engines. In particular, the advent of the Ford financed Cosworth DFV V8 in 1967 would transform the entire commercial and sporting landscape of the F1 business.

This reliable, compact and efficient off-the-shelf F1 engine would usher in the era of 'every-man' Grand Prix racing. It was the ultimate irony that the engine that enabled F1 to thrive and expand for well over a decade should eventually be eclipsed by those developed under rules that the DFV had originally been seen to make totally redundant.

One of the most vocal critics of the turbo in F1 was Keith Duckworth, the man behind the Cosworth Ford DFV. In the late 1970s or early 1980s, if you wanted a really brisk argument in the pit lane, the easiest means of securing it was to ask Keith what he thought about the new generation of turbos.

Duckworth reckoned, quite rightly in theory, that this arbitrary equivalency formula made no sense

whatsoever. What he advocated was a fuel-flow formula that would, in his view, encourage truly innovative engineering.

"When the rules were written back in 1963, only the word 'supercharged' was used, and 'turbocharging' was not mentioned at all," Duckworth told Graham Robson, the author of *Cosworth, the Search For Power* (Patrick Stephens Limited, 1990).

"In a supercharged engine, you can affect the weight of charge getting into the cylinder, albeit at the cost of taking work off the engine to drive the compressor. Then you only have the stroke of the piston to do the expansion work, which brings its own limits.

"On the other hand, a turbocharger is an air compressor driven by a turbine, and the turbine itself is an expansion motor. Therefore a turbocharger not only allows you to 'fiddle the books', but it allows you an unlimited expansion capacity as well. It means that the effective capacity of a turbocharged engine has an entirely different meaning to that of a supercharged engine."

The F1 turbo era began inauspiciously with that tentative Renault V6 outing at Silverstone, but by 1982/83, it was certainly into top gear, with engines from Ferrari, BMW, Honda, TAG-Porsche, Alfa Romeo and Hart joining those of the French car maker that had started the trend. At its absolute zenith, this chapter of Grand Prix racing history spawned some of the most spectacular and powerful F1 cars of all time, power outputs brushing the 1000bhp mark – even in race trim – on some occasions in 1986.

Thereafter a progressive reduction in turbo boost pressure over the next two seasons produced a gentle tactical retreat from the world of forced-induction Grand Prix cars. The final race of the turbocharged era was won by Alain Prost's McLaren MP4/4-Honda at Adelaide at the end of the 1988 season.

There could hardly have been a more appropriate combination of driver, chassis and engine to claim that distinction, bringing the curtain down on an era that, short though it may have been, was rich in technical variety and memorable motor racing.

The first seeds of the turbocharged F1 engine had been sown in the early 1970s, although perhaps not intentionally. Renault began its serious contemporary motor racing involvement in low-key fashion, starting with a 2-litre, four-cam V6 built around an iron cylinder block for the then-prestigious European 2-litre Sports Car Championship.

This engine was developed for use in the equally high-profile European Formula 2 Championship and powered the Elf 2 single-seater driven by Jean-Pierre Jabouille to victory in that series in 1976. Jabouille would later play a key role in the history of Renault's F1 involvement, and would score the company's first victory in the 1979 French Grand Prix at Dijon.

At this stage in the story, the French car maker's main priority was to develop a machine powered by a turbocharged version of the V6 that was capable of winning the Le Mans 24-hour sports car classic. That was duly achieved in 1978, when Jean-Pierre Jaussaud and Didier Pironi won the famous event, after which Renault swung its full attention and effort behind its fledgling F1 programme, which, by then, had been running for almost a year.

A reduction in the stroke of the 2-litre V6 had brought the engine down to 1.5 litres, but it quickly became obvious that there were serious shortcomings to be surmounted. From the driver's standpoint, the most obvious was 'turbo lag', which meant that there was a delay between the driver opening the throttle and the power chiming in. This would provide a major headache for pretty well all the turbo F1 teams over the next few years.

The concept of turbocharging was originally applied by the aviation industry as a method of sustaining intake manifold pressure at altitude on piston-engine aircraft. At higher altitudes, the rate at which

Above: **Where it all started. The 1.5-litre Renault turbo V6, which transformed the face of F1 racing after its debut in the 1977 British GP at Silverstone.**

Right: **Guy Ligier's team had a brief winning interlude at the start of the 1979 season, when Jacques Laffite, seen here with chief engineer Gérard Ducarouge, won both the Argentine and Brazilian Grands Prix. Paddock wags suggested that 'Duca's' set-up notes had been scrawled on an empty Gitanes packet and had been lost when he accidentally threw it away!**
Photos: Bernard Cahier

air can be introduced into a combustion chamber to mix with incoming fuel is obviously reduced by the lower barometric pressure.

At sea level, air density is 1 bar – around 14 pounds per square inch – but at 3000ft, the density of the air drops to 0.85 bar. Thus a piston-engine aircraft progressively loses performance the higher it flies, in the same way that a car engine loses performance when it is being operated at high altitude.

The great advantage of turbocharging over supercharging is that the former consumes little in the way of power to drive itself. In contrast to a gear-driven supercharger, which would need up to 70bhp just to drive it, the turbocharger simply produces back pressure in the exhaust manifold, against which the pistons have to fight on the exhaust stroke.

STRAWS IN THE WIND DURING 1979

Although Jody Scheckter won the 1979 World Championship for Ferrari, a combination of Michelin radial rubber and bulletproof reliability contributed more to his success than the qualities of the 312T4 chassis. More significant by far that year was the emergence of the Williams team, and the near collapse of both Lotus and McLaren. Frank Williams, the son of a Second World War bomber pilot, was motor racing's original self-made man. Throughout the 1960s, he'd lived on his wits as he abandoned his career as a budding Formula 3 racer and concentrated on wheeler-dealing in second-hand racing cars.

In those days, the Williams team was a tiny operation with little more than 50 people working out of a small factory on a trading estate alongside the railway lines in Didcot, a far cry from its swish headquarters today at Grove, near Wantage, with its cathedral-like

entrance hall, 30 acres of grounds and workforce in excess of 250.

Williams himself has come a long way since he sought employment as a Campbell's Soup salesman in the mid-1960s to raise sufficient money to race his Austin A35. Eventually he graduated to international Formula 3, financing his racing by selling spares to fellow competitors on a nomadic basis at minor-league European events, but he finally gave up driving in 1966 to support the career of his close friend, brewery heir Piers Courage.

Demonstrating considerable financial ingenuity, Williams eventually raised sufficient cash to go Grand Prix racing in 1969 with a private Brabham-Ford driven by Courage. Second places in the Monaco and US Grands Prix were a tremendous boost to their reputations and, as we have seen, the following year they continued together using an Italian-built de Tomaso chassis.

Sadly, Williams was to have his first taste of personal tragedy when the debonair Courage was killed when the de Tomaso crashed and caught fire in the Dutch Grand Prix at Zandvoort. Compounding his grief, the disaster left Williams virtually bankrupt, but, not for the first time in his career, he picked himself up and relaunched his assault on the F1 'big time'.

In 1976, Williams decided to sell up, having received a financial offer he could not refuse from Austro-Canadian oil magnate Walter Wolf. Yet, although handsomely paid, Frank quickly found himself uncomfortable with his role as right-hand man to his new employer. In 1977, he decided to start from scratch, running a private March and establishing Williams GP Engineering.

To design the team's own cars, he took on Patrick Head, then no more than a promising young engineer.

Above: Fans take a drenching of champagne from the podium after the 1980 Belgian Grand Prix at Zolder.

Top right: Alan Jones demonstrated a toughness and single-minded approach that meshed perfectly with the character of the emergent Williams squad.

Above right: Two Swiss winners. Nineteen-forty-nine British GP victor Toulo de Graffenried congratulates compatriot Clay Regazzoni after his similar achievement 40 years later.

Right: Enduring partnership. Patrick Head and Frank Williams.

Photos: Bernard Cahier

The two men met in a London hotel where Williams asked, "Are you prepared to work 24 hours a day to achieve motor racing success?" Head's response took him aback.

"No," he replied, "because anybody who has to do that must be very badly organised." Head got the job and, two years later, penned the superb Williams FW07, which rewrote the parameters of Grand Prix car design at a stroke.

The Williams FW07 would develop the ground-effect concept pioneered by Lotus to fresh levels of performance, its chassis being considerably stiffer than that of the Lotus 79, which fell off the front-running pace in 1979. It did not make its race debut until the fifth round of the title chase, but Alan Jones and his team-mate, Clay Regazzoni, quickly indicated that it was a highly promising proposition. For the British Grand Prix, Jones would be the man to beat.

After an initial skirmish with Jabouille's Renault turbo, Jones stormed off into the distance, only to be sidelined by a cracked water pump. That let Regazzoni through to achieve the historic distinction of the Williams team's first win.

Jones won four more races for the team that season to end up third in the World Championship on 40 points net, trailing new champion Scheckter (51 points net) and Gilles Villeneuve (47 net).

"Undoubtedly when we did the FW07, a great deal of the basic thinking centred on what Lotus had done

with the 79," said Head. "Although, to be honest, from the outset I really didn't fully understand the function of ground effect, and it became very clear at the end of 1978 that we needed to get more time working in a wind tunnel.

"In fact, the entire aerodynamic design of the car was based on a single week's work in the Imperial College wind tunnel, in what amounted to the first wind tunnel work I'd ever done in my life.

"One notable area we made a significant improvement on was the front wing set-up, because the Lotus 79 had huge nose wings on it which damaged the airflow to the side pods. We twigged very early on that a ground-effect design would really be better without front wings, which is why we had tiny little neutral-profile trim tabs on FW07 from the start, and it even raced on a few occasions without any front wings at all."

Williams and Head were on their way. In 1980, the updated FW07B, still equipped with full sliding skirts, emerged as the car of the year and carried Alan Jones to the World Championship. It is no coincidence that Williams now had its own wind tunnel and, in 1979, had recruited a specialist aerodynamicist, the highly respected Frank Dernie, factors that helped the team sustain its performance edge into the following year.

Jones was joined in the team by former Brabham, Ferrari and Lotus driver Carlos Reutemann, who won the Monaco Grand Prix and finished third in the final point standings. Jones won five of the season's 14 Grands Prix and deservedly took the title after a head-to-head-battle with the young Brazilian, Nelson Piquet, who had emerged as a world-class contender

at the wheel of the Gordon Murray-designed Brabham BT49-Ford at the end of the previous year.

Brabham owner Bernie Ecclestone had decided to ditch the unreliable new Alfa Romeo V12 engines that had been developed for 1979 to facilitate a ground-effect chassis design. Niki Lauda thought the new engines were awful, and their inconsistent performance through the summer of 1979 contributed to his decision to retire from the cockpit.

The Alfa 1260 was a 60-degree, 78.5 x 51.55mm V12 that developed an impressive 525bhp at 12,300rpm. It didn't work largely because its oil scavenging was inadequate and, at its worst, was horrifyingly unreliable. Add to that the fact that the detailed specification of the V12s varied from unit to unit, and the whole exercise left the Brabham team in a pretty alarming situation. The switch to Cosworth Ford DFVs in time for the 1979 Canadian Grand Prix came too late to retain Niki's interest, and he walked away from F1 midway through the first practice session in Montreal.

THE EMERGENCE OF McLAREN INTERNATIONAL

Late in 1979, Formula 2 team owner Ron Dennis made contact with former Chaparral Champ car designer John Barnard, who had been recommended to him by the Williams team's chief designer, Patrick Head. Barnard, who had served his motor racing apprenticeship at Lola, the Huntingdon based manufacturer of production racing cars, assumed Dennis was looking for somebody to design and build a Formula 2 car for him. Only when they met did Barnard fully appreciate that Dennis had F1 ambitions – a happy meeting of minds, as things turned out, for John had some exciting plans of his own on that particular front.

The British engineer believed that it would be possible to manufacture an extremely light and very strong chassis from carbon fibre, then regarded as a highly esoteric material, the use of which had previously been confined to the aerospace industry.

As Dennis worked meticulously to calculate what sort of budget would be needed to launch an F1 team of his own, developments elsewhere gave a well-timed fillip to his efforts. The McLaren team's deteriorating form since James Hunt had won the World Championship in 1976 had naturally been a matter of some concern to Marlboro, its title sponsor. As a result, Marlboro engineered an amalgamation of the team and Dennis's Project 4 organisation, which had gained considerable success in the second-division formulas. Under the terms of the merger, which was announced in September 1980, McLaren chief Teddy Mayer's 85-per-cent stake in the original Team McLaren became 45 per cent of the new company, McLaren International, which sustained his position as the largest single shareholder. Yet it was the energy of Dennis and his Project 4 partner, Creighton Brown, that began to transform the team's image.

On the engineering front, Dennis and Barnard successfully concluded a deal with the US Hercules aerospace company for the supply of the carbon-fibre composite panels that would be bonded together to form the chassis of the radical new McLaren MP4. Smooth and sleek, with beautifully fitted body panels and finished with great attention to detail, the MP4 may only have had a Cosworth Ford DFV in its engine bay, but it was a major contribution to the process of raising the team's game.

Alain Prost had partnered John Watson during the final year of the old Team McLaren regime in 1980, but the young Frenchman switched to Renault at the end of the season, as he was deeply concerned about the number of chassis breakages sustained by the old M29, which had replaced the unsuccessful M28 in the middle of the 1979 season.

Prost's abrupt departure from the team gave Watson the chance to restore his tarnished reputation; he was joined in the line-up for 1981 by the erratic Andrea de Cesaris, who, to be frank, was a bit of a liability and only earned his drives through his close relationship with Marlboro. Happily everything went to plan, with Watson scoring the revamped team's first win at Silverstone after René Arnoux's Renault had wilted with engine trouble. Five years had passed since John had scored his sole previous F1 victory for the American Penske team in the 1976 Austrian Grand Prix, and this latest success had come not a moment too soon.

For 1982, Dennis would hit the headlines by persuading Niki Lauda to come out of a retirement that had lasted two-and-a-half years and, while McLaren would continue with Cosworth Ford DFVs for the moment, the management began to lay plans for the team's own turbocharged engine. Dennis was ambitious and Barnard totally uncompromising when it came to engineering the cars, so it was unlikely that either of them would be satisfied with any of the existing turbos on the Grand Prix scene.

THE BATTLE TO CONTROL FORMULA 1

Between 1979 and 1983, the most important aspect of Grand Prix motor racing had precious little to do with the action taking place out on the circuit. It was the battle for the commercial heart of Formula 1 that really attracted the attention of the media, a high-profile contest with subtle undertones that was fought out between Bernie Ecclestone, on behalf of the F1 teams, and the sport's governing body.

During the 1970s, the Formula 1 Constructors' Association (FOCA) had become a powerful and influential grouping under Ecclestone's presidency. Its rise to prominence might have been ignored for the most part by the sport's administrators, the Commission Sportive Internationale (CSI), which later changed its title to the Fédération Internationale du Sport Automobile (FISA), but if, during that period, you were a race organiser, then the only person you had to speak to was Ecclestone.

The Brabham proprietor organised the financial arrangements for the races on behalf of the team owners. Organisers did not pay out on a published prize scale; they handed the whole amount over to FOCA, which then distributed it among its members in accordance with a complex formula.

Some insiders believed matters had almost got to the point where FISA was effectively being bypassed by the commercially astute Ecclestone. For legal, administrative and historical reasons, it certainly sanctioned the races, but its authority had been progressively diluted by the time volatile Frenchman Jean-Marie Balestre was elected FISA president at the end of 1978. From the very start of his tenure, sparks flew.

At a stroke, FOCA's unimpeded push towards overall F1 dominance appeared to have been checked. Balestre was an eccentric extrovert who seemed to like nothing better than playing the role of Napoleon. But he was no fool and no pushover.

Born in 1920, Balestre had enjoyed a colourful and action-packed career. He had served in the French Resistance during the war and carried out covert activities against the German forces occupying his country. When, in the late 1970s, photographs began to circulate of him apparently wearing a German uniform, he took unsuccessful legal action to prevent their publication. He explained that he had been a double agent who had been ordered to infiltrate the enemy, and insisted that he was once arrested by the Gestapo, tortured and condemned to death. Only the Allied invasion had saved him.

During the post-war years, he had helped set up an important Paris based publishing group and founded the FFSA (Fédération Française du Sport Automobile) in 1952, at a time when a handful of regional race organising clubs dominated the administration of French motor sport.

In his new role as FISA president, Balestre played hardball from the start. At the first race of the 1979 season, John Watson's McLaren M28 tangled with Jody Scheckter's Ferrari 312T3 and caused the race to be flagged to a halt. Watson suspects that Balestre's robust intervention may have been behind the stewards' decision to penalise him with a draconian fine.

In 1980, apparently with an eye to improving safety by reducing the lap speeds of F1 cars, Balestre announced that sliding aerodynamic side skirts would be banned from the start of the following season. This decision put FOCA on red alert. The organisation's members were predominantly the British based specialist F1 teams who relied on their technical ingenuity in chassis design to get the best out of Cosworth Ford DFV engine performance. They now suspected that Balestre was attempting to undermine their competitive edge at a time when both Renault and Ferrari were developing 1.5-litre turbocharged machines that, while they clearly had powerful engines, were seriously lacking when it came to chassis technology.

Right: **Man with a mission. Fiery Frenchman Jean-Marie Balestre's emergence as FISA president led to a confrontation with Bernie Ecclestone and the teams over ultimate control of the sport.**

Opposite: **Didier Pironi drove with spine-tingling commitment for Ligier in 1980, earning himself a move to Ferrari for 1981.**

Photos: Paul-Henri Cahier

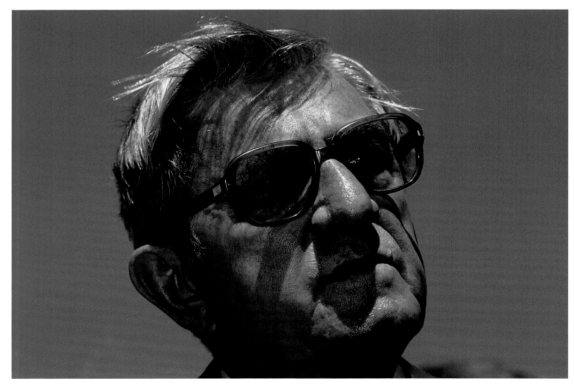

FERRARI JOINS THE TURBO BRIGADE

The first turbo Ferrari, the 126CK, was a case in point. It may have been equipped with a powerful engine, but when it made its public debut in practice for the 1980 Italian Grand Prix at Imola, its chassis looked crude and basic. Its construction followed long-established Ferrari practice, with a multi-tubular spaceframe overlaid with stressed alloy panelling. Rocker-arm suspension activated inboard coil-spring/dampers all round, and power was transmitted through a transverse gearbox, as on its successful T-series predecessors, but the whole package was a touch makeshift and unsophisticated.

For this new generation of Ferrari F1 cars, a 120-degree, 81 x 48.4mm, 1496.43cc V6 engine had been produced. The four-cam unit had its inlet camshafts on the outside and exhaust camshafts on the inside of the vee, enabling short exhaust pipes to run from each bank of cylinders to feed into the turbines and compressors, which were mounted just behind the large central fuel cell.

Power output from the Ferrari V6 was claimed to be in the region of 540bhp, initially around 60bhp more than the outmoded flat-12. Ferrari spent much of the winter of 1980/81 refining the performance of this KKK turbocharged engine, but Mauro Forghieri and his colleagues also took the opportunity to investigate a different system of forced induction, which had been developed by the Swiss Brown-Boveri organisation. This system, known as the Comprex, was a directly driven supercharger with the exhaust gases providing the pressure waves to compress incoming air as it entered the inlet manifold. Unlike the exhaust-driven turbochargers, the Comprex system seemed to have no throttle lag, while the turbine/compressor units came up to speed once the throttles were opened.

Tests during the off-season indicated that the new system had genuine potential. Drivers Gilles Villeneuve and Didier Pironi – who had replaced Jody Scheckter on the South African's retirement from racing at the end of 1980 – quickly reported that the immediate throttle response from the Comprex system certainly seemed an improvement. But there were some distinct problems to be overcome and eventually it was shelved.

The 1981 season yielded Ferrari two Grand Prix victories with the 126CK. Both were scored by Gilles Villeneuve, one through sheer driving brilliance in Monaco, the other by shrewd tactics and total consistency at the head of a jinking queue of cars during the Spanish Grand Prix at Jarama.

Yet the Ferrari 126CK was far from the integrated design that would be needed to remain competitive in the years to come. The rival McLaren team had introduced its carbon-fibre composite chassis soon after the start of the 1981 season and, while the safety bonuses accruing from such developments were considerable, the rigidity offered by such construction techniques was absolutely crucial when it came to retaining the torsional strength of chassis. This would become an increasingly important factor for designers to take into account as the new generation of turbocharged engines increased their power output in leaps and bounds over the next few seasons.

In fact, by the start of the 1981 season, there were no fewer than four turbocharged F1 engines poised to do battle. However, while the Hart 415T joined the fray at the first race in Europe, BMW's four-cylinder production-based unit would not be seen in competitive action until the following year. The trusty Renault EF1 was now producing around 540bhp at 11,500rpm. The Ferrari 126CK had been developed to offer around 20bhp more than its French counterpart, but in time the BMW M12/13 would come to be regarded as perhaps the most powerful of all these forced-induction engines.

A ROCKY PATH TO F1 CONSENSUS

It was perhaps ironic that Nelson Piquet should drive to his first World Championship in 1981 at the wheel of the Ecclestone owned Brabham BT49. By this time, Ecclestone had left the day-to-day running of the Brabham team to his trusted lieutenants, most notably chief designer Gordon Murray, while he attempted to deal with the contentious issues arising from the battle with FISA.

The first major confrontation had come the previous season. Balestre had started the year by threatening that any driver who failed to attend the pre-race briefing would be fined. Some of the FOCA teams attempted to encourage their men not to go, apparently anxious that they should not be seen to be bossed about by what was often perceived as a weak governing body.

Suddenly, a crisis arose. At Monaco and Zolder, several drivers did not appear and Balestre said that the culprits would be suspended. FOCA accused FISA of being confrontational and demanded that the penalties be rescinded.

At the time, these individual scuffles seemed sufficiently serious to be taken at face value. Yet it was the sub-text to the disputes, several of which erupted over different, seemingly separate issues over a period of three seasons, that was much more important.

Ecclestone had shrewdly recognised the potential for growth of televised sports, and was determined that he and the teams should have their share of a goose that seemed set to continue laying golden eggs into the distant future. Bernie was right on target and would become one of the richest men in Britain as a result of that perspicacity.

The preliminary skirmish between FOCA and FISA came to a head over a sanctioning dispute at the 1980 Spanish Grand Prix. In the end, the race went ahead, but Ferrari, Renault and Alfa Romeo did not participate. They all had commercial interests in the motor industry and could not risk alienating FISA – and therefore its parent, the FIA – by competing in what was, to all intents and purposes, a pirate event.

Alan Jones won the race for Williams, but the result was not allowed to count for the World Championship. The same thing happened at the following year's South African Grand Prix. FOCA had made plans to combat the sliding-skirt ban by taunting FISA with threats of a breakaway World Championship organised by the 'World Federation of Motor Sports', which would run its series for cars still using these aerodynamic appendages.

In fact, the World Federation of Motor Sports didn't exist, and its rather grand-looking statutes, circulated

in a document at the time, had been cooked up by Ecclestone's legal adviser and collaborator, Max Mosley, of whom motor racing in general and F1 in particular would hear a great deal more in his future role as president of the FIA.

FOCA lost this second confrontation with FISA. Running on rag-tag used tyres, the F1 teams managed to produce some semblance of a motor race at Kyalami to open the 1981 season. But, again, Reutemann's victory in a Williams was not permitted to stand.

Eventually, just prior to the Long Beach Grand Prix, FISA and FOCA reached a rapprochement with the signing of the Concorde Agreement, a wide-ranging document that laid out the procedures whereby regulations could be changed. While acknowledging FISA's role as the sporting power, effectively it left financial control in the hands of the constructors.

Thus the 1981 season continued without sliding skirts, and the whole World Championship programme was blighted by the need to build ridiculously complicated suspension systems that enabled the competing cars to conform to a 6cm ground-clearance rule when they were checked in the pits, while still being able to run as close to the ground as possible out on the circuit.

Brabham's Gordon Murray and his colleague, David North, came up with the best way around the rule. They devised a system of soft air springs that the aerodynamic load compressed as speed built up, dropping the team's BT49C contender down to a ground-effect

stance. As the speed dropped away again when the car arrived in the pit lane, so it rose on its suspension to meet the 6cm requirement.

The system worked brilliantly at Buenos Aires, where Piquet ran away with the Argentine Grand Prix, the third race of the title chase, and the rest of the field erupted in fury. Rivals objected on the basis that the Brabhams were running flexible skirts – not sliding skirts – and, in the view of the Williams team for one, this was not legal.

Murray simply shrugged the protests aside, accusing his rivals of being bad losers, but then FISA issued a rule clarification on the subject and the whole issue of the complex Brabham suspension system became irrelevant when several of the cars arrived for the Belgian Grand Prix fitted with suspension lowering switches in the cockpit. The FISA officials figuratively threw up their hands in horror, but took no action, and that effectively was the end of that.

Eventually everything settled down, and the 1981 World Championship was clinched by an exhausted Piquet in the final race of the season in sweltering conditions in Las Vegas. Nelson struggled home fifth after his arch-rival for the title, Reutemann, faded to an inexplicable eighth after starting from a dazzling pole position.

Reutemann relinquished the title with such astonishing docility that Piquet was simply amazed. "He braked early to let me pass when I came up behind him," he recounted. "He made it so easy for me,

Opposite: Carlos Reutemann in his well-sponsored driving suit. The Argentine driver had the talent to win a championship, but never quite strung everything together.

Below: Brabham's Nelson Piquet and Charlie Whiting intently check practice times of their competitors.
Photos: Bernard Cahier

I couldn't believe it."

The quiet Argentinian was surely one of the most outstanding F1 drivers never to win a World Championship. Yet he was a complex character. After the 1981 British Grand Prix, ensconced in a comfortable points lead, he bet the author that he would not win the title. Two races into the 1982 season, he abruptly decided to retire, a couple of months before the Falklands conflict erupted in the South Atlantic.

BATTENING DOWN THE HATCHES FOR RENEWED STRIFE

As Ferrari and Renault gradually began to get into the competitive swing of things with their turbocharged F1 cars, so the British based teams, aligned with FOCA, began to worry that they might be hard pressed to win many races in the foreseeable future. Most of these teams relied on Cosworth power, but, with the rival turbos nudging their way towards 580bhp, going into battle with a 480bhp naturally aspirated V8 was calculated to cause more than a few problems. So the British teams sat down and worked out a clever ruse by which they could redress the balance of power. Quite literally.

For many years, it had been the accepted practice to top up oil and water to normal levels before cars were submitted for post-race scrutineering, thereby bringing them back up to the regulation minimum weight. Now the Cosworth powered teams were thinking along the same lines, but to subtly different effect.

Lotus, Brabham, McLaren and the others all decided to fit their cars with reservoirs to carry water for brake cooling purposes. These were filled up at the start of the race and, claimed the teams, the water was then used to cool air entering the brake ducts, with

the result that it was all consumed by the end of the event. Then the containers were refilled, and when the cars were scrutineered they would make the minimum weight limit as required.

However, many people suspected that the entire contents of the water containers were dumped at the first corner. A cynical view, perhaps. The truth, however, was even more convoluted. In many cases – some would say most – the water bottles were never filled in the first place. Therefore, the Cosworth runners were running beneath the minimum weight limit in an effort to make up for their lack of horsepower.

This issue was first highlighted at the 1981 Monaco Grand Prix, where Piquet's Brabham BT49C qualified on pole, just ahead of the mercurial Gilles Villeneuve's Ferrari 126CK, a much heavier machine altogether with its full fuel load. The vexed question of underweight racing cars was now firmly in the spotlight. Everybody in the pit lane tended to pick their words with care, but Ligier driver Jacques Lafitte grasped the nettle in an interview carried by the French sporting newspaper, *L'Équipe*.

"Piquet has two cars, one ultra-light, which he uses in practice, and then his race car, which is to normal weight," he claimed. "A regular Brabham is already on the weight limit. Good for them. But the practice car has carbon-fibre brake discs which save 12 kilos, and I'm told that the car also has a tiny fuel tank, much lighter than the normal one.

"The car should be weighed as soon as Piquet stops, before the mechanics can touch it But no, no one will do anything, because it's a Brabham, owned by Ecclestone. Nobody can touch him. Everybody is frightened of him."

Yet, as we shall see later on, Brabham was not alone in pursuing this strategy.

Above: Gilles – Little Big Man.

Above left: **Fateful day. Zolder, 8th May, 1982. Gilles Villeneuve sits in the pit lane in his Ferrari before practice.**

Photos: Paul-Henri Cahier

MORE TROUBLE WITH THE SCALES OF JUSTICE

The issue of cars running under the weight limit bubbled along through 1981 and then erupted again at the 1982 Brazilian Grand Prix. But this time, it almost triggered another terminal split between FOCA and FISA.

Nelson Piquet's Brabham BT49D won the race, ahead of Keke Rosberg's Williams FW07C, with Alain Prost's Renault turbo RE30B finishing third. During the course of the race, Piquet's featherweight Brabham had hustled Gilles Villeneuve, driving the heavier and less wieldy Ferrari turbo, into an error, and the Canadian had spun off the circuit into a barrier.

However, the stewards of the Rio race were having none of the FOCA teams' subterfuge. They disqualified Piquet and Rosberg, thereby handing the race to Prost's Renault. The Brabham and Williams teams appealed, but a Court of Appeal convened by FISA upheld the disqualification. In turn, the FOCA teams claimed that this disqualification constituted a change in the rules. For its part, the governing body retorted that, far from being a change in the rules, it was merely a clarification.

Of course, nobody really expected the FOCA aligned teams to take this lying down. Yet FOCA dramatically over-played its hand with a stubborn display of trades-union-style muscle when it came to the San Marino Grand Prix at Imola. En masse, the FOCA teams boycotted the event, with the result that it was contested only by Ferrari, Renault, Osella, Toleman, ATS (unrelated to the earlier entrant of that name) and the renegade Tyrrell team, which, despite its alignment with FOCA, found itself obliged to take part at the insistence of its Italian sponsor.

In what was seen at the time as an effort to placate his furious FOCA colleagues, during the course of the San Marino GP weekend, Tyrrell fired the first volley in the next major argument, namely a formal protest against all turbocharged cars competing at this event on the basis that their engines included turbines and, since turbines were banned by the F1 regulations, these were effectively illegal secondary power units.

The race was won by Didier Pironi's Ferrari 126C2 after the Frenchman had tricked his team-mate, Gilles Villeneuve, on the final lap. Pironi effectively gained his success against team orders and, 13 days later, Gilles was killed practising for the Belgian Grand Prix at Zolder. It was the start of a nightmare season for Ferrari, which would see Pironi's career ended by horrendous leg injuries sustained during practice for the German Grand Prix.

It was also the season that effectively saw the FOCA teams cut and run into the turbo enclave. At the end of the day, they were in the racing business, and winning races meant you had to go faster than the opposition. In 1982, that meant having a turbocharged engine.

CHAPTER NINE: 1982–87
IF YOU CAN'T BEAT THEM...

In scorching heat, the grid rolls away on the warm-up lap before the start of the 1984 British Grand Prix. Nelson Piquet's Brabham is on pole, ahead of the McLarens of Prost and Lauda. De Angelis (Lotus), Rosberg (Williams) and Warwick (Renault) complete the top six qualifiers.
Photo: Paul-Henri Cahier

BY the summer of 1982, the Formula 1 scene was starting to settle down again. Renault's turbo-cars were getting seriously into their stride and the Ferrari 126C2s, much more sophisticated machines than their immediate predecessors with chassis built around 'folded up' Nomex honeycomb/aluminium sandwich sheeting, were also becoming very competitive, although the Italian team's season had been sadly punctuated by the accidents to Gilles Villeneuve and Didier Pironi.

Meanwhile, Bernie Ecclestone had very shrewdly been hedging his bets as far as Brabham was concerned. The team had tested a BMW four-cylinder turbocharged engine as early as the 1981 British Grand Prix, where Nelson Piquet had appeared in the BT50 prototype during practice, but the unit was not raced until the start of the following year.

From the outset, the BMW board took the view that, for promotional reasons, it was extremely important that any Grand Prix involvement should be seen to rely upon a production-based engine. Chief designer Paul Rosche was able to draw on considerable technical data from the 2.1-litre turbocharged 320 saloons, which the US end of the McLaren operation had been running in the IMSA category across North America. In 1980, therefore, Rosche was able to take the first steps towards developing the BMW M12/13 F1 engine, which was based on the BMW 2002's four-cylinder block.

It did not take long for the BMW Motorsport engineers to discover that the standard production blocks performed at their optimum when aged. Two- or three-year-old blocks from cars that had covered as much as 100,000km on the road had less inherent stress in their structure than newer examples. Apart from the machining away of around 5kg of superfluous metal, such as stiffening ribs and water channels on the inlet side, however, the blocks remained fundamentally unmodified from the basic production examples.

The twin-overhead-camshaft, four-valves-per-cylinder engines, which initially were supplied to the Brabham team on an exclusive basis, had a bore and stroke of 89.2 x 60mm for a capacity of 1499cc. The steel crankshaft ran in five main bearings, and short, forged-alloy Mahle pistons with very rugged titanium connecting rods were employed to withstand the much higher loads to which the units were subjected.

Fitted with a single KKK turbocharger and employing a 6.7:1 compression ratio, the engine's initial output was quoted as 557bhp at 9500rpm, although eventually it would achieve almost twice that figure in high-boost qualifying form during the course of its F1 competition career.

Of course, after the 1981 season had been punctuated by arguments about the rules and technical controversies, it was ironic that 1982 should kick off with a major row involving the drivers. Niki Lauda, returning to F1 to drive for McLaren, provided the catalyst for this unfortunate confrontation. While examining the paperwork that accompanied his FISA superlicence prior to the start of the season, he realised that the governing body had issued the licence in conjunction with a specific team. It was not, if you like, a 'stand alone' licence issued individually to the Austrian.

The drivers quickly concluded that FISA and the team owners had conspired to establish a restrictive cartel, making them nothing more than pawns in a big-budget chess game. They threatened a strike unless things were changed and, partly at least, carried out their threat by missing first practice for the South African Grand Prix at Kyalami.

Eventually the strike was broken by an apparent compromise, which did not prevent FISA from imposing fines on those who had transgressed. It was an unsatisfactory episode that did not reflect well on the drivers, but its significance was largely swamped by wider issues engulfing the sport at that time, most notably the 'water bottle' scam.

Meanwhile, on the technical front, one of the biggest problems facing the F1 teams was to resolve the lazy throttle response of the turbo engines. Renault's answer had been to squirt a jet of fuel into the turbo, which ensured that the turbines kept spinning when the driver was off the throttle.

Ferrari chose to tackle the same problem by linking the compressor manifold to the exhaust manifold by means of a valve that opened to pass compressed air into the turbines when the throttles closed. Once the driver went back on to the throttle, the valve closed and stopped combustion from occurring within the turbines. This was developed into a highly efficient system, although secondary problems arose in terms of higher wear on the turbine blades and bearings. As a consequence, the system was revised for 1982 with modifications to the turbines, compressors and boost control valves.

The Italian team also sought to address the question of increasing combustion chamber temperatures with the help of a key development from the team's fuel supplier, Agip. Following a principle that was used to cool jet engines, the Agip fuel technicians developed a highly complex system whereby a globule of water could be encapsulated within a globule of petrol, lowering the temperature of the fuel as it entered the combustion chamber. At the point of combustion, the water turned to steam, 'exploding' the surrounding petrol in a process that offered improved atomisation and better control of the mixture within the combustion chamber.

Meanwhile, the Brabham BT50-BMW had scored its first victory in the 1982 Canadian Grand Prix at Montreal with Nelson Piquet at the wheel, a performance made easier, perhaps, by the fact that the race start had been postponed to the late afternoon following a tragic fatal accident at the first start.

Yet again, the Ferrari team would be at the centre of the disaster. Pironi stalled his pole-position 126C2 and, as the pack scattered to avoid him, F1 novice Riccardo Paletti slammed his Osella straight into the back of the stationary red car. Although he was removed to hospital promptly by helicopter, Paletti died soon afterwards from multiple injuries.

As the ambient temperature dropped dramatically in the late afternoon, so the charge temperature to the BMW's turbo engine dropped sympathetically. Nelson had no trouble in keeping ahead of his team-mate, Riccardo Patrese, in the Cosworth DFV-engined BT49D.

Brabham also reintroduced the concept of mid-race refuelling, chief designer Gordon Murray having worked out that this was the quickest theoretical means of covering a race distance. It certainly made sense. The Brabhams needed to run as light as pos-

Opposite: **The BMW M12/13 four-cylinder, production-based turbo-charged engine was developed into one of the most formidably powerful units ever to be installed in an F1 car, producing around 1100bhp with qualifying boost.**
Photo: Paul-Henri Cahier

Above: Niki Lauda and Keke Rosberg battle in the non-turbocharged McLaren and Williams respectively. The Finn swam against the turbo tide to win the 1982 World Championship for Frank's outfit.

Above right: Keke Rosberg with his ever-present cigarette, in the days when this was not politically incorrect for a sportsman.

Right: An elated John Watson celebrates his McLaren victory in the 1982 Belgian GP at Zolder, where he took a late lead after Rosberg half spun with locked rear brakes.

Photos: Paul-Henri Cahier

sible for as many laps as possible, given that they required a massive 47 gallons to get through a Grand Prix distance – 11 gallons more than a corresponding Cosworth-engine machine.

Murray and his colleagues judged that starting the Brabham-BMWs on soft tyres and a half fuel load would enable them to stop, refuel and still be in front at the end of the race. They first tried the strategy in the British Grand Prix at Brands Hatch, but, ten laps into the race, Piquet had only opened a three-second advantage over Niki Lauda's McLaren-Cosworth DFV, which would eventually win when the Brazilian's engine failed.

Later, in the Austrian Grand Prix, Patrese would retain the lead during one of these highly publicised stops, only to suffer an engine failure shortly afterwards. The Brabham-BMWs would certainly sustain a reputation for being fast and fragile.

ROSBERG GETS THE JOB DONE

Through all this controversy, mechanical mayhem and off-track politicking, the feisty, extrovert Keke Rosberg picked his way through other people's debris to take the 1982 World Championship at the wheel of the naturally aspirated Williams FW08. Having joined Williams only at the start of the 1982 season, following Alan Jones's retirement from F1, he drove his heart out from start to finish. Although he won only a single Grand Prix, it was certainly an unusual year, in that no other driver won more than two races.

"Sure, it was frustrating not to have a turbo," said Keke, "but there was no point in complaining about it. Anyway, I think I proved that a Cosworth car could

be competitive on all but the fastest circuits when I put FW08 on pole for the British Grand Prix at Brands Hatch."

Despite this, Keke's opposite-lock style would drive Williams technical director Patrick Head to despair. "I've told him that if he could only tidy up his driving style, he would be even quicker than he is," said Patrick. Rosberg just puffed on a cigarette and replied that his style seemed to work pretty well, thanks very much.

There was also one occasion when Frank Williams – who hated Keke's smoking and made him leave the team motorhome when he wanted a drag – made the mistake of suggesting that Rosberg's occasional first-lap 'moments' could be attributed to a certain lack of physical fitness.

"That's bullshit," replied the indignant Finn. "We were starting the races with low tyre pressures so that they came up to precisely the correct pressure when they warmed up. It was necessary to manhandle the car on the opening lap because it was extremely twitchy until the tyres warmed up."

At the end of the year, although Ferrari clinched the Constructors' Championship with 74 points to McLaren's 69, Rosberg squeezed home to win the drivers' title with 44 points to the 39 each of John Watson and Didier Pironi.

It's worth reflecting that seldom has a contemporary World Championship been won with fewer points than Rosberg amassed in 1982. To put it in perspective, he clinched the title with two fewer points than Mika Häkkinen squandered through a combination of driver and McLaren team error in 1999 up to the Italian Grand Prix alone. Ironically, by then, Rosberg was Häkkinen's business manager.

Above: Nelson Piquet heads for victory on the first lap of the 1983 Italian Grand Prix. The Brabham driver leads Alain Prost, Elio de Angelis, Niki Lauda *et al.*

Right: Alain Prost came close to taking the title for Renault in 1983. The Frenchman was pilloried by his home press for his 'failure' to land the championship. He moved to McLaren for the 1984 season.

Far right: The last of 155 Grand Prix wins for the Cosworth DFV and its DFY derivative. Michele Alboreto's Benetton-liveried Tyrrell 011 heads for victory in the 1983 Detroit Grand Prix, with Eddie Cheever's Renault in hot pursuit.

Photos: Paul-Henri Cahier

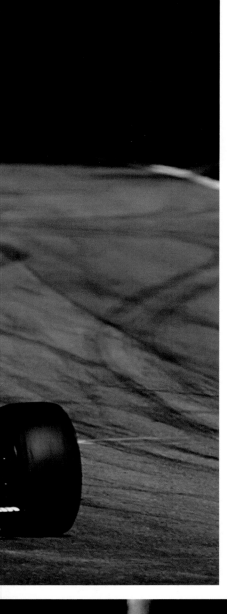

NEW UNDERBODY RULES PUT DESIGNER IN A FLAT SPIN

Ground-effect aerodynamics were swept away for the 1983 season when FISA decreed that all cars should have flat bottoms from the start of the year. More welcome was the news that there would be stability of engine regulations through to the end of 1985, plus a reduction in minimum weight to 540kg and, from the start of 1984, a cut in fuel tankage from 250 to 220 litres.

Most immediately affected by this was Gordon Murray. Outsiders believed that he had an inside line, via Ecclestone, to the FISA decision making process. Yet he and his employer had remained confident that there would be no changes to the rules affecting undercar aerodynamics for 1983.

Encouraged by the obvious potential of the in-race refuelling strategy, Murray had decided to take this concept a step further for 1983 with a 'half tank' chassis, dubbed the BT51, complete with a radical new transmission that had been designed to get the best out of ground-effect aerodynamics. Suddenly, on 3rd November, 1982, Murray realised that the new car would have to be scrapped.

And so he started again. Brabham had to produce a totally new car to the latest flat-bottom rules, and it had to be ready for the Brazilian Grand Prix on 13th March. That was the deadline and there was absolutely no question of missing it.

More to the point, there was no realistic prospect of reworking the outdated BT50-BMW into some sort of

stop-gap machine conforming to the new regulations. In anticipation of the BT51, Murray had requested that BMW alter the routing of the exhaust pipes and turbocharger specifically to fit the new car. There was no way in which these modified engines could be installed into the back of the BT50.

The BT52 was duly readied in time for its race debut. It was a distinctively different machine that owed virtually nothing to the long line of Murray-designed Brabhams stretching back to 1973. The new car had no side pods, and the chassis looked dramatically slim as a result.

Piquet started the 1983 campaign as he meant to go on, storming to victory in the Brazilian Grand Prix at Rio, and he kept the BT52 pretty well in play for the rest of the season. In-race refuelling would remain an integral component in F1 race strategy throughout the year, although it would be banned for 1984, and the Brabham mechanics came to be regarded as possibly the most accomplished of all in this respect.

Yet Renault's Alain Prost would give Piquet a good run for his money. He won the French Grand Prix and also scored maximum points in Belgium, Britain and Austria. The introduction of Ferrari's new carbon-fibre composite 126C3 at Silverstone helped keep Maranello in contention, with René Arnoux adding victories in Germany and Holland to his earlier win in Canada, but although the Italian team would retain its Constructors' Championship crown, the main issue of the drivers' title came down to a battle between Prost and Piquet.

Put simply, Renault took its eye off the ball and Nel-

son's Brabham-BMW began to pick up the pace over the last four races of the season. The French team's failure to grasp the seriousness of the situation could be judged by the fact that they romanced a plane load of journalists to Kyalami for the final championship round in the confident expectation that Prost would clinch the title.

It was incredibly naïve. Piquet, who had won the two previous races at Monza and Brands Hatch, ran at a blistering pace in the early stages, easing back to finish third, behind team-mate Riccardo Patrese and the Alfa Romeo 183T of Andrea de Cesaris after Prost had succumbed to engine failure.

However, much controversy surrounded the specification of the fuel sample that was taken from Piquet's car. On the face of it, this exceeded the octane limits laid down by the rules, but nobody seemed to want to do anything about it. The results stood and the whole issue was forgotten.

WILLIAMS FORGES HONDA PARTNERSHIP

Honda had been away from Formula 1 for a full 14 seasons by the time the tiny UK based Spirit team began experimenting with the 1.5-litre Honda RA 163-F V6 turbocharged engine at the start of the 1983 season. The Japanese company wanted to compete in F1 at the highest possible level, but started on a characteristically cautious note in partnership with Spirit, with whom it had already operated in Formula 2. Behind the scenes, however, Honda had taken a strategic decision of even greater significance. In the early months of 1983, the Japanese company had forged a long-term deal with Frank Williams.

At a time when John Barnard was precisely laying down the guidelines for the new TAG turbo, Williams technical director Patrick Head could have been forgiven a twinge of envy when the first lumpy, untidy 80-degree V6 Honda engine arrived at the team's Didcot factory. The package also contained two turbochargers, but little else. It was down to Williams to evolve a means of installing the engine into a chassis, to say nothing of finalising such ancillaries as radiators and general plumbing for the turbo and exhaust systems.

Head and his aerodynamicist, Frank Dernie, produced what amounted to a development chassis for the first Honda V6, the Williams FW09, which was still constructed around an aluminium honeycomb chassis; Williams would not make the move to carbon-fibre composite chassis until 1985. The FW09 made its race debut in the 1983 South African GP.

Above: **Three wins gave René Arnoux a good tilt at the 1983 World Championship, but the popular, if erratic, French driver eventually finished third in the points standings, behind Piquet and Prost.**

Above right: **Jacques Laffite never quite got to grips with the Williams-Honda FW09B during his second season with the British team.**

Above far right: **Keke Rosberg scored possibly the best win of his career at the Monaco Grand Prix in 1983, driving the Williams FW08C.**

Right: **The 1983 San Marino GP at Imola yielded a fine Ferrari win for Patrick Tambay. Here, the Maranello team personnel join the track invasion after the race.**

Photos: Paul-Henri Cahier

Above: **The Porsche-built TAG turbo V6, which had been commissioned by McLaren, made its debut in the 1983 Dutch GP and carried Niki Lauda to his third World Championship the following year.**

Photo: Paul-Henri Cahier

McLAREN KEEP TAGS ON THE OPPOSITION

No such engineering compromises would be accepted by the McLaren directors in their efforts to ensure that the team had the best turbocharged F1 engine in the business by the end of the 1983 season. Ron Dennis approached this challenge in a methodical fashion. Having discussed the matter in detail with John Barnard, he decided that there were too many limitations involved in using any of the existing turbocharged F1 engines. With the Renault, there was a lack of exclusivity; with the BMW, installation problems, and so on. Consequently Dennis approached Porsche, who had considerable accumulated experience of turbocharging sports car engines stretching back through the previous decade.

When Dennis arrived on Porsche's doorstep, the management may have been bracing themselves for the usual enquiry as to whether they would be interested in supplying F1 engines for the McLaren team. They were not. But the question Dennis asked them was very different. He approached Porsche as a potential customer, asking whether the German company would be prepared to make a state-of-the-art turbocharged F1 engine with McLaren funding the project. Barnard would have the final say in its configuration: "Too many engine designers give absolutely no thought to how it is going to be installed in a chassis," he noted. "They get it running on a test bed and then wonder why the chassis designer isn't interested. With the Porsche project, I had the final say."

Meanwhile, Dennis pulled out all the stops and persuaded Techniques d'Avant Garde, a long-established international trading company founded by the Franco-Lebanese Ojjeh family, to back the project. Mansour Ojjeh was already an enthusiastic supporter of F1 as a Williams team sponsor, but the relationship with Dennis and McLaren would become far

Left: The Ferrari V6 turbo that achieved four wins in 1983.

Below: Nearly a winner. Andrea de Cesaris came close to giving Alfa Romeo a victory with the 183T during the 1983 season.

Photos: Paul-Henri Cahier

wider ranging. Today McLaren International is part of the TAG McLaren Group, a high-technology conglomerate that has expanded way beyond the pure motor racing orbit.

With the funding secure, Barnard was in a position to lay down his specific design requirements to Hans Metzger, the leader of the Porsche design team. He wanted an aluminium-alloy V6 configured with a vee angle no greater than 90 degrees, with all the pumps and other ancillary equipment positioned at the head of the engine and room for upswept exhaust pipes, which would enable it to be fitted into an ideal ground-effect concept.

"I would not compromise," said Barnard. "We had to have the right turbos. I made them pull in bolt heads which extended outside the overall prescribed profile of the engine, re-engineer various casings and so on. The work went back and forth between us."

The end result had a bore and stroke of 82 x 47.3mm,

giving a capacity of 1499cc. Initially Porsche claimed a power output of 600bhp, at least 75bhp more than the best available Cosworth DFY V8 (a derivative of the legendary DFV), at the time of the TAG turbo's debut in 1983. A single KKK turbocharger was piped into the exhaust manifolding on each cylinder bank, and the engine was equipped with a Bosch electronic management system.

Much of the early development work of the TAG turbo was carried out by John Watson and Niki Lauda at Porsche's Weissach test circuit with prototype engines installed in 956 sports-racing cars. Early problems included throttle lag and oil breathing shortcomings, but eventually these were ironed out. Barnard was aghast when those changes to the FIA technical regulations in the autumn of 1982 effectively ruled out many of the benefits of his carefully crafted engine configuration intended for a ground-effect chassis. But there were other considerations.

SENNA WIN MIGHT HAVE HELPED PROST TO 1984 TITLE

IRONICALLY, if Ayrton Senna had won the 1984 Monaco Grand Prix in the Toleman TG84-Hart, Alain Prost might well have ended up with that year's World Championship. To understand the logic of this contention, one must go back to 1981, when Toleman first decided to make the jump into F1 after winning the previous year's European F2 Championship with the Toleman TG280, which was powered by a 2-litre engine built by Brian Hart's small specialist company.

Toleman's ambitious managing director, Alex Hawkridge, persuaded Hart to develop his own 1.5-litre, four-cylinder turbocharged engine on an exclusive basis. This started the team on a long road strewn with technical pitfalls as Hart and his engineers effectively taught themselves all about F1 turbo technology.

By 1983, the lead Toleman 183B-Hart, driven by Derek Warwick, had steadily developed into a competitive proposition. The Englishman scored the team's first World Championship points with a fourth place in the Dutch GP at Zandvoort, followed by a sixth at Monza, a fifth at the Grand Prix of Europe at Brands Hatch and another fourth in the final race of the season, the South African GP at Kyalami.

Even so, Warwick had decided to leave Toleman and sign for Renault, opening the way for one of the most exciting drivers of all time to make his debut on the F1 World Championship stage.

"Late in 1983, we were testing at Silverstone when Alex arrived in the Toleman helicopter accompanied by a young man with remarkably intense eyes who had been blowing everybody off in F3," recalled Brian Hart.

"Alex said, 'This is Ayrton Senna, our new driver for next year – 1984.' I was very excited, as I'd been to a couple of F3 races where he and [Martin] Brundle had been battling it out.

"Clearly the guy was unusually talented. But this was absolutely typical of Alex; who else could have pulled off something like this? Senna had tested for Williams, tested for McLaren, but Alex managed to persuade him that he should come to join the Toleman team.

"By the start of the 1984 season, Rory [Byrne, Toleman's designer] had really got a handle on the flat-bottomed aerodynamics with the new TG184, but the real story of that year was Ayrton. What an incredible bloke, as well as being an unbelievably quick, motivated and complete racing driver.

"He rang me up in the winter. 'This is Ayrton,' he said. 'As you know, Alex has signed me. I want to know all about the engine, what boost we're going to use, how I should drive it.' I thought, 'Hang on, you haven't even driven it yet.' But this approach was absolutely characteristic of his determination to understand every detail of the car he would race."

The highlights of the season came at Monaco, where Ayrton was only narrowly beaten into second place by Prost's McLaren as the race was flagged to a premature halt on a near-flooded track, and Estoril, where Ayrton took the Toleman TG184-Hart to a brilliant third place, behind a Prost-Lauda McLaren 1-2.

"Despite Senna crossing the line ahead of Prost, Clerk of the Course Jacky Ickx stopped the race so the order on the lap before gave victory to Prost," remembered Hawkridge. "My enthusiasm for F1 never recovered from that cruel blow. Brian deserved that win, as did the team."

Paradoxically, if Senna had won and the race had gone to its prescribed distance, it would have been better for Prost. As it was, Alain scored 4.5 points for a half-distance win. Second place in a full-distance race would have netted him six points. In those circumstances, he might well have gone on to win the World Championship by a single point – rather than lose it by half a point.

Above: **Alain Prost who was pipped to the 1984 title by just half a point.**

Above left: **Niki Lauda clinches the 1984 World Championship with second place, behind team-mate Prost in the Portuguese Grand Prix at Estoril.**

Left: **A youthful Aryton Senna holds Lauda's arm aloft in triumph on the podium after the Austrian's victory in the 1984 British Grand Prix. Senna finished in third place with the Toleman-Hart.**

Photos: Paul-Henri Cahier

McLAREN-TAGS SET THE AGENDA

At the start of the 1984 season, Niki Lauda suddenly found himself presented with an unexpected challenge. Instead of continuing to be paired with John Watson, a man whose qualities he knew well, he was joined in the McLaren squad by Alain Prost, who had been dropped by the Renault team after the World Championship debacle of 1983.

Prost later admitted that he had been signed by Dennis for a song, but that he had been happy to agree to the contract if it meant he could put the whole Renault episode behind him. Lauda now found himself up against a very fast and ambitious new partner. There would be plenty of hard work ahead.

The new McLaren MP4/2-TAGs proved to be the class of the field in 1984. They were fast and reliable, and handled well, all these qualities backed up by first-class standards of preparation on the part of McLaren International. In addition, the TAG V6s were adequately frugal when it came to fuel consumption, a major consideration in view of the ban on in-race refuelling and the reduction in maximum fuel capacity to 220 litres.

At the end of the day, Prost won seven races and Lauda five, but Niki took the championship by the wafer-thin margin of half a point. Thus between them, they won 12 of the season's 16 races, the only interlopers being Ferrari new boy Michele Alboreto, who triumphed in the Belgian Grand Prix at Zolder after the McLarens had suffered engine failures caused by fuel specification problems; Nelson Piquet, whose Brabham BT53 was victorious in Montreal and Detroit; and Keke Rosberg, who took the Williams FW09 – a veritable bucking bronco – to a memorable win in the one-off Dallas Grand Prix.

Continued on page 251

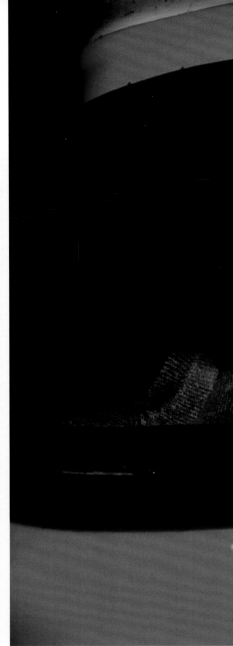

Above: **Nigel Mansell spent five years at Lotus without a victory. A switch to Williams would to change all that...**
Photo: Paul-Henri Cahier

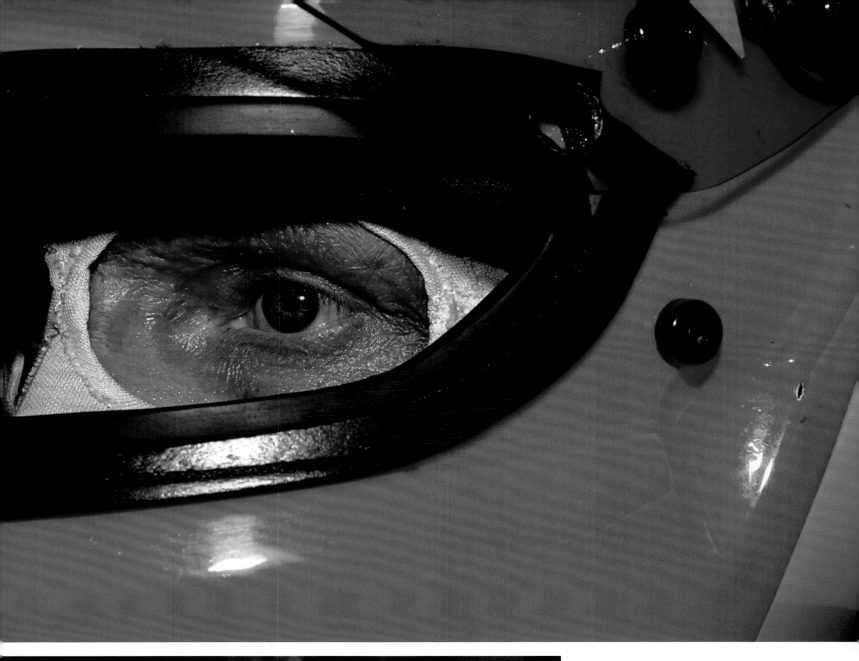

Above: Blue-eyed boy. Lost in thought, Niki Lauda gazes from his helmet.

Left: Stefan Bellof drove a stupendous race to finish third for Tyrrell in the 1983 Monaco GP, the dynamic German rising star closing on Prost and Senna all the way to the finish. Unfortunately, Tyrrell was excluded from the 1984 championship for a rule infringement.
Photos: Paul-Henri Cahier

WILLIAMS JOINS THE TURBO FRONT LINE

The 1985 season brought two developments of considerable significance for the Williams-Honda team: British driver Nigel Mansell was signed up to partner Keke Rosberg, and Patrick Head's engineering department produced its first carbon-fibre composite monocoque.

Williams was late in following the prevailing trend to carbon-fibre composite chassis construction, just as it had been late on the turbo bandwagon. This reflected a degree of natural caution on the part of Head, who wanted to be certain that Williams could remain on top of the engineering aspects of such developments when the decision was finally taken to make such a crucial change of direction.

"There were also aspects of the behaviour of certain carbon-fibre/honeycomb materials which I wasn't terribly impressed about," he explained.

"In addition, we had experienced two massive shunts with FW06 and FW07 monocoques – at Watkins Glen in 1978 when Alan Jones's car broke a hub shaft, and at Silverstone during testing in 1980, when Carlos Reutemann went straight into the vertical sleepers on the outside of Copse Corner – and had been extremely impressed with the way our aluminium monocoques had withstood the impacts.

"I had also always attempted to take a practical approach towards the cost involved in producing an F1 car, and I think in those days we were talking in terms of a cost increase of around 100 per cent between an aluminium and a carbon-fibre chassis.

"At that time, I had a tendency to say, 'Well, this may be a little bit nicer, but it will cost ten times as much, so we won't do it.' I had always tried to keep costs down to a reasonable level and was quite shocked when we had some carbon-fibre panels made for experimental purposes and, when I got the quote, it seemed absolutely astronomic.

"I think that made me a little bit wary about dealing with a sub-contractor from that point onwards, and I decided we would accumulate all the expertise in-house before embarking on a major carbon-fibre chassis development programme."

A total of nine moulded carbon-fibre composite Williams FW10 chassis were built during the course of the season. Rosberg would win at Detroit and Adelaide, sandwiching the first two victories of Mansell's F1 career at Brands Hatch (the Grand Prix of Europe) and Kyalami.

In the early part of the year, the FW10s were powered by modified 1984 D-spec Honda engines, but the revised E-spec arrived in time for Montreal, while a new six-speed transmission was used to handle the reputed 1000/1250bhp qualifying capability offered by the Japanese V6s.

At the end of the 1985 season, Rosberg moved to McLaren. He'd been cautious about having Mansell in the Williams team, having heard rumours that he was difficult to get on with, and by the time he found that his misgivings had been exaggerated, he was committed to making the change. To replace him, Frank Williams did a deal with Nelson Piquet for a reputed $3 million, wooing the Brazilian away from Bernie Ecclestone's Brabham team, which many had believed was his spiritual home.

For 1986, fuel capacity was restricted to 195 litres,

prompting Head to produce yet another brand-new turbo-car, the FW11, which would come to be regarded as the definitive Williams-Honda and would last to the end of the 1987 season. The FW11 design represented a turning point in the progress of the Williams team's design and manufacturing capability. Thanks to the benefits of a costly computer aided design/manufacturing system, the new Williams set fresh standards of detail finish and fit throughout the car.

Unfortunately Frank Williams would not be at the pit wall for the 1986 season. A couple of weeks prior to the Brazilian Grand Prix, the team principal was driving back to Nice airport after the final off-season test session at Paul Ricard when his Ford Sierra rental car crashed into a field. The team's public affairs manager, Peter Windsor, was a passenger in the car and emerged unhurt, but Frank sustained very serious back injuries that left him a tetraplegic and confined to a wheelchair to this day.

In 1985, the Williams-Hondas had flexed their muscles, but the McLaren-TAGs still had the upper hand. Prost was a model of consistency, adding victories in Brazil, Monaco, Britain, Austria and Italy to his mounting tally, and posting six other podium finishes. Despite losing another win at Imola, when his car was found to be underweight, he clinched his first World Championship with two races remaining, while Lauda rounded off his distinguished career with a fine victory in Holland.

In 1986, however, it was significantly different. The

Continued on page 254

Above: **A thoughtful Ayrton Senna scored the first of his 41 GP wins in atrocious conditions in the 1985 Portuguese GP at Estoril.**

Opposite: **Nigel Mansell takes his Williams FW10 through Paddock Bend in a shower of sparks on the way to his debut win in the 1985 European GP at Brands Hatch.**

Photos: Paul-Henri Cahier

251

Right: Elio de Angelis was a consistent finisher in his Lotus during the 1985 season with 11 top-six finishes.

Below: After coming so close in 1984, Alain Prost made no mistake the following year, taking five wins, including this one at Monaco.

Photos: Paul-Henri Cahier

Right: A switch to Michelin tyres marginalised Nelson Piquet and the Brabham team in 1985. A notable exception, however, was his win in the French Grand Prix, where the Italian rubber was unbeatable.

Opposite: Boom! Jonathan Palmer's Zakspeed blows a turbo.

Photos: Paul-Henri Cahier

Williams-Hondas took the initiative and would hold it through two glorious, Constructors' Championship winning seasons.

The smaller fuel cell of the FW11 enabled Williams to follow the trend of laying their drivers back into a semi-reclined driving position. The chassis was slightly longer than that of the FW10, as was its F-spec Honda PA 163-E engine. The Williams-Hondas could run consistently fast in race trim with the drivers instructed to adjust their turbo boost across four possible settings controlled from the cockpit.

According to Patrick Head, position one was a fuel conservation mode; two and three were race boosts at a higher or lower level; and position four was a 50/60bhp burst of 'overtaking boost' that could be used sparingly for very short periods. In practice, Mansell and Piquet usually juggled the settings between two and three during the course of a race. It says everything about the relative power/fuel efficiency of the Honda and TAG engines that Prost's McLaren finished the 1986 British Grand Prix at Brands Hatch in third place – but lapped by the victorious Mansell and Piquet.

With the help of fuel supplier Mobil's chemists, Honda was now pursuing the same route as that followed by Wintershall on BMW's behalf a couple of years earlier, opting for high-density aromatic 'hydrocarbon' fuels. A significant step towards Honda's increase in race power output to over 900bhp could be attributed to this development path, which helped the injection system to atomise its fuel more completely, ensuring that nothing was wasted in the cylinder's combustion chamber.

Meanwhile, Mansell developed into a natural winner. In 1986, he triumphed in the Belgian, Canadian, French, British and Portuguese Grands Prix, losing his grasp on the World Championship only when a rear tyre burst at 200mph on the back straight in the final race at Adelaide, when it seemed as though he had

it in the bag. Mansell would have to wait another six years before being crowned World Champion.

Mansell's misfortune should have handed the title to Piquet, but Nelson was called in for a precautionary tyre change. Ironically, he had no problems, but now had to settle for second in the race, behind Prost in the McLaren-TAG. Thus the Frenchman became the first title holder since Jack Brabham in 1960 to retain his crown with 72 points net to Mansell's 70 (net) and Piquet's 69. However, this was a season in which the all-conquering McLaren International squad experienced a major internal shift of emphasis, with chief designer John Barnard leaving the organisation he had helped establish more than five years earlier.

The 1986 season was also marked by the final victory for the four-cylinder BMW turbocharged engine, which powered Gerhard Berger to a good win in Mexico City, where his Pirelli tyres enabled him to enjoy a non-stop run, in contrast to most of his rivals. This was also the maiden Grand Prix victory for the Benetton team, which had its roots in the British Toleman F1 operation. By the start of 1985, Toleman was finding the financial burden of Grand Prix racing increasingly onerous, and the team faced that season without a tyre contract. Eventually it bought the tiny Spirit organisation's tyre contract and recruited Benetton as a major sponsor, but at the end of the year, the Italian clothing company bought the team outright.

Despite the impressive pace of the Williams-Hondas in 1986, it had been only a few races into the season before Piquet began to get very irritated over his status within the team. He firmly believed that he'd been guaranteed full number-one status and that Mansell should play second fiddle. This misunderstanding, if you like, eventually caused a breach between Nelson and Williams at the end of 1987.

"What Nelson thought he was being guaranteed was a repeat of the Reutemann fiasco of 1981, when

Above: Britsh Grand Prix, 13th July, 1986. Nigel Mansell and Nelson Piquet battle for the lead in their Williams FW11-Hondas. Such was their dominance that they lapped third-placed Alain Prost's McLaren.

Left: Exhilaration for Mansell on the podium following his Brands win.

Far left: The Detroit skyline gave a different dimension to the classic European tracks. Eddie Cheever (substituting for regular Patrick Tambay) prepares for the coming action with his Beatrice Lola.

Photos: Paul-Henri Cahier

255

we controlled, or tried to control, the second driver," said Williams, recalling the way the Argentinian, who had been recruited as number two to Alan Jones, disobeyed team orders and won that year's Brazilian Grand Prix ahead of his team-mate.

"What in fact had been discussed was that, in a classic case of one driver leading the championship and needing every bit of support, then we would control his team-mate.

"But he was not given unconditional priority over the second driver. We took the view that if they were both in the running for the World Championship, they would have to fight it out between them."

Elsewhere on the F1 landscape, Renault's works team had shown dwindling form since Prost's departure at the end of 1983. Derek Warwick and Patrick Tambay took over the driving duties for the next two seasons, but neither managed to score a single victory, as the machinery was never quite up to the job.

With the impressive young Brazilian, Ayrton Senna,

moving to Lotus from Toleman at the start of 1985, it was clear that Renault would be better served by its prime customer, Lotus having used Renault turbo power with steadily increasing success since 1983, and the factory team withdrew from F1 at the end of the season. In 1986, Senna, who had won in Portugal and Belgium the previous year, posted eight pole positions, although he took maximum points only twice during the course of the season. One of these victories was a sensationally well-judged, split-second win over Nigel Mansell's Williams FW11 in the Spanish Grand Prix at Jerez, by what was officially the closest winning margin in F1 history.

For 1986, Renault Sport's chief engineer, Bernard Dudot, produced the first pneumatically activated valve gear system for the French V6. The saving in mass and weight enabled the engine's rev limit to be increased initially from 11,000 to 12,000rpm, but later to over 13,000rpm, which would hand Senna around 900bhp in race trim.

For qualifying purposes, Lotus would use the EFI5-spec Renault V6 with water injection and its turbo waste gates blanked off, the engine surviving concentrated bursts of 5-bar over-boost to catapult Ayrton to the front of the grid on so many occasions. With sparks cascading from its undertray as it scraped the ground to gain the maximum possible downforce, and with a haze of unburnt hydrocarbons trailing ominously in its wake, the all-black Lotus 98T with its brilliant yellow-helmeted driver strapped in behind the wheel projected a formidable image of suppressed menace and power.

PIQUET TAKES THIRD WORLD CHAMPIONSHIP

Nelson Piquet liked nothing more than working with his engineers to develop a technical edge over his rivals, and the Brazilian driver had to pull every ounce of strategic know-how out of the bag to win the 1987 World Championship.

Top: **After emerging as contenders for the 1985 World Championship, Michele Alboreto and Ferrari were left struggling in 1986.**

Above: **Brabham also dropped the ball with the troublesome BT55 lowline chassis. Bernie Ecclestone oversees operations on Riccardo Patrese's car at Spa.**

Left: **Derek Warwick, a doughty competitor who never quite got the right drive at the right time.**

Photos: Paul-Henri Cahier

Armed with the revised Williams FW11B, Piquet knew his biggest opposition would come from his team-mate, Nigel Mansell. It seemed as though the Englishman had the early advantage, winning the San Marino Grand Prix at Imola with relative ease after Piquet had been sidelined on medical advice after crashing heavily during practice due to a tyre failure.

Mansell won again in the French Grand Prix at Paul Ricard, following that up with a dynamic chase through the field at Silverstone to pass Nelson after a brilliant double-bluff manoeuvre going into Stowe Corner on the penultimate lap. This was Mansell at his absolute best, wringing the last drop of speed from a dominant racing car in front of his adoring home crowd. Those who took in the shell-shocked expression on Piquet's face at the post-race press conference were in no way surprised when he announced that he would be switching to Lotus the following year.

Yet this was not the end of the matter. Piquet bounced back with wins at Hockenheim and Budapest, took second to Mansell in Austria, then won the Italian Grand Prix at Monza through sheer cleverness.

Williams was developing its own 'reactive' suspension system – what might be described as a simplified version of the computer controlled 'active' system being used by Ayrton Senna in the rival Honda-engine Lotus 99T – and Nelson reckoned it would give him an advantage at Monza. Honda was now supplying its very powerful V6 turbo engines to Lotus, since Renault had withdrawn from all engine supply contracts at the end of the previous year.

Unhappy experiences with the prototype Lotus active system in its early years had left Mansell feeling rather cool towards such accessories, so the Englishman opted for the standard car, but Nelson took the gamble. Piquet was pretty sure of what he was about.

The week before, he had completed a race distance at Imola over a minute faster than Mansell's winning average three months earlier.

In the end, Piquet won the World Championship because Mansell crashed out in practice at Suzuka and missed the last two races. Even so, he had finished with Williams.

"I didn't come into this team to compete with another driver," he said. "I had a contract as number-one driver and they screwed up the whole thing. Technically they were the best team I worked with, but I didn't join them to apply my experience to setting up cars for a team-mate who then made it difficult for me to win races."

FERRARI BACK IN THE WINNER'S CIRCLE

Meanwhile, Ferrari had been struggling to get back into the winner's circle, last occupied for the team by Michele Alboreto at the 1985 German Grand Prix at the rebuilt Nürburgring.

Enzo Ferrari had personally sanctioned the dramatic steps planned to shake the whole organisation back into some semblance of order. After John Barnard left his post as chief designer with McLaren in the summer of 1986, the elderly patriarch gave the British engineer the green light to establish his own Ferrari design studio in the UK.

In his new role as technical director of the Ferrari team, one of Barnard's main priorities was the development of a brand-new car for the 3.5-litre naturally aspirated regulations, which would come into force at the start of 1989. As far as the future of the 1.5-litre turbocharged project was concerned, he had arrived a little late in the day to have much of an impact on the F1/87, which was the handiwork of engineer Gustav Brunner.

Above: **Nelson Piquet (6) just managed to out-fox his Williams team-mate Nigel Mansell to take his third World Championship in 1987.**

Top left: **Fingertip control. The gear shift of the McLaren, as polished as Alain Prost driving.**

Left: **Benetton's Gerhard Berger emerged as the find of the 1986 season. Here the Austrian works his Pirelli's at Spa.**

Photo: Paul-Henri Cahier

NELSON PIQUET: BRAIN BAFFLES BRAVADO

NELSON Piquet was the sort of driver who relished going on to the Grand Prix starting grid secure in the knowledge that he secretly harboured a technical advantage that might give him a crucial performance edge over his rivals. In that respect, the Brazilian driver, who had been born in Rio on 17th August, 1952, was one of the most cerebral of World Champions. During testing, for example, he would always be working at developing the best car set-up for the race, rather than aiming for the out-and-out fastest lap time he could manage.

Like his compatriot, Ayrton Senna, Piquet would win three World Championships during a Grand Prix career that spanned 204 races from 1978 to 1991. His father had been keen for him to develop his talent for tennis, packing him off to California during his teenage years for a programme of intensive coaching. Yet the attraction of karts, cars and motorcycles exerted an overwhelming pull on the young Brazilian and ultimately would shape his personal ambitions.

Piquet initially made his mark in the Brazilian national Formula Super Vee series before setting out for Europe, where he finished third in the 1977 European Formula 3 Championship. The following year, he switched to the British F3 scene, winning no fewer than 13 races and clinching the BP Championship.

He made his F1 debut in the 1978 German Grand Prix at Hockenheim, at the wheel of an Ensign; drove a private McLaren M23 in the Austrian, Dutch and Italian races; and then joined the works Brabham-Alfa team alongside Niki Lauda and John Watson for the final Grand Prix of the year in Montreal.

In 1979, Piquet replaced Watson as Lauda's team-mate in Bernie Ecclestone's Brabham squad. The team struggled with Alfa Romeo V12 engines for

much of the season before Bernie decided that they were really getting nowhere. He took the decision to switch to Cosworth Ford V8 power, the new Brabham BT49 proving competitive from the outset.

At virtually the same moment, Nelson found himself unexpectedly propelled into the role of team leader when Lauda decided, abruptly and with immediate effect, to retire midway through first practice for the 1979 Canadian Grand Prix. Thereafter Nelson would, unconsciously perhaps, mould the Brabham team around him. He got on well with chief designer Gordon Murray and all the mechanics, being very much one of the boys. His first Grand Prix victory came in Long Beach in 1980, and he followed it up with further wins in the Dutch and Italian Grands Prix. He finished second in the World Championship, losing out to Williams driver Alan Jones in the final race of the season.

The following year, Piquet bagged his first title, edging out an overwrought Carlos Reutemann in a torrid finale beneath the scorching Nevada sun in Las Vegas. In 1982, the Brabham squad switched from Ford V8 to BMW turbo power, heralding a mechanically troubled year with only a single win for Piquet. Yet his shrewd commitment to the Brabham-BMW development programme would reap rewards in 1983, when he snatched his second World Championship after a down-to-the-wire confrontation with Alain Prost and the factory Renault team.

This peak of achievement was followed by two relatively bleak seasons and, frustrated by Brabham's fruitless switch to Pirelli rubber in 1985, allied to Ecclestone's reluctance to pay him what he believed was his market value, Piquet stunned the F1 world by announcing a change of team for 1986.

Bernie might not have been willing to hike his pay from $1.1 million to $3 million, but Frank Williams certainly was. Thus Nelson switched to the Williams-Honda squad alongside Nigel Mansell.

Piquet relished the performance edge offered by the Williams-Hondas in 1986 and 1987, but was less impressed with Mansell's unwillingness to fulfil a supporting role. Nelson believed he had been promised number-one status, but in fact his contract stipulated equal treatment and priority access to the spare car. Nothing more.

In 1986, both Piquet and Mansell were pipped by McLaren rival Alain Prost in the battle for the championship, a state of affairs that left the Brazilian driver feeling particularly irked. His tactical and strategic approach would duly pay off with a third world title in 1987, but he was no happier with the Williams way of operating and moved to Lotus in 1988, taking the Honda engine contract with him.

Unfortunately the Lotus 100T proved no match for the dominant McLaren-Hondas of Alain Prost and Ayrton Senna. In 1989, Lotus lost its Honda engine supply and Piquet suddenly found himself slumping to the role of a midfield runner, forced to use uncompetitive Judd V8s.

Another change of team was needed. In 1990 and 1991, he switched to Benetton, winning three more races and benefiting from a bonus system that paid him $100,000 per championship point scored. He recorded his final win in the 1991 Canadian Grand Prix, after which his front-line racing career came to a painful end when he crashed heavily during practice for the 1992 Indianapolis 500, sustaining extensive foot injuries from which, happily, he made a full recovery.

In 1987, the performance of the cars was further capped by a restriction of turbo boost pressure to 4 bar in conjunction with a fuel capacity maximum of 195 litres. For the new season, Ferrari discarded its long-serving 120-degree V6 and replaced it with a 90-degree (Tipo 033) unit transmitting its power through a longitudinal gearbox.

The new engine was eclipsed by the front-line Honda opposition, but then that was a fate shared with just about every other F1 powerplant in 1987. What worsened Ferrari's plight, however, was the mechanical unreliability displayed by the new V6.

Barnard found himself spending too much time fiddling about with the 1987 car, when he should have been toiling away on the new 3.5-litre project. Coincidentally, Michele Alboreto became vastly disillusioned over the manner in which Barnard, in his opinion, was trying to operate like "a brain surgeon attempting a complicated operation over the telephone" from his base in England.

This confrontation between the willful Italian driver and the single-minded British designer came to a head at Hockenheim over the German Grand Prix weekend. Thanks to Ferrari's inclination towards believing anything and everything its senior management read in the media, Alboreto's remarks to *L'Équipe*, the French sporting newspaper, resulted in Barnard being hauled over to Germany for what amounted to a time wasting trial by press.

Despite all these distractions, by the end of the season, Ferrari was beginning to get itself under control again. Gerhard Berger – signed from Benetton at the start of the season – would have won the Portuguese GP at Estoril, had he not spun off under pressure from Prost's McLaren. But the Austrian made up for this with a superb victory in the revived Japanese GP at Suzuka, a race from which Alboreto also emerged with considerable credit, having climbed through to fourth place after his clutch had gone solid at the start, causing him to stall the car and then get away last after a push-start.

Ferrari's first win in almost two-and-a-half years brought to an end the team's longest spell in F1 without a race victory. Berger immediately repeated this with a similarly impressive win in the Australian GP at Adelaide, Alboreto taking second after Ayrton Senna's Lotus-Honda, the original runner-up, was disqualified for a rule infringement relating to extra brake cooling ducts that had been fitted especially for the race.

The McLaren-TAGs reached their sell-by date in 1987, but Prost scored three more race wins to take his career total to 28 victories. At last, Jackie Stewart's record of 27 wins, which had stood since 1973, had been broken.

Opposite: **Nelson Piquet who, having clinched his third World Championship at Williams in 1987, decamped to Lotus – along with the Honda engines.**

Below: **Satoro Nakajima, who was part of the Honda package with Lotus.**
Photos: Paul-Henri Cahier

CHAPTER TEN: 1988–93
SENNA VERSUS PROST

Class of the field: the McLaren-Honda MP4/4s of Ayrton Senna and Alain Prost surge into the first right-hander at the start of the 1988 Portuguese Grand Prix at Estoril, while Ivan Capelli's Leyton House-Judd leads the pursuing pack.

Photo: Paul-Henri Cahier

Above: **A new F1 era dawned as Ayrton Senna and McLaren begin a fabulously successful partnership.**

Opposite: **A Honda technician fettles one of the Japanese car maker's 1.5-litre V6 turbo engines installed in Prost's McLaren MP4/4.**

Photos: Paul-Henri Cahier

McLAREN-HONDA achieved a stranglehold on Formula 1 during the final season of turbo competition and the early years of the 3.5-litre formula, but the bitter rivalry between Ayrton Senna and Alain Prost ensured that interest in Grand Prix racing had never been greater. Squeezed out of McLaren by the Brazilian, Prost waged a fierce, but ultimately unsuccessful battle to retain the crown after switching to Ferrari in 1990 and eventually captured his fourth title following a move to Williams-Renault in 1993.

Meanwhile, there had been a spectacular advance in the use of high technology, fuelled by the cash available from major sponsors and the motor industry, with the result that computer controlled driver aids were beginning to usurp the role of the driver.

After three seasons with Lotus, Senna had decided to move on for 1988. The young Brazilian had forged a unique collaborative bond with Honda, and the Japanese car maker was keen to continue working with him. That meant that he would either have to go to Williams, to replace 1987 World Champion Nelson Piquet, or move to McLaren, which had clinched a deal to use Honda power in place of its previous TAG V6s.

This was a classic case of F1 musical chairs, and even the most casual observer could work out that three into two would leave somebody dejected on the sidelines. In the event, it was Williams who lost the Honda engines, despite the fact that it had a firm contract through to the end of 1988.

McLAREN-HONDAS DOMINATE FINAL TURBO SEASON

Williams was told it could keep its Honda engines as long as it agreed to have Japanese driver Satoru Nakajima in the second car. Frank Williams and Patrick Head were not interested and chose to go it alone with naturally aspirated Judd V8s in what would be a transitional season between the turbo and new non-turbo eras. Piquet's popularity with Honda ensured that Lotus retained its engine deal when the Brazilian moved there from Williams. McLaren, of course, won on all fronts.

The 1988 season would see two different types of car competing in the FIA Formula 1 World Championship, both qualifying equally for points in both the drivers' and constructors' title battles. On the one hand, a team could choose to run under the 3.5-litre naturally aspirated rules to a 500kg minimum weight limit, a formula that would become obligatory the following season. On the other, it could opt for a final fling with the 1.5-litre turbos. Many people believed they hadn't got a chance, restricted as they were by a 2.5-bar boost limitation, a 150-litre maximum fuel capacity and a 540kg minimum weight limit.

One such individual was FISA President Jean-Marie Balestre, who, speaking at a meeting at Estoril in late 1986 to announce this interim season, made a remark that matched anything a professional politician could have produced in its capacity for being wide of the mark.

Right: Boy with a new toy. Gerhard Berger replaced Stefan Johansson at Ferrari for 1988.

Below: The arrival of Gerhard Berger and John Barnard had the secondary effect of making Michele Alboreto feel distinctly unwanted at Maranello, and the Italian driver soon headed for the exit door.

Photos: Paul-Henri Cahier

"I promise you, gentlemen, in 1988, no way for the turbos," said Balestre. He would have been correct in that prediction had it not been for the McLaren-Hondas. They won 15 out of the season's 16 races. If they hadn't been there, the laurels would have been pretty evenly spread between naturally aspirated and turbocharged machinery. But they were.

Ironically, there was one team that might have challenged McLaren, had it made subtly different arrangements for its 1988 engine supply deal. At the start of 1987, the Benetton team had decided to switch from BMW to Ford power, taking over supplies of the Cosworth-built 120-degree V6 turbo that had been used by the Haas Lola team the previous season. Although not the most obviously powerful of the turbo generation, its wide cylinder angle enabled it to be packaged extremely tightly within the B187 chassis, which made for a notably effective aerodynamic profile.

Additional development progress was made with the Ford turbo throughout the 1987 season, during which Italy's Teo Fabi was joined in the driver line-up by Thierry Boutsen, the popular Belgian replacing Gerhard Berger, who had gone off to Ferrari. Boutsen and Fabi both made it to lower placings on the rostrum during the course of the season, finishing eighth and ninth in the drivers' championship, and helping the team to earn 28 points – and fifth place – in the constructors' contest.

It is a matter of debate just how close the Ford V6 turbo came to winning its first Grand Prix in a Benetton. Nobody will ever know, because its development was brought to an abrupt halt by the latest change in the F1 engine regulations. The days of the turbo had suddenly become numbered, and naturally aspirated engines, this time of 3.5 litres capacity, which had been re-admitted to F1 in 1987, would be the only permitted power source from 1989 onwards.

Ford decided to concentrate its resources on developing the new naturally aspirated Cosworth DFR, and it was this engine that was supplied to Benetton in 1988. With hindsight, the team would have done better to have stuck with the turbo, even under the restrictive new regulations.

Had Benetton used the Ford turbo in 1988, it is quite possible that Honda would not have enjoyed the performance advantage that helped the McLaren team to dominate the World Championship.

Of course, in 1988, McLaren didn't go into battle with just the benefit of Honda engines. By recruiting Senna to drive alongside Prost, it had also assembled one of the very strongest driver line-ups ever seen in F1. However, the rivalry between the two men developed to an uncomfortable level of intensity: they were too different, yet too similar, at one and the same moment. Prost eventually came to believe that his position in the team was being undermined, but Senna

Above: **Ayrton Senna heads for victory in the 1988 Hungarian GP. Prost took second place in this race to give McLaren its seventh 1-2 finish in the first ten races of that season.**
Photo: **Paul-Henri Cahier**

ALAIN Prost combined mental astuteness and considerable speed with an economy of physical effort behind the wheel. He ran hard and fast, but like Niki Lauda – his teenage hero – he let the car do as much of the work as possible.

Prost always performed when it really mattered. Within three laps of the start of his first F1 test at Paul Ricard in late 1979, he was right on the pace, and McLaren team manager Teddy Mayer was rummaging through his briefcase, looking for a draft contract and a pen.

First time around, he stayed just a single year at McLaren. Unfortunately it would be 1981, before McLaren International, a revised and revamped company motivated and shaped by the ambitious Ron Dennis, began to play a significant role on the Grand Prix scene. By then, Prost was committed to a three-year deal with the Renault works team.

In 1983, Alain came close to the World Championship, but it slipped from his grasp in the closing races of the year as rival BMW raised the engine development stakes and provided Nelson Piquet's works Brabham with more power. Renault failed to respond to this obvious challenge and lost the title at the last Grand Prix of the season in South Africa.

Cast as the fall guy for this failure, Prost returned to McLaren in 1984, prepared to take peanuts from Ron Dennis as long as it got him away from Renault. He and his McLaren-TAG team-mate, Niki Lauda, carved up that season between them. Prost won seven races, Lauda five. Yet it was Niki who took the championship by the slender margin of half a point.

Prost had arrived at McLaren with nine Grand Prix victories under his belt. He finished 1984 with 16 to his credit and added another five in 1985, when he finally became France's first World Champion. He would retain the title in 1986, although he needed a bit of bad luck to strike at the more powerful rival Williams-Hondas of Nigel Mansell and Nelson Piquet to do so. In the event, Alain dodged through to win the championship at the last race of the year.

By 1987, the McLaren-TAG was past its best Even so, Alain's third win that season was his 28th, making him the most successful Grand Prix driver to date, eclipsing Jackie Stewart's record of 27 wins, which had endured since 1973. His final tally stood at 51 victories, and his position at the head of the all-time winner's list looked unlikely to be challenged... Until Michael Schumacher and Ferrari rewrote the record books.

The 1988 season witnessed another critical sea change at McLaren. The team signed a long-term deal to use Honda engines, and Ayrton Senna joined Prost to produce the most formidable line-up on the contemporary Grand Prix scene. Suddenly Alain found himself in exactly the same situation as that in which he had put Niki Lauda, back in 1984.

At the end of the season, Senna won the World Championship with eight wins to Prost's seven. The two drivers continued together in 1989, only for their personal relationship to fall apart after Senna apparently reneged on a no-overtaking agreement on the opening lap at Imola. Tensions between the two men increased, and Prost decided to leave at the end of the season to join Nigel Mansell at Ferrari. But not before he'd clinched his third title following a controversial collision between the two McLaren drivers in the Japanese Grand Prix.

Sadly Prost's initially successful partnership with Maranello became seriously unravelled in 1991. Mansell had left the team at the end of the previous season, and Prost found it difficult to work with team manager Cesare Fiorio. The team had a poor year, and this, combined with some intemperate remarks to the media,

resulted in Prost being dismissed with one race still to run.

He sat out the following season, but he still wanted to race. Renault and Elf, his old partners, were keen to get him back behind the wheel of a front-running car, and in 1993 he was signed up to drive a Williams-Renault.

Prost rounded off what would be his final season in Formula 1 with victories in the South African, San Marino, Spanish, Canadian, French, British and German Grands Prix. His new team-mate, Damon Hill, certainly put him under pressure, but inevitably Alain seemed capable of pulling a little extra out of the bag every time he looked seriously challenged.

He retired largely because he didn't want to be paired with Senna again in 1994. The two men even discussed it by telephone, Ayrton urging Alain that, this time, it might work out; Alain thought otherwise.

Clearly it gave Alain considerable satisfaction that he and Senna seemed to be approaching a personal rapprochement on the day prior to the Brazilian's fatal accident at Imola in the 1994 San Marino Grand Prix. It was as if they had both suddenly realised the truth of the previous ten years. Each had been feeding off the other to sustain his competitive instinct and passion behind the wheel.

simply regarded his confrontational stance as a pragmatic means by which he could stamp his identity on the McLaren team.

In the run-up to the new partnership with Honda, the McLaren team also reorganised its technical department. Former Brabham chief designer Gordon Murray was recruited to handle the management and administration side of the design process, leaving Steve Nichols free to become project leader of the design team that would produce the 1988 season challenger, the MP4/4.

From a structural standpoint, the carbon-fibre composite chassis of the latest McLaren was subject to fresh design requirements. Under revised safety regulations applicable from the start of 1988, the foot pedals had to be drawn back by 20cm from their previous position to put the driver's feet behind the front wheel centre-line. However, this was offset by the shorter centre section required to accommodate the 150-litre fuel cell, resulting in a modest overall 4cm increase in the wheelbase of the 1987 chassis.

More than ever, in 1988, the McLaren hallmark was attention to minute detail, but the engine was perhaps the key factor in the team's success, although it also had the advantage of Prost and Senna in the driving seats and a much better chassis than the similarly powered Lotus 101 driven by Piquet and Nakajima.

Honda's new 'XE2' and 'XE3' twin-turbo V6s offered better economy or enhanced top-end performance respectively, depending on the circuit require-

ments. Honda attempted to improve its turbo response by the use of ceramic turbine wheels, and opted for a 79 x 50.8mm bore and stroke in conjunction with a 9.4:1 compression ratio and near-flat-headed pistons, which made a major contribution to the sought-after fuel efficiency.

The engines incorporated a new small-diameter clutch, which enabled the Japanese company to build them lower, dropping the crankshaft centre-line a full 28mm from its 1987 level. McLaren matched this development by producing a three-axis gearbox that raised the drive line sufficiently to facilitate the use of an upswept, aerodynamic rear under-tray, in addition to reducing potentially wearing driveshaft angularity.

Honda's engine management system was refined to fresh levels of efficiency on this latest V6, air intake temperatures being of absolutely paramount importance to its efficient functioning. The temperature of the air flowing into the engine was regulated to as close to 40°C as possible by opening the intercooler's bypass valve at the appropriate moment. In addition, there was a temperature control system that utilised a heat exchanger fed by water from the cooling system, the flow through the exchanger being controlled by a solenoid valve.

The amount of fuel remaining in the McLaren's tanks at any point while racing was calculated by computer and displayed to the driver, enabling Senna and Prost to select the correct balance of boost pressure, intake air temperature, fuel temperature and air/fuel mix

Left: **Alain Prost may have been a four-times World Champion, but this photograph captures the Frenchman in a somewhat introspective and sombre mood.**

Below: **The turbochargers on the Honda engine (silver, in foreground) were almost as large as the V6 itself.**
Photos: Paul-Henri Cahier

GNOLO

during the course of the race. Even in conditions of marginal fuel consumption, this latest Honda RA163-E variant produced around 630bhp, still about 40bhp more than the best of the naturally aspirated cars.

During that remarkable final season of turbo competition, Ayrton Senna won eight races, Alain Prost seven. The World Championship battle went right down to the penultimate race of the season, Senna finally clinching the title with a decisive victory over the Frenchman in the Japanese Grand Prix at Suzuka.

McLaren boss Ron Dennis has had great drivers before and since, but there has never been anything that has come close to the high-tension static that positively crackled between the ascetic Brazilian and his French colleague. When Senna arrived in the McLaren enclave at the start of 1988, Dennis might have believed he was a good team player; the reality was that he was anything but that. Senna, a charismatic combination of towering ego, presence and talent, simply dominated every F1 team for which he drove.

Prost had been McLaren's 'baby', the sitting tenant ever since the start of 1984. During that first season with the revamped team, the Frenchman had shown a thing or two to Niki Lauda about dodging through gaps in traffic. Four years later, the driving boot was very firmly on the other foot.

By 1988, Prost had become the seasoned campaigner, unwilling to put everything on the line for a kamikaze qualifying lap, risking all by going for gaps that might close before he got to them. But the Frenchman judged that he would be able to match Senna on race-craft and tactics, if not on sheer qualifying speed.

It proved to be an electrifying season and, although it passed more or less without incident, the relationship between the two drivers was certainly far from harmonious. Whereas Prost favoured a calm and sympathetic team environment, Senna thrived on tension and confrontation as a means of heightening his competitive edge.

Alain found the whole experience extremely stressful, but Ayrton clearly revelled in every minute of it.

By the time they arrived at the 1988 Portuguese Grand Prix, Prost was beginning to fight back after Senna had won four straight races through July and August. And it was at Estoril that things very nearly became physical between the two McLaren drivers.

Senna got it into his head that Prost had squeezed him out towards the left-hand kerb as they sprinted to the first corner, although a quick glance at the TV tapes revealed that the Frenchman – as you'd expect – had done nothing out of the ordinary. Never mind, Ayrton led from the second start, the race having been stopped due to a startline shunt among the tail-enders, only for Alain to come swooping out of his slipstream at 170mph as they came past the pits at the end of the opening lap.

Amazingly, Senna lunged to the right and tried to pincer his so-called team-mate against the pit wall, but Prost kept his foot hard on the throttle and forced his way through, the pit signal boards being hastily pulled back for fear of actually hitting the roll-over bar on the Frenchman's car.

Make no mistake, this was crassly dangerous driving on Senna's part. Yet neither the stewards nor the McLaren management, for some reason cowed by the sheer force of Senna's character, opted to intervene.

After winning the race, Prost tore Senna off a strip behind the closed doors of the team's motorhome. "I hadn't appreciated you were prepared to die to win the World Championship," he told the startled Brazilian. Later he added to a friend, "If he wants the title that badly, he can have it."

Senna duly won the championship that year, and the two men stayed together as McLaren team-mates in 1989. Yet if a fragile peace had existed between them in 1988, now it was torn asunder after what Prost regarded as Senna's brazen duplicity.

SENNA AND PROST AT EACH OTHER'S THROATS

For the 1989 San Marino Grand Prix at Imola, Prost suggested to Senna a first-lap no-passing pact: whoever made the best start in their 3.5-litre Honda RAI09E V10-engine McLaren MP4/5 should lead through the uphill left-hander at Tosa, after which they would be free to race unfettered. Ayrton agreed.

At the start, Senna got away first, but the race was stopped after only four laps following a huge accident involving Gerhard Berger's Ferrari, from which the Austrian driver was lucky to emerge with only superficial injuries. After a delay, the race was restarted. This time, Prost got the jump on the Brazilian, but Senna

slipstreamed past him on the run down to Tosa in apparent breach of their private agreement. The blue touch paper had been well and truly ignited.

Prost confronted Senna and again gave him a dressing down. He was not, he told him, a man whose word could be relied on. Ron Dennis was understandably keen to nip this confrontation in the bud and engineered a meeting between the two men during a test at Pembrey the following week.

Senna was persuaded to apologise, fighting back tears of frustration as he did so. But the relationship was long gone. Before Monaco, the next race on the calendar, Prost gave an interview to *L'Équipe* in which he said, "At a level of technical discussion, I shall not close the door completely, but for the rest I no longer wish to have any business with him. I appreciate honesty and he is not honest."

The ultimate embarrassment for McLaren came later that year when the two drivers, once again locked in a fierce struggle for the World Championship as the season neared its climax, collided while battling for the lead of the Japanese Grand Prix. Prost, who had removed the tail strip from his car's rear wing only moments before the parade lap in the interests of straight-line speed, led from the start and seemed to have the edge. But Ayrton produced a superhuman lap to haul up on to his tail as they approached the tight chicane before the start/finish straight with only six of the race's 53 laps to go.

It had to happen. Senna braked incredibly late, two wheels shaving the grass on the inside. But Prost wasn't having it. As Ayrton kept coming, the Frenchman – who by now had had enough of his intimidation – closed the door. The two cars skidded to an interlocked halt in the middle of the track.

Prost hopped out and walked away. Senna beckoned for the marshals to help restart his car and accelerated

back into the race through the chicane. Later he was disqualified. McLaren made an unsuccessful appeal, and the whole episode degenerated into a morass of bitterness and recrimination. Prost would become World Champion as a result

Twelve months later, with Alain now driving for Ferrari, Senna would exact his revenge by ramming him deliberately off the road at 130mph on the first corner of the race. The FIA stewards did nothing, nor again did the McLaren management. It was one of motor racing's most outrageous scandals, made all the more pathetic by the idiotic apologies offered for Senna's behaviour by many leading lights within the sport who should have known better.

Less than four years later, on the eve of Senna's death at Imola, the two men seemed to have achieved a genuine rapprochement. Prost, by now retired, had returned as a television commentator. For Ayrton, it was as if the penny had dropped, as if he'd suddenly realised just how much of his motivation behind the wheel had come from trying to beat the little French-

man with the crooked nose when they were rivals on the track.

Throughout this enthralling period, it was almost as if every other driver had been pushed to the sidelines in some sort of supporting role. Even Nigel Mansell, who left Williams after a frustrating 1988 season struggling with the 3.5-litre Judd V8 engine, had to wait until the sunset years of the McLaren-Honda alliance before he could get a serious look in.

Mansell joined Ferrari in 1989 and celebrated his arrival with a fortuitous win in the Brazilian Grand Prix at Rio, armed with the John Barnard-designed Ferrari 640 complete with its 3.5-litre naturally aspirated V12 engine and electro-hydraulic automatic gearchange. That season he would also win superbly in Hungary, where he beat Senna's McLaren MP4/5 into second place after a great fight. Berger would add another victory in Portugal in September, but shortly afterwards it was announced that Barnard would be leaving the team.

Continued on page 276

SENNA ON TECHNIQUE

Ayrton Senna put more mental firepower into his driving technique than possibly any other F1 competitor of his era. In the 1990–1991 edition of AUTOCOURSE, he graphically described to the late Denis Jenkinson just how much intensity and personal focus were required for his breathtaking pole-position lap at the 1988 Monaco Grand Prix at the wheel of the McLaren MP4/4-Honda.

"Monte Carlo, 1988, qualifying. What happened was that we had race tyres, not qualifying tyres, so it was lap after lap, not just one lap. We had the turbo car. I went out, had a good lap, another lap. I was on pole, then the next lap with a bigger margin, and I was going more and more and more and more.

"I got to the stage when I was over two seconds faster than anybody, including my teammate [Alain Prost], who was using the same car, same engine, everything. That was the direct comparison and over two seconds. It wasn't because he was going slow, but because I was going too fast. I felt at one point that the circuit was no longer really a circuit, just a tunnel of Armco. But in such a way that I suddenly realised that I was over the level that I considered … reasonable. There was no margin whatsoever, in anything.

"When I had that feeling, I immediately lifted. I didn't have to, because I was still going. I immediately lifted. Then I felt that I was on a different level. I didn't fully understand that level and I still don't understand it a bit better, but I'm still far away from satisfying my own needs as to how it works in that [mental] band.

"So I backed off and came slowly into the pits. I said to myself, 'Today that is special. Don't go out any more. You are vulnerable. For whatever reason, you are putting yourself in a situation where you are doing it more in a subconscious way.'

"I could not really cope with that in a manner that I could find easy."

Above: Alessandro Nannini's Benetton-Ford seen against a typical backdrop at the Autodromo Enzo y Dino Ferrari, long-time home of the San Marino GP.

Left: Alain Prost won the 1989 World Championship and promptly took his number 1 to Ferrari.

Right: Johnny Herbert, still recovering from his appalling leg injuries, put in some gritty performances for Benetton before being dropped. Note the bike to aid him around the paddock.

Photos: Paul-Henri Cahier

Top: After a year out of Formula 1, Martin Brundle returned with the Brabham team.

Above: Brundle's team-mate, Italian Formula 3 hot-shot Stefano Modena, had loads of talent, but was ultimately found wanting in the Grand Prix cauldron.

Left: Nigel Mansell's switch to Ferrari was sensational, *'Il Leone'* winning for the team at the first time of asking in Brazil.

Photos: Paul-Henri Cahier

PROST AND MANSELL IN CONFLICT

Prost won the 1989 World Championship with 76 points (net) to Senna's 60, while Riccardo Patrese wound up third on 40 points during the first year of the nascent Williams-Renault partnership, using the French company's 3.5-litre V10, which had been quietly developed behind the scenes ever since the 1.5-litre turbo project had been shelved at the end of 1986.

Having tired of the tensions involved in being Senna's team-mate, Prost decided to switch to the Ferrari team in 1990 to partner Mansell, while Berger moved in the other direction to take on what would prove to be very much a number-two seat in the McLaren-Honda squad.

Prost and Mansell were a volatile pairing, particularly as everything seemed to go the Frenchman's way during the first half of the season. By the time they arrived at Silverstone for the British Grand Prix, Prost had already won three races and would bag his fourth on Nigel's home soil when the Englishman's gearbox went haywire after he had qualified superbly in pole position and led commandingly in the early stages. In a knee-jerk response to his disappointment, Mansell announced that he would retire from racing at the end of the year.

Thereafter, everything went wrong for Mansell. He retired an only lightly damaged car at Hockenheim; hurt his wrist in a silly collision with Berger's McLaren in Hungary; and then trailed around in midfield after being forced to take the spare car following a first-corner shunt that caused the Belgian GP to be red-flagged at the end of the opening lap.

What happened next was that Ferrari negotiated for Jean Alesi to replace Mansell in 1991. Once that was tied up, the British driver announced that he had changed his mind about retirement – largely due to overwhelming pressure from his adoring fans – and signed for Williams. Prost, meanwhile, found his position in the Ferrari team undermined when Mansell, in his view at least, ganged up with Senna to thwart his efforts in the Portuguese GP at Estoril.

At the start, Mansell's pole-position Ferrari 641 veered across in front of Prost, allowing Senna to take an immediate lead. Ayrton eventually finished second, behind Nigel, with Alain third.

"Ferrari doesn't deserve to be World Champion," said the furious Prost after climbing from the cockpit. "It is a team without directive and without strategy trying to win against a well-structured team like McLaren. Berger helped Senna to the maximum to win the race."

A week later, Prost won the Spanish Grand Prix at Jerez, where Mansell finished second. Then came the Japanese GP at Suzuka, where Alain's hopes of becoming the first Ferrari World Champion driver in 11 years were wiped out when Senna used his McLaren as a battering ram going into the first corner, wiping both cars out of the race.

"If everybody wants to drive in this way, then the sport is finished," said Prost. He was right, of course. Fiat Vice-President Cesare Romiti best summed it up when he hinted that Ferrari might consider withdrawing from F1. "We do not feel part of this world without rules," he noted. Ferrari Chairman Piero Fusaro also called upon FISA President Jean-Marie Balestre to legislate against such wayward driving tactics.

Either way, Ferrari's hopes of a World Championship had been wrecked. Senna took his second title with 78 points to Prost's 71 (net).

Alain went into the 1991 season with Alesi as his partner, but there would be no more Grand Prix victories coming Ferrari's way. Prost also found himself increasingly at odds with the team and, in particular, the team manager, the politically minded Cesare Fiorio, who was ditched midway through the campaign. Yet it would not be enough.

As the season wore on, Prost came under attack

by the influential Italian media, but he would not be intimidated. "This is the last straw in a ridiculous sequence of events," he said. "I suppose it was the same for John Barnard when he was working here, but I never imagined the influence of the press would be so considerable."

In the end, after a season in which Steve Nichols's latest updates of Barnard's original design – the 643 replacing the 642 at the French GP – failed to win a single race, Prost was fired before the final round of the title chase. His offence was having described the 643 as "a truck". But his judgement was correct, and the Ferrari management's stubbornness had cost them the services of one of the very greatest Grand Prix drivers of all time.

MANSELL'S RETURN TO WILLIAMS PROVES WELL TIMED

By the end of 1990, Williams was poised to stage a major recovery as a winning force; as we have seen, in late summer, the team had opened negotiations that would return Nigel Mansell to its fold.

Frank Williams suspected that his former driver might have made a hair-trigger decision to retire after his misfortunes with Ferrari and successfully coaxed him into changing his mind. With Renault raising the stakes with the latest version of its V10 engine, running to 14,000rpm with its pneumatic valve gear, and a new chassis benefiting from aerodynamic input from new chief designer Adrian Newey, Mansell did not need much persuading.

Mansell duly signed, and the Williams FW14 proved to be a highly competitive tool from the outset. Had mechanical problems not blighted the car early in the season, Nigel might have made an even more serious bid for the 1991 World Championship. But Ayrton Senna, in his new McLaren MP4/6, powered by Honda's RA121E V12 engine, won the first four races of the season to earn a worthwhile points cushion.

Despite this, Mansell won the French, British, German, Italian and Spanish Grands Prix in dominant style, carrying his bid for the championship all the way to the penultimate race at Suzuka, where Senna finally clinched the crown after the Williams driver ended up in a gravel trap.

The 1991 season also saw two very important developments that would have a profound effect on the F1 landscape in the long term. Firstly, leading F3000 entrant and wheeler-dealer Eddie Jordan made the huge jump into F1 with the Gary Anderson-designed 1991 challenger powered by leased Cosworth Ford HB V8 engines. Secondly, at the Belgian Grand Prix, Jordan made a car available for a promising young German lad who qualified seventh at his first attempt, only for the clutch to fail almost at the start. His name was Michael Schumacher.

Benetton engineering boss Tom Walkinshaw had seen Schumacher racing Mercedes sports cars against his own Jaguars and suspected that he was something really special. Now Walkinshaw had no doubts whatsoever. He rightly judged that Benetton could offer Schumacher more than Jordan at this stage in his career. Ever since Flavio Briatore had been brought in to run the team in 1989, Benetton had made steady progress. His task was aided by the arrival of John Barnard as technical director and the team's continuing partnership with Ford, which supplied its 'works' operation with a succession of Cosworth-developed V8s, although ironically Barnard left Benetton midway through the 1991 season, shortly after his B191 design had scored its first victory in Canada.

The fortnight separating the Belgian and Italian Grands Prix saw frantic negotiations to get Schumacher out of his Jordan contract and into a Benetton. With Bernie Ecclestone taking a hand in the contractual debate, the deal was eventually done, leaving Jordan temporarily humiliated and vowing legal retribution.

Roberto Moreno was duly replaced in the Benetton squad, briefly taking over Schumacher's vacated Jordan; Michael found himself lining up alongside Nelson Piquet, who was starting his 200th Grand Prix, at Monza. Some people felt that Piquet was past his best, but, while the veteran Brazilian could perhaps no longer demonstrate the sort of form that had carried him to his three World Championship titles, his huge experience would prove enormously helpful to Schumacher.

At Monza, Michael started as he meant to go on, outrunning Piquet all weekend to finish fifth in the race, just over ten seconds ahead of the Brazilian. The rest of the 1991 season went quite smoothly for Schumacher, who finished sixth in Portugal and Spain, but retired after a mechanical failure and a collision in the other two races.

Yet there would be no stopping the Williams-Renaults in 1992. Fitted with state-of-the-art electronic driver aids, such as traction control, active suspen-

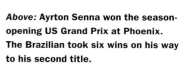

Above: Ayrton Senna won the season-opening US Grand Prix at Phoenix. The Brazilian took six wins on his way to his second title.

Left: On a wing and a prayer. Eddie Jordan breezed into Formula 1 and immediately made a big impression.

Right: The unlucky Roberto Moreno, who was forced to make way for Schumacher at Benetton.

Far right: Michael Schumacher made his debut for Jordan at the 1991 Belgian Grand Prix, but was spirited away to Benetton by the next race.
Photos: Paul-Henri Cahier

AYRTON SENNA: F1'S HOLY WARRIOR

PERHAPS unique in the intensity of his commitment to his chosen sport, Ayrton Senna ranks as one of the very greatest Grand Prix drivers of all time, not merely in the period covered by this volume. Dynamic and highly committed, even when he was a junior driver on the lower rungs of the racing ladder, Senna was always bold and aggressive, whether in driving technique or in dealing with the top teams.

In 1983, McLaren offered to fund Senna's British Formula 3 Championship programme in exchange for an option on his services. Many youngsters in that position would have jumped at such an opportunity, but Ayrton declined politely. He told Ron Dennis that he would generate his own finance and chart his own path through the motor racing maze.

Senna graduated to Formula 1 with Toleman after winning the 1983 F3 title, which ironically earned him a test drive with McLaren. Instantly the Toleman team was won over by the brilliant young Brazilian. At the wheel of its Hart turbo-engine TG184, he finished a superb second in Monaco and third in Portugal, beaten only by the McLarens of Prost and Lauda.

Senna switched to Lotus the following year and scored his first Grand Prix victory in the second race of the season, held in pouring rain at Estoril. This spellbinding example of high-speed car control was followed by five more Lotus victories during his three seasons with the team, but it wasn't until he joined the McLaren-Honda squad at the start of 1988 that he really began to notch up the wins at a quite dramatic rate.

Few drivers in history have ever applied so much mental focus to the business of Formula 1. Ayrton was forever probing, exploring and analysing every means of gaining an edge. It took him little more than a season of intense psychological warfare to unseat Alain Prost from his position at McLaren, driving him into the arms of the rival Ferrari camp.

The highly confrontational attitude towards Prost, which developed during their second year together at McLaren and intensified thereafter, was seen by many as nothing more than a reflection of Senna's competitive spirit. It was not enough for him simply to succeed. He had to do so from a position of total dominance. Even if that meant crushing the morale of his opposition.

It was also the view of many colleagues that Senna lacked not only a sense of humour, but also a degree of perspective. He almost exclusively reserved the former for his close friends, who came from within or around his closeted family environment.

Yet perhaps the tensions that brewed up between Prost and Senna in 1988/89, to some extent, were inevitable. Prost wanted to protect his position, Senna to undermine it. Prost had been central to all McLaren's success since 1984, but now he could see the balance of power shifting decisively in Senna's favour.

Senna was not a man who could accept defeat This was graphically demonstrated when he deliberately pushed Prost's Ferrari off the circuit on the first corner of the 1990 Japanese Grand Prix, after being frustrated in his attempt to move pole position to the other side of the track. This episode suggested that his messianic zeal might extend to discarding considerations of his own personal safety, let alone that of anybody else on the circuit.

The difference between the two drivers was that, in a car that Alain liked and was set up specially for him, he was untouchable, unbeatable. But Ayrton could drive anything, no matter how badly it handled. That was the case in his last, fateful race at Imola. The Williams FW16 was probably not a car that should have been on pole position at that stage in its development. It was in pole position because Ayrton was driving it. Michael Schumacher, whose Benetton was following Senna in the early stages, later said he could see that the Brazilian was having problems with his car. But Ayrton Senna was never a man to take it easy.

sion and automatic gearchange, the Williams FW14B, powered by the even more powerful Renault RS4 engine, enabled Mansell to blitz his way to the World Championship with nine victories. He also started all but two of the 16 races from pole position. Senna and McLaren were defeated, and Mansell had the title wrapped up by the Hungarian Grand Prix in the middle of August.

For McLaren, the 1992 season produced something of a humiliation. Although the new MP4/7 was probably the most sophisticated and beautifully made chassis McLaren had produced so far, Honda's latest V12 engine was certainly lagging behind in terms of power. Unbeknown to those outside the team's senior management, Honda had advised McLaren chief Ron Dennis early in the season that it would not be continuing in F1 in 1993. As a result of this decision, the Japanese company slowed its technical development, and McLaren personnel were left to smile bravely, taking responsibility for disappointing performances in an effort to be politically tactful.

At Ferrari, meanwhile, Jean Alesi had yet to win his first race. It would be a long haul for the talented Frenchman, who had first come to prominence with Tyrrell in 1989 and then stunned the world with two storming second places to Senna's McLaren in the 1990 Phoenix and Monaco Grands Prix. After being tutored by his friend, Prost, in 1991, Alesi found himself forced into the Ferrari team leadership the following year. Partnered by Ivan Capelli, he was unable to produce much in the way of hard results.

In the race following Mansell's 1992 title clincher, there was an almost symbolic endorsement of F1's new order when Michael Schumacher returned to Spa-Francorchamps on the first anniversary of his debut outing in the Jordan. With the Benetton B192-Ford, he now took his maiden victory in treacherously wet/dry conditions, winning by nearly 40 seconds from Mansell's Williams-Renault.

By this stage, Mansell was a very rich man. In 1991, he had earned a reputed £4.6 million, and he stayed on to win the title the following year for a slightly increased £5 million fee. For 1993, Williams's connections with Elf and Renault steered the team towards signing Alain Frost – who had sat out the 1992 season – as Riccardo Patrese's replacement.

For his part, Mansell had serious doubts over whether this would work, feeling apprehensive about being paired with Prost after his experience at Ferrari in 1990. But a fee of £937,000 was agreed as additional compensation for having to relinquish his absolute number-one status. It looked as though a deal had been struck.

If Mansell had been able to sign the Williams deal early, all would have been well. However, Elf, whose profits had fallen by 23 per cent during the first six months of 1992, then had second thoughts about how much it wanted to spend on F1. Williams offered Mansell a substantially lower figure. He refused.

The matter came to a head at the 1992 Italian Grand Prix, where Nigel convened a press conference to announce that he would be quitting F1 at the end of the season. A last-minute intervention by a Williams emissary, who arrived with word from Frank that a deal could be reached, came too late. Mansell was already midway through his statement. The partnership had passed beyond the point of no return.

Continued on page 284

Opposite: **Ayrton Senna totally focused.**

Below: **After narrowly missing out on the 1986 title, Nigel Mansell ran away with the 1992 crown. Eight wins from the first ten races put the title in his grasp at Hockenheim before the month of July was out.**
Photos: Paul-Henri Cahier

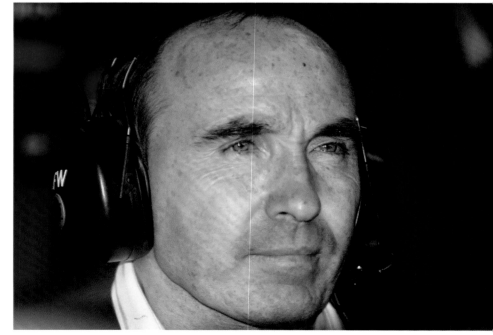

Top: Jean Alesi struggling at Ferrari.

Above: A feisty and sometimes combative relationship developed between Nigel Mansell and Williams technical director Patrick Head, but it yielded brilliant results.

Right: Sir Frank Williams, one of the bedrock personalities of F1 over the last 40 years.

Photos: Paul-Henri Cahier

Above: Michael Schumacher confirmed his special talent with a maiden victory at the 1992 Belgian Grand Prix.

Left: After three years of playing second fiddle to Senna at McLaren, Gerhard Berger opted for a return to Ferrari for 1993.

Photos: Paul-Henri Cahier

As the cars stream down Craner Curves on the opening lap of the 1993 European Grand Prix, Ayrton Senna already lies fourth. The Brazilian would soon dispatch Wendlinger's Sauber and the Williamses of Damon Hill and Alain Prost.

Photo: Paul-Henri Cahier

McLAREN FORCED TO TURN TO FORD

At the end of the 1992 season, McLaren duly relinquished its partnership with Honda and had to cast around for an alternative source of engines. While this task was not the work of a moment, Ron Dennis secured a supply of Renault engines by the expedient of agreeing to purchase the Ligier team, the idea being to switch its powerful French V10s to the McLarens and find Ligier some new engines to use.

However, although Dennis obtained the agreement of Renault that McLaren could run the engines on Shell fuel and lubricants for at least one season – an important consideration, since Shell had been a major McLaren sponsor for many years – the idea was vetoed by Elf, Renault's long-established fuel partner, and that was that.

Instead, McLaren opted to become a customer for the Cosworth Ford HB V8 at a reputed cost of £6 million, an investment that would be supplemented by techni-

cal input from TAG Electronic Systems, a McLaren associate company specialising in the development of sophisticated automotive electronic systems.

The Ford V8 was installed in the brand-new McLaren MP4/8 chassis, which may have been giving away 50bhp to the Williams FW15C-Renault, but Senna's genius behind the wheel allowed him to squeeze out no fewer than five wins during the course of 1993. These included his breathtaking victory in the one-off Grand Prix of Europe at Donington Park on Easter Monday where, in torrential rain, he saw off the Williams duo of Damon Hill and Alain Prost to score what many people regarded as the best win of his career.

Yet Senna was not an easy man to live with in 1993. He was alternately frustrated and embittered that McLaren could not get its hands on the latest-specification Ford HB engines, which were reserved for the rival Benetton squad as a central plank of its factory deal. Senna had also demanded a fee of $1 million per

race and initially agreed to compete only on a race-by-race basis. In a classic piece of brinkmanship, he was partying in a São Paulo discotheque on the eve of first practice for the San Marino Grand Prix.

Only an overnight Alitalia flight to Rome, a private jet to Bologna, a helicopter to Imola and a motorcycle pillion ride eventually got Ayrton to the paddock minutes before the first timed session. Earlier, he had kept everybody guessing by testing a Penske Indy car in North America before deciding to remain in F1. If it frayed Ron Dennis's nerves, the McLaren boss never showed his frustration.

Prost, meanwhile, was having a frustrating time in his role as Williams team leader, but for different reasons. He had returned to F1 after his season out of the cockpit in 1992, only to be propelled headlong into a confrontation with FISA President Max Mosley, who, in a dramatic change of roles, had replaced Jean-Marie Balestre in 1991.

They clashed over FISA's efforts to change the rules to make F1 more interesting. For 1993, the cars were slightly narrower (down from 215 to 200cm) and rear wheel rim widths were reduced from 18 to 15in, but during the course of the season, it was decided that the costly computer controlled driver aids would be stripped from the cars for 1994.

This provoked squeals of indignation from such teams as Williams and McLaren, which had made great technical progress in these areas. In addition, the 1993 season also saw a prohibition of the use of the spare car in practice and qualifying, and the introduction of limits on the number of laps permitted on both practice days.

On the face of it, these changes might have been made with a view to saving money, but there was certainly one man in the field who cursed them from the outset. This was Indy car star Michael Andretti, who had been recruited to drive the second McLaren alongside Senna. He never got into the swing of the Grand Prix business and was replaced by Mika Häk-

kinen, the team's young test driver, with three races of the year remaining.

Prost won seven of the first ten races and clinched the 1993 World Championship by taking second place to Schumacher's Benetton in the Portuguese Grand Prix at Estoril, where earlier he had announced that he would be retiring for good at the end of the season. Senna went on to win the final two races of the year at Suzuka and Adelaide, thereby consolidating his second place in the championship on 73 points – 26 behind Prost's total.

Although Prost may have ended his Formula 1 career feeling a little unwanted within the wider political situation surrounding Williams and Senna, Patrick Head remembers the Frenchman as one of the most outstanding performers in terms of mechanical sympathy.

"You could see with Alain that he was more concerned with looking after his tyres, rather than deliberately thinking about the fuel load," said Head, recalling the turbo era and its fuel-restriction rules.

"He would drive a quite conservative race for the first ten to twenty laps or so, because he did not see the point of using mega amounts of boost while he had 240 litres of fuel on board. If he really gave it the big power, he would destroy the tyres.

"When we were running Keke Rosberg and he was roaring off into the lead, we would think, 'No problem,' when we checked that Prost was down around 15th place. But then the quick laps would start to come in from Prost and he would be on you like a rash, while Keke's tyres were going off. Prost's attitude was that he did not want to use a lot of fuel while he had to take it easy on the tyres. He would save the power and fuel until later."

The second Williams was driven by the team's former test driver, Damon Hill, who had been promoted to fill the void created by Mansell's departure. The son of the late Graham Hill, Damon was as focused and single-minded as his father, and had

carried out excellent test and development work for the team over two seasons.

Hill got the job after Frank Williams had dithered for a while, first offering a deal to Häkkinen, then talking to Martin Brundle before deciding on a modest £200,000 retainer for Hill. Frank can be a shrewd negotiator, but after Damon had won the Hungarian, Belgian and Italian Grands Prix for the team, he must have looked like the bargain of the age.

For the 1994 season, Senna decided to switch to Williams, while McLaren, who had clinched a deal to use the new Peugeot V10 F1 engine, relied on Häkkinen and Brundle. Ferrari would retain its established pairing of Gerhard Berger and Jean Alesi, while Benetton and Ford braced themselves for a major push forward with Michael Schumacher.

DOUBLE DISASTER AT IMOLA

Ayrton Senna struggled with the new Williams FW16 for the first two races of the 1994 season, spinning off in front of his home crowd at Interlagos and then tangling Häkkinen's McLaren-Peugeot on the first corner of the Pacific Grand Prix at Japan's TI-Aida circuit.

In-race refuelling was part of the revised technical challenge facing the F1 teams from the start of the 1994 season, but, although Ayrton was slightly wrong-footed by the winning pace of Michael Schumacher's new Ford Zetec-R V8-engine Benetton B 194 in those first two races, improvements to the Williams made him more confident about his prospects for the San Marino Grand Prix at Imola.

Yet this would be the bleakest weekend F1 had known since the 1960 Belgian Grand Prix claimed the lives of British drivers Chris Bristow and Alan Stacey. During Saturday qualifying, Austrian novice Roland

Ratzenberger was killed when his Simtek-Ford crashed at 190mph on the approach to the Tosa hairpin after the nose section of his car, loosened in an earlier off-track excursion, flew off at a crucial moment. The 31-year-old from Salzburg was the first driver to be killed in an F1 car since the Italian, Elio de Angelis, had died testing at Paul Ricard at the wheel of a Brabham BT55-BMW during the summer of 1986. Senna, in particular, felt deeply moved by the whole episode and discussed the possibility of not racing with the FIA medical delegate, the respected neurosurgeon, Professor Sid Watkins.

On race day, it seemed as though everything was coming unstitched. JJ Lehto's Benetton stalled on the grid and was rammed from behind by Pedro Lamy's Lotus, scattering wreckage all over the start/finish line. Debris also flew into the grandstand and injured several spectators, thankfully none seriously.

The safety car – a new F1 development that mimicked Indy car racing's pace-car concept – was de-

Left: The day the music died. Ayrton Senna on the starting grid for the 1994 San Marino GP at Imola, in the Williams FW16 he had put on pole.

Below: A youthful Rubens Barrichello was very lucky to escape with his life after a massive accident in practice at Imola that put him in hospital.

Bottom: The much-loved Professor Sid Watkins, who for twenty-six years served as the FIA Formula One Safety and Medical Delegate.

Photos: Paul-Henri Cahier

ployed to slow the field and to give the marshals a chance to clear up the mess. For three laps, the cars were kept down to cruising speed. When the safety car pulled off, Senna led the pack around to complete its fifth lap of the afternoon.

Despite his car bottoming out dramatically in a shower of sparks on the fast Tamburello left-hander after the pits, Senna held on to lead from Schumacher by 0.6s at the end of lap six. Going into lap seven, the Brazilian's Williams FW16 suddenly twitched dramatically and slammed off the track into the retaining wall at Tamburello. The race was red-flagged to a halt while Senna was removed by helicopter to hospital in Bologna, where he was offically declared dead from massive head injuries a few hours later.

It was a shattering blow to the F1 community, but life had to go on and the restarted race was won by Schumacher's Benetton from Nicola Larini's Ferrari – the Italian subbing for the injured Jean Alesi – and Häkkinen's McLaren.

Top: In the aftermath of the tragedy, modifications were made to a number of circuits, including the emasculation of Spa's daunting Eau Rouge. Pole-position starter Rubens Barrichello's Jordan is chased by Schumacher's Benetton and Alesi's Ferrari.

Photos: Paul-Henri Cahier

Above: Ayrton Senna's death shocked the world.

THE AFTERMATH OF THE ACCIDENT

The implications of the Senna accident were a matter of acute concern for all those involved in F1. But it would be two-and-a-half years before the long-awaited trial of Frank Williams and five others on charges of culpable homicide eventually took place in Bologna. Williams and his co-defendants, Patrick Head, chief designer Adrian Newey, FIA race director Roland Brunseyraede, and Imola track officials Federico Bendenelli and Giorgio Poggi were not present. Nor did the law require them to be so.

It was clear that the prosecution was set on pressing home its contention that badly welded alterations to the steering column on Senna's Williams had caused a pre-impact failure that had sent car and driver into the retaining wall of the flat-out Tamburello left-hander at 193mph. The indications were that investigating magistrate Maurizio Passarini lent no credence to photographic evidence, published in the previous week's *Sunday Times*, showing Senna about to run over debris on the circuit.

However, there was evidence to consider that Senna may have pressed too hard on cold tyres after several laps of running at much reduced speed behind the safety car while debris from the start-line collision was removed from the straight in front of the pits.

Senna had arrived at Imola vowing that "the World Championship starts here", and he was known to be suspicious that there was something not quite right about his key rival Schumacher's Benetton. Subsequently it was established that this car had an illegal electronic 'launch control' system contained within its software systems, but the FIA accepted that it had not been used.

The implication was that Ayrton might have overdriven in the heat of the moment, his determination to get the better of Schumacher causing him to press too hard before his tyres were up to temperature. In this condition, his car might have been particularly nervous to drive over the bumps of the Tamburello corner, and this could have contributed to a rare error.

Interestingly, safety car driver Max Angelelli admitted that he had been very worried that the breathless Opel used for the job was not quick enough. He said that a Porsche Carrera RSR would have been more appropriate and recalled Senna pulling level with him, motioning him to speed up. "I could see from his eyes that he was very angry," he recounted.

More than a year would pass before the defendants were finally acquitted, but the controversy would linger on even as late as 1999, when rumours circulated that the prosecuting magistrate was considering lodging an appeal for a retrial.

NIGEL MANSELL: THE PEOPLE'S FAVOURITE

BY the time Nigel Mansell retired from racing, he was the most successful British Grand Prix driver ever, with a total of 31 career victories, a record that placed him fourth in the all-time winners stakes, behind Alain Prost, the late Ayrton Senna and Michael Schumacher.

Mansell fought his way up to Formula 1 with the same blend of absolute commitment and physical pugnacity he had applied to the business of driving a racing car. Having cut his teeth in karting and established himself as a proven winner in Formula Ford, he eventually got his F1 break when he was invited to test a Lotus 79 in the summer of 1979.

Colin Chapman was deeply impressed with the brash young man's tenacity and determination, and gave him his F1 chance in the 1980 Austrian Grand Prix. It was typical of Mansell that he drove much of the race in acute discomfort from petrol burns caused by a fuel cell

leaking its contents into the cockpit. He would not give up until the engine had expired.

Mansell was signed up as a regular Team Lotus driver alongside Elio de Angelis in 1981, but while Chapman's faith in his ability never wavered, Nigel found himself robbed of a close friend and mentor when the Lotus founder died from a sudden heart attack in December 1982.

He remained with Lotus through to the end of 1984, but real success did not come his way until he moved to Williams the following year. He scored his first victory in the Grand Prix of Europe at Brands Hatch with the Williams FW10-Honda, after which the wins came cascading in his direction.

Another nine seasons would pass before Mansell, who had won the 1992 World Championship in a Williams FW14B-Renault, posted his final Grand Prix victory at the wheel of a Williams

FW16 at Adelaide. In 1989 and 1990, he had interrupted his stormy romance with Williams by spending two seasons driving for the Ferrari squad, during which the Italian fans nicknamed him *'Il Leone'*.

Mansell was braver than Dick Tracy, more accident prone than John Prescott and more confrontational than Mike Tyson. Yet he seldom gave less than 100 per cent effort when he was behind the wheel, and his presence would always guarantee a hysterical capacity crowd at Silverstone for the British Grand Prix.

Williams technical director Patrick Head recounted an anecdote that puts Mansell's character into context. "I remember Nigel's race at Montreal in 1986," he said. "I told him to turn his boost down from 3.6 to 3.5, or whatever. He was in the lead, but needed to save fuel, so I got on the radio and said, 'Change the boost to 3.5.'

"There was a long silence, then he

came on the radio saying, 'I don't want to turn the boost down, I'll be beaten.'

"So I had to say to him, 'Turn your effing boost down.' There was no reaction and I got even angrier. 'Turn your effing boost down and do what you're told!'

"So he did and the lap time went a second slower. But he was determined to show he was better than the situation. So the next lap, he made up half a second, and then another half-second on the following lap, so that he was back doing the same times as before, but with less turbo boost.

"Once he had the time back down, the radio clicked on: 'Today's the day the teddy bears have their picnic,' came over the airwaves. Nigel was singing *Teddy Bears' Picnic* while going round the circuit as he broke the lap record, lap after lap.

"He was just making the point that we were not going to screw him that way."

Ayrton Senna (right) and Michael Schumacher line up on the front row of the grid for the 1994 Pacific Grand Prix at Japan's very remote TI circuit.

Photo: Paul-Henri Cahier

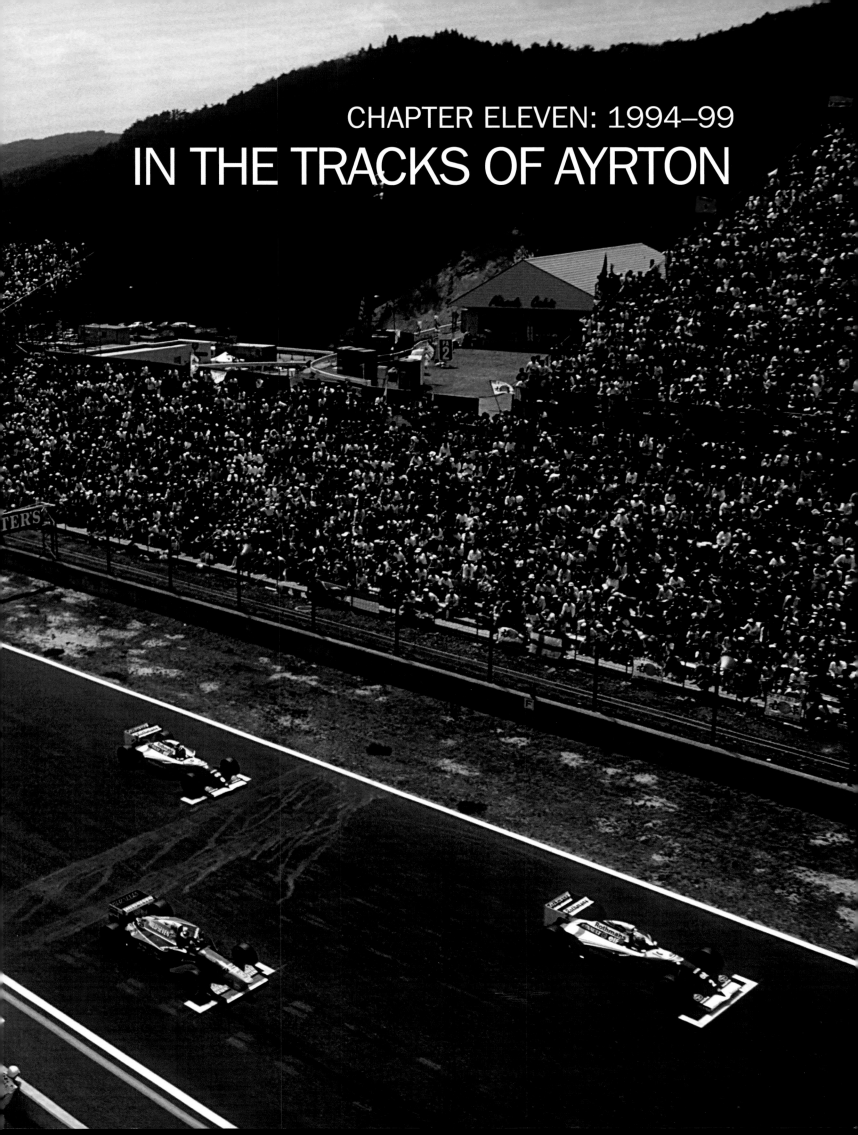

IN THE TRACKS OF AYRTON

Above right: Damon Hill celebrates on the upper step of the Barcelona podium after winning the 1994 Spanish GP for Williams. Michael Schumacher (left) and Tyrrell's Mark Blundell were second and third.

Above, far right: The Ford Zetec-R V8 engine that propelled the Benetton to the 1994 title.

Right: Schumacher quickly became the man to beat during 1994 in the wake of Ayrton Senna's death.

Photos: Paul-Henri Cahier

AS the dust settled in the aftermath of Ayrton Senna's fatal accident and the sport began to grapple with its long-term consequences, one thing quickly became very clear. The baton had now passed to Michael Schumacher as the leading exponent of the F1 technique. Just as Jim Clark had taken over from Stirling Moss, and Jackie Stewart had eventually inherited the mantle of his fellow Scot, so Schumacher set the pace in 1994 and 1995 at the wheel of his Benetton.

The start of the 1994 season had seen Ford back Benetton's factory effort with the all-new 65-degree Zetec-R V8, which owed nothing in terms of shared parts to its immediate predecessor. It certainly benefited greatly, however, from the technical lessons learned from a shelved Ford V12 F1 programme, particularly in the areas of heat rejection, crankshaft configuration and the use of ceramics in the cylinder head design.

Sharing Cosworth's optimism were the Benetton design staff, headed by Ross Brawn, Rory Byrne and Pat Symonds, whose new B194 chassis was a logical development of the previous year's machine, which had won the 1993 Portuguese GP.

Senna's death triggered an immediate programme of rule changes from the FIA, which had absorbed FISA, its sporting arm, the previous year, with Max Mosley becoming president of the parent organisation. Truncated diffusers and shortened front wing endplates were required with effect from the Spanish Grand Prix, and a reduction in engine size from 3.5 to 3 litres from the start of the 1995 season was also announced.

At Williams, Damon Hill found himself forced to shoulder the team leadership after the Brazilian's death, a task that he performed with admirable resilience. Hill won in Spain, but it was clear that Williams's engine partner, Renault, felt it could give only qualified support for his new status as team leader. They pressured Williams to rehire Nigel Mansell, who, having won the 1993 Indy car championship with a Newman/

Haas Lola-Ford, was having a much less happy time in his second season in the US based series.

Mansell was duly paid £900,000 for a one-off drive in the French Grand Prix; he also secured agreement for a £2 million compensation fee if Williams did not wish to take up his services and confirm a £7 million deal for 1995. Mansell drove in a total of four races for Williams in 1994, ending the season with a comfortable victory in Australia.

When Mansell was not available, Hill was partnered by the young Scot, David Coulthard, a Formula 3000 graduate promoted from the role of test driver.

Schumacher began a run of domination that was dramatically frustrated by a major confrontation with the authorities following events at the British Grand Prix at Silverstone. On the final parade lap, he breached the rules by overtaking Hill's Williams. After a considerable delay, the German driver was shown a black flag together with his race number, indicating that he had been given a stop-go penalty for this transgression, but he enraged the governing body by staying out on the circuit while Benetton directors Flavio Briatore and Tom Walkinshaw argued at length with the stewards.

Michael eventually pulled into the pits to serve his penalty and finished the race in second place, behind Hill, with Benetton incurring a fine of $25,000. At a special meeting of the FIA World Motor Sports Council, however, he was subsequently disqualified from the results, while Benetton's fine was increased to $500,000 as a punishment for its failure to obey the instructions of race officials. In addition, Schumacher was given a two-race ban, although the team lodged an appeal, which at least allowed him to race in the German Grand Prix at Hockenheim a few days later.

Hockenheim produced another problem for Benetton, the team's second driver, Jos Verstappen, being lucky to escape all but uninjured after a refuelling conflagration during a routine pit stop. Schumacher retired with engine problems, allowing Gerhard Berger's

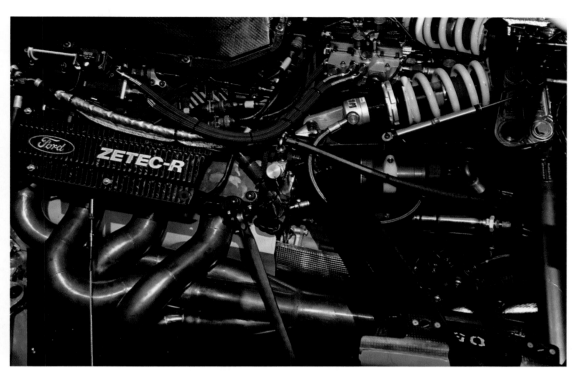

Ferrari an easy win, but the Benetton ace bounced back in Hungary, beating Hill's Williams with an audacious three-stop strategy to the Englishman's two stops.

Benetton was fortunate to escape from the Hockenheim fuel fire without an additional penalty: the fuel rig used for Verstappen's car had a filter missing, illegally speeding up its flow rate. There were some ambiguities, however, that prevented the team from facing further sanction, but Michael's two-race suspension was upheld, and he duly missed the Italian and Portuguese Grands Prix – having previously been disqualified from first place in Belgium after excessive wear had been detected in the B194's under-car skid block when it was checked after the race.

Hill won all three of those races to vault into contention for the World Championship, although in reality this was a somewhat artificial situation, in the sense that the various transgressions committed by Schumacher and his team had cost the German driver the chance of winning another 40 championship points from four races, when the Silverstone disqualification was added to the other setbacks.

Michael returned to the fray at Jerez, where he won the European Grand Prix, but he was beaten into second place by Hill in the rain soaked Japanese Grand Prix at Suzuka three weeks later. Then Schumacher rounded off the season by clinching the 1994 World Championship in intensely controversial fashion by apparently ramming Hill out of the Australian Grand Prix in Adelaide.

Whether Schumacher made an innocent error, or took a pragmatic decision to take out Hill after he himself had inflicted potentially terminal damage on his Benetton by side-swiping a wall, has never been satisfactorily resolved. Suffice it to say that the 1994 season was one that the F1 fraternity was happy to put behind it.

It was not simply that Senna, one of the sport's greatest ever exponents, had died in such tragic circumstances. The controversy surrounding the various Benetton issues had also contributed to an uncomfortable climate of suspicion that F1 found difficult to purge from its image.

The 1994 season also saw new Sporting Director Jean Todt getting into his stride at Ferrari, even though Berger's win at Hockenheim was as far as any Maranello revival went. At the opposite end of the scale, Lotus, whose fortunes had been administered by the tenacious and committed former Benetton team manager, Peter Collins, ever since 1991, withdrew from the F1 stage after being overwhelmed by financial problems. Thus ended a strand of F1 continuity that had endured ever since Graham Hill and Cliff Allison had given the Lotus 12s their debut at Monaco 36 years earlier.

At McLaren, the Peugeot V10s proved hideously unreliable, consuming fuel and lubricants in pretty well equal measure. Martin Brundle stormed home second to Schumacher at Monaco, leaving team owner Ron Dennis to make his memorable observation that "second is just the first of the losers" when he found the Peugeot lads celebrating after the race.

It was an undeniably harsh judgement, but correct. The McLaren-Peugeot relationship was going nowhere. Similarly, Mercedes-Benz was becoming in-

creasingly frustrated by its relationship with the Swiss Sauber team.

Eventually Mercedes motor sport manager Norbert Haug brokered a deal with Dennis to switch the German V10 engines to McLaren for 1995. As part of the deal, Dennis also arranged for Peugeot to move its engines to the Jordan team, replacing the promising Brian Hart V10s that it had used for the previous two seasons.

When Mercedes-Benz set out to dominate F1 racing in the 1990s, it turned to British technology to propel it to the top of the victory rostrum. Instead of building its own engines, the famous German car maker bought a stake in Ilmor Engineering, the specialist race engine builder established by Mario Illien and his partner, Paul Morgan, in 1983.

Illien is a formal, reserved Swiss with a burning passion for racing engines. "I always wanted to be involved with engines since I was a kid," he said. "It is, if you like, a childlike passion which has never left me. But the nature of this business, with all its pressures, is such that you simply have to be passionate about it. Otherwise you quite simply can't put in the hours which it requires."

In 1979, Illien had joined Cosworth, the maker of Ford's F1 engines, where he met Morgan. In 1983,

Above: Damon Hill scored the finest victory of his career in the 1994 Japanese GP at Suzuka, beating Michael Schumacher into second place and thus deferring the World Championship decider to Adelaide the following weekend. Benetton was convinced that Damon would make another refuelling stop in the closing stages, but he confounded its predictions by staying out in the torrential conditions.

Left: Despite Jean-Pierre Jabouille's optimistic gestures, McLaren boss Ron Dennis looks unconvinced. The McLaren-Peugeot alliance lasted for one fruitless season, and the team cut a deal with Mercedes for 1995.

Far left: On the way out. Alex Zanardi and Mika Salo in their penultimate appearances with Lotus 109-Mugen-Hondas, before the Lotus team finally called it a day at the end of the 1994 season.

Above far left: Mario Illien was the driving force behind Ilmor Engineering, who built the Mercedes F1 engines for many years.

Photos: Paul-Henri Cahier

Above: Michael Schumacher leads Damon Hill at the start of the 1995 Canadian Grand Prix.

Right: : Flavio Briatore and Michael Schumacher celebrate Benetton's victory in the 1995 Pacific GP.

Far right: Johnny Herbert took full advantage of a collision between Damon Hill and Michael Schumacher to win the 1995 British Grand Prix.
Photos: Paul-Henri Cahier

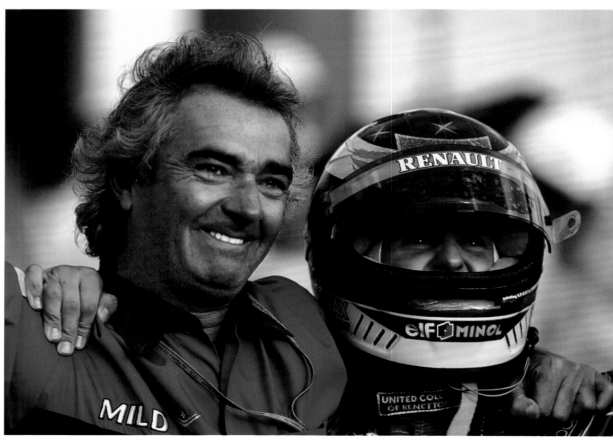

they decided to go it alone in an audacious move to beat their former employer at its own game.

"When we left Cosworth, we considered carefully which racing category to tackle and concluded that taking on Cosworth's monopoly in US Indy car racing would make most sense," said Illien.

With backing from legendary Indy car team owner Roger Penske, General Motors and, subsequently, Mercedes-Benz, Ilmor became firmly established as a leading race engine builder. Eventually, under the Mercedes banner, it made a concerted assault on Formula 1 with the Sauber team in 1994. But it soon became clear that Sauber was unlikely to develop into a fully competitive prospect.

RENAULT GOES WITH BENETTON

For the 1995 season, Renault agreed to expand the supply of its works engines to include Benetton. Frank Williams and his colleagues were not happy about this, but knuckled down to concentrate on developing their new FW17 to the point where it was more competitive than the Benetton B195. On balance, the FW17 would end up with the performance edge. But Hill found himself increasingly outclassed by Schumacher.

For Damon, the off-season had been a time to sit and consider what was required to beat the German. You could tell that he was still smarting over the way in which the 1994 World Championship had been resolved, but he knew only too well that Schumacher regarded F1 racing as much a mind game as anything else. So not only did Damon have to keep control on the track, capitalising on the Williams FW17's performance advantage for as long as possible while Benetton played catch-up, but also he had to avoid be-

coming embroiled in any psychological battle with his great rival.

In qualifying for the first Grand Prix of the season at Interlagos, Hill pipped Schumacher for pole, but the Williams and Benetton efforts in that event were thwarted by a discrepancy in their Elf fuel specifications. Schumacher led the race initially, but Hill vaulted ahead at the first refuelling stops, thereafter pulling away before spinning to a halt with broken rear suspension.

That left Schumacher an easy run to victory from Coulthard, the Scot having been signed for the high-profile Williams drive alongside Hill in preference to the high-priced Mansell. As expected, however, both drivers were excluded for the apparent fuel discrepancy. Both teams appealed and the FIA International Court of Appeal duly reinstated them in the results, accepting that there were valid differences of opinion over whether or not the fuel discrepancy offered any performance benefit, although they were not allowed their Constructors' Championship points for first and second places.

Hill would surge on to score wins in both the Argentine and San Marino Grands Prix, after which his title challenge progressively fell apart. Most notable among his slips were collisions with Schumacher's Benetton that eliminated the two contenders from the British and Italian Grands Prix, Benetton number two, Johnny Herbert, ducking through to take victory on both occasions.

Hill admittedly scored a good win in Hungary, which he optimistically described as a "payback race", but it did not signal a major shift in his fortunes. In fact, as Schumacher stormed on to clinch his second World Championship, Hill floundered increasingly,

Above: **With Nigel Mansell retired, the flags flew at Silverstone for new hero Damon Hill.**

Above right: **A fresh-faced David Coulthard took his maiden win for Williams at the 1985 Portuguese Grand Prix.**

Opposite, top: **Tamburello corner at Imola, one year after Ayrton's accident and now an informal shrine to the great Brazilian driver's memory.**

Oppposite, bottom: **An emotional win for Jean Alesi, who scored his only F1 win at the 1995 Canadian Grand Prix.**
Photos: Paul-Henri Cahier

culminating in a truly awful performance at Suzuka for the Japanese Grand Prix, where he seemed to be spinning in all directions.

It was certainly a frustrating period for Frank Williams and Patrick Head, neither of whom had ever been inclined to take a sympathetic stance towards any psychological problems experienced by their drivers. By mid-season, they had already decided that Coulthard wasn't quite the ticket after his failure to beat Schumacher's Benetton in the German Grand Prix at Hockenheim, where Hill had spun off at the start of the second lap.

The pleasant Scot, who had been grappling with tonsillitis for much of the season, would be replaced by that year's Indy car champion and Indy 500 winner, Jacques Villeneuve, the son of the famous Ferrari ace who had been killed at Zolder in 1982. Hill, who had signed his 1996 contract in August 1995, was safe for one more year with the Williams team, but at Suzuka Williams and Head vowed to replace him at the end of the following season with German rising star Heinz-Harald Frentzen, who had made his F1 debut with Sauber in 1994.

It is difficult to understand why they needed to take that decision so early in the day. Hill dug deep into his personal resources and then stormed back into contention with a fine win in the 1995 Australian Grand Prix in Adelaide, the final race of the season. It would set the scene for his performances in 1996.

MANSELL'S McLAREN INTERLUDE

In the McLaren camp, there had been pressure from Marlboro, the team's title sponsor, to secure the services of a top-line driver for the first year of the Mercedes partnership in 1995. The only front-rank performer

available was Nigel Mansell, and the alliance turned out to be a fiasco. Some years before, Ron Dennis had offered the view that Mansell was the one driver he really would not want to have at McLaren, but now force of circumstance had thrown them together.

The 41-year-old veteran's taste for F1 success had been reawakened by those outings for Williams in 1994, but now he found that the new McLaren MP4/10 Mercedes was simply not up to scratch. Its engine had abrupt throttle response and power delivery, qualities that aggravated the poor balance of the chassis.

As if this wasn't enough, McLaren also had to expend many man-hours designing and building an enlarged monocoque to accommodate the British driver. Eventually Mansell drove only in the San Marino and Spanish Grands Prix, touring into the pits after a difficult time wrestling with the car in the latter event before apparently throwing in the towel.

Before the next race of the season in Monaco, Dennis and Mansell agreed to dissolve their partnership. The disentangling of their contractual relations was at least conducted with a professional formality that impressed Dennis, even though he was happy to be released from the pressure created by such a demanding driver at a time when McLaren's product did not match up to Mansell's ambitions.

McLaren saw out 1995 with Mark Blundell partnering Mika Häkkinen, and the team made steady progress with Mercedes, although the final race, the Australian Grand Prix in Adelaide, was blighted by a terrible practice accident in which Mika sustained quite serious head injuries. Initially there was some doubt as to how well he might recover, but happily the Finn returned to robust health in time for the start of the 1996 season.

Right: Damon Hill made up for his disappointment in 1994 by winning the World Championship for Williams two years later. In doing so, he became the only second-generation F1 title holder, emulating the achievements of his late father, Graham, in 1962 and 1968.

Below: Schumacher marked his first victory for Ferrari with a brilliant drive in the wet conditions at the 1996 Spanish Grand Prix.

Below right: Joy for Olivier Panis produced a surprise – and very impressive – victory for the Ligier team in the 1996 Monaco GP.

Photos: Paul-Henri Cahier

HILL WINS THE 1996 WORLD CHAMPIONSHIP

Damon Hill's remarkable resolve paid off in 1996. He began the year with victory in the Australian Grand Prix – now the opening race and held in Melbourne – and fended off a season-long challenge from his increasingly confident new team-mate, Jacques Villeneuve, to take the World Championship.

With the Canadian moving in at Williams, Coulthard took up a pre-arranged vacancy in the McLaren-Mercedes squad, replacing fellow Briton Mark Blundell, who had been a former Williams test driver. Meanwhile, Villeneuve would enjoy more than 10,000km of pre-season testing with his new team. Seldom, if ever, had there been a better-prepared F1 newcomer.

Villeneuve would win four races during his maiden season. An irreverent non-comformist, he brought a refreshingly open-minded approach to F1. He was a racer through and through, cowed by none of his rivals, and a man who firmly believed that one racing car was pretty much like another, whether F1, Indy car or whatever. He scored his first F1 victory in only the fourth race of the season, winning the European Grand Prix at the new Nürburgring in a split-second finish ahead of Michael Schumacher, the German double World Champion having switched from Benetton to Ferrari. Quite clearly, Hill now faced his most dangerous opposition from within his own team.

Continued on page 306

Monza, 8th September, 1996.
Michael Schumacher delivers a Ferrari
victory to the *tifosi* on home soil for
the first time since Gerhard Berger
in 1988.
Photos: Paul-Henri Cahier

Hill had started the season noting that every driver since 1990 who had won the opening race had gone on to take that year's World Championship. "It is a tradition I intend to continue," he said, having scored a rather fortuitous victory in the first race of the season after Villeneuve had been slowed by fluctuating oil pressure.

He was as good as his word, although if there was a tinge of disappointment attaching to his title bid, it was probably when a rare Renault engine failure prevented him from winning the Monaco Grand Prix, an event in which his late father, Graham, had triumphed no fewer than five times.

The realisation that his contract would not be renewed, and that he was effectively being replaced by Frentzen – despite claims to the contrary – was quite a blow for Hill. But Damon shrugged aside the disappointment as best he could, sat back and relished his role as F1's first second-generation World Champion driver.

The 1997 season duly delivered more of the same, with Williams still decisively on top and clinching another Constructors' Championship. Jacques Villeneuve took the drivers' crown, while Michael Schumacher was left to repent at leisure the dubious piece of driving that beached his own title hopes in a Jerez gravel trap.

Technically, Schumacher was the best driver, even though Villeneuve's talent developed apace during the course of the season. Michael's victorious performances in the rain at Monaco and Spa were absolutely from the top drawer. He also had luck on his side when he won in Canada, and the assistance of a compliant team-mate at Suzuka, where Eddie Irvine balked the opposition while Michael made good his escape.

Of course, at Williams, no such preferential treat-ment was on the menu. Not that Villeneuve needed much help from Frentzen, even though the German newcomer produced a fine victory in the San Marino Grand Prix at Imola.

For his part, in 1997, Hill was lured by a £5 million retainer into driving for the Arrows team, now under the control of Tom Walkinshaw. With the team using Yamaha V10 engines, it was always going to be a long shot, but the prospect of running on Bridgestone tyres during the Japanese company's first season of F1 involvement looked like a reasonable gamble. In the event, Hill was unable to provide the motivation that Walkinshaw believed was the team's due from such a highly-paid driver and, apart from a strong run to second place in Hungary, pretty well wasted his time.

Meanwhile, McLaren-Mercedes was busy assembling a serious World Championship challenge. In the autumn of 1996, Williams's highly respected chief designer, Adrian Newey, effectively suspended himself on full pay after indicating that he wanted to leave the team he had worked for since 1990.

Newey's reputation as one of the sport's top aerodynamicists had been confirmed by the succession of excellent Williams-Renault designs from 1992 through to 1996. He had disagreed with Frank Williams and Patrick Head over the decision to ditch Damon Hill, but also had wanted more influence in the company as a whole.

It might have been possible to salvage Newey's relationship with Williams had he been offered a shareholding in the company. Eventually, after protracted negotiations over the issue of an early termination of his contract, however, he joined the McLaren-Mercedes squad as technical director in the summer of 1997.

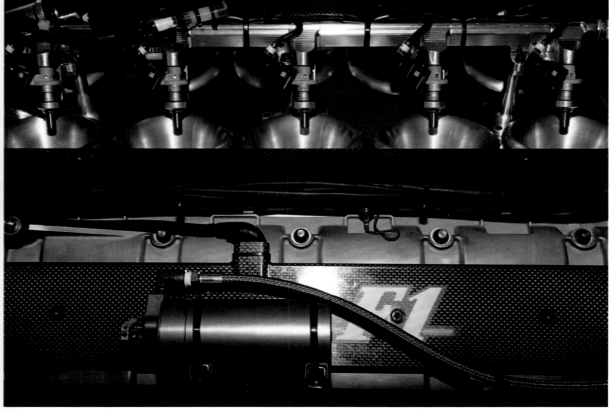

Above: Heinz-Harald Frentzen replaced Damon Hill at Williams, but failed to match up to the Englishman's achievements.

Left: The all-conquering Renault V10 that powered Benetton (1995) and Williams (1996–7) to three successive World Championships.

Opposite: No hard feelings. Adrian Newey defected from Frank Williams to join McLaren for 1997 and soon set about reviving the Woking team's fortunes.

Photos: Paul-Henri Cahier

Opposite, top: Stewart's Rubens Barrichello scored a brilliant second place behind Michael Schumacher in the wet 1997 Monaco Grand Prix.

Opposite, bottom: Stewart Grand Prix's great day. Winner Johnny Herbert, team patron Jackie Stewart and third-placed Rubens Barrichello celebrate their 1-3 finish in the 1999 European Grand Prix.

Below: The single-minded Jean Todt, taking Ferrari back to the top.

Photos: Paul-Henri Cahier

STEWART ARRIVES ON THE SCENE

After Benetton switched to Renault power at the end of 1994, Ford turned its attention to an alliance with the Swiss constructor, Sauber. This endured for two seasons, but even before the end of 1995, it was becoming doubtful whether Sauber would develop into a front-line team, and plans were laid for a totally new F1 operation run by Jackie Stewart and his son, Paul. This was finally confirmed at the start of 1996, and the first Stewart SF1-Ford, designed by Alan Jenkins and powered by the latest Ford Zetec-R V10 engine, took to the tracks the following year, driven by Rubens Barrichello and F3 graduate Jan Magnussen.

It proved to be a difficult first season for the fledgling F1 team, highlighted by a magnificent second place for Barrichello in Monaco in the pouring rain. On too many other occasions, the Ford V10 failed spectacularly, and the sight of Stewart SF1s parked at the side of various circuits was a regular feature of Grand Prix racing in 1997.

By the end of the season, Ford's top brass freely admitted that they had become tired of being labelled half-hearted in their commitment to F1 and indicated their seriousness of purpose by unveiling a totally new Zetec-R V10 engine, built by their long-time partner, Cosworth Engineering.

If anything, 1998 was slightly worse than Stewart's maiden season, the team scoring a measly five points, one fewer than they had managed with Barrichello's second place in Monaco the previous year. In the middle of 1998, Magnussen was replaced by Jos Verstappen, and there followed a major shake-up for 1999. Ford produced the excellent CR-1 V10, which immediately propelled the Stewart SF3 into the role of regular top-six contender, with Johnny Herbert scoring the team's first victory in the Grand Prix of Europe at the Nürburgring.

In the summer of 1999, the Stewarts sold the team to Ford for an estimated $95 million. Barely four months

later, in one of the most audacious pieces of rebranding seen in motor racing's most senior category, its new owners announced at the Frankfurt Motor Show that the cars would race under the Jaguar Racing banner from the start of the 2000 season.

"Jaguar has a long and distinguished record in motor sport," said Dr Wolfgang Reitzle, chairman of Jaguar. "We have won Le Mans seven times and we have twice been Sports Car World Champions. We have also won the Monte Carlo Rally as well as countless other events. The next logical move is F1.

"The move into F1 will undoubtedly benefit Jaguar technologically. It will also clearly promote a wider recognition of the Jaguar brand as we significantly expand our product range over the next few years."

Ford, which had purchased Jaguar ten years earlier, also confirmed that Eddie Irvine, who at that point shared the lead at the head of the World Championship points table, would quit Ferrari to become number-one driver from the start of 2000.

The emergence of Jaguar as an F1 contender was highly significant on two counts. Firstly, it revived the sporting pedigree of a company whose links with front-line motor sport stretched back to the immediate post-war years. Secondly, it served as another major endorsement of Grand Prix racing's commercial pulling power among the world's major car makers.

At a time when tobacco sponsorship in Grand Prix racing was being scaled down prior to a complete ban from 2006 onwards, Jaguar chose to go head-to-head with Mercedes, who had recently arranged an option to purchase a 40-per-cent holding in McLaren, and BMW, the Williams team's engine supplier from the start of 2000, in a battle that would expand as other major car makers bought into top Grand Prix teams.

Ford Motor Company's vice-president and chief technical officer, Neil Ressler, commented, "The need to solve problems quickly breeds a nimble and innovative culture which we will be able to transfer to the road car development programmes. I regard the technology transfer as one of the biggest single benefits of Jaguar's decision to enter F1."

Engines for the team would continue to be designed, developed and built by Cosworth, which was acquired by Ford in 1998. Trevor Crisp, Jaguar's chief engineer for powertrain engineering, was named as head of the F1 engine development programme.

FERRARI CLIMBS BACK INTO CONTENTION

As we have seen, at the end of 1995, Michael Schumacher confirmed that he would be leaving Benetton to join Ferrari for the following season. Maranello was really getting its corporate shoulder behind Jean Todt's efforts to achieve an F1 revival, and recruiting Schumacher was another key element in that rebuilding process.

Michael would be joined in the team by Ulsterman Eddie Irvine, who had spent the previous two seasons with the Jordan team, learning the ropes alongside Rubens Barrichello. By this stage, John Barnard was back in charge of the engineering department at Ferrari, again being allowed to establish a UK design studio to carry out the crucial research and development programmes.

Schumacher found the new V10 powered Ferrari

Above: Jacques Villeneuve with Mika Häkkinen and David Coulthard on the rostrum after the French-Canadian driver clinched the 1997 World Championship with a third-place finish for Williams in the European GP at Jerez. Coulthard was instructed to hand the race win to Häkkinen, the Finn having never won in F1 before.

Right: Villeneuve at speed in the Williams FW19, taking victory in the 1997 Italian Grand Prix.

Photos: Paul-Henri Cahier

F310 promising, if not an unqualified success, from the start of the 1996 season. "We are pretty much on schedule," he commented, "and I really want to take the first two or three races more as testing [sessions] rather than go for race results."

As things transpired, Michael retired from his first Ferrari race with brake problems. That left Irvine to come home third on his first run for the legendary Prancing Horse.

In the early races of the year, the new F310 struggled. Transmission problems meant that the previous car's rear end had to be used for a couple of races, and the atmosphere in the team was not helped when Ferrari President Luca di Montezemolo made some observations about the car that were construed as being critical of Barnard's efforts.

Montezemolo carefully reserved praise for the engine department, even though there was evidence that the new 3-litre V10 was still around 30bhp down on the previous year's V12. "It depends how you measure it," observed Barnard. "Whether you take the readings from the dynamometer or calculate what it's producing when it is installed in the car."

Montezemolo added, "Last year, we took a very important decision to make a V10-cylinder engine. This was to have a better power unit, not only from the viewpoint of performance, but also economy, heat dissipation and ease of installation.

"I think we have made good progress with this engine at a time when the engine in F1 is definitely important, but less than before. I think that is demonstrated [by the way] that Benetton and Williams, which both use the same engine, were almost two seconds apart in qualifying here at the Nürburgring.

"For 1996, we at Ferrari were also obliged to do a brand-new car. My approach is that I generally prefer an evolutionary approach, but with the switch to the V10-cylinder engine, its dimensions were very different from the V12 and we were obliged to make a totally new car from a clean sheet.

"To be honest, I expected altogether a more competitive car, I will admit. But on the other hand, I know that it was necessary to pay a big price, particularly in the first half of the season, because we have everything new, even the fuel. The drivers, the chassis, the engine and the gearbox.

"We know that our engine is making very steady progress, but the first priority was to make the engine reliable. Now, after the first three races, we are involved in a deep investigation of the chassis in conjunction with John Barnard, because the interpretation of the rules for driver protection [introduced for 1996] theoretically leaves us with the possibility of having to think of a new chassis. But I sincerely hope not, both from financial and timing reasons. In the meantime, we will concentrate on working on the car, which is obviously very late indeed."

For his part, Barnard remarked, "To be honest, I'm a bit fed up with this pantomime, and I'm looking forward to some serious Shakespearian theatre at some time in the future. It's the usual situation: we're [Ferrari Design and Development] here as a scapegoat, and the moment something goes wrong, they start popping off at us. I can only assume that there is tremendous pressure from Turin."

Later that season, Barnard would finally tire of what he regarded as the endless politicking of the Ferrari team. He left and his place was taken by former Benetton designers Ross Brawn and Rory Byrne, who, unlike their predecessor, were happy to relocate to Italy.

VILLENEUVE DENIES FERRARI THE TITLE

Many F1 insiders would have wholeheartedly approved had Ferrari been able to celebrate its 50th anniversary by securing either the 1997 Drivers' or Constructors' World Championship. As things transpired, throughout that season, the team was not a sufficiently consistent scorer to fend off Williams in the battle for the constructors' title, and a down-to-the-wire shoot-out between Maranello's team leader, Michael Schumacher, and Jacques Villeneuve ended in tears with the German vilified in the European media for trying to ram the Williams driver out of the final race of the season, the European Grand Prix at Jerez.

This strategy backfired dramatically on Schumacher, although the FIA World Motor Sports Council took a lenient view of his alleged malfeasance. Despite expectations of draconian fines, possible race suspensions or even a points penalty that would see him start the following season with a negative points total, FIA President Max Mosley announced that the German would be stripped of his second place in the World Championship and be required to carry out some road safety campaign work on an FIA/European Union initiative in 1998.

Many F1 insiders regarded this as little more than a slap on the wrist, but Mosley explained that it was intended as a deterrent, aimed at anybody who had a mind to transgress the rules in the future.

"It sends a message to all drivers at all levels of the sport that, if you do something you shouldn't do, when the championship is at issue, you will be excluded from that championship," he said. "You cannot possibly gain anything by engaging in an illegitimate act."

At the start of the season, Ferrari President Luca di Montezemolo had said that it was the team's ambition to improve on its 1996 record of three wins. Schumacher had obliged with five victories, so from that standpoint it was a case of mission accomplished. Perhaps the biggest sin of which Michael had been guilty was to have raised Maranello's expectations so high that when the final disappointment arrived, the sense of anti-climax and pain was felt even more acutely.

Thus it was left to Jacques Villeneuve in the Williams FW19-Renault to win the World Championship in only his second season of F1 driving. The 26-year-old former Indy car champion survived a wobbly mid-season slump to bounce back and take the title against the odds. Even exclusion from the Japanese Grand Prix, a somewhat harsh, if admittedly self-induced penalty for a trifling offence, failed to ruffle his calm, despite the fact that he went into the final race one point behind title favourite Schumacher.

If Villeneuve's outspoken personality was hailed by some as a welcome breath of fresh air, the fact remains that the French-Canadian driver was the latest beneficiary of the Williams team's technical excellence. Like Nigel Mansell, Alain Prost and Damon Hill before him, Villeneuve was the throttle jockey who profited,

Above: **Silver dream racer. McLaren's Mika Häkkinen took the first of his back-to-back titles in 1998, clocking up an impressive eight victories.**

Centre: **Exaltation from Damon Hill on the victory podium following his 1998 Belgian Grand Prix win.**

Far right, top: **Ralf Schumacher seems none too happy with life!**

Far right, bottom: **On the way up. Giancarlo Fisichella switched from Jordan to Benetton.**

Photos: Paul-Henri Cahier

assuring the British team of its ninth Constructors' Championship in only 17 years. It was a remarkable achievement and an all-time record.

There were other achievements worth noting in 1997. The McLaren-Mercedes alliance scored its first three wins, returning Ron Dennis's team to the top step of the rostrum for the first time in its post-Ayrton Senna era.

Giancarlo Fisichella, Ralf Schumacher, Jarno Trulli and Alexander Wurz all signalled that there was another generation of F1 hopefuls waiting in the wings, while Damon Hill was left to go into 1998 as Grand Prix racing's 'Senior Citizen' following the retirement of the ever popular Gerhard Berger, who, having won brilliantly for Benetton at Hockenheim, rounded off his distinguished career with a hard-fought fourth place at Jerez, less than two seconds behind Mika Häkkinen's victorious McLaren.

McLAREN AND FERRARI: HEAD TO HEAD IN '98

The rule makers again sought to put a brake on F1 lap speeds in 1998, introducing a new breed of narrow-track car running on grooved tyres. The move was effective as far as it went, although much of the on-paper speed reduction was cancelled out by the intensity of the tyre war between Bridgestone and Goodyear. It was clear, however, that, had these changes not been brought in, lap speeds would have spiralled dangerously out of control.

The popularity of Grand Prix racing remained remarkable, with Bernie Ecclestone pursuing plans for the sport to be in pole position for the forthcoming digital television revolution, although his monopoly on F1 television rights continued to attract the questioning – and certainly very protracted – scrutiny of EU Competition Commissioner Karel van Miert.

The 1998 season was good for Ecclestone and the competing teams because a new Concorde Agreement was finally approved, signed, sealed and delivered. Frank Williams and Ron Dennis had stood out against signing in 1997, because they considered the other teams had failed to understand precisely what intellectual property rights they were signing away.

Eventually a new deal was formalised, which provided for between $9 and $23 million in annual television revenue for the 11 competing teams, with provision for a 12th in anticipation of Honda entering with its own factory team at the start of 2000. However, this never actually came to pass.

Meanwhile, the McLaren design team reckoned it had expended more than 12,000 man-hours over the winter of 1997/98 in attempting to claw back aerody-

namic downforce lost to the new regulations. The new MP4/13 also had a completely revised Mercedes-Benz FO 110G V10 engine, which weighed around five per cent less than its immediate predecessor.

McLaren had gambled on leaving the build programme for the new car as late as possible, Adrian Newey and his technical group reasoning that the team's serious development work for the new regulations had not really started until his arrival in August 1997. "Williams and the others had been hard at it since February or March," he said enigmatically, "so we had a steep learning ramp to climb."

McLaren also switched to Bridgestone tyres for 1998, having decided that, as Goodyear had indicated its intention to withdraw from F1 at the end of the season, it made sense to be among the advanced guard developing a relationship with what was set to become Grand Prix racing's sole tyre supplier.

Newey conceded that the change had cost the team a crucial extra week or so in terms of finalising the car's detailed suspension geometry, but this was judged well worth the effort. "The harder you use those tyres, the faster you go," reported Mika Häkkinen. "You can slide the car a lot and the rubber will sustain its grip. At last I can drive the car in the way I have always wanted to."

Once the season began, the MP4/13 was quite simply the class of the field, even after its asymmetric braking system was removed voluntarily by the team prior to the Brazilian GP, after a protest initiated by Ferrari. The car proved versatile, quick and generally moderately reliable. The Merc V10s were less so, crucial engine failures at Monaco and Monza sidelining Coulthard, who suffered another retirement when the throttle mechanism fell apart at Montreal. A counterfeit gearbox bearing also found its way into the McLaren supply chain to cause Häkkinen's retirement at Imola.

The lowest point of the year for the team came in the Belgian Grand Prix at Spa-Francorchamps, where Häkkinen was eliminated in a collision at La Source on the opening lap, while Coulthard had his rear wing ripped off later in the race when Michael Schumacher's Ferrari F300 slammed into the back of him in torrential rain while attempting to lap the Scot.

Schumacher three-wheeled back to the pits after his right front wheel was torn off in the impact and had to be restrained from assaulting Coulthard as the two men squared up to each other in a fury. Meanwhile, Michael's misfortune handed the lead to Damon Hill, the Englishman having moved from Arrows to the Jordan team at the start of the season.

Jordan had spent three years using Peugeot's promising V10, but had made the switch to Mugen-Honda power at the start of 1998. Initially the Gary Anderson-designed Jordan 198 had proved very troublesome to set up. To see Hill just scraping home ahead of a Minardi, lapped by Häkkinen's winning McLaren, in Monaco that season was to see a team on the verge of a major crisis.

Thereafter a fine effort reversed Jordan's fortunes during the second half of the year, and Hill surged home the winner at Spa, a few yards ahead of his team-mate, Ralf Schumacher, the younger brother of the Ferrari ace, who was fast making a reputation for himself as one of F1's most outstanding rising stars.

Ferrari, meanwhile, was having a storming season, and it was really beginning to look as though the Italian team's consistency and reliability would finally pay off with a World Championship. The F300 was a logical evolution of the previous year's F310B, although Ferrari Technical Director Ross Brawn admitted that under the new regulations, basic elements in the design, such as the centre of gravity, were even more critical. The cockpit of the new car had been moved back by about 10cm to facilitate the use of shorter side pods

while still conforming to the more exacting lateral impact tests introduced for 1998 and lowering the centre of gravity, a change also assisted by a slightly wider fuel tank and lower engine position.

Ferrari also switched to a longitudinal gearbox to transmit the power from its outstandingly reliable V10 developed by Paolo Martinelli's engine group. Rory Byrne remained as chief designer, working closely with Brawn.

Maranello was playing for high stakes. The team's sporting director, Jean Todt, opened the year by saying that anything less than winning the World Championship simply wasn't acceptable. The Frenchman had been in charge of Ferrari's F1 fortunes since the summer of 1993, and now, five years down the road, the level of expectancy was running on over-boost.

From the start of the season, it seemed as though Ferrari had been wrong-footed in the biggest possible way by the McLaren-Mercedes-Bridgestone alliance. Goodyear had been slow off the mark developing tyres for the new grooved regulations, and its new wider front cover – which would prove crucial in boosting Ferrari's fortunes – was also later than hoped for, but it was worried that it did not have a rear cover to match.

Once Goodyear got into the swing of the season, Ferrari could exploit its mechanical reliability to great advantage. Schumacher's win in Buenos Aires was followed by second place at Imola and third in Spain. Then came Monaco and one of the season's biggest disappointments. Michael qualified fourth, but finished down in tenth place after a collision with Alexander Wurz's Benetton.

Monaco was followed by three more decisive wins: at Montreal, Magny-Cours and Silverstone. All were controversial. In Canada, Schumacher pushed off Heinz-Harald Frentzen's Williams as he rejoined the track after a pit stop – careless, but possibly not deliberate – while in France, McLaren was left crying foul after an aborted start gave Michael a second chance following a poor getaway from the grid first time around. On his second attempt, he made no mistake and won easily, while Irvine fended off the McLarens in the opening phase of the race.

Silverstone saw Häkkinen give the German a rare wet-weather driving lesson, but the Ferrari driver emerged triumphant after Mika spun, although inevitably his victory was overshadowed by the controversy surrounding the ten-second stop-go penalty that Michael took after passing the chequered flag to win the race. This may have been technically correct to the letter of the rule book, but it allowed an absurd anomaly to enter the pages of history.

By this stage in the year, Ferrari was coming under close scrutiny from McLaren, who believed its rival was using some sort of asymmetric braking system, similar to that which the Mercedes backed team had removed from its own cars in Brazil, following objections from Ferrari. This was in addition to a suspicion that Ferrari was using an engine mapping system that effectively duplicated the effects of the now-banned traction control devices, although this was less of an issue, since most teams in the F1 field were attempting

Opposite: Michael Schumacher took the Ferrari F399 to victory at Monza in 1998.

Below: Jean Alesi, reflecting on F1 life as a midfield runner with Sauber.
Photos: Paul-Henri Cahier

to develop similar technology behind the scenes.

Unquestionably Hungary was Schumacher's finest race of the season, a combination of fine pit-wall strategy and Michael's committed genius at the wheel, ensuring that McLaren went down to an embarrassing defeat. Then came Spa and Schumacher's crucial stumble: over-wound and overwrought at the sight of Coulthard's McLaren ahead of him in a ball of spray, he made a momentary misjudgement. It could have cost him the title.

Monza brought with it a slice of good fortune when the faster McLarens hit trouble, allowing Schumacher and Irvine to post a 1-2 for Maranello. But at the Nürburgring, Ferrari found its Goodyear tyre choice insufficiently soft for the job. "It was a bit of a contrast to 1997, when we dreaded hot races," Brawn reflected. "This year's compounds have generally been very good in high temperatures, but we were too hard at the Nürburgring and couldn't get the grip."

Eddie Irvine had second places in France and Italy, plus his first ever front-row qualifying position at the Nürburgring, as consolation for the fact that he had yet to win a Grand Prix.

"I suppose being Michael's team-mate is good in a way, because you are measuring yourself against the very best," he said. "You are always aiming to climb Mount Everest every day you get into the car, whereas if there was somebody else in the other car, it would just be a gentle stroll up the Alps, wouldn't it?

"If you are running the team, everything goes your way. If you say something which is ignored because somebody in the team is more powerful, as Michael is here at Ferrari, then it's not good for your pysche.

Michael is a bit of a phenomenon, isn't he? It's a pisser, but it's true!"

The confrontation between Häkkinen and Schumacher reached its climax at the final race of the season, the Japanese Grand Prix at Suzuka, where Michael qualified on pole, ahead of his rival. A tingling sense of anticipation could almost be felt through the track surface itself as Häkkinen's sleek grey and silver McLaren-Mercedes took up its place alongside Schumacher's brilliant red Ferrari on the front row of the grid. Around the parade lap they went, pausing in their positions to await the starting signal, only for the whole procedure to be aborted after Jarno Trulli's Prost-Peugeot stalled down in 14th place.

The rules require that anybody who stalls and causes a restart should be put to the back of the grid. So off they went on their second parade lap.

Back on the grid, Schumacher pulled for first gear, the car lurched forward and stalled. "The engine stalled because the clutch did not free itself, and I don't know why," he explained later, "All the work this weekend was then wasted, as I had to start from the back." Subsequently it was concluded that the problem had been caused by overheating hydraulics, which had affected the way in which the clutch mechanism engaged.

With the start aborted again, the scarlet Ferrari had to go to the back of the grid for the second restart. That allowed Häkkinen a clear run through to a decisive win and the World Championship title with 100 points, 14 more than Schumacher, who fought back through the field, only for a rear tyre to explode and cause his retirement. McLaren number two, David Coulthard, finished a distant third overall on 56 points.

JORDAN IN THE ASCENDANT

The 1999 season promised more of the same, with McLaren-Mercedes and Ferrari the most obvious contenders, although Benetton, Williams and the new British American Racing team all held out high hopes for progress with the Renault-derived Supertec V10 engines that had been raced by Williams and Benetton under the Mecachrome label in 1998.

Goodyear having retired from the F1 scene, the FIA still went ahead with another speed reducing rule change, requiring that front tyres be deprived of more grip through the addition of a fourth circumferential groove. Most of the drivers were soon up in arms over these changes, which many insisted made the cars absolutely impossible to drive. Yet despite some processional races early in the season, the 1999 World Championship contest would turn out to be an electrifying affair, full of unexpected drama.

Aiming for a second straight season of domination, McLaren produced the superbly engineered new MP4/14, which was powered by an even lighter 72-degree Mercedes FO11H V10 developing an estimated 785bhp at 16,700rpm from the start of the season. With extra weight trimmed off the entire chassis/engine package, the new car offered even more scope for the strategic placement of ballast.

Mika Häkkinen and David Coulthard used the new cars from the start of the season, despite some serious consideration being given to running uprated MP4/13s at the first race if the new car did not prove quick enough in testing.

Ranged against the McLarens at the front of the field were the new Ferrari F399s, being evolutionary versions of the 1998 car, but equipped with seven-speed longitudinal gearboxes to make the most of the 780bhp at 17,000rpm offered by the type 048 V10 developed by Paolo Martinelli's engine department. Michael Schumacher was poised to start his fourth season with the team, partnered by the dutiful Eddie Irvine, whose contract still required him to give the German driver priority in his bid to win the Italian team's first Drivers' World Championship for 20 years.

At Williams, RaIf Schumacher and former CART champion Alex Zanardi formed a new driver line-up, replacing Jacques Villeneuve and Heinz-Harald Frentzen, who had moved to British American Racing and Jordan respectively.

Jordan, meanwhile, started the season in an upbeat mood after very promising tests with the new Mike Gascoyne-developed 199 chassis, which was powered by a further uprated Mugen-Honda MF301HD engine pumping out a reputed 765bhp. Damon Hill continued as team leader, with Frentzen – ironically the man who had displaced him at Williams in 1997 – alongside him.

The McLarens seemed set to dominate the first race in Australia, but technical problems sidelined both Häkkinen and Coulthard, leaving Irvine's Ferrari to beat Frentzen's Jordan. Schumacher's Ferrari was beset by gearchange problems that caused him to finish out of the points.

Häkkinen managed to get McLaren's score off the ground with a win at Interlagos, but the first signs of

Above: David Coulthard drenches his team-mate, Mika Häkkinen, after the Finn was crowned 1998 World Champion.

Left: The McLaren MP4/13-Mercedes V10s of Häkkinen and Coulthard lead the field at the start of the 1998 Monaco Grand Prix.

Photos: Paul-Henri Cahier

the Constructors' Champion's potential vulnerability came at Imola, where Mika crashed inexplicably while leading the San Marino Grand Prix and Coulthard simply couldn't get on terms with Schumacher's winning Ferrari.

Michael backed this up with a superb win in Monaco, soundly beating Häkkinen into third place, behind Irvine, but the Finn bounced back to head a McLaren 1-2 in Spain. Then the tables were turned in Canada, where the German driver crashed heavily while leading and the McLaren team leader took the win.

Unpredictable wet/dry conditions, allied to a shrewd Jordan refuelling strategy, helped Frentzen to victory in the French Grand Prix at Magny-Cours, but then the title chase took on a whole new complexion when Schumacher crashed heavily on the opening lap of the British Grand Prix at Silverstone, sustaining a broken right leg.

With Häkkinen's McLaren being prudently withdrawn from the battle after shedding its left rear wheel, the number-two drivers picked up the gauntlet to produce a close-fought battle all the way to the chequered flag, Coulthard just winning from Irvine. The former's McLaren had the performance edge over the Ferrari, and the Scot drove with great restraint and self-discipline to conserve his machinery, edging away from Irvine in the closing stages when he realised the race was all but won.

On a day inevitably clouded by the sombre sight of Ferrari's brilliant team leader clattering away to hospital in a medical helicopter, Coulthard's win represented a crucial moment of restoration for the easy-going 28-year-old, who had last tasted victory in the 1998 San Marino Grand Prix.

Schumacher's nightmare began in the first few yards of the race, when the advantage of his front-row starting position immediately slipped away as Häkkinen and Coulthard surged their McLarens into first and second places. As if to add insult to injury, Irvine's Ferrari swept majestically around the outside of the German ace going into Copse, pushing him back to fourth place.

Down through the luridly quick ess-bend at Becketts, Schumacher came hard at Irvine and slipstreamed on to his tail as the two Ferraris accelerated up to 185mph on the Hangar Straight. Irvine glanced in his mirror and dutifully allowed just enough room for Schumacher to have free passage down the inside into the tricky Stowe right-hander, which tightens up on itself as it leads around into the Vale.

Suddenly things went wrong. Instead of cuffing a gentle arc to the right, Michael locked up his front brakes. From then on, everything was lost. The Ferrari skidded on to the gravel trap, which did virtually nothing to reduce his speed, and slammed head-on into the retaining tyre wall.

The horrifying impact ripped off the front end of the Ferrari monocoque. Schumacher caught his breath and began to lift himself from the shattered F399. After a moment's effort, he slumped back into the cockpit as marshals swarmed around the car. He had sustained a double fracture below his right knee, and would have to wait for the ambulance to arrive before being released from the wreckage and taken off to the

medical centre, jauntily waving to his fans from the stretcher.

"I had to touch the brakes to avoid David [Coulthard] going into Becketts on the first lap, and it's possible that Michael may have touched me and damaged his front wing," said Irvine. "All I know is that he came flying past me all locked up. I think he just out-braked himself."

On the face of it, this seemed the logical view. Schumacher had been frustrated by the handling of his car during the race morning warm-up and had made a quick-fix change to the set-up in an effort to improve things. Then he was jumped into Copse by Irvine and, in his anxiety to stay in touch with the McLarens, might just have been willing to take one risk too many as he slammed into Stowe.

In fact, having examined all the technical data at its disposal, the Ferrari team concluded that a rear brake malfunction had caused the accident.

The incident was also an endorsement of the overall high safety standards that had come to be taken for granted over the previous few years and had been encouraged by both the F1 constructors and the FIA. When one considers that many drivers in the 1990s regularly walked away uninjured from the sort of impacts that tore apart Jochen Rindt's Lotus 72 during the Austrian's fatal accident at Monza in 1970, it is a graphic illustration of how effectively technology was applied to making Grand Prix racing a safer and more secure professional sport.

Meanwhile, at Silverstone, Ralf Schumacher's Williams finished third after vaulting ahead of Frentzen's Jordan, while Damon Hill, who had decided that he

would retire from racing at the end of the season, took fifth at the chequered flag. Jordan was ever present and increasingly in touch at the front of the field.

Häkkinen's misfortunes now multiplied dramatically. He was pushed off on the opening lap of the Austrian Grand Prix after an over-ambitious passing move by Coulthard on the second corner. As if this wasn't bad enough, Irvine dodged through to win after the McLaren team failed to keep Coulthard sufficiently well briefed about the Ferrari's progress. Häkkinen recovered to finish third.

At Hockenheim, a 200mph rear tyre failure sent Häkkinen sailing into a tyre barrier and left Irvine to saunter home for his second win in as many weeks, ahead of Schumacher's stand-in, Mika Salo. Häkkinen regained his composure to win from Coulthard in Hungary, but then the positions were reversed at Spa, where the Scot notched up his second win of the season in the Belgian Grand Prix, after an unruly first-corner barging match between the two McLaren drivers.

By this time, the apparent lack of team orders discriminating between the two McLaren-Mercedes drivers was the subject of intense media scrutiny. In an effort to appear even handed – understandably so, perhaps, since both Häkkinen and Coulthard had signed identical contracts in this respect – the management wanted to give them both a fair chance.

Even so, while they might have been forgiven for discounting Irvine's chances after his surprise midsummer victories in Austria and Germany, they seemed to ignore Frentzen in the ever improving Jordan, who was coming up on the rails as a strong outsider.

TOBACCO WARS FUND F1 EXPANSION

IT was at the start of the 1968 season that Colin Chapman's Team Lotus rewrote the sponsorship book by accepting funding from the Player's tobacco company, at a stroke replacing his cars' distinctive green and yellow livery with the rather gaudy red, white and gold of the Gold Leaf cigarette brand.

At the time, this was regarded as imaginative and up-to-the-minute promotion in tune with the mood of the day. This tone continued well into the 1970s, when Lotus carried the distinctive and classier black and gold livery of the JPS brand.

At the height of the JPS sponsorship programme, with Lotus enjoying great success, the cigarette company adopted an extremely lofty attitude towards those scribes who still referred to the cars as Lotus-Fords. Its argument was that they were officially entered in the World Championship as John Player Specials. Needless to say, this did not wash. Not for long, anyway.

In 1972, the giant Philip Morris organisation was persuaded to sponsor the fading BRM team under its Marlboro brand. The sponsorship lasted for just two seasons before Marlboro switched to McLaren, a partnership that would endure for 23 seasons.

It was Marlboro's marketing managers who really showed how to make sponsorship effective and, in the process, the sport as a whole became dramatically dependent on its money. Not only was the company active at the highest level in Formula 1, but also it sponsored junior formulas in an effort to bring on F1 drivers of the future, notably the British Formula 3 Championship, which spawned such talents as Ayrton Senna, Martin Brundle and Johnny Herbert.

In 1984, Marlboro made a huge commercial leap by gaining space on the side of the Ferrari F1 cars, even though the company founder, Enzo Ferrari, had been critical of tobacco sponsorship's arrival in F1 more than a decade earlier.

Initially the Marlboro/Ferrari deal was excused on the basis that the sponsor simply contributed to driver retainers and no more, but since Enzo Ferrari's death in 1988, Marlboro backing for the famous Italian team became the biggest single sponsorship deal in Grand Prix racing, worth in excess of £35 million annually.

Yet the role of the tobacco companies as Grand Prix motor racing's most prolific paymasters came under gradual threat from as early as 1983, when Britain followed Germany's example and banned competing teams from carrying sponsorship identification on their cars and transporters.

It was a measure of the success of subliminal advertising, however, that the substitution of 'McLaren' for 'Marlboro' on the red and white McLarens and, subsequently, of 'Racing' for 'Rothmans' on the Williams-Renaults was scarcely noticed by a large proportion of race fans and, more particularly, of television viewers.

Up until the late 1990s, tobacco companies involved in F1 sponsorship remained cautiously relaxed about any further restrictions, feeling that, to a large degree, they had pre-empted the planned government legislation by their voluntary restrictions. However, by the start of the 1999 season, things were changing. Ironically, F1's newest team, British American Racing, almost unwittingly played a crucial role in helping the FIA prove to the European Union that it was not giving the tobacco companies an easy ride.

British American Racing, whose number-one driver was 1997 World Champion Jacques Villeneuve, ran into a head-on confrontation with the FIA and its president, Max Mosley, over the issue of dual branding.

BAR's intention of running one of its cars in red and white Lucky Strike livery and the other in dark blue 555 identification was not acceptable under the F1 rules, which require both of a team's cars to be fielded in substantially the same livery.

Despite an agreed arbitration hearing, which went against BAR, Craig Pollock, the team's managing director, went one step further and lodged an official complaint with EU Competition Commissioner Karel van Miert over what he regarded as the FIA's anti-competitive stance. This was a breach of the Concorde Agreement, and BAR was summoned to appear before the FIA's World Council five days after the Australian Grand Prix.

The matter was resolved without further sanction, but there was much more to this than simply the issue of an ambitious newcomer rocking the F1 boat. For some time, the FIA had been keen to be seen to be responsive to the anti-tobacco lobby, while at the same time orchestrating a well-ordered retreat from reliance on the industry's funds to comply with the European Union's requirement that the sport should dispense with tobacco sponsorship from 2006. Pollock's attempt to bring two brands on to the Grand Prix stage for the price of one had given Mosley an opportunity to take a tough line.

"We feel their attempt to run two tobacco sponsors is going too far," said Mosley. "Several governments make concessions and allow teams to run with tobacco advertising, but one mustn't overdo it."

However, with a firm line having been drawn for the end of F1 tobacco sponsorship, it soon became clear that both the cigarette companies and motor racing's governing body had become alert to the important issues involved.

A shift of emphasis in terms of F1 funding was clearly looming on the distant horizon. Increased involvement by major motor manufacturers quickly signalled the path ahead. By the end of 1999, Ford had purchased Stewart Grand Prix, Mercedes-Benz had taken a $250 million 40-per-cent stake in the TAG McLaren Group and BMW had entered F1 after forging a commercial partnership in addition to a five-year engine supply deal with Williams.

When Häkkinen inexplicably threw away victory in the Italian Grand Prix at Monza with a spin while leading, Frentzen dodged through to take the win and moved into third place in the World Championship, two points ahead of Coulthard and just ten points – a single win – behind the dead-heated Häkkinen and Irvine.

However, McLaren boss Ron Dennis was not about to be bullied by the media into changing the nature of his contractual relations with the team's drivers. In his view, his policy had served McLaren pretty well for more than a decade and he was anxious to play fair with the men he employed behind the wheel.

"During the course of the season, we work strenuously to treat both our drivers evenly and ensure that they are both equally favoured in terms of chances to win the World Championship," he insisted.

"Having said that, when we are seeking to close down the championship from a threat by another team, it is only logical to help the driver who has the best mathematical chance of doing so. This is entirely different from deciding at the start of the season that one driver is a number one and will be specifically favoured over the number two, irrespective of the status of the World Championship."

Nevertheless, Häkkinen's slip at Monza gave a timely boost to Irvine's title chances. The Ferrari driver could only finish a disappointed sixth on his team's home turf, unhappy with the F399's fast-circuit performance on this occasion, but he and Häkkinen were now level on 60 points with three races left to run. "We got out of jail today," said Irvine thankfully.

This really was turning into the World Championship nobody seemed to want to win. The European Grand Prix at the Nürburgring followed, where Johnny Herbert gave the Stewart-Ford squad a memorable maiden victory, the veteran British driver calling his tyre stops to perfection in tricky wet/dry/wet conditions.

McLaren and Ferrari again bombed out. Häkkinen was called in for a premature first tyre change and eventually scraped home in fifth, while Coulthard crashed out of the lead, a slip that finally wiped out his hopes of the title. Mika now led by two points with two races to run.

The penultimate event of the season was the inaugural Malaysian Grand Prix at Kuala Lumpur's magnificent new government funded Sepang circuit. After endless pre-race uncertainty, Michael Schumacher made a brilliant return to the cockpit, qualifying in pole position and driving a defensive, tactical race into second place, behind Irvine.

This proved a hugely controversial episode, for not only did Schumacher ruthlessly balk Häkkinen, keeping the frustrated McLaren driver bottled up in third place all the way to the flag, but then both Ferraris were excluded from the results at post-race scrutineering after their aerodynamic side deflectors ('bargeboards') were found to have infringed the permitted dimensions.

On the face of it, this handed Häkkinen his second straight World Championship, but Ferrari lodged an appeal against the disqualification. The following Saturday, the FIA Court of Appeal, in a highly controversial and questionable interpretation of the technical rules, reversed that exclusion, reinstating Irvine and Schumacher in first and second places.

Häkkinen now had it all to do at the Japanese Grand Prix, going into the final event of the season four points behind Irvine. But the Finn regained his composure quite brilliantly to dominate the race, winning from Schumacher and Irvine to retain his championship crown by two points.

By way of consolation, Ferrari clinched the constructors' title for the first time in 16 years, which many people regarded as a fair division of the season's spoils. In reality, of course, it was a case of McLaren losing the constructors' crown rather than Ferrari winning it, but it was all grist to the mill for the news-hungry media, setting up the prospect of yet another enthralling struggle for supremacy at the start of the new millennium.

Above: **Mika Häkkinen takes the chequered flag at Suzuka to confirm his second World Championship by a mere two points from Ferrari's Irvine.**

Opposite: **British American Racing's dual-liveried car was seen as a step too far by the authorities, who banned such graphic contrivances thereafter.**
Photos: Paul-Henri Cahier

Michael Schumacher aboard the
Ferrari F2002 in which he claimed
the third of his five consecutive World
Championship titles.
Photo: Paul-Henri Cahier

THE late 1990s had effectively seen Michael Schumacher warming up for his principal act. He'd switched from Benetton-Renault to Ferrari at the start of 1996 and, through the subsequent ten seasons during which he wore Maranello's bright red overalls, he was always a contender for the title crown. In so many ways, Michael had become the most rounded and complete performer on the championship stage, and it was no surprise to anybody in the F1 business when he finally began rattling away those World Championships.

Ferrari's F1-2000 was a good machine, but ranged against his old rival, Mika Häkkinen at McLaren, bursting through to take his first Ferrari championship would not be the work of a moment for Schumacher. By mid-season, he had been 22 points ahead, yet by three-quarter distance, he was several points behind. But, leaving aside all the detail, this was probably the first season in which the Ross Brawn-engineered Ferrari had genuinely showed itself to be evenly matched with the contemporary McLaren-Mercedes.

The F1-2000 was a totally new package powered by a brand-new V10 engine, the vee angle of which had been opened from 80 to 90 degrees, a move that allowed Brawn and his team to lower the car's over-

all centre of gravity, which substantially improved its aerodynamics. Schumacher opened the season with victories in the Australian, Brazilian and San Marino GPs, but while any chance of success in Spain went out of the window due to a chaotic pit stop, which saw Ferrari chief mechanic Nigel Stepney ending up with a broken leg, and the failure of an overheated rear suspension link snatched Monaco from the team in the closing stages, Ferrari built up a tactical momentum that was hard to stop.

One could say with good reason that McLaren's chances were badly damaged by Häkkinen's engine failure in the inaugural US GP at Indianapolis, but Brawn and Schumacher always impressed with their clever tactics, most notably in Michael's title clinching performance at Suzuka, where he took on extra fuel at the first stop to gain the flexibility of a longer middle stint.

"And Michael paced himself beautifully, so as not to alert Häkkinen too much," recalled Brawn with great satisfaction. "Then, as soon as Häkkkinen was in the pits for the second time, bang! Michael did the business. It was a race we won which they should have won." More crucially, that elusive championship crown was Ferrari's at long last.

Left: **Hear no evil for BAR's Jock Clear and Jacques Villeneuve.**

Below: **Schumacher takes victory in the rain at Montreal, just one of nine wins for the German on his way to the 2000 championship.**
Photos: Paul-Henri Cahier

MIXED FORTUNES AT McLAREN

With Mika Häkkinen taking four wins and David Coulthard three at the wheel of the impressive McLaren-Mercedes MP4/15, the 2000 campaign certainly looked like creating envy among all the rivals of the famous Woking based team. Yet psychologically both men seemed under even more pressure than usual. Perhaps worn out by the efforts involved in stringing together consecutive title crowns in 1998 and 1999, Häkkinen took a mid-season break, obviously missing no races, but a sufficient rest to recharge his batteries.

Coulthard, for his part, went into the season knowing that his place in the McLaren squad was under scrutiny. "It is very important for him," said McLaren managing director Martin Whitmarsh, in what was a brutally frank assessment of the Scot's position, even by the unyielding standards of the F1 business.

"David is intelligent enough to realise that we considered other drivers for this season. When he is strong and performing, he is very good. What he has to do now is to take those peaks and turn them into a plateau. There is no sentimentality here; we have to have the best drivers. David has earned his position in the team and knows this is the year to prove his capability." In the end, the popular Scot would remain as a member of the McLaren line-up until the close of 2004.

As things transpired, Coulthard would be faced with a situation during the course of the year that would test his personal resilience in far more dire circumstances than anybody could possibly have imagined. Ten days after beating Häkkinen to post an impressive victory in the British GP at Silverstone, Coulthard had literally come within inches of death when his chartered private jet skidded off the runway while making an emergency landing at Lyons airport, an accident that tragically resulted in the deaths of both the pilots.

Only a few days after this disaster, Coulthard proved his mettle by finishing second to Häkkinen in the Spanish GP at Barcelona, a race where he was on the receiving end of another bout of aggressively defensive driving from Michael Schumacher. On this occasion, Michael's weaving was so blatant that it received comment not only from the Scottish driver, but also from McLaren team principal Ron Dennis.

"The behaviour at the start is the second time that Michael has pushed things right to the edge," said Dennis. "You don't win these races by having a passive approach, certainly, but there are limits which would not be crossed."

Clearly, Coulthard's tragic experience further sharpened his awareness of the dangers lurking both on and off the circuit. Later in the year, he would call for heavy penalties to be imposed on the organisers of the Italian Grand Prix after a Monza track marshal was fatally injured by flying debris following a multiple collision on the opening lap of the race.

"I think the race should have been stopped," he commented, "not continued while he lay at the side of the track receiving emergency medical treatment." From a purely pragmatic viewpoint, this also marked the end of Coulthard's World Championship challenge, as the sprint to the title was now mathematically between Häkkinen and Schumacher for the balance of the season.

"To say I am disappointed is an understatement, really," he said. "I've had fewer obstacles on the track this year, but I'm still tripping at the last hurdle. I've got to do my best in these last few races, then try again next year."

Above: **Rubens Barrichello tries unsuccessfully to contain his tears of joy on the rostrum at Hockenheim after scoring his maiden F1 triumph in the 2000 German GP at the wheel of a Ferrari.**

Left: **The unmistakable profile of Schumi.**

Right: **Up yours! The FIA took a dim view of David Coulthard giving Michael Schumacher the finger as they battled for the lead of the 2000 French GP; the Scot apologised for the gesture afterwards.**

Photos: **Paul-Henri Cahier**

Right: An elated Juan Pablo Montoya celebrates his first GP win for BMW Williams at Monza in 2001.

Below: Jenson Button made his F1 debut impressively for Williams in 2000. It was the start of a long and unpredictable journey that would eventually lead the popular British driver to the 2009 World Championship crown.

Photos: Paul-Henri Cahier

CAR MAKERS FLEX THEIR F1 MUSCLES

The 2000 season was also a key turning point in recent F1 history, marking a fresh surge of interest from some of the sport's biggest car makers, including Mercedes, BMW, Ford, Toyota and Honda, all of whom were attracted by the commercial possibilities offered by an association with one of the most highly visible of international sports.

Mercedes was well established, of course, as McLaren's long-term engine partner, but now its parent company, DaimlerChrysler, decided to exercise its option to purchase 40 per cent of the TAG McLaren Group, an investment that was thought to value the business in the region of £700 million. Later it would also yield a joint project for the development of the Mercedes SLR McLaren high-performance road car and would further cement an F1 alliance that continues on-track to this day.

Meanwhile, although Williams experienced its third season without a race win, a brand-new engine supply deal with BMW returned the iconic Munich based car maker to the Grand Prix grids. BMW had not been involved in the sport's most senior category since the turbo era of the 1980s, when its high-boost, four-cylinder forced-induction engines carried Nelson Piquet to the 1983 title for the Brabham team, which at that time was owned by Bernie Ecclestone.

F1 in the new millennium called for a more ambitious approach. Whereas BMW's turbo programme had been overseen by respected engineer Paul Rosche and a small group of technicians, almost working in the corner of the factory, the 2001 programme saw BMW establish a dedicated engineering centre for the new breed of V10 engines at its Munich headquarters. It was very much a transitional season, the promising driver pairing of Ralf Schumacher and Jenson Button climbing as steep a learning curve as the team.

Button, who'd impressed everybody when he had tested a Prost-Peugeot at Barcelona towards the end of 1999, admitted that he could hardly believe his ears when Frank Williams rang up to touch base. Williams was hugely impressed with Button's personality, but decided to check out his initial impressions with BMW's newly appointed competitions manager, Gerhard Berger. The latter watched Jenson during his first Williams test at Jerez and was convinced that he was something special – not only with his consistency and control behind the wheel, but also with his complete composure out of the cockpit.

Trouble was, Frank Williams had a long-term commitment that guaranteed Juan Pablo Montoya a place in the team from the start of 2001, so Button was warned that he would have to do something really impressive if he were to have a hope of keeping the Colombian out of the team for the following year.

"Jenson rattled Ralf's cage and he did not like it one little bit," said one well-placed Williams insider, "and he was out to lunch certainly in the last two races of the season." There was much potential to be unlocked from this second Anglo-German alliance on the F1 starting grid, but as technical director Patrick Head crisply observed, 36 championship points weighed against the 170 scored by Ferrari and 152 by McLaren was "pretty feeble".

BMW Williams would quickly build momentum, and in 2001 Ralf Schumacher would take four race victories, including beating his brother, Michael, in the first sibling 1-2 in F1 history at Montreal, one of the few occasions when the younger Schumacher managed to claim an edge. The Williams FW23 also carried Montoya to his first win in the Italian GP at Monza and, taken in the round, the Williams squad began to look once again like a potential World Championship challenger for the first time since Jacques Villeneuve's successful title onslaught of 1997.

The same could not be said for Ford's F1 ambitions. In the summer of 1999, Jackie Stewart and his family sold their Stewart Grand Prix operation to Ford for a figure reputed to be in the region of £100 million. Shortly afterwards, the Detroit automotive giant decided to rebrand the team under the Jaguar name, but there were moments when the organisation, if high on image, seemed to be worryingly short on substance.

Eddie Irvine and Rubens Barrichello effectively swapped roles, Irvine switching from Ferrari and the Brazilian taking his place at Maranello. Irvine's arrival

Below: **Ralf Schumacher scored the first win of his and BMW Williams's career in the 2001 San Marino GP.**
Photos: Paul-Henri Cahier

Above and above right: **Eddie Irvine took third place for Jaguar in the 2001 Monaco GP, just one of two podium finishes he managed during his three-year stint with the team, which would later be reborn as Red Bull Racing.**

Right: **After the highs of 1999 with Stewart Grand Prix, Johnny Herbert had a miserable 2000 season in the Jaguar team, failing to score a single point.**

Photos: Paul-Henri Cahier

at Jaguar confirmed what the team already suspected, namely that it was way off the standard required from an aerodynamic viewpoint. Irvine would stay there for three seasons, during which time he managed to achieve just two podium finishes, third at Monaco in 2001 and the same result in Italy the following year.

In a sense, Jaguar's failure to make its mark in F1 reflected Ford's unwieldy management structure at senior levels, with various personalities dipping in and out to no lasting effect over the five-year programme. Eventually Ford decided to call time on the whole programme at the end of 2004, selling the team to Red Bull, reputedly for just a dollar, on the condition that the new owner assumed all the company's existing commercial obligations. That sowed the seeds of the front-running Red Bull Racing operation that would challenge for the 2010 World Championship with a strong driver pairing of Sebastian Vettel and Mark Webber.

Ford's decision to divest itself of its F1 commitment was based on its failure to make a compelling case to stay in the sport, although one was bound to speculate whether there might have been a different outcome had the team actually managed to achieve

more when it was on the circuit. Ford's decision also seemed strangely perverse, given that the manufacturer had given so much vocal support to the GPWC power base, an alliance of car manufacturer-linked teams that was struggling to cut a better deal with commercial rights holder Bernie Ecclestone over the distribution of F1 income.

Renault, meanwhile, decided to purchase the Benetton F1 squad, while Honda continued to make progress supplying its works engines to the BAR squad and planning at the same time to expand that supply to encompass a second team, Jordan, for 2001. On the eve of first practice for the Belgian GP at Spa-Francorchamps, FIA President Max Mosley was one of the key guests who attended the formal announcement of Toyota's intention to start racing in F1 from the start of 2002. Add to that continuing speculation that a consortium of the car makers involved in F1 was considering making an offer to purchase a stake in Bernie Ecclestone's SLEC empire and, as the new millennium dawned, it seemed as though no self-respecting automobile manufacturer could resist scrambling for a slice of the F1 pie. It was not to prove an open-ended commitment, by any manner or means.

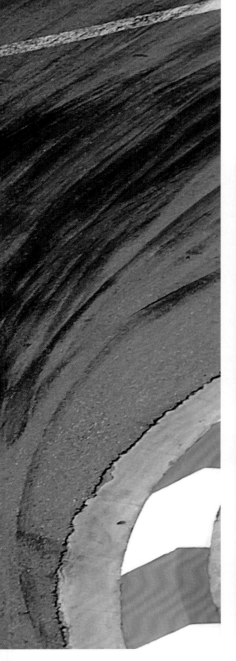

Above: Classic Monte Carlo backdrop. Michael Schumacher rounds Leows hairpin on his way to winning the 2001 Monaco Grand Prix.

Right: Two of the sport's most seasoned and senior engineers, Rory Byrne of Ferrari and Patrick Head of Williams, chatting on the grid at Imola, 2001.

Far right: Mika Häkkinen in the McLaren MP4/16 during the 2001 season, his last in front-line racing action. He would later race for Mercedes in the DTM after his retirement from F1.

Photos: Paul-Henri Cahier

Going into 2001, Ferrari effected such a seamless transition from its previous campaign that the two seasons appeared little more than a single 34-race series dominated by Michael Schumacher. Having at last broken Ferrari's apparent World Championship jinx, neither Michael nor Maranello was minded to let the trophy slip from their grasp, the effort being buttressed by Jean Todt's brilliantly focused management capability.

Yet there was never any doubt that Ferrari was Schumacher's ship and Schumacher's alone. Rubens Barrichello received a firm reminder of that when he was ordered to move over and gift Michael second place, behind David Coulthard's McLaren, in the Austrian GP. The Brazilian was understandably miffed, but in truth he was simply being reminded of the rules of the game. Twelve months later, when he was required to duplicate this manoeuvre, but this time relinquishing the actual race win, Rubens found it difficult to be philosophical. Or Todt in any way contrite, come to that.

HÄKKINEN CALLS IT A DAY

For Schumacher, there was never any shortage of bright-eyed young talents all champing at the bit for an opportunity to take on the great man should the right car and opportunity present themselves. As for Michael, respect for other drivers was often only proffered grudgingly, or so it seemed, but his unspoken respect for Mika Häkkinen had always been something easily discerned as the two men gradually worked their way to the front of the starting grids throughout the 1990s.

For almost a year, the Finnish driver had been toying with the idea of taking a sabbatical at the end of 2002. And that indeed is what he did. His decision was aided by the fact that the McLaren MP4/16 lacked the raw engine power and crisp handling required if he

was going to have a decent chance of taking on Schumacher's Ferrari F2001 at the very front of the pack. Like his team-mate, David Coulthard, Mika picked up only a couple of Grand Prix wins during 2001, at Silverstone and Indianapolis. But there were signs that the stress was getting to him, most notably at Monaco, where he felt so spooked about the handling of his car that he retired it after just 15 laps. How much of that was the car, or its driver, was difficult to say.

In many ways, that US GP success could be ranked as the best victory of the entire 2001 World Championship season. Häkkinen endured a catalogue of frustrations, including engine failure during Friday free practice, an accident in the race morning warm-up and the disappointment of being dropped from second to fourth on the grid when his best time was disallowed after he missed the red warning light at the end of the pit lane, also during the warm-up.

Despite this, Mika got his head together superbly, running a hugely disciplined race to make a one-stop refuelling strategy work for him, winning in a style that one would hardly have associated with a man about to take a sabbatical from his chosen sport. But Häkkinen stuck to his guns, softening the surprise with which his announcement had been greeted in some quarters by assuring his fans that it was his intention to return to F1 in 2003. Yet the sport is like an express train, waiting for nobody who is less than totally committed. In the event, Mika's fourth place at Suzuka, 2002, was the last finish of his F1 career.

And yes, it was a race that had been won by Michael Schumacher, now with 123 points under his belt at the end of this remarkable season, which saw Coulthard trailing in second place on 65. Most of Ferrari's opposition was simply left clinging to the shattered remains of its early-season ambitions. At the sport's most exalted level, the gap between the haves and have-nots seemed to be widening, not narrowing.

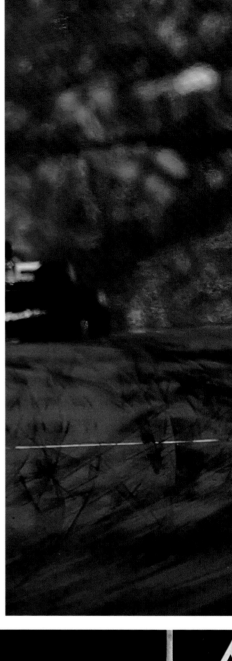

WILLIAMS BID THWARTED BY TYRE RULES

After four race wins in 2001, Williams had a disappointing 2002, with Ralf Schumacher delivering just a single victory in Malaysia, but Sir Frank's team bounced back impressively in 2003 with a car that was capable of challenging for the championship. After a slow start, Montoya drove brilliantly to win at Monaco, where Ralf managed pole position, Initially the younger Schumacher had the edge, but after Silverstone, where he put a wheel over the kerb, breaking one of the guide vanes that sent the water temperature off the clock, the advantage swung towards Juan Pablo.

Schumacher blotted his copybook somewhat in the French GP at Magny-Cours. The two Williams FW25s were very closely matched in this event, but Montoya thought the team had unfairly favoured Ralf as he completed his out lap after refuelling; he expected to be in the lead, only to find Schumacher coming out of the pits ahead of him. The Colombian lost his temper over the radio, telling the team what he thought of their biased tactics. Later he was summoned to the Williams factory for a severe dressing down.

Montoya did not like this, but he was wise enough not to let it get in the way of his increasing title momentum, helped by BMW's impressive P83 V10 engine and Michelin's steadily improving rubber. "Towards the latter part of 2002, the Michelin tyres took a big step forward in terms of their durability and stability," recalled Patrick Head. "We started to be in a position where we were less influenced by the heavy graining that had made it very difficult to develop the car.

"That was a big advantage to us. Michelin certainly did a great job in 2003, even if work still needed to be done on their wet-weather tyres."

There was, however, a rather tense moment that threatened to overshadow the title battle in the run-up to the Italian GP at Monza. Controversy over the legality of Michelin's F1 tyres was triggered after Bridgestone tipped off Ferrari that it considered the French company's products, in certain circumstances, could infringe the rule specifying that the front contact patch must not exceed 270mm. "This looked as though it could develop into a major rumpus and, given the perpetually febrile atmosphere which seemed to exist between Ferrari and most of its front-running rivals, gave way to speculation that Maranello were simply bad losers," continued Head.

The FIA technical delegate, Charlie Whiting, wrote to all the team principals, outlining the changes in the way the tread patterns on the front tyres would be checked in future. He advised, "With immediate effect, any part of a front tyre which we consider to have been in regular or systematic contact with the track will be deemed tread and will be taken into account when measuring the width of the tread as defined in the regulations."

In the end, Michelin made a new batch of tyres prior to the Italian GP to ensure that its contracted front-runners – Williams, Renault and McLaren – erred on the side of caution as far as the FIA's edict was concerned. The race went off without any worries, Schumacher's Ferrari F2003-GA – so called after the late Fiat patriarch, Gianni Agnelli, who had died earlier in the year – delivering a fairytale victory from Montoya's Williams. Ralf Schumacher stood down after a huge testing shunt at the circuit, his place being ably filled by test driver Marc Gené, who drove very respectably to finish fifth.

Continued on page 339

Above: Rubens Barrichello leads Michael Schumacher on his way to split-second victory in the 2002 Hungarian Grand Prix. Third-placed Ralf Schumacher tries to hang on to the Ferraris with his Williams-BMW.

Left: McLaren's David Coulthard at work between the armco barriers during the Monaco GP.

Far left: Bad boys. After Rubens Barrichello handed Michael Schumacher a last-corner victory in the 2002 Austrian GP, Ferrari hamfistedly tried to atone by allowing Barrichello to take top place on the podium. The FIA did not approve and handed the team a hefty fine.

Photos: Paul-Henri Cahier

Above: Michael Schumacher and Ross Brawn on the podium following the 2002 Brazilian Grand Prix.

Right: Allan McNish and Mika Salo were tasked with the challenge of taking the new Toyota F1 team into championship action.

Photos: Paul-Henri Cahier

Above: Final adjustments for Sauber team-mates Felipe Massa and Nick Heidfeld.

Left: Max Mosley and Ron Dennis usually had little to laugh about in each other's company.

Top: Peter Sauber, replete with his trademark cigar.

Photos: Paul-Henri Cahier

Above: Fernando Alonso makes his mark with his first Grand Prix win in the 2003 Hungarian Grand Prix.

Left: Giancarlo Fisichella finally wound up as the unlikely winner of the 2003 Brazilian Grand Prix after the race was stopped prematurely.

Right: Ever the high-profile, effervescent showman, Ferrari President Luca di Montezemolo celebrates Schumacher's Monza win in 2003.

Photos: Paul-Henri Cahier

With only two races left to the end of the season, Montoya led the pursuit of Schumacher, but dropped to third place in the title stakes, behind McLaren rising star Kimi Räikkönen, who had scored his first Grand Prix victory earlier in the season at Sepang.

It was Kimi's extraordinary consistency that allowed him to get to the end of the season still in with a chance of wresting the championship from Michael Schumacher, although the reason that he was eventually unsuccessful in that quest was down to the fact that McLaren slipped from the competitive high wire when it came to developing its new MP4/18 contender. Instead, he and David Coulthard had to rely on the upgraded MP4/17D for the entire season, a car that was good enough, perhaps surprisingly so, to win the first two races of the year.

It had been McLaren's intention to make the MP4/18 a very special production indeed, but its development cycle was strewn with problems. Never mind the fact that it twice failed the FIA side-impact test, it was also beset by excessive vibration from the all-new, lighter and lower Mercedes F0110P V10 engine, which triggered unwanted knock-on effects in terms of secondary component failures.

ONE-SHOT QUALIFYING INTRODUCED

Another major change to the rules in 2003 was the introduction of one-lap, Indy-style qualifying, which most people judged to be a fascinating development, if not perhaps the unqualified success one might have hoped, given the fact that the second Saturday qualifying session would now effectively become the opening stint of the race from the standpoint of fuel strategy.

Cars would then be confined to a *parc fermé* area and no additional fuel could be taken aboard before they took their places on the starting grid the following day. This made life a little more difficult for the television commentators, who now had to use inspired guesswork as much as inside knowledge to interpret just how heavy the fuel loads were when assessing an individual car's performance in the battle for grid positions.

Of course, F1 being the highly competitive business it is, such rule changes certainly did not please everybody, to the point where the Williams and McLaren teams went to arbitration with the argument that this was a clear breach of the governing body's rules, a dispute that would drag on beyond the completion of the racing season.

ALONSO SHOWS HIS METTLE

Fernando Alonso made his F1 debut in 2001, at the wheel of a Minardi. A young protégé of Flavio Briatore's FB Management company, he drew huge attention from the watching media in the press room at Monaco when the in-car camera feed from the cockpit of his Minardi was aired. Quite simply, this was a man who had something special about him, and it was no surprise when he was promoted to the role of Renault F1 test driver in 2002, a post that often involved the personable young Spaniard hanging around the team's catering truck at the Grand Prix, helping out where and when he could.

Midway through 2002, it was announced that Jenson Button would be leaving Renault to join BAR-Honda the following season, although it was a matter of some debate as to whether Jenson jumped or was given an encouraging push to help him leap overboard. It was certainly the right decision for Alonso, who made a totally seamless and trouble-free transition to the sport's senior league.

From the word go, Fernando looked like a potential race winner. He qualified superbly on pole in Malaysia, led the opening stages and wound up third to claim the first podium of his F1 career. He hounded Michael Schumacher's Ferrari to second place at Barcelona, a

performance that helped whip up huge enthusiasm for the sport in his native land, to the point where, just a week later, when he demonstrated one of the Renault cars through the streets of Madrid, an estimated 100,000 fans turned out to cheer him on.

Finally, at Budapest, Alonso became the youngest winner in the history of the official World Championship, beating the long-established record held by the late Bruce McLaren. At 22 years, 26 days old, he was three months younger than the New Zealander had been when he had triumphed in the 1959 US Grand Prix at Sebring, driving a works Cooper-Climax.

The young Spaniard won from pole position in torrid conditions that nudged the track temperature at the airless Hungaroring to well above the 40-degree mark to beat Kimi Räikkönen's McLaren MP4/17D by just under 17s.

"With ten laps to go, I was hearing noises from the engine and the gearbox in my mind," said an elated Fernando after the race. "It was fantastic. I needed this victory to grow up this year and have more chance next season. I came here knowing that I had a good chance of finishing on the podium. Then in the first stint, I started thinking I could win, because after 12 laps or so, I was 20 seconds ahead."

Alonso reeled off the season in sixth place in the World Championship, cementing his reputation as one of the most exciting new talents since Michael Schumacher had arrived on the scene more than a decade earlier. Ironically Fernando would not post a

race victory for Renault in 2004. That distinction fell to team-mate Jarno Trulli with his start-to-finish victory through the streets of Monte Carlo.

However, while that proved to be the high point of Trulli's career, never to be repeated, Alonso would really get into his stride from the start of 2005. And once the young man from Oviedo got a taste for success, nobody would seriously break him of the habit.

MONTOYA OPTS FOR A McLAREN MOVE

At the end of 2004, Juan Pablo Montoya decided to accept an invitation to join McLaren as team-mate to Kimi Räikkönen, leaving David Coulthard to accept the challenge of transferring to the Red Bull Racing squad, which had sprung from the flickering embers of the Jaguar organisation.

In the final race of the 2004 season, there was a curious symmetry about the result, Montoya's Williams-BMW easing out future team-mate Räikkönen's McLaren-Mercedes in a battle that was so close that on one occasion they ran down the pit lane side by side as they rejoined the contest following a refuelling stop.

Both Montoya and Räikkönen would win more Grands Prix in the future, but anybody who predicted that this would be the last Williams victory for many years would surely have been derided had they offered such a viewpoint at the end of 2004.

Yet the shifting sands of F1 fortune often contribute

Above: Jenson Button took pole position for the 2004 San Marino Grand Prix at Imola for BAR. The British driver had a hugely impressive season, finishing third in the Drivers' Championship behind the all-conquering Ferrari pairing of Schumacher and Barrichello.

Opposite: To the delight of the home crowd, Michael Schumacher skips to the podium following his win in the 2004 German Grand Prix. Third-placed Fernando Alonso was just part of the supporting cast as the Ferrari juggernaut rolled on.

Photos: Paul-Henri Cahier

to wildly unpredictable results. At the time of writing (April 2010), Williams still has to add another race win to its glittering tally of victories. As for the drivers concerned on that memorable day at Interlagos, Räikkönen would go on to win the 2007 World Championship for Ferrari, then quit circuit racing in favour of rallying at the start of 2010, while Montoya would survive an intermittently successful spell with McLaren before switching to the NASCAR series in the USA, an environment where he felt more comfortable and relaxed, just as he had done during his pre-F1 Champ car heyday.

MIXED FORTUNES FOR BUTTON

Jenson Button finally scored his first F1 podium finish with the BAR-Honda, taking third place in the 2004 Malaysian GP at Sepang. Then he put in such an impressive run to qualify on pole for the San Marino GP at Imola, finishing second to Michael Schumacher's Ferrari, that even the seasoned Ross Brawn was moved to comment favourably on the young Englishman's performance.

"Jenson had a good race. I am very impressed with him," said the Ferrari technical director. "The signs were there when he was at Williams, and his present form just goes to show that when a driver gets the right engineers, the right environment and the team believe in him, then he raises his game.

"For him to have taken pole position ahead of Schumacher was fantastic, and he is learning to work with the team. He is going to become very hot property over the next couple of years."

Only a few months later, Jenson went from hero of the hour to paddock pariah when he became tangled up in an unseemly sequence of events that saw his contract fall under the scrutiny of the FIA Contracts Rec-

ognition Board. Jenson had received an invitation to rejoin the Williams team, but if he thought that such a state of affairs would be meekly accepted by BAR team principal David Richards, then he was seriously mistaken.

The breach between Jenson and BAR came just after his superb drive to second place in the German GP. His then-manager, John Byfield, sent a fax to Richards, advising him that the driver would not be staying in 2005 and would be returning to Williams. It was not just the substance of the fax, but the manner in which it attempted to invoke what was claimed as a legitimate escape route, that really annoyed the BAR team principal.

"There is absolutely no question, we have a valid contract with Jenson," said Richards robustly. "If anything, I feel sorry for Jenson at this present moment for being so misled. Both myself and Geoff Willis, our technical director, have been attempting to call him for the last 24 hours, but without any success. This is a quite extraordinary situation."

Frank Williams weighed in confidently: "There has been a long-term relationship between the Williams team and Jenson," he said. "We have maintained that relationship to the present day, and I am delighted that one of the most talented drivers in F1 has accepted the opportunity to return to the team."

It took another couple of months for the FIA Contracts Recognition Board to rule that Button's BAR contract for 2005 was valid and took precedence over any contract with Williams. As an interesting footnote, David Coulthard claimed he was the only logical choice to take the now-empty seat alongside Mark Webber at Williams in 2005. But in the end, it was Nick Heidfeld who claimed the vacant spot, and DC moved to Red Bull to perform a crucial role in the team's rise towards the top.

Jenson Button's Brawn-Mercedes is dwarfed by the magnificent pit and hotel complex of the Yas Marina circuit, which hosted the Abu Dhabi Grand Prix for the first time in 2009.
Photo: Paul-Henri Cahier

Above: Fernando Alonso celebrates stemming the Schumacher/Ferrari tide at last after clinching the 2005 World Championship with victory for Renault in the Chinese GP.

Above right: Takuma Sato's BAR-Honda holds off the tyre-smoking Ferrari of Rubens Barrichello at the 2005 Bahrain Grand Prix.

Right: Kimi Räikkönen could sometimes deliver truly seismic race performances, and his last-lap victory over Giancarlo Fisichella's Renault at Suzuka in 2005 was one of the very best of the Finn's F1 career.

Photos: Paul-Henri Cahier

THE 2005 season was one of those seminal F1 turning points, where it seemed that one could simply draw a line between momentous eras in the sport's history. From the touchlines, it looked as though the combined efforts of Michael Schumacher, Ferrari and Bridgestone had driven Maranello's GP effort right over a precipice and out of the winning business.

The most obvious beneficiary of this drop-off in form by the man who had dominated the decade so far was Fernando Alonso, the young Spaniard now ripe for graduation to F1's front rank, his natural driving talent so obviously complemented by his tactical acuity that almost inevitably he drew comparisons with the likes of Jackie Stewart, Alain Prost and Niki Lauda as another classic example of an F1 driver who had peaked at precisely the optimum moment.

"I have to say, I think Alonso is extraordinary," said Lauda. "The more pressure he has, the better he drives. I've never seen any driver of that age so completely composed and consistent. Okay, he may have made a mistake at Montreal [where he hit the wall] but, speaking for myself, I reckon I would have made many more mistakes if I had been in that position at that age. He is a huge asset to the sport as a whole. I think he is perfect." Three years later, the Austrian would be making precisely the same comment to the author about Lewis Hamilton.

Therefore it was no surprise that Alonso emerged as the sport's youngest World Champion since Emerson Fittipaldi, who had taken the title for Lotus in 1972. He was also a great racer, and the manner in which he dominated the 2005 San Marino Grand Prix at Imola, driving just quickly enough to fend off the omnipresent Schumacher's Ferrari F2005, was an indication of the man's sheer quality, as if another were needed.

In 2005, all Alonso's eight race victories were earned on merit. He squeezed every ounce of potential from the excellent Renault R25, decisively eclipsing his respected team-mate, Giancarlo Fisichella, in the process. The Renault's only vulnerable point was that it was quite hard on its rear tyres, and the rival McLaren MP4/20 tended to have a performance edge in qualifying. Ferrari, of course, was off the radar.

"I don't think the McLaren was necessarily the better car," said Renault's executive director of engineering, Pat Symonds. "Everything is relative. The R25 was a superb car, but unfortunately the McLaren was slightly quicker, so therefore there was room for improvement. We didn't use our tyres as well as McLaren did. We were a little bit hard on them, after years of maybe suffering the other way."

Yet this brilliantly successful career was about to deliver an unwelcome sting for Alonso, even though at the time it was very difficult to anticipate. Fernando clinched the 2005 title crown with an energetic run to third place in the Brazilian GP, following in the wheel tracks of the McLarens of Montoya and Räikkönen.

On the rostrum, McLaren team principal Ron Dennis made a discreet inquiry. Would Alonso like to be part of the McLaren squad in 2007 once his final year with Renault had been played out? He agreed to the deal almost before the exhausts were stilled at the end of 2005.

In 2006, Alonso had another brilliant season, retaining his championship and posting another seven race wins. This was the season when the engine regulations were amended to 2.4-litre V8s, but such was Fernando's seamless transition from the previous year that it prompted Pat Symonds to comment wryly that the only real mistake the World Champion had made was to sign a contract with McLaren. As it turned out, he might have been right. For the moment, however, all he had to contend with was Michael Schumacher's final season with Ferrari, during which Michael ruined Fernando's potential pole winning lap at Monaco, and what was perceived as an unjust qualifying penalty at Monza for allegedly impeding Felipe Massa's Ferrari. Then in 2007, the real fun would begin.

By the time Alonso signed for McLaren, the pit-lane consensus was that the Spaniard would probably be replacing Räikkönen in the Woking line-up, as the Finn was being tipped to join Ferrari, which he duly did. Perhaps Alonso reckoned that automatically meant that his team-mate would be Juan Pablo Montoya – a piece of cake to handle. But it turned out to be a young and hungry Lewis Hamilton.

Fernando was in for one hell of a fight against the British newcomer, who had been groomed for stardom by McLaren since he had been a teenage karting sensation. Alonso won the second race of the year, in Malaysia, but by the time of the Monaco race, round five, the lid was off their intense personal rivalry. Alonso won the race, chased hard across the line by Hamilton. Neither was happy, as privately both drivers suspected

that the team had favoured their team-mate. Fleetingly it looked as though McLaren might be found guilty of illegally imposing team orders, but FIA officials cleared the team of any such offence.

The rivalry between the two men spilled over again at the Hungarian GP, where, as at Monaco, each driver believed the other had been favoured. During qualifying, Hamilton found himself forced to queue in the pit lane behind the other McLaren-Mercedes, and there was a spirited exchange on the radio between the team engineers and the two drivers. Late on the Saturday evening, McLaren team principal Ron Dennis, Alonso and Hamilton were called before the stewards, who ruled that Alonso had impeded Hamilton and docked him five grid places. It was the beginning of the end of Alonso's tenure with McLaren.

Behind the scenes, their relationship was close to boiling over after Alonso threatened to tell the FIA what he knew – or thought he knew – about the simmering controversy that would end with McLaren being fined $100 million by the FIA for being in possession of technical information relating to the rival Ferrari F2007, which had been leaked to the team by one of the Maranello engineers. Ron Dennis indicated that, in a desire for closure, McLaren would not appeal the punishing ruling that was widely regarded as one of the most excessive and unreasonable penalties ever imposed by the governing body.

At the end of the day, it was perhaps ironic – and symbolic of the tensions in their relationship – that Alonso and Hamilton tied for second place in the World Championship on 109 points, just a single point behind Ferrari recruit Kimi Räikkönen, who hauled back a 17-point deficit over the final two races of the year.

In 2008, Alonso would return to Renault, where he would win the inaugural Singapore GP night race un-

Above: Fernando Alonso basks in the satisfaction of having beaten his impressive young McLaren team-mate to victory in the 2007 Monaco GP, while third-placed Felipe Massa stares directly at the Cahier camera lens.

Left: Victory and a second world title confirmed at Suzuka for Alonso as he embraces his pit crew.

Far left: Alonso's Renault leads Räikkönen's McLaren at the start of the 2006 Canadian Grand Prix.

Photos: Paul-Henri Cahier

der controversial circumstances and back this with a superb win in Japan. After this, he marked time with the French squad through 2009 before finally securing a berth at Ferrari for 2010. It was the team where most people in the pit lane believed he rightly belonged.

MIXED FORTUNES FOR FERRARI

Ferrari's 2005 challenge fell apart, reducing Michael Schumacher and Rubens Barrichello to the role of bit-players, largely because of Bridgestone's inability to produce a tyre that would sustain its performance through the rigours of qualifying and a full race distance, as required by the newly instigated regulations.

Ferrari's programme started a little on the late side and never quite made up that lost ground. The need to redesign the aerodynamically below-par transmission package quite late in the day meant that the team had to run an updated F2004M in the first couple of races and did not debut the F2005 until Bahrain, the third round of the title contest.

Ross Brawn was anxious that none of the blame for this state of affairs should be pinned on Aldo Costa, the new chief designer, who had taken over from the veteran Rory Byrne. Clearly, however, while it was extremely satisfying being Bridgestone's prime runner when things were going well, it was less so when rival Michelin had the upper hand. As things turned out, Ferrari's only win in 2005 was Schumacher's success in the controversial 'Indy 200', otherwise the United States Grand Prix, where the Michelin runners were all withdrawn from the race after it had been decided that their tyres could not stand the forces involved in handling the final banked turn out on to the start-line straight.

"When you operate in isolation, as Ferrari does as the main Bridgestone runner, you don't quite know where you are," said Brawn. "But in a sense, that doesn't matter, because you are in a partnership, and the aim is to win races. But there are no cross-reference points. It has been very frustrating."

At the end of the season, Barrichello decided that for 2006 he would try his luck alongside Jenson Button in the BAR-Honda squad, leaving Schumacher to go into his final season of F1 with Ferrari paired with the emergent Felipe Massa. It hadn't been the best of years for the Prancing Horse, but at least things could only get better from this point onwards.

BAR-HONDA SUSPENDED IN FUEL-TANK CONTROVERSY

Button was well satisfied to have taken third place in the 2005 San Marino Grand Prix, behind Fernando Alonso's Renault and Michael Schumacher's Ferrari, but the young British driver could never have imagined what would unfold as his car was submitted to the post-race scrutineering process.

Although the stewards gave the car a clean bill of health, the FIA took the extraordinary decision to appeal against that decision and referred the matter to an FIA Court of Appeal in Paris just over a week later. Button's car had spent a protracted six-hour spell in the scrutineering bay after the race. Weighed immediately after the race, it had tipped the scales at 606kg, comfortably above the 600kg minimum weight

limit, but after it had been drained of fuel, it weighed only 594kg.

The team travelled to the next race at Barcelona knowing that the decision would be delivered on the Thursday prior to the start of practice. When the verdict was made public, it sent shock waves reverberating through the paddock. The team was handed a three-race suspension, including disqualification from third place at Imola, plus a suspended six-race ban that could be triggered at any time during the balance of the season in the event of a rule infringement on any other occasion.

"The facts of the case are very clear," said FIA President Max Mosley. "The team was asked to pump the fuel out of its car. It left 15 litres in the tank and told us it was empty. Under the circumstances, we feel BAR has been treated rather leniently."

However, the court stopped short of endorsing the FIA's contention that BAR had committed a fraudulent act in concealing the details of an apparently hidden fuel tank on Button's car. However, it concluded that the team had "displayed a highly regrettable negligence and lack of transparency."

The team was stunned, initially promising that it would appeal the court's verdict. But at the end of the day, team principal Nick Fry decided that it would be politically more astute to take the ruling on the chin and put a brave face on their abject disappointment.

TYRE FIASCO RUINS US GP AT INDY

Ralf Schumacher never had much luck in the US Grand Prix at Indianapolis. In the 2004 race, he had crashed his Williams-BMW heavily as he came out of the banked turn 13 – turn one for the classic Indy 500 oval race, which is run in the other direction – and by the end of the first day's practice in 2005, Michael's younger brother was experiencing an uncomfortable sense of *déjà-vu*.

In 2005, the consequences of his accident at the wheel of the Toyota TF105 were far more serious indeed. Michelin, tyre supplier to most of the front running cars in the field, immediately put up its hand and confessed that its tyres were unsuitable for the circuit. But this potentially dire and extremely serious situation was compounded by the FIA's inertia in helping to resolve the unfortunate and embarrassing issue.

To mitigate the problem, and reduce the strain on its tyres, Michelin wanted the organisers to erect a chicane to slow the cars coming into turn 13. There was a clear precedent for taking such a step, the teams citing the 1994 Spanish GP at Barcelona, where the drivers had threatened to strike if such a chicane had not been added to the track layout.

A number of options were discussed. None seemed realistic in the cold light of day. One suggestion was to run the race behind the safety car, another to make the Michelin-shod cars detour through the pit lane on every lap. Michelin attempted to salvage the situation by flying in some Barcelona-spec tyres on race morning, but these proved to be of the same construction as the original Indy tyres, albeit with a different compound. They were not the answer either.

At the end of the day, the FIA resolutely refused permission for a chicane to be added to the circuit and, as the six Bridgestone-shod competitors – two Ferraris,

Above: Rubens Barrichello (left) after finishing second in the six-car 2005 US Grand Prix at Indianapolis, an unfortunate farce that spelled the end of F1's romance with the 'Brickyard'. Ferrari's Ross Brawn, the FIA's Herbie Blash and race winner Michael Schumacher look on.

Right: Irate American fans demand their money back.

Far right, top: Under pressure. BAR team principal Nick Fry with Michelin's Pierre Dupasquier.

Far right, bottom: The damaged Michelin tyre that sparked the safety issues at Indianapolis.

Photos: Paul-Henri Cahier

two Jordans and two Minardis – took up their places on a strangely empty starting grid, the Michelin runners all coasted slowly into the pits at the end of the formation lap and called it a day even before the starting signal had been given.

The bitterly disappointed crowd was left with the ludicrous sight of the two Ferraris racing each other, Schumacher eventually beating Barrichello by 1.5s, with Tiago Monteiro's Jordan third after 73 sterile laps.

Max Mosley's subsequent summons to all the Michelin teams to appear before the FIA's World Motor Sport Council the following week served merely to harden their belief that the sport's governing body was pursuing an overtly political agenda against them for rebelling against the proposed 2008 Concorde Agreement while simultaneously exploiting the chaos to create a situation where F1 could become the preserve of a single tyre supplier.

FIRST TURKISH GRAND PRIX AT ISTANBUL

Fitting the Turkish GP into an already crowded World Championship schedule was never going to be the work of a moment, but at least there was a three-week gap following the previous race in Hungary, which brought to an end an unprecedented helter-skelter of eight races spread over the previous 11 weekends.

The Istanbul Park circuit shared its anti-clockwise configuration with only two other circuits on the World Championship calendar, Imola and Interlagos. Yet it was the constructional challenge that stretched track designer Hermann Tilke's team to their limits.

"We needed to blast away a lot of rock," said Tilke, "but we were already experienced in that from our work in Bahrain. There we moved approximately a million cubic metres of rock. Here, the excavation totalled about three million cubic metres. We even had to case a small river that now runs underneath the circuit in a concrete channel!"

Tilke added, "It is very important to my team and I that our race tracks make it apparent which country is hosting F1. In Bahrain, it was the desert; in Shanghai, we made use of the river delta environment; and for the Istanbul track, we used oriental elements that you no longer see all that often here because Turkey has become a very modern country in respect of its architecture."

Come the race itself, Kimi Räikkönen underlined yet again that the McLaren-Mercedes MP4/20 was probably the quickest car of the year, totally dominating the race from the start to post a runaway victory by just over 18s from Fernando Alonso's Renault R25. Good though the performance was, he would lack the overall consistency to beat Fernando to the title.

GRAND PRIX
DE FRANCE

...URS 200...

Above: **Another good day at the office. Michael Schumacher acknowledges his mechanics after winning the 2006 French Grand Prix.**

Above right: **Schumacher signals his defeat of Alonso in the 2006 Chinese Grand Prix.**

Right: **There is nowhere like Monza, particularly when a Ferrari is the winner. Here the *tifosi* enact the obligatory track invasion after Michael Schumacher's 2006 Italian Grand Prix win.**

Photos: Paul-Henri Cahier

SCHUMACHER BACK IN CONTROVERSY

Michael Schumacher's ability to clad his character with an almost impervious coating of 'Teflon' was thrown into the sharpest possible relief during practice for the 2006 Monaco Grand Prix, which at the time was to be his final visit to the streets of the principality before hanging up his helmet for good at the end of the season.

Yet any suggestion that Michael might have been inclined to ease his pace slightly as he set out on the road towards the end of a glittering career would have been naïvely optimistic. Battling for pole position through the streets of the Grimaldi principality, he suddenly skidded his Ferrari 248 F1 to a halt under braking for Rascasse in a rather obvious attempt to thwart Alonso's Renault, then midway around what looked like a quicker lap and about to usurp his position on pole.

After examining the evidence at some length, the Monaco stewards decreed that they were "left with no alternative but to conclude that the driver deliberately stopped his car on the circuit in the last few minutes of the qualifying at a time when he had thus set the fastest lap time."

Rather than accept the ruling with a modicum of dignity and good grace, Ferrari boss Jean Todt let rip with an indignant critique of the decision, reawakening memories of his similarly self-absorbed defence of the team's decision to instruct Rubens Barrichello to relinquish victory in the 2002 Austrian Grand Prix.

"Ferrari notes with great displeasure the decision of the race stewards, which is to delete the times set by Michael Schumacher in qualifying for the Monaco Grand Prix," he fumed. "We totally disagree with it. Such a decision creates a very serious precedent, ruling out the possibility of driver error. Michael was on his final timed lap and he was trying to put his first place beyond doubt, as could be seen from the fact that his first split time was the best and could have seen him do another very good lap.

"With no real evidence, the stewards have assumed he is guilty."

Renault team principal Flavio Briatore missed no opportunity to aim a barbed remark in the direction of Maranello. "It is disgusting," he said. "This is the way Ferrari manages."

Others also did not pull their punches. "It was the cheapest, dirtiest thing I have ever seen in F1," said Keke Rosberg, the 1982 World Champion. "He [Schumacher] should leave F1 and go home. I think he's underestimated our intelligence by trying to claim it was a driving mistake. I mean, give me a break."

Ironically Keke's remark would bounce back to prominence four years later, when his son, Nico, found himself paired with the veteran Schumacher, now 41, who was making a much debated return to the cockpit with the Mercedes team, previously the Honda and Brawn operation. It was just what Rosberg Junior could have done without. From the very start of 2010, the younger German looked like a schoolboy who had been told to stand in the corner by the Mercedes management and only speak when spoken to, leaving centre-stage clear for the great Michael to expound his philosophy to a rapt audience.

At Monza in 2006, Michael won the Italian Grand Prix yet again, but he was still the centre of controversy after Fernando Alonso delivered another scathing critique of his professional behaviour. This, remember, was at the race meeting where Michael had announced that he would definitely be retiring at the end of the season. But Alonso was not minded to let him go without a few more critical parting shots.

Alonso's ire had been stoked up after qualifying, when he had been found guilty of compromising

Felipe Massa's last hot lap as he came out on a warm-up lap, despite the fact that the Brazilian's Ferrari had almost certainly benefited from the Renault driver's slipstream down the back straight. Perhaps reluctantly, but in line with other decisions during the course of the year, the stewards had disallowed Alonso's three best times, plunging him from fifth to tenth on the grid.

Alonso was furious, but still had more to say on race day. Comparing Schumacher's departure with the dramatic retirement of the French footballer Zinedine Zidane in the World Cup final that June, where he had been sent off for head-butting the Italian player Marco Materazzi, Alonso said, "Zidane retired with more glory than Michael Schumacher. Michael is the most unsporting driver with the largest number of sanctions in the history of F1. But that does not take away the fact that he has been the best driver and it has been an honour to battle against him. Everyone has their time and things will be more equal now."

Not satisfied with that, Alonso then launched an attack on what he regarded as institutional bias in favour of Schumacher and Ferrari. "In F1, there are commercial and political interests," he noted. "We are talking about the most successful driver in history, and a little bit of help has never gone amiss. Quite often, they go over the line of what is acceptable."

Continued on page 358

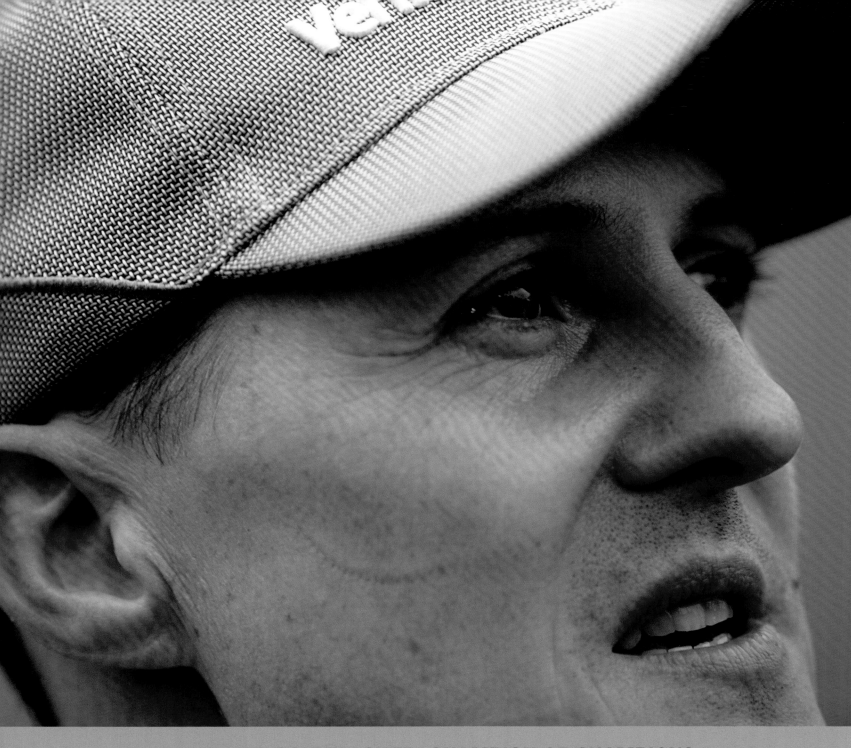

MICHAEL SCHUMACHER: CHAMPION OF CHAMPIONS

MICHAEL Schumacher had two World Championships to his credit before he joined Ferrari at the start of 1996. A decade later, he had added another five title crowns to that tally, all won with Ferrari, a team that he shaped and moulded into his personal fiefdom in conjunction with his loyal collaborators, Jean Todt and Ross Brawn. In so doing, the ascetic, committed and super-fit German driver demonstrated that absolute number-one status was the best way of getting the job done consistently at the highest level of this challenging sport. Forget equal status, Michael wanted nothing of that. If he was to deploy his genius to maximum effect, he wanted a clear run at the opposition, unfettered by irritations within his team. Ferrari was happy to oblige, and they

rode to glory together, winning not just five titles, but five on the trot between 2000 and 2004.

At home in Germany, Michael rode through much of the past two decades on a tidal wave of popular support, which probably transcended any similar public displays of adulation towards fellow German sporting legends, such as Boris Becker and Jürgen Klinsmann.

By the time an accident at Silverstone interrupted his 1999 season, the 31-year-old Ferrari driver had amassed no fewer than 35 Grand Prix victories. That put him six away from Ayrton Senna's tally of 41, and a more challenging 16 short of Alain Prost's all-time record. But that was just the start. By the time he retired at the end of 1996, he had 91 victories on the record board.

There is something compellingly attractive about the 'little boy lost' demeanour of this lad from the wrong side of the tracks who has made the 'big time'. Michael's father was a bricklayer; his mother ran the hamburger stand at the little go-kart track at Kerpen where the future champion first cut his competitive teeth as a boy.

He may seem slightly surly and uninterested when faced with one of the obligatory press conferences that take place daily at each Grand Prix for a number of selected celebrities. He ducks questions, replies with sweeping and anodyne generalities, and generally manages to look slightly morose.

On his own, however, Schumacher is better value. Like the late Ayrton Senna, he weighs his replies carefully behind a mask of slightly distant for-

mality. But, as Eddie Irvine, his Ferrari team-mate over four seasons to 1999, said, "Michael is always pretty intense. There is nothing lighthearted about Grand Prix racing for him. He is there to win and nothing else."

It was in 1989 that Willi Weber recruited the young Michael Schumacher to drive for his F3 team, and the two men have never looked back, becoming richer than their wildest dreams together. Schumacher's third place in that year's German F3 championship put him on the map.

Thanks to such performances, Weber was able to negotiate a deal for him to join the Mercedes-Benz sports car racing team, where Schumacher, Karl Wendlinger and Heinz-Harald Frentzen were shrewdly promoted as Germany's new generation of future

and David Coulthard to continue driving the McLarens that *were* powered by its engines.

Mercedes insiders hinted that Schumacher carried with him a little too much controversial baggage: the collision with Damon Hill that resolved the 1994 World Championship, and the incident with Jacques Villeneuve at Jerez in 1997 for example. By contrast, Ferrari wanted the very best driver available and was prepared to put up with everything to keep him. Yet everything comes to he who waits…

Under such circumstances, it seemed quite understandable that Ferrari was prepared to accept Michael's requirement that the team sign an acquiescent number-two driver who was prepared to play second fiddle. However, Eddie Irvine had grown tired of that role by the middle of the 1999 season and decided to switch to the new Jaguar F1 operation as team leader for the new millennium. Rubens Barrichello willingly took over his position.

In days gone by, of course, the F1 team owners called the shots. Enzo Ferrari bestrode the Grand Prix world like an irascible automotive colossus, paying his star drivers a few hundred dollars a month and invariably heightening the tension between them by failing to nominate a team leader.

In the era of Michael Schumacher, the best driver in the world dictated the terms at Ferrari. He knew just how difficult it really is to win a World Championship and did not intend to let the interests of his team-mate get in the way of his own towering ambition.

Schumacher burst on to the Grand Prix scene in the summer of 1991, when he was invited to test at Silverstone for the Jordan team, coincidentally later the employer of his younger brother, Ralf.

"It was instantly clear that Michael was very special," said Eddie Jordan. "We tested him on the South Circuit at Silverstone, which in those days was a fairly hair-raising place. Within a few laps, he was braking 15 metres later for the kink before the pits than anybody else who had previously driven the car, and we were signalling him that he should come in, because we thought he was going too quickly too soon.

"But Michael knew what he was doing. Within five minutes, we were convinced that he was pretty special."

Ken Tyrrell recognised the same sort of natural talent in Schumacher that he had seen in Jackie Stewart more than 40 years ago. "It is that terrific ability to put in a fantastically quick first lap at the start of a race," he said.

"Stewart was exactly the same, easily the best of his generation. Now Schumacher, but we all want to see Michael challenged, otherwise he could run away with all the championships."

Michael's first Ferrari victory came in the pouring rain at Barcelona in 1996. He followed that up with two equally fine wins at Spa and Monza, but the Ferrari didn't consistently come on to the pace until the second half of the year. It was too late to mount a title challenge, but the omens were certainly promising for 1997.

Luca di Montezemolo, Ferrari's high-profile president, made it the team's priority to win more races in 1997 than it had the previous year. Michael duly delivered, almost doubling the tally to five. But then came the vital fumble at Jerez that handed Villeneuve the World Championship, and left Michael facing more criticism and doubt.

Even the controversy at Jerez, where he rammed his Ferrari into the side of Villeneuve's overtaking Williams in an effort to settle the outcome of the championship by what was universally condemned as a 'professional foul', failed materially to dent his popularity.

There were short-term criticisms, but Schumacher quickly regained his status in the eyes of the fans. The so-called punishment of being disqualified from second place in the World Championship brought with it an obligation for him to help with a European road safety campaign backed by motor racing's governing body, the FIA. The exercise was deftly turned into something of a PR triumph for the Ferrari driver.

Surely 1998 had to be the year when the World Championship would be Ferrari's. Six wins were firmly under Michael's belt by the time he lined up in pole position at Suzuka, and it was even money as to whether he would finally get the job done.

Then, at the first restart, he stalled the engine. It was an episode that served as a reminder that even the greatest drivers are human. He was consigned to the back of the grid and eventually retired with a punctured tyre, leaving Mika Häkkinen to win both race and championship.

Yet again, Michael had proved that he possesses a dazzling talent, an almost magical touch, behind the wheel. Yet, like the late Ayrton Senna, whose mantle he assumed, he could display a tendency towards arrogance and intolerance of others. When he bundled Heinz-Harald Frentzen's Williams off the road at Montreal, he could scarcely bring himself to make a grudging apology. After hitting the back of David Coulthard's McLaren in the rain at Spa, he completely lost control of his temper. Yet the driving genius still transcended his weak and vulnerable points.

Then, in 1999, Schumacher suffered the biggest setback of his career so far. On the opening lap of the British Grand Prix at Silverstone, he crashed under braking for Stowe Corner and slammed into the tyre barrier. Having already won the San Marino and Monaco Grands Prix in splendid style, the German driver now had to recover from a broken right leg and accept that his title hopes were at an end for another year.

Then, suddenly, it all clicked. The first five seasons of the new millenium passed in a scarlet blur as Schumacher delivered race victory after race victory. Yet even during his most dominant period, he was no stranger to controversy, most notably when he skidded to a halt at Rascasse during qualifying for the 2006 Monaco GP, thwarting World Champion Fernando Alonso's bid for pole position. As a result, he received a significant grid penalty, even though the Ferrari top brass remained defiantly unapologetic in the aftermath of this unfortunate incident.

By the end of 2006, Schumacher was ready to retire, and he walked away from the Ferrari garage seemingly for the last time. Yet he was back in the pit lane the following year as a team advisor, clearly restless and eager for a fresh challenge. By the summer of 2009, he was ready to toy with the notion of standing in for the injured Felipe Massa after the Brazilian received head injuries during qualifying at the Hungaroring. That prospect fell at the last hurdle when the lingering effect of an earlier neck injury caused him to put his ambitions on hold. But he'd got a taste of it now.

The 'smell of the grease paint and the roar of the crowd' were too much for him to resist. Michael Schumacher would be back behind the wheel of a car run by Ross Brawn in 2010 – one with a three-pointed star on its nosecone at long last. The story would continue.

racing stars. Schumacher trusts Weber's judgement completely. "If they have a new sponsor or a contract, Willi will do all the negotiations," said a Schumacher camp insider. "If the terms seem to Willi's liking, he will then present them to Michael.

"This is a serious partnership; they are business colleagues and close friends. Willi knows that his main priority is to take all the worries off Michael's shoulders. It is very important that he has his mind free for what he does best, the racing."

Ironically, it seemed that Schumacher might never drive a Mercedes-engined car in Formula 1. At a Mercedes shareholders' meeting in the summer of 1998, board director Jürgen Schrempp emphasised that the car company wanted Mika Häkkinen

HORNER STEERS NEWEY INTO THE ARMS OF RED BULL

The emergence of Red Bull Racing as one of the sport's most formidable World Championship contenders was among the outstanding F1 achievements of the first decade of the 21st century. When it was announced in the summer of 2004 that Jaguar Racing was being sold by its owner, Ford, a decision justified on the basis that the manufacturer could discern no continuing commercial benefit from an involvement in F1, there were fears that its Milton Keynes factory would become a ghost town.

Thanks to the far-sightedness of Dietrich Mateschitz, the millionaire co-founder of the Red Bull energy drink manufacturer, however, the team was given the opportunity to change its identity for the second time in its short life. The net result was that the operation originally founded as Stewart Grand Prix in 1996, and sold by Jackie and Paul Stewart to Ford at the end of 1999 for a reputed £35 million, was now sold by Ford to Red Bull for a nominal dollar, on the condition that the new owner assumed all its financial obligations.

Thus, at the start of November 2004, Red Bull acquired the core assets of Jaguar Racing, which, in terms of hardware, amounted to the keys of the factory and the designs for the car that would become the Cosworth propelled Red Bull RB1. It seemed to many people that Red Bull could look forward to a midfield existence of modest achievement, but those

sceptics would be confounded by the single-minded determination and focus that the Red Bull organisation brought to bear on its new acquisition.

For the 2005 season, Red Bull recruited the entrepreneurial Christian Horner, boss of the ultra-successful Arden F3000 operation, as team principal and shrewdly employed former McLaren ace David Coulthard as the number-one driver to create a rock-solid foundation on which to build the team. DC started the year with an encouraging fourth place in Australia, while the second car was shared between rising stars Vitantonio Liuzzi and Christian Klien. Meanwhile, as the team was steadily building up a strong technical infrastructure back at base, its vibrant and youthful marketing image was underpinned by the colourful and capacious 'Energy Station', which was one of the biggest and most off-beat team hospitality areas anywhere in the paddock.

Horner quickly came to be regarded with considerable respect within the F1 paddock, much as he had been among the F3000 community. He was a team principal who knew of that about which he spoke. He'd raced himself up to F3000 level and even briefly tested an F1 Lotus at Hethel in the early 1990s. In his mid-thirties, Horner could talk to the team's drivers with a depth of understanding and insight that belied his relative youth.

Horner was one of the driving forces behind Red Bull's switch from Cosworth to Ferrari engines for the 2006 season, the year when Coulthard posted the team's first podium finish with a third at Monaco. At

the same time, the progress in expanding the engineering base continued apace with the recruitment of Adrian Newey to head up the technical staff in the summer of 2005. Newey was – and remains – possibly the most innovative and daring F1 engineer in the business. He arrived at Red Bull having crafted the World Championship winning machines for Williams and McLaren throughout the 1990s and, ironically, he had almost joined Red Bull in its previous incarnation as Jaguar, but McLaren boss Ron Dennis persuaded him to stay where he was. Eventually, however, he decided that he wanted a fresh challenge, and Red Bull was the place where he would find it.

"In truth, when I joined Williams and McLaren, they were teams that had won championships and clearly had the infrastructure to be capable of doing so in the future," said Adrian. "It meant they were able to get to the point of winning races and championships quite quickly, whereas Red Bull Racing was a very different case, which was what appealed to me. It was a very young team, which offered me the opportunity to be centrally involved in developing not only the design of the car, but the whole infrastructure of the engineering team."

Coulthard continued to lead the team through 2006, still using Ferrari engines, but Newey and Horner were insistent that either Maranello progressed this relationship from a simple supplier/customer deal or Red Bull would look elsewhere. The net result was that the team switched to Renault power in 2007, with Mark Webber joining Coulthard on the driving strength, while Scuderia Toro Rosso, the Red Bull number-two team, took over the Ferrari engine deal. This worked out well in the long term, with a young kid called Sebastian Vettel

winning the 2008 Italian GP in an STR-Ferrari.

By 2009, the team was ready to fly. Coulthard had decided to retire, and Vettel moved across to partner Webber, while Newey's RB5 challenger, the epitome of taut, tight and economical technical packaging, proved a formidable contender from the outset, even though initially the team did not follow the 'double diffuser' route, the adoption of which gave such an early advantage to Jenson Button's run to the championship in the Brawn-Mercedes.

Not that the absence of a double diffuser seemed to matter much. Vettel's sheer genius earned him 2009 wins in China, Britain, Suzuka and Abu Dhabi, while Webber stepped up to the plate with victories at the Nürburgring and Interlagos. The lanky Australian had done a superb job, raising his game to match his young team-mate's level of performance, and Red Bull went into 2010 looking as though it had possibly the strongest line-up in the business.

Moreover, as Newey explained, the 2009 success gave the team the momentum to continue its strong performances in 2010. "For 2010, the regulation changes had been relatively small and meant any research for the 2009 car was relevant to this season," he said. "As a result, there was much less of a choice to be made between 2009 and 2010 development.

"We initially concentrated on the challenges of almost doubling the size of the fuel tank for the no-refuelling regulations and what impact the narrower front tyre would have. Most of the rest of the chassis work was the new aero optimisation and accommodating the extra 70-odd kilogrammes of fuel."

From the start of the 2010 season, Vettel and Webber were right on the pace, although not until Malay-

Above: **Mark Webber, Christian Horner and Sebastien Vettel celebrate their 1-2 finish in the 2009 Abu Dhabi Grand Prix. World Champion Jenson Button looks pleased just to have gained third place behind the rampant Red Bulls in the season's finale.**
Photo: **Paul-Henri Cahier**

sia, the third round of the title chase, did they produce their first win of the year with a 1-2 grand slam. Yet it was the psychological effect of what Red Bull was achieving that really mattered.

You could see the resigned sense of despair in Jenson Button's eyes after the World Champion could only qualify fifth at Barcelona, where Webber and Vettel stitched up the front row with ease.

"It should be a walk in the park for the Red Bulls," said Jenson. "It's their race to lose…" That was a *real* compliment, and a reminder of just how far the team had come in a little over five years.

HAMILTON ALMOST WINS TITLE

Lewis Hamilton's debut season with the McLaren-Mercedes team was simply astonishing. The key to the depths of talent offered by F1's first black driver had nothing whatsoever to do with his ethnicity; that counted as much on the starting grid as Tiger Woods's skill with a five iron. The keys to Hamilton's remarkable success were his rounded personality and composure away from the field of battle.

McLaren had last risked appointing a driver with no race experience in 1993, when it had signed Michael Andretti as team-mate to Ayrton Senna. It had not been a productive experience, and Andretti had been dropped before the end of the year. The doubters may have made much of the fact that Hamilton had wrecked a car during pre-season testing at Valencia, but signing him up had been a no-risk strategy. His CV had reflected his dominant performance in both Euro F3 and GP2, while the best part of 1000 hours spent on McLaren's bespoke in-house simulator had ensured that he had arrived at Melbourne for the Australian GP as the best prepared freshman of all time.

Hamilton scored a podium finish with third place

in the first race of the season in Melbourne, trailing race winner Kimi Räikkönen's Ferrari and Alonso in the other McLaren. He followed that up with second places in Malaysia, Bahrain and Spain to surge into the lead of the World Championship only four races into the season. Another second at Monaco preceded wins at Montreal and Indianapolis; in the latter event, he beat team-mate Alonso in a straight fight.

By the time he had finished third at Silverstone in the eighth round of the title chase, Lewis was 12 points in front of Alonso at the head of the championship table. Then the Spaniard narrowed the gap with a fine victory in the European GP at the Nürburgring, hauling up to just two points adrift, but Hamilton scored a flawless win in Hungary and began to pull away again. However, it was in the rain soaked Japanese GP at the revamped Mount Fuji speedway that Alonso's title challenge really came unstitched. He crashed heavily, while Lewis won the race to put himself 12 points clear of the Spaniard with two races to go. But Räikkönen was also coming up in his rear-view mirror in the Ferrari…

Suddenly the cards fell in a different direction. Going into the pit lane at Shanghai, Lewis made a crucial slip and skated into the gravel trap, handing Kimi the race win, ahead of Alonso. At the final race, in Brazil, Hamilton's challenge was thwarted by a gearchange glitch. Felipe Massa relinquished the race victory to Räikkönen, who thus squeezed through to take the title by a single point.

Lewis would have to wait another 12 months before grasping the 2008 championship at the São Paulo track, this time taking the crown by a single point from Massa, who had won the race and could hardly have done more. It didn't seem fair in a way, but life is never fair. Certainly not in F1, anyway.

Continued on page 364

Right: Lewis Hamilton makes a perfect arc across the sodden Suzuka track on his way to his superb win in the 2007 Japanese Grand Prix.

Inset: Lewis and his father, Anthony, were inseparable on their way to top.
Photos: Paul-Henri Cahier

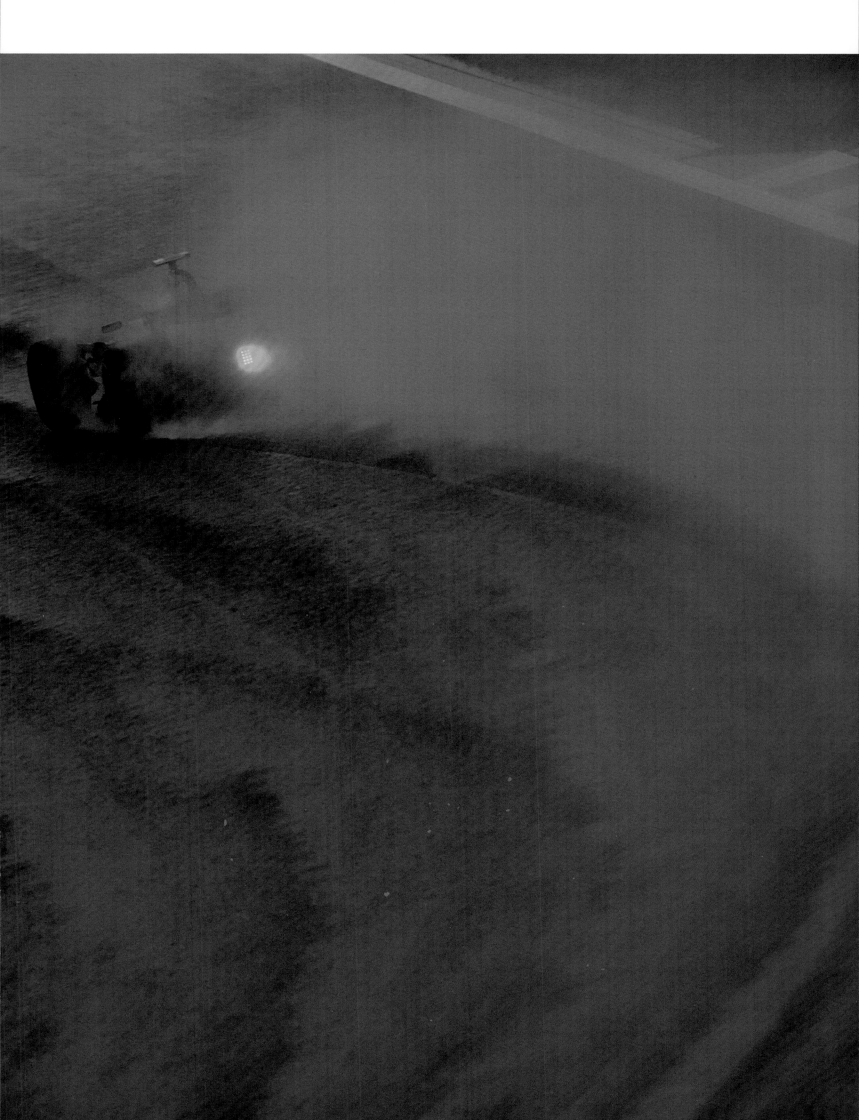

Above right: Lewis Hamilton took the 2008 World Championship in only his second season racing at the top level.

Opposite: Ron Dennis spent three decades at the helm of McLaren before stepping aside from the team's racing activities at the end of 2008.

Below: Martin Whitmarsh capped 20 years of service at McLaren by taking over as F1 team principal at the start of the 2009 season.

Photos: Paul-Henri Cahier

McLAREN ATONES FOR ESPIONAGE ALLEGATIONS

After the end of the 2007 F1 season, McLaren stunned the F1 community by making a public and wide-ranging apology to both Ferrari and the sport's governing body for its illegal use of Ferrari technical data, for which it had already been fined £50 million and lost all its Constructors' World Championship points from the 2007 season.

Following a detailed technical examination of both its current and newly designed 2008 challenger, the MP4/23, the team acknowledged that Ferrari data was more widely disseminated within its organisation than previously had been realised. McLaren admitted that it "greatly regrets that its own investigations did not identify this material" and had written to the World Motor Sport Council to apologise.

This demonstrated how anxious the British team was to draw a line under an acutely embarrassing episode that had begun when their disgraced chief designer, Mike Coughlan, had been found in possession of over 700 drawings 'allegedly' supplied by Ferrari engineer Nigel Stepney.

Had McLaren been forced to wait until February 2008, after a planned meeting of the FIA World Motor Sport Council, for its new car to be formally signed off for use, any modifications that might have been required to satisfy the governing body may have had to be rushed or perhaps not even completed prior to the first race in Australia.

The McLaren group chief operating officer, Martin Whitmarsh, sent a letter to the FIA, which, in the interests of transparency, it published together with a formal press statement. He also wrote to the World Motor Sport Council to apologise that it had taken an FIA investigation to find this information and express the team's deep regret that its understanding of the facts had been improved as a result of the FIA inspection rather than its own investigations.

McLaren conceded that "this entire situation could have been avoided if we had informed Ferrari and the FIA about Nigel Stepney's first communication when it came to our attention. We are, of course, embarrassed by the successive disclosures and have apologised unreservedly to the FIA World Motor Sport Council."

Furthermore, to avoid even the possibility of Ferrari information influencing its performance during 2008, McLaren offered a set of detailed undertakings to the FIA that imposed a moratorium on development in relation to certain technical systems on the car.

As if all this ritual humiliation was not enough for a team that had always prided itself on its high standards of probity and integrity, McLaren felt it necessary to conduct a thorough review of its policies and procedures regarding the recruitment and management of staff. Happily, the FIA agreed with the team's wish to move on from this most unfortunate episode and the case was closed.

RON DENNIS: PLAYING THE LONG GAME

RON Dennis has a total commitment to excellence and attention to detail that has driven the McLaren F1 team to sustained success throughout the past 30 years. Essentially a private man, whose fundamentally reserved character sometimes makes him seem rather aloof, he still loves motor racing with the same passion that brought him into the sport as a junior mechanic for Cooper almost 45 years ago.

Although Dennis chose to stand down as McLaren F1 team principal, relinquishing the role to his long-time right-hand man, Martin Whitmarsh, at the start of the 2009 season, he remains fascinated and intrigued by any technical and commercial challenge, whether it be on the race track or stemming from his new role as head of McLaren Automotive. Even more significantly, he has been one of the defining figures within F1 over the past three decades, helping to shape and influence not only the development of McLaren as a business, but also the sport as a whole.

Under Ron's regime, the McLaren Group has grown into a wide-ranging and cutting-edge organisation. Its diverse interests range from racing, the development of a new road car, through marketing to electronics. The group employs upwards of 1700 staff at its technical centre near Woking, which was opened by the Queen in 2004.

Dennis took effective control of the struggling McLaren F1 team in 1980 and revived its fortunes to brilliant effect, winning the World Championship in 1984, '85, '86, '88, '89, '90 and '91. That was followed by a dramatic performance slump, from which the team emerged in 1997 to add further World Championships to that tally in 1998, 1999 and 2008, in partnership with engine supplier Mercedes-Benz.

"I have a belief that everything is important in life, and everything is important when you are trying to achieve high levels of success in any business, certainly in F1," said Dennis.

"I believe that at all times you should have the best, or at least try to have the best. This is not simply about money, it is mainly about commitment. We try to instil it into the very fibre of everyone's approach to their work for the team." It is this basic attitude that underpins every aspect of the McLaren operation.

Dennis has always been particularly adept at lateral thinking and projects a shrewd understanding of Grand Prix racing that extends beyond the simple, obvious scenario of cars running around a circuit. Unlike some of his contemporaries within the ranks of F1 team owners throughout much of the past three decades, he also understands that success in F1 may depend on playing what he described as "the long game".

In essence, that has meant investing in improvements in McLaren's design and manufacturing infrastructure. In this respect, there is no short cut to success. It involves sustained hard work and self-belief that can be made more frustrating and demanding by the inherent complexity of the F1 machine.

"When you look at many sports, you realise the role equipment plays in the overall equation is very small," he said. "By contrast, a Grand Prix car is one of the most complex pieces of equipment you could ever place in the hands of a sportsman. That is why it is so enormously difficult to win a Grand Prix."

Reflecting on the 2009 season, Dennis gained satisfaction from the way in which the team had turned around the fortunes of the MP4/24. "It was a very difficult first season for Martin to experience in the role of team principal. I like to think that I was supportive of his efforts to tackle the challenge, but did not interfere. It is a credit to the team that we turned a slow car into a winning package during the course of the season, something which many manufacturer backed teams have singularly failed to do in the past."

Ron denied any suggestion that somehow he had been forced to drop out of F1 by the so-called 'Spygate' episode in 2007, or the subsequent controversy at the 2009 Australian GP involving Lewis Hamilton, which led to the dismissal of the team's sporting director, Dave Ryan.

"I don't think there has ever been a case of my having a gun held to my head to force me into doing anything I have not wanted to do," he said in measured style. "But there have been times when I have chosen to do something which, although perhaps not something I really want to do, I judge to be in the best interests of the company.

"To take an example, I was bitterly disappointed that we did not win the 2007 World Championship because I think we deserved it, and Lewis deserved to win the World Championship in his first season. Okay, so in 2008 Lewis and McLaren won the championship, but I can assure you that, had he won it in 2007, I can absolutely positively guarantee that I would have stood down as team principal and would have stopped being involved in F1. I was absolutely resolute about that."

SEBASTIAN VETTEL – A PRECOCIOUS TALENT

Above: **The infectious grin of Vettel, which is so endearing.**

Top: **Vettel gave Toro Rosso a fairytale victory in the 2008 Italian Grand Prix.**

Photos: **Paul-Henri Cahier**

WITHIN seconds of the start of his F1 debut, Sebastian Vettel picked up a speeding fine. And his right foot has been flat to the floor ever since. Vettel's big chance came in F1 when he succeeded Robert Kubica as the BMW Sauber team's third driver in the second half of the 2006 season, collecting that penalty for exceeding the pit-lane speed limit at Istanbul Park only a few moments into Friday practice for the Turkish Grand Prix, which also saw him finish the day at the top of the time sheets.

Born on 3rd July, 1987 in Heppenheim, Germany, Vettel has been an absolutely outstanding talent from the moment he slipped behind the wheel of a kart in 1995, when he was just eight years old. By 2003, aged 15, he won five of the 19 races in his debut season in Formula BMW, and the following year he took the German title with an astonishing 18 wins out of 20 races. His was a talent obviously born for F1, and that promise was sustained through F3 and World Series by Renault en route to test outings with Williams and BMW Sauber during his relentless march towards the sport's most senior category.

While his performance on track was very impressive, the BMW Sauber team was also instantly struck by his composure and self-confidence for one so young. The authority with which he spoke and his attractive brand of self-deprecating humour stood out as much as his sheer speed on the circuit.

Sebastian finally got his chance to race a year later, standing in for the injured Kubica at the United States Grand Prix. Still only 19, he qualified seventh and finished eighth, becoming the youngest man to score a championship point. Later in the 2007 season, he moved to a permanent seat at Scuderia Toro Rosso. He made a lasting impression on future team-mate Mark Webber during the monsoon-hit Japanese Grand Prix at Fuji, before bouncing back a week later to secure fourth place at an equally waterlogged Chinese Grand Prix.

Confirmed for 2008, Vettel didn't have the best start to his first full season, crashing out of the first four races, mostly as a result of being dragged into other driver's accidents. Happily he quickly shrugged aside any reputation of being accident prone to score points at Monaco, Montreal, Hockenheim, Valencia, Spa, Singapore, Fuji and Interlagos. But the high spot was his stupendous victory in the Italian GP at Monza, where he also became the youngest driver in F1 history to take pole and then the youngest winner. If anybody had been uncertain about Vettel's star quality, such lingering doubts were now removed.

Elevated to the senior Red Bull team for 2009, Vettel won his second, and Red Bull Racing's first, victory at the third race of the year. He followed it with a string of podium and solid points scoring finishes, establishing himself as a firm championship contender with a second, commanding victory in the British Grand Prix. He finished the season strongly with further victories in Japan and Abu Dhabi. These, together with four other podium finishes, took him to second place in the Drivers' Championship.

Never off the front row of the starting grid for the first five races of the 2010 World Championship season, Vettel only managed to score a single victory in the Bahrain GP prior to the F1 circus returning to Europe for the Spanish round of the title chase. Yet the manner in which he drove the last few laps to third place at the Circuit de Catalunya, his Red Bull RB6 almost totally out of brakes and forcing him to rely on engine braking alone to slow the car, very publicly signalled the depth of his genius on a day when he had to bite the bullet and watch team-mate Mark Webber storming to an unchallenged win.

VETTEL USHERS IN A NEW GENERATION

They crowded into Monza in their customary thousands, packing the grandstands to the rafters in keen anticipation of a Ferrari-versus-McLaren showdown, only to find that the World Championship contest between Lewis Hamilton and Felipe Massa had been reduced to a secondary issue. Instead, the *tifosi* sat sodden and bewitched throughout the 2008 Italian GP as an engaging young kid with a ready smile and a wacky sense of humour that embraced *Little Britain* and *Monty Python* drove into the F1 record books before their very eyes.

Sebastian Vettel had started from pole position in his Ferrari powered Toro Rosso STR3 in the same conditions of heavy rain that had seen him vault to the top of the timing sheets the previous afternoon. The sophisticated view from more seasoned observers was that the Toro Rosso driver might have been hard pressed to maintain his performance edge if the track dried out completely, but when the rain finally eased after a dozen or so laps, the young Vettel was over 6s ahead of Heikki Kovalainen's second-place McLaren-Mercedes, and he controlled the race with consummate skill and confidence.

"It was difficult to realise what had happened," said Vettel, whose wide-eyed innocent delight wooed the crowd into paroxysms of delight.

"It was unbelievable seeing everybody going crazy all the way round the circuit. To see the people in the team, from my family going mad, and then to listen to my national anthem, I started to cry. I think everybody in the team can go to sleep tonight thinking we were winners."

FELIPE MASSA NARROWLY BEATEN FOR THE TITLE

Just as there was huge sympathy for Lewis Hamilton when he was pipped to the 2007 championship by Kimi Räikkönen at Interlagos, so the crowds' hearts went out to Felipe Massa a year later after the Brazilian drove his Ferrari to a dominant victory in his home Grand Prix, but ended up just one point behind Hamilton in the final title reckoning.

As Hamilton battled on rain tyres in the closing seconds of the race, he managed to claw his way past Timo Glock's fifth-place Toyota a couple of corners from the chequered flag, just as Massa was on the point of celebrating his championship success. But fifth was enough for Hamilton to get the job done, even though there were those hypersensitive cynics in the paddock who believed that Glock somehow deliberately had backed off to help Lewis clinch the championship. It was all fanciful stuff that Massa – to his credit in a moment of abject disappointment – had managed to remain above.

"I have been through completely mixed emotions," said Felipe with great dignity and composure. "When I crossed the line, the positions meant I was going to be champion, but Rob [Smedley, his engineer] was on the radio keeping me informed. That's racing though and I am still happy with the way I drove.

"There are always explanations for what happens in life, and if things worked out like this today, it's just the way it was meant to be."

Top: **Alonso raises his eyes towards the skies as Felipe Massa fights back the tears following his victory in the 2008 Brazilian GP – a success that left him one point short of the World Championship, which was claimed by Lewis Hamilton.**

Above: **Robert Kubica gave BMW its sole Grand Prix win as a manufacturer at the 2008 Canadian Grand Prix.**

Photos: Paul-Henri Cahier

RENAULT ROW AS PIQUET DELIBERATELY CRASHES AT SINGAPORE

When Fernando Alonso had decided to leave the McLaren team after his frustrating 2007 campaign, the only realistic option for the hapless Spaniard was to back-track to Renault, where he was welcomed with open arms, even though most people – correctly – judged that this was a temporary expedient before some way could be arranged for him to be recruited by Ferrari.

Thus strong results were few and far between for the double World Champion in 2008, but even the most cynical pit-lane insiders would have been hard pressed to imagine that his victory in the inaugural Singapore GP night race would remain the centre of fevered controversy a year later.

It was one of the biggest scandals in F1 history. Forget the fact that Alonso won the race. At the time, nobody gave a second thought to the fact that his teammate, Nelson Piquet, had spun into the wall after 14 laps, an incident that had triggered the deployment of the safety car and had given Fernando a tactical leg-up as he climbed through the field.

Yet unknown to its senior management, the Renault squad was nursing a squalid secret. Piquet had crashed deliberately and had done so with the alleged complicity of Flavio Briatore, the team principal, and the team's executive director of engineering, Pat Symonds.

For his part, Piquet was ready to confess to his involvement in this duplicity shortly after the 2008 race. Word had already reached the FIA that something was amiss, but the governing body knew it could not initiate action on rumour alone. Helpfully, however, it signalled that if Piquet made a formal complaint, he would not be penalised. The Brazilian driver duly attended the offices of the governing body and made a legal statement.

The net result was that Briatore was banned indefinitely from further involvement in the sport by a meeting of the FIA World Motor Sport Council in Paris the week before the 2009 Singapore race. Symonds

received a five-year suspension. Only much later, after Jean Todt had taken over from Max Mosley as FIA president, were those draconian penalties reduced. But, for all his apparent candour, it was an episode that seemed to mark the end of the road for Piquet Junior's F1 dream.

BUTTON WINS WORLD CHAMPIONSHIP – AND JOINS McLAREN

A few weeks before the start of the 2009 F1 season it seemed possible that Jenson Button might be without a drive. Honda, running scared ahead of a horrifying global recession, had decided they were to withdraw from F1 and sell their team, setting a trend that would be followed by BMW and Toyota before the end of the season.

Yet the team was saved by Ross Brawn who headed up an audacious management buy-out, the team was on the grid in Australia and Jenson was on his way to five wins out of the first six races in the brilliant Brawn-Mercedes BGP 001. This remarkable run ended with a mid-season dip in form which started at Silverstone where Sebastian Vettel and Mark Webber produced a brilliant dry weather reprise of the Red Bull 1-2 which they had earlier delivered in torrential rain in China to interrupt Jenson's sequence of wins by taking round 3 of championship.

In the second half of the year Button's team-mate Rubens Barrichello frequently demonstrated a slight edge over the British driver just as he had sometimes done during his halcyon days alongside Michael Schumacher at Ferrari. Rubens won magnificently at Valencia and Monza on two glorious days when Jenson had no answer to him. Increasingly he also had his hands more than full keeping abreast of Red Bull's steady advance with Vettel and Webber becoming stronger by the race as the season wore on.

Nevertheless, Jenson surged to maturity during the course of this campaign and, even though the second half of his season lacked the overt dominance of the first, the 29-year old kept his composure superbly to

Continued on page 374

Far left: Nelson Piquet Junior crashed deliberately in the inaugural 2008 Singapore GP, supposedly to give the advantage to team-mate Fernando Alonso.

Centre left: The colourful Flavio Briatore was held responsible for masterminding the 'crashgate' scandal and was suspended from involvement in the sport as a result.

Left: The rear end of the all-conquering 2009 Brawn-Mercedes.

Below: Jenson Button enjoyed a sensational run of wins at the start of the 2009 season, which included a runaway win in the Monaco Grand Prix. Brawn team-mate Rubens Barrichello (left) and Kimi Räikkönen complete the top three finishers.
Photos: Paul-Henri Cahier

Right: Jenson Button steam-rollered the opposition on his way to the 2009 title. His win in Bahrain (right) was one of six in seven starts.

Below: After years of knocking on the door, Mark Webber really came of age with Red Bull in 2009, taking wins in the German and Brazilian Grands Prix.
Photos: Paul-Henri Cahier

Left: So near – and yet so far. Toyota's eight seasons in Formula 1 failed to provide a victory, leading the Japanese car giant to withdraw from the Grand Prix arena at the end of 2009.

Far left: Sebastian Vettel bathed in the early evening glow while winning the 2009 Abu Dhabi Grand Prix for Red Bull.

Photos: Paul-Henri Cahier

THE RISE OF BERNIE ECCLESTONE

GOING into the 2010 F1 season, Bernie Ecclestone was approaching his 80th birthday, but the sport's supreme powerbroker continued to preside over the relentless expansion of the World Championship, just as he had done for the previous 35 years. He has the energy and motivation of a man half his age, as well as a razor-sharp brain that generally keeps him some distance ahead of those with whom he is doing business.

By any standards, Ecclestone is an intriguing character. On the one hand, he can be a ruthless negotiator, deploying brain power and intellect that few can match. On the other hand, he can be one of the boys when socialising with those on the inside of motor racing whom he has known for a long time. From his muted grey motorhome, which stands on pole position just inside the paddock gates at every European Grand Prix, Bernie knows what most people in F1 are up to before they know themselves.

So where did this all start? Bernie was born in 1930, the son of a trawler captain from Suffolk. His family later moved to Kent, where he grew up, demonstrating his entrepreneurial skills from an early age in the school playground by buying and selling pens and cakes, anything that came his way. He quickly learned to live on his wits and developed an independent streak that helped make him the billionaire tycoon he is today. The 2010 *Sunday Times* 'Top 1000 rich list' placed him 38th with a worth of around £1.4 billion, even after a costly divorce from his wife Slavica. Many people on the inside of F1 just smile at what they regard as an ultra-conservative assessment of Bernie's real worth.

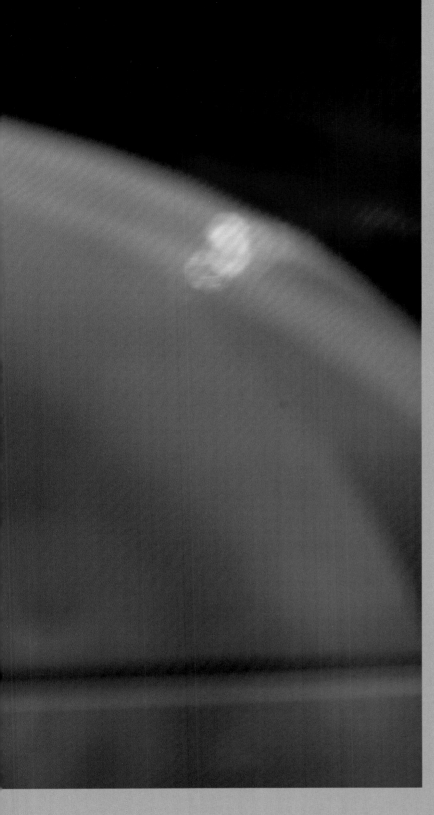

His interest in motor racing stretches back to the immediate post-war era, when he raced a motorcycle on the grass track at Brands Hatch, later graduating to an F3 Cooper 500. In 1958, he made an unsuccessful effort to qualify a Connaught for the Monaco GP, by which time he was managing the interests of the British driver Stuart Lewis-Evans, who was competing in the Vanwall team alongside Stirling Moss and Tony Brooks.

After Lewis-Evans suffered fatal burns when he crashed in the Moroccan Grand Prix at Casablanca, Bernie dropped out of the F1 scene to concentrate on developing his car dealing and property interests. When he reappeared eight years later, he was looking after the interests of the dynamic Austrian driver Jochen Rindt, who would be killed at Monza practising in his Lotus 72 for the 1970 Italian GP. Rindt's daughter, Natascha, would later work for Ecclestone's television production company before becoming a pilot and flying the FIA's Learjet, used by the governing body's president, Max Mosley.

By this point, however, Ecclestone had more ambitious plans. He would purchase the Brabham F1 team from its co-founder, Ron Tauranac, and when he took control at the start of 1972, he placed his foot firmly on the bottom step of a ladder that eventually would carry him to multi-millionaire status.

By 1979, it was clear that Ecclestone's burgeoning power base, the F1 Constructors' Association, was in a strong position to stake a claim for a bigger share of the television income generated by the World Championship, which, on the face of it, accrued to the sport's governing body, FISA, the motor sport division of the FIA. Yet it had been Bernie's tireless efforts that had generated the income for the sport and, quite reasonably, FOCA believed it should take a bigger slice of the cake. But with the controversial Jean-Marie Balestre installed as FISA president, this wouldn't happen without a fight.

The dispute became a fundamental battle over precisely who controlled motor racing, and the early 1980s became a turbulent period in the sport's history as a result, with some races being boycotted and others taking place outside the official World Championship. Eventually this led to an accommodation being reached between FOCA and FISA that was enshrined in the so-called Concorde Agreement. This, renewed on a number of occasions, has since governed the way in which the commercial and sporting aspects of F1 are controlled and administered.

It has not always been an easy balancing act to maintain. In 1997, when Williams, McLaren and Tyrrell held out for better terms and initially declined to sign a new Concorde Agreement, more than 60 drafts were circulated and debated before a final deal was struck.

In 2005, Ecclestone pulled off another major business coup when he negotiated the sale of a controlling interest in his F1 Group to British investment firm CVC Capital Partners, the then 75-year-old remaining on the payroll as chief executive, even though he had sold his 25-per-cent stake in the business.

As part of the deal, CVC established a new company, Alpha Prema, which would hold the 48-per-cent stake of Munich bank Bayerische Landesbank and the 25 per cent held by Ecclestone's family trust, Bambino Holdings, in SLEC Holdings, which controlled a number of companies that run the F1 industry. The other stakeholders in SLEC Holdings were JP Morgan Chase and Company and Lehman Brothers Holdings, Inc.

The monetary terms of the deal were not disclosed, and the agreement was subject to approval by the European Commission and endorsement by the FIA, both of which obviously were secured.

CVC Capital Partners had laid out a well-chartered plan for Alpha Prema that henceforth would run Formula 1. Its shareholders were CVC Capital Partners, Bambino Holdings (Ecclestone seems to have bought back a stake in Alpha Prema on behalf of the trust), Ecclestone himself and the F1 management team.

At the time, the acquisition was seen as an effort to foil a move to float a rival F1 series, proposed from 2008, by an organisation opposed to Ecclestone and called the Grand Prix Manufacturers Association (GPMC). It had been set up by BMW, Daimler-Chrysler, Renault, Toyota and Honda, all of whom wanted a bigger say in how the sport was administered.

At the 2005 German GP weekend at Hockenheim, this newly branded alliance of nine F1 teams and five car manufacturers presented FIA President Max Mosley with a package that outlined their views on the way in which they believed the sport should develop over the coming years.

"Considering the fact that the alliance represents 90 per cent of the current grid, and views from stakeholders such as circuits, broadcasters, sponsors and fans are included, the teams and manufacturers are confident that the FIA will consider their proposals very carefully," said a GPMA statement.

"Where possible, costs should be significantly reduced, providing sporting spectacle and competition are not compromised. The vision is for a fair and transparent sport with well-funded and highly competitive teams on every row of the grid with the best drivers competing on the most exciting race tracks around the world."

The footnote to this, of course, would soon become evident. Ecclestone successfully quashed the car manufacturers' ambitions. By the end of 2009, BMW, Toyota and Honda had quit the sport. And Bernie Ecclestone was still calling the shots.

CHAPTER THIRTEEN

Above right: Sir Jackie Stewart at Monza, marking the 40th anniversary of his first World Championship win in 1969 with helmet and trophy.

Right: Ross Brawn sold a major shareholding in his team to Mercedes for the 2010 season.

Below: Max Mosley and his successor, Jean Todt ,who took over as the president of the FIA in 2009.

Photos: Paul-Henri Cahier

senior management would hold 24.9 per cent of the team's equity, the Abu Dhabi based Aarbar investments would hold 30 per cent, and Daimler AG would take 45.1 per cent. The team would continue to be run from its current headquarters at Brackley in Oxfordshire.

It had been thought that Button would remain with the team alongside Nico Rosberg, the preferred Mercedes nominee, for 2010, but there were suggestions at the time that Button was never at the top of the Mercedes list and that he would join McLaren, despite the fact that Daimler, the parent company of Mercedes, had announced a structured sale of its 40-per-cent stake in the McLaren group by 2011.

In switching to McLaren, Button was going against advice from F1 grandees, including Sir Stirling Moss, Sir Jackie Stewart, Niki Lauda and Martin Brundle, all of whom felt that he might have bitten off more than he could chew by taking on Lewis Hamilton on his home turf in equal cars. But, for Button, the prospect of going head to head with the man regarded by many in the pit lane as possibly the fastest of all, would be an integral element of the defence of his title crown.

MOSLEY SUCCEEDED BY TODT IN TOP JOB

At the end of the 2009 season, FIA President Max Mosley made good his promise to stand down from his post, and Jean Todt, the former Ferrari F1 team principal who had presided over Michael Schumacher's glory years at Maranello, was elected overwhelmingly as his successor, becoming one of the most powerful men on the international motor sporting scene.

Mosley vigorously endorsed Todt's candidature, making no secret of the fact that he believed the Frenchman was the right man from the job. The FIA member clubs clearly agreed, and the bid by the former World Rally Champion, Ari Vatanen, to be elected to the position was comprehensively defeated, as Mosley correctly predicted.

"Jean is unquestionably the outstanding motor sport manager of his generation, and arguably of any generation," said Mosley. "Teams run by him have won the World Rally Championship, cross-country rallies, including the Paris-Dakar, the Le Mans 24-hours and, in the last 15 years, one F1 World Championship after another."

There can be no argument with that, particularly in view of the fact that the FIA presidency covers every

clinch the title with a storming fifth place finish at Interlagos in the penultimate race of the year. What happened next shook the F1 community to the core. Jenson signed a long-term deal to join McLaren.

The decision by the newly crowned World Champion to turn his back on the team that had been built from the ashes of the Honda outfit by Ross Brawn came on the day that it was announced that Mercedes-Benz had purchased a controlling interest in Brawn GP, and that it would field its cars under the Mercedes banner in 2010.

Under the new set-up, Ross Brawn and the other

Above: **Damon Hill worked tirelessly to ensure that the British Grand Prix at Silverstone maintained its place on the F1 calendar.**

Top: **An aerial view of the revised Silverstone track, which would be in place for the 2010 Grand Prix.**

Photos: **BRDC**

aspect of the automobile and automobile industry in modern life, not just F1 and the other strands of the sport. Yet traditionally it has been F1 where the governing body has manned the barricades and earned its reputation, rightly or wrongly, as an authoritarian and often unsympathetic administrator.

POSTCRIPT: BRITISH GP SEES OFF DONINGTON CHALLENGE

The protracted and often painful negotiations to secure the future of the British Grand Prix were successfully concluded early in December 2009, when the British Racing Drivers' Club announced that it had secured a 17-year deal to continue staging the race at the former wartime RAF base, which has been at the very core of UK motorsport for the past 60 years.

The news brought a welcome end to a painful period in British motorsport, after Donington Park had failed, as expected, to upgrade its track facilities to meet the terms of a similar 17-year deal that had been signed with commercial rights holder Bernie Ecclestone in the summer of 2009.

"The title of Silverstone as the home of British motor sport has come true," said Damon Hill, the BRDC president, who had won the 1996 World Championship driving for Williams. "It is a place for all motor sport. Everybody in the BRDC loves motor sport and we are looking forward to hosting the Moto GP as well as the British GP."

He added, "It is not easy to enter into a contract of this magnitude, and you have to take on a lot of responsibility, but the BRDC wanted this relationship to continue. Everyone was well aware that the British Grand Prix was not just a sporting event, but the dynamo of the industry in this country. Losing it would have been damaging, and perhaps there would have been no coming back.'

Hill's obvious delight was echoed later in the morning when Gordon Brown appeared at the BRDC annual awards lunch to present Jenson Button with the Richard Seaman trophy, in memory of the British Mercedes driver who had been killed in the 1939 Belgian GP. "This puts Britain at the centre of world racing for 17 years to come," said the prime minister.'

Yet Silverstone remains hopeful that it can pack in a capacity 90,000-strong crowd year after year, tapping into the emotional soul of the fanatical British fans at a time when they have two World Champions in the form of Lewis Hamilton and Jenson Button to entertain them royally. All in all, the saga behind cementing the British Grand Prix's place on the 2010 international calendar had been a lurid one, but one entirely in keeping with the tortuous and unpredictable relationship that has existed between Bernie Ecclestone and the BRDC for two decades.

For his part, after weeks of telling the BRDC to sign or bow out of the F1 business, and despite all the distractions caused by the failure of Donington Park to meet its commitment to take on the GP contract, Ecclestone admitted that he was happy that the deal had finally been done with Silverstone. But he still could not resist a parting shot.

"It's been a long and tiring nonsense," he was reported as saying. "They could have done this whole thing months and months ago."

EXPANSION IS THE KEY

WHEN the inaugural F1 World Championship kicked off with the British Grand Prix at Silverstone on 13th May, 1950, there were just six such events making up the series, all of them in Europe. Ignore, if you will, that curious statistical anomaly of the Indianapolis 500 being an official round of the World Championship through to 1960, the year after the first official US Grand Prix had taken place at the Sebring circuit in Florida, where Jack Brabham had clinched the first of his three World Championships. There was no crossover worth mentioning between the F1 brigade and the 'roundy round' boys at the Brickyard.

No, the World Championship proper did not stray out of Europe until 1953, when Alberto Ascari won the Argentine GP at Buenos Aires. Even then, the championship was being run under F2 technical regulations, so you could say that Juan Manuel Fangio's victory in Argentina the following year, with the graceful Maserati 250F, was the first proper championship F1 race to take place outside Europe. Morocco followed in 1958, then the USA in 1959, followed by a three-year break before South Africa joined the party in 1962, with Mexico coming aboard in 1963.

Since then, F1's commercial tentacles have reached out to leave precious few areas of the world untouched by its high-octane experience.

Looking back over the past decade, the 2004 season saw the addition of two spectacular new events, in the form of the Bahrain and Chinese Grands Prix. Bahrain's exotic desert location added to the sense of expectancy as the F1 teams rolled into the Gulf sheikdom for the first time. The grandstands and pit complex at the Sakhir circuit loomed into view like an ocean liner emerging from the mist as one travelled through the arid desert landscape about 30km south of Manama, the capital city of Bahrain.

Nobody doubted that the Bahrain authorities had done a brilliant job in building the Herman Tilke-designed circuit in just 18 months, and unfavourable comparisons with some of the older established European races, many of which do not benefit from such government funding, was understandable in the prevailing highly-political F1 environment.

"My message to some of the European circuits is, 'Watch your backs,'" warned commercial rights holder Bernie Ecclestone. "This is an F1 *World* Championship. Nobody wants

to abandon the European races. What we want them to do is to raise their standards. They will never raise it to the sorts of levels achieved here in Bahrain, but they can raise it."

Although Sakhir was a brand-new circuit, the teams began preparing for the track well before the season began. Pat Symonds, Renault's executive director of engineering, explained that preliminary work began as soon as the first accurate circuit map had been published, from which the trajectory of the car along the racing line could be described mathematically in three dimensions.

"Once the circuit configuration has been finalised, detailed maps are issued by the FIA and work can begin," he said. "The boundaries of the tarmac are digitised and fed into the first stage of the simulation program to determine the ideal racing line. This is what a skilled driver does intuitively."

Michael Schumacher and Rubens Barrichello posted a Ferrari 1-2 finish at the end of the first Bahrain Grand Prix. Schuey was curiously off form, however, when it came to the first Chinese Grand Prix, held later that year on the splendid Shanghai circuit, another Tilke architectural *tour-de-force*, and Barrichello dominated proceed-

ings to score a commanding win.

There was much more variety to come. In 2008, Singapore staged the first World Championship GP to be held under floodlights after dark, setting itself a commercial and technical challenge that could herald a new era in the sport's history.

The inaugural event on the tight and tortuous Marina Bay circuit represented the culmination of almost 30 years of lobbying by the Singapore Motor Sports Federation to bring back motor racing to the island city-state after the end of the original free-formula event that had taken place in 1973.

In the late 1980s, preliminary talks had been held with Bernie Ecclestone about the possibility of running a World Championship Grand Prix on a permanent circuit. In the event, the project never got off the ground, but the Singapore waterfront finally reverberated to the roar of F1 exhausts for the first time in 2008.

"There are many advantages to holding a night race," said Colin Syn, the deputy chairman of the race organisers. "The later start time will ensure maximum exposure of the race in Singapore to the important European television markets, while in Asia too, a late Sunday evening broadcast gains maximum market exposure."

The timing of the race weekend programme raised a raft of completely new challenges, as Williams technical director Sam Michael explained: "Singapore is a new circuit on the F1 calendar that promises lots of action, even if only for the fact that it's our first ever night race. Running at night will bring new challenges for all the teams, from the driver having to adjust himself to different levels of visibility to team personnel having unusual sleeping and eating patterns!

"To add to the excitement of the night race, there is also a strong possibility of rain during the evening, which is normal in such a humid climate."

The issue of reflective glare, not only from the lights illuminating the circuit, but also from the battery of camera flash bulbs from the packed grandstands, was also thought to pose a particular visibility problem in the event of a wet race, so much so that German helmet manufacturer Schubert developed a special visor to be used by its contracted drivers, among them Kimi Räikkönen, Felipe Massa and Nick Heidfeld.

However, Lewis Hamilton brushed aside any worries that adapting to the different schedule would be a problem. "The race will be quite a fun challenge, and I like a challenge!" he insisted. "I've never raced at night before, but I don't think it is going to be a problem. It doesn't seem to be a problem in other sports, and there have been huge preparations for this, so I think it will be great."

F1's desire for further expansion and ever bigger prize funds then brought Abu Dhabi on to the F1 calendar for the first time in 2009. The emirate would host the final race of the season and become the second round of the World Championship to be staged in the Gulf region after the Bahrain event, introduced five years earlier.

Work began on the Yas Marina circuit in February 2007, after the franchise had been awarded to Abu Dhabi for a renewable seven-year term until 2016. Although the sport's hierarchy welcomed such further expansion of the F1 calendar, particularly at a time of economic depression, the emergence of another lavishly funded fixture in the Middle East had the secondary effect of ratcheting up the

commercial pressure on cash strapped European races.

With Donington Park putting a brave face on its efforts to be ready for the 2010 British GP, the French race having dropped off the calendar for the time being, and the German round of the title chase alternating between the Nürburgring and a financially strained Hockenheim, you could argue that the time is ripe for as much expansion to new venues as the sport can take. And the stakes are being raised all the time.

The developer of the Yas Marina circuit claimed that it would be the most technologically advanced in the world ahead of its first event, and the reality was in no way a disappointment. Certainly it encompasses unique features, among them the Yas Marina hotel, which actually straddles a section of the circuit, offering guests an unparalleled view of the action. By common consensus, the Abu Dhabi GP not only was a huge success, but also it raised the bar yet again, setting fresh standards by which others will be judged. Onwards and upwards seems to be the catchphrase in Bernie's World. More now than ever.

Left: Bahrain offered a spectacular addition to the calendar with its splendid grandstand providing far reaching views for the spectators on a traditional style of track.

Below: Abu Dhabi's jaw dropping Yas Marina street circuit offered a satisfyingly contrasting atmosphere to Bahrain with its nighttime racing.
Photos: Paul-Henri Cahier

Grand Prix Season-by-Season Tables 1950–2009

Compiled by David Hayhoe (Grand Prix Data Book)

The following tables display the complete season performance records for drivers who scored points or achieved a pole position during the season.

It was common practice in the 1950s for drivers to share a car. In these situations, a driver's best result in the race is shown.

Points shown in brackets are those scored but not counted towards the final championship total.

The Indianapolis 500 featured in the F1 World Championship from 1950 until 1960. These race results are not included in the tables.

KEY:

=	shared				
ap	also practiced				
dq	disqualified				
ew	entry withdrawn				
exc	excluded				
nc	non classified				
npq	non pre-qualified				
nq	non qualified				
ns	non started				
p	pole position				
r	retired				
*	driver died during the year				
(F2)	Formula 2 category				

Grand Prix races

A	Austria	LV	Caesars Palace, Las Vegas (USA)
ABU	Abu Dhabi (United Arab Emirates)	MA	Morocco
AUS	Australia	MAL	Malaysia
B	Belgium	MC	Monaco
BR	Brazil	MEX	Mexico
BRN	Bahrain	NL	Netherlands
CDN	Canada	P	Portugal
CH	Switzerland	PAC	Pacific
CHN	China	PES	Pescara (Italy)
D	Germany	RA	Argentina
DAL	Dallas (USA)	RSM	San Marino
DET	Detroit (USA)	S	Sweden
E	Spain	SIN	Singapore
EUR	Europe	TR	Turkey
F	France	USA	United States of America
GB	Britain	USAE	USA East
H	Hungary	USAW	USA West
I	Italy	ZA	South Africa
J	Japan		

1950

Pos	Driver	Car-Engine	GB	MC	CH	B	F	I	Points
1	Giuseppe Farina	Alfa Romeo	p1	r	1	p4	7r	1	30
2	Juan Manuel Fangio	Alfa Romeo	r	p1	pr	1	p1	pr	27
3	Luigi Fagioli	Alfa Romeo	2	r	2	2	2	3	24 (4)
4	Louis Rosier	Tabot Lago	5	r	3	3	6=	4	13
5	Alberto Ascari	Ferrari	-	2	r	5	ns	2=	11
6	B Bira	Maserati	r	5	4	-	-	r	5
7	Peter Whitehead	Ferrari	-	ns	-	-	3	7	4
8	Louis Chiron	Maserati	r	3	9	-	r	r	4
9	Reg Parnell	Alfa Romeo	3	-	-	-	-	-	4
		Maserati	-	-	-	-	r	-	
10	Dorino Serafini	Ferrari	-	-	-	-	-	2=	3
11	Yves Giraud-Cabantous	Talbot Lago	4	-	r	r	8	-	3
12	Raymond Sommer *	Ferrari	-	4	r	-	-	-	3
		Talbot Lago	-	-	-	r	r	r	
	Robert Manzon	Simca Gordini	-	r	-	-	4	r	3
14	Philippe Étançelin	Talbot Lago	8	r	r	r	5=	5	3
15	Felice-Bonetto	Maserati-Milano	-	-	5	-	r	-	2
		Milano-Speluzzi	-	-	-	-	-	ns	
16	Eugène-Chaboud	Talbot-Lago	-	-	-	r	5=	-	1

1951

Pos	Driver	Car–Engine	CH	B	F	GB	D	I	E	Points
1	Juan Manuel Fangio	Alfa Romeo	p1	p9	p1=	2	2	pr	1	31 (6)
2	Alberto Ascari	Ferrari	6	2	2=	r	p1	1	p4	25 (3)
3	Froilán González	Talbot Lago	r	-	-	-	-	-	-	24 (3)
		Ferrari	-	-	2=	p1	3	2	2	
4	Giuseppe Farina	Alfa Romeo	3	1	5	r	r	3=	3	19 (3)
5	Luigi Villoresi	Ferrari	r	3	3	3	4	4	r	15 (3)
6	Piero Taruffi	Ferrari	2	r	-	-	5	5	r	10
7	Felice Bonetto	Alfa Romeo	-	-	-	4	r	3=	5	7
8	Reg Parnell	Thin Wall Ferrari	-	-	4	-	-	-	-	5
		BRM	-	-	-	5	-	ns	-	
9	Luigi Fagioli	Alfa Romeo	-	-	1=	-	-	-	-	4
10	Consalvo Sanesi	Alfa Romeo	4	r	10	6	-	-	-	3
11	Louis Rosier	Talbot Lago	9	4	r	10	8	7	7	3
12	Emmanuel de Graffenried	Alfa Romeo	5	-	-	-	-	r	6	2
		Maserati	-	-	r	-	r	-	-	
13	Yves Giraud-Cabantous	Talbot Lago	r	5	7	-	r	8	r	2

1952

Pos	Driver	Car-Engine	CH	B	F	GB	D	NL	I	Points
1	Alberto Ascari	Ferrari	-	p1	p1	1	p1	p1	p1	36 (17.5)
2	Giuseppe Farina	Ferrari	pr	2	2	p6	2	2	4	24 (3)
3	Piero Taruffi	Ferrari	1	r	3	2	4	-	7	22
4	Rudi Fischer	Ferrari	2	-	11=	13	3	-	r	10
5	Mike Hawthorn	Cooper-Bristol	-	4	r	3	-	4	nc	10
6	Robert Manzon	Gordini	r	3	4	r	r	5	14	9
7	Luigi Villoresi	Ferrari	-	-	-	-	-	3	3	8
8	Froilán González	Maserati	-	-	-	-	-	-	2	6.5
9	Jean Behra	Gordini	3	r	7	-	5	r	r	6
10	Ken Wharton	Frazer Nash-Bristol	4	r	-	-	-	r	-	3
		Cooper-Bristol	-	-	-	-	-	-	9	
11	Dennis Poore	Connaught	-	-	-	4	-	-	12	3
12	Alan Brown	Cooper-Bristol	5	6	-	22	-	-	15	2
13	Maurice Trintignant	Ferrari	ns	-	-	-	-	-	-	2
		Simca Gordini/Gordini	-	-	5	r	r	6	r	
14	Paul Frère	HWM	-	5	-	-	r	-	-	2
		Simca Gordini	-	-	-	-	-	r	-	
	Eric Thompson	Connaught	-	-	-	5	-	-	-	2
	Felice Bonetto	Maserati	-	-	-	dq	-	5	2	2

1953

Pos	Driver	Car-Engine	RA	NL	B	F	GB	D	CH	I	Points
1	Alberto Ascari	Ferrari	p1	p1	1	p4	p1	p8=	1	pr	34.5 (12.5)
2	Juan Manuel Fangio	Maserati	r	r	pr	2	2	2	p4=	1	27.5 (1.5)
3	Giuseppe Farina	Ferrari	r	2	r	5	3	1	2	2	26 (6)
4	Mike Hawthorn	Ferrari	4	4	6	1	5	3	3	4	19 (8)
5	Luigi Villoresi	Ferrari	2	r	2	6	r	8=	6	3	17
6	Froilán González	Maserati	3	3=	r	3	4	-	-	-	13.5 (1)
7	E de Graffenried	Maserati	-	5	4	7	r	5	r	r	7
8	Felice Bonetto*	Maserati	r	3=	-	r	6	4	4=	r	6.5
9	Onofré Marimón	Maserati	-	-	3	9	r	r	r	r	4
10	Maurice Trintignant	Gordini	7=	6	5	r	r	r	5	4	4
11	Oscar Gálvez	Maserati	5	-	-	-	-	-	-	-	2
	Hermann Lang	Maserati	-	-	-	-	-	-	5	-	2

1954

Pos	Driver	Car-Engine	RA	B	F	GB	D	CH	I	E	Points
1	Juan Manuel Fangio	Maserati	1	p1	-	-	-	-	-	-	42 (15.14)
		Mercedes-Benz	-	-	p1	p4	p1	1	p1	3	
2	Froilán González	Ferrari	3	4=	r	1	2=	p2	3=	-	25.14 (1.5)
3	Mike Hawthorn	Ferrari	dq	4=	r	2	2=	r	2	1	24.64
4	Maurice Trintignant	Ferrari	4	2	r	5	3	r	5	r	17
5	Karl Kling	Mercedes-Benz	-	-	2	7	4	r	r	5	12
6	Hans Herrmann	Mercedes-Benz	-	-	r	-	r	3	4	r	8
7	Giuseppe Farina	Ferrari	p2	r	-	-	-	-	-	-	6
	Luigi Musso	Maserati	ns	-	-	-	-	-	r	2	6
9	Roberto Mières	Maserati	r	r	r	6	r	4	r	4	6
10	Stirling Moss	Maserati	-	3	-	r	r	r	10	r	4.14
11	Onofré Marimón *	Maserati	r	r	r	3	ns	-	-	-	4.14
12	Robert Manzon	Ferrari	-	-	3	r	9	ns	r	r	4
13	Sergio Mantovani	Maserati	-	7	ns	-	5	5	9	r	4
14	B Bira	Maserati	7	6	4	r=	r	-	-	9	3
15	Umberto Maglioli	Ferrari	9	-	-	-	7	3=	-	-	2
16	André Pilette	Gordini	-	5	-	9	r	-	-	r	2
17	Elie Bayol	Gordini	5	-	-	-	-	-	-	-	2
	Luigi Villoresi	Maserati	-	5	r=	ns	-	r	r	-	2
		Lancia	-	-	-	-	-	-	-	r	
19	Alberto Ascari	Maserati	-	-	r	r	-	-	-	-	1.14
		Ferrari	-	-	-	-	-	r	-	-	
		Lancia	-	-	-	-	-	-	pr	-	
20	Jean Behra	Gordini	dq	r	6	r	10	r	r	r	0.14

1955

Pos	Driver	Car-Engine	RA	MC	B	NL	GB	I	Points
1	Juan Manuel Fangio	Mercedes-Benz	1	pr	1	p1	2	p1	40 (1)
2	Stirling Moss	Mercedes-Benz	4=	9	2	2	p1	r	23
3	Eugenio Castellotti	Lancia	r=	2	pr	-	-	-	12
		Ferrari	-	-	-	5	6=	3	
4	Maurice Trintignant	Ferrari	2=	1	6	r	r	8	11.33
5	Giuseppe Farina	Ferrari	2=	4	3	-	-	-	10.33
		Lancia	-	-	-	-	-	ns	
6	Piero Taruffi	Ferrari	-	8=	-	-	-	-	9
		Mercedes-Benz	-	-	-	-	4	2	
7	Roberto Mières	Maserati	5	r	5=	4	r	7	7
8	Jean Behra	Maserati	6=	3=	5=	6	r	4	6
9	Luigi Musso	Maserati	7=	r	7	3	5	r	6
10	Karl Kling	Mercedes-Benz	4=	-	r	r	3	r	5
11	Paul Frère	Ferrari	-	8=	4	-	-	-	3
12	Froilán González	Ferrari	p2=	-	-	-	-	-	2
13	Cesare Perdisa	Maserati	-	3=	8	-	-	-	2
14	Luigi Villoresi	Lancia	r	5	-	-	-	ns	2
	Carlos Menditéguy	Maserati	r	-	-	-	-	5	2
16	Umberto Maglioli	Ferrari	3=	-	-	-	-	6	1.33
17	Hans Herrmann	Mercedes-Benz	4=	ns	-	-	-	-	1

1956

Pos	Driver	Car-Engine	RA	MC	B	F	GB	D	I	Points
1	Juan Manuel Fangio	Lancia Ferrari	p1=	p2=	pr	p4	1	p1	p2=	30 (3)
2	Stirling Moss	Maserati	r	1	3=	5=	pr	2	1	27 (1)
3	Peter Collins	Ferrari	r	-	-	-	-	-	-	25
		Lancia Ferrari	-	2=	1	1	2=	r	2=	
4	Jean Behra	Maserati	2	3	7	3	3	3	r	22
5	Eugenio Castellotti	Lancia Ferrari	r	4=	r	2	10=	r	8=	7.5
6	Paul Frère	Lancia Ferrari	-	-	2	-	-	-	-	6
7	Chico Godia	Maserati	-	-	r	7	8	4	4	6
8	Jack Fairman	Connaught	-	-	-	-	4	-	5	5
9	Luigi Musso	Lancia Ferrari	1=	r	-	-	-	r=	r	4
10	Mike Hawthorn	Maserati	3	-	ns	-	-	-	-	4
		BRM	-	ns	-	-	r	-	-	
		Vanwall	-	-	-	10=	-	-	-	
11	Ron Flockhart	BRM	-	-	-	-	r	-	-	4
		Connaught	-	-	-	-	-	3	-	
12	Alfonso de Portago	Lancia Ferrari	-	-	-	r	2=	r=	r	3
13	Cesare Perdisa	Maserati	-	7	3=	5=	7	ns	-	3
14	Harry Schell	Vanwall	-	r	4	10=	r	-	r	3
		Maserati	-	-	-	-	-	r	-	
15	Louis Rosier*	Maserati	-	r	8	6	r	5	-	2
16	Luigi Villoresi	Maserati	-	-	5	r	6	r	r=	2
17	Nano da Silva Ramos	Gordini	-	5	-	8	r	-	r	2
	Horace Gould	Maserati	-	8	r	-	5	r	-	2
19	Olivier Gendebien	Ferrari-Lancia Ferrari	5	-	-	-	-	-	-	2
		Lancia Ferrari	-	-	-	r	-	-	-	
20	Gerino Gerini	Maserati	4=	-	-	-	-	-	10	1.5
21	Chico Landi	Maserati	4=	-	-	-	-	-	10	1.5

1957

Pos	Driver	Car-Engine	RA	MC	F	GB	D	PES	I	Points
1	Juan Manuel Fangio	Maserati	1	p1	p1	r	p1	p2	2	40 (6)
2	Stirling Moss	Maserati	p8	-	-	-	-	-	-	25
		Vanwall	-	r	-	p1=	5	1	1	
3	Luigi Musso	Lancia Ferrari	r	-	2	2	4	r	8	16
4	Mike Hawthorn	Lancia Ferrari	r	7r=	4	3	2	-	6	13
5	Tony Brooks	Vanwall	-	2	-	1=	9	r	7	11
6	Masten Gregory	Maserati	-	3	-	8	4	4	10	10
7	Harry Schell	Maserati	4	r	5	r	7	3	5=	10
8	Peter Collins	Lancia Ferrari	6=	r	3	4=	3	-	r	8
9	Jean Behra	Maserati	2	-	6	r	6	r	r	6
10	Stuart Lewis-Evans	Connaught	-	4	-	-	-	-	-	5
		Vanwall	-	-	r	7	r	5	pr	
11	Maurice Trintignant	Lancai Ferrari	-	5	r	4=	-	-	-	5
12	Wolfgang von Trips	Lancia Ferrari	6=	7=	-	-	-	-	3	4
13	Carlos Mendiléguy	Maserati	3	r	r	r	-	-	4	4
14	Roy Salvadori	BRM	-	nq	-	-	-	-	-	2
		Vanwall	-	-	r	-	-	-	-	
		Cooper-Climax	-	-	-	5	(F2)r	r	-	
15	Giorgio Scarlatti	Maserati	-	r=	-	-	10	6	5=	1
16	Alfonso de Portago*	Lancia Ferrari	5=	-	-	-	-	-	-	1
	Froilán González	Lancia Ferrari	5=	-	-	-	-	-	-	1

1958

Pos	Driver	Car-Engine	RA	MC	NL	B	F	GB	D	P	I	MA	Points
1	Mike Hawthorn	Ferrari	3	r	5	p2	p1	2	pr	2	2	p2	42 (7)
2	Stirling Moss	Cooper-Climax	1	-	-	-	-	-	-	-	-	-	41
		Vanwall	-	r	1	r	2	pr	r	p1	pr	1	
3	Tony Brooks	Vanwall	-	pr	r	1	r	r	1	r	1	r	24
4	Roy Salvadori	Cooper-Climax	r	4	8	11	3	2	9	5	7	-	15
5	Peter Collins*	Ferrari	r	3	r	r	5	1	r	-	-	-	14
6	Harry Schell	Maserati	6	-	-	-	-	-	-	-	-	-	14
		BRM	-	5	2	5	r	5	r	6	r	5	
7	Maurice Trintignant	Cooper-Climax	-	1	9	-	-	8	3	8	r	r	12
		Maserati	-	-	7	-	-	-	-	-	-	-	
		BRM	-	-	-	r	-	-	-	-	-	-	
8	Luigi Musso*	Ferrari	2	2	7	r	r	-	-	-	-	-	12
9	Stuart Lewis-Evans*	Vanwall	-	r	pr	3	r=	4	-	3	r	r	11
10	Phil Hill	Maserati	-	-	7	-	-	-	-	-	-	-	9
		Ferrari	-	-	-	-	-	-	(F2)5	-	3	3	
11	Wolfgang von Trips	Ferrari	-	r	-	3	r	4	5	r	-	-	9
	Jean Behra	Maserati	5	-	-	-	-	-	-	-	-	-	9
		BRM	-	r	3	r	r	r	4	r	r	-	
13	Juan Manuel Fangio	Maserati	p4	-	-	-	4	-	-	-	-	-	7
14	Cliff Allison	Lotus-Climax	-	6	6	4	r	r	5	-	7	10	3
		Maserati	-	-	-	-	-	-	-	r	-	-	
15	Jack Brabham	Cooper-Climax	-	4	8	r	6	6	(F2)r	7	r	(F2)1	3
16	Jo Bonnier	Maserati	-	r	10	9	8	r	r	r	-	-	3
		BRM	-	-	-	-	-	-	-	-	r	4	

Masten Gregory and Carroll Shelby shared a Maserati in Italy where they finished 4th. Consequently they were ineligible for points.

1959

Pos	Driver	Car-Engine	MC	NL	F	GB	D	P	I	USA	Points
1	Jack Brabham	Cooper-Climax	1	2	3	p1	r	r	3	4	31 (3)
2	Tony Brooks	Ferrari	2	r	p1	-	p1	9	r	3	27
		Vanwall	-	-	-	r	-	-	-	-	
3	Stirling Moss	Cooper-Climax	pr	r	-	-	r	p1	p1	pr	25.5
		BRM	-	-	dq	2	-	-	-	-	
4	Phil Hill	Ferrari	4	6	2	-	3	r	2	r	20
5	Maurice Trintignant	Cooper-Climax	3	8	11	5	4	4	9	2	19
6	Bruce McLaren	Cooper-Climax	5	-	5	3	r	r	r	1	16.5
7	Dan Gurney	Ferrari	-	-	r	-	2	3	4	-	13
8	Jo Bonnier	BRM	r	p1	r	r	5	r	8	r	10
9	Masten Gregory	Cooper-Climax	r	3	r	7	r	2	-	-	10
10	Harry Schell	BRM	r	r	7	4	7r	5	7	r	5
11	Innes Ireland	Lotus-Climax	-	4	r	ns	r	r	r	5	5
12	Olivier Gendebien	Ferrari	-	-	4	-	-	-	6	-	3
13	Cliff Allison	Ferrari	r	9	-	-	r	-	5	r	2
14	Jean Behra*	Ferrari	r	5	r	-	-	-	-	-	2
		Behra Porsche	-	-	-	ns	-	-	-	-	

1960

Pos	Driver	Car-Engine	RA	MC	NL	B	F	GB	P	I	USA	Points
1	Jack Brabham	Cooper-Climax	r	dq	1	p1	p1	p1	1	-	4	43
2	Bruce McLaren	Cooper-Climax	1	2	r	2	3	4	2	-	3	34 (3)
3	Stirling Moss	Cooper-Climax	p3=	-	-	-	-	-	-	-	-	19
		Lotus-Climax	-	p1	p4	ns	-	dq	-	p1	-	
4	Innes Ireland	Lotus-Climax	6	9	2	r	7	3	6	-	2	18
5	Phil Hill	Ferrari	8	3	r	4	12r	7	r	p1	-	16
		Cooper-Climax	-	-	-	-	-	-	-	-	6	
6	Olivier Gendebien	Cooper-Climax	-	-	-	3	2	9	7	-	12	10
7	Wolfgang von Trips	Ferrari	5	8r	5	r	11r	6	4	5	-	10
		Cooper-Maserati	-	-	-	-	-	-	-	-	9	
8	Richie Ginther	Ferrari	-	6	6	-	-	-	-	2	-	8
		Scarab	-	-	-	ns	-	-	-	-	-	
9	Jim Clark	Lotus-Climax	-	-	r	5	5	16	3	-	16	8
10	Tony Brooks	Cooper-Climax	-	4	r	r	5	5	r	-	r	7
		Vanwall	-	-	-	-	-	r	-	-	-	
11	Cliff Allison	Ferrari	2	nq	-	-	-	-	-	-	-	6
	John Surtees	Lotus-Climax	-	r	-	-	-	2	pr	-	r	6
13	Graham Hill	BRM	r	7r	3	r	r	r	r	r	r	4
14	Willy Mairesse	Ferrari	-	-	-	r	r	-	-	3	-	4
15	Jo Bonnier	BRM	7	5	r	r	r	r	r	-	5	4
16	Henry Taylor	Cooper-Climax	-	-	7	-	4	8	ns	-	14	3
17	Carlos Mendiléguy	Cooper-Maserati	4	-	-	-	-	-	-	-	-	3
	Giulio Cabianca	Cooper-Castellotti	-	-	-	-	-	-	-	4	-	3
19	Lucien Bianchi	Cooper-Climax	-	-	-	6	r	r	-	-	-	1
	Ron Flockhart	Lotus-Climax	-	-	-	6	-	-	-	-	-	1
		Cooper-Climax	-	-	-	-	-	-	-	-	r	
	Hans Herrmann	Porsche	-	-	-	-	-	-	6	-	-	1

Stirling Moss shared his car with Maurice Trintignant in Argentina and so were both ineligible for points for their 3rd place.

1961

Pos	Driver	Car-Engine	MC	NL	F	GB	D	P	I	USA	Points
1	Phil Hill	Ferrari	3	p2	p1	p9	p2	p3	1	-	34 (4)
2	Wolfgang von Trips*	Ferrari	4r	1	2	r	1	2	pr	-	33
3	Stirling Moss	Lotus-Climax	p1	4	8	r	r	1	r	r	21
		Ferguson-Climax	-	-	-	-	dq=	-	-	-	
4	Dan Gurney	Porsche	5	10	6	2	7	7	2	2	21
5	Richie Ginther	Ferrari	2	5	3	15r	3	8	r	-	16
6	Innes Ireland	Lotus-Climax	ns	-	r	4	10	r	r	1	12
7	Jim Clark	Lotus-Climax	10	3	12	3	r	4	r	7	11
8	Bruce McLaren	Cooper-Climax	6	12	r	5	8	6	3	4	11
9	Giancarlo Baghetti	Ferrari	-	-	1	r	-	1	r	-	9
10	Tony Brooks	BRM-Climax	13r	9	13	r	9	r	5	3	6
11	Jack Brabham	Cooper-Climax	r	6	r	r	4	r	r	pr	4
12	John Surtees	Cooper-Climax	11r	7	5	r	r	5	r	r	4
13	Jack Lewis	Cooper-Climax	-	-	9	r	r	9	4	-	3
14	Olivier Gendebien	Emeryson-Maserati	nq	-	-	-	-	-	-	-	3
		Ferrari	-	-	4	-	-	-	-	-	
		Lotus-Climax	-	-	-	-	-	-	-	11=	
15	Jo Bonnier	Porsche	12r	11	7	7	5	r	r	6	3
16	Graham Hill	BRM-Climax	r	8	r	6	r	r	r	5	3
17	Roy Salvadori	Cooper-Climax	-	-	-	8	6	10	6	r	2

1962

Pos	Driver	Car-Engine	NL	MC	B	F	GB	D	I	USA	ZA	Points
1	Graham Hill	BRM	1	6r	p2	9r	4	1	1	2	1	42 (10)
2	Jim Clark	Lotus-Climax	9	pr	1	pr	p1	4	pr	p1	r	30
3	Bruce McLaren	Cooper-Climax	r	1	r	4	3	5	3	3	2	27 (5)
4	John Surtees	Lola-Climax	pr	4	5	5	2	2	r	r	r	19
5	Dan Gurney	Porsche	r	r	-	1	9	p3	13r	5	-	15
		Lotus-BRM	-	-	ns	-	-	-	-	-	-	
6	Phil Hill	Ferrari	3	2	3	-	r	r	11	-	r	14
		Porsche	-	-	-	-	-	-	-	ns	-	
7	Tony Maggs	Cooper-Climax	5	r	r	2	6	9	7	7	3	13
8	Richie Ginther	BRM	r	r	r	3	13	8	2	r	7	10
9	Jack Brabham	Lotus-Climax	r	8r	6	r	5	-	-	-	-	9
		Brabham-Climax	-	-	-	-	-	r	-	4	4	
10	Trevor Taylor	Lotus-Climax	2	r	r	8	8	r	r	12	r	6
11	Giancarlo Baghetti	Ferrari	4	-	r	-	-	10	5	-	-	5
12	Lorenzo Bandini	Ferrari	-	3	-	-	-	r	8	-	-	4
13	Ricardo Rodríguez*	Ferrari	r	ns	4	-	-	6	14r	-	-	4
14	Willy Mairesse	Ferrari	-	7r	r	-	-	-	4	-	-	3
15	Jo Bonnier	Porsche	7	5	-	10r	r	7	6	13	-	3
16	Innes Ireland	Lotus-Climax	r	r	r	r	16	-	r	8	5	2
17	Godin de Beaufort	Porsche	6	nq	7	6	14	13	10	r	11r	2
18	Masten Gregory	Lotus-Climax	r	-	r	-	-	7	-	-	-	1
		Lotus-BRM	-	nq	r	r	-	-	12	6	-	
19	Neville Lederle	Lotus-Climax	-	-	-	-	-	-	-	-	6	1

1963

Pos	Driver	Car-Engine	MC	B	NL	F	GB	D	I	USA	MEX	ZA	Points
1	Jim Clark	Lotus-Climax	p8r	1	p1	p1	p1	p2	1	3	p1	p1	54 (19)
2	Graham Hill	BRM	1	pr	r	3	3	r	16r	p1	4	3	29
3	Richie Ginther	BRM	2	4	5	r	4	3	2	2	3	r	29 (5)
4	John Surtees	Ferrari	4	r	3	r	2	1	pr	9r	dq	r	22
5	Dan Gurney	Brabham-Climax	r	3	2	5	r	r	14r	r	6	2	19
6	Bruce McLaren	Cooper-Climax	3	2	r	12r	r	r	3	11r	r	4	17
7	Jack Brabham	Lotus-Climax	9	-	-	-	-	-	-	-	-	-	14
		Brabham-Climax	-	r	r	4	r	7	5	4	2	13r	
8	Tony Maggs	Cooper-Climax	5	7r	r	2	9	r	6	r	r	7	9
9	Innes Ireland	Lotus-BRM	r	-	-	-	-	r	-	-	-	-	6
		BRP-BRM	-	r	4	9	dq	-	4r	-	-	-	
10	Lorenzo Bandini	BRM	-	-	-	10	5	r	-	-	-	-	6
		Ferrari	-	-	-	-	-	-	r	5	r	5	
11	Jo Bonnier	Cooper-Climax	7	5	11	r	r	6	7	8	5	6	6
12	Gerhard Mitter	Porsche	-	-	r	-	-	4	-	-	-	-	3
13	Jim Hall	Lotus-BRM	r	r	8	11	6	5	8	10r	8	-	3
14	Godin de Beaufort	Porsche	-	6	9	-	10	r	nq	6	10	10	2
15	Jo Siffert	Lotus-BRM	r	r	7	6	r	9r	r	r	9	-	1
16	Trevor Taylor	Lotus-Climax	6	r	10	13r	dq	8	-	r	8	-	1
17	Lodovico Scarfiotti	Ferrari	-	-	-	-	-	6	ns	-	-	-	1

Graham Hill was awarded no points for his 3rd place in France, because he was push-started on the grid.

1964

Pos	Driver	Car-Engine	MC	NL	B	F	GB	D	A	I	USA	MEX	Points
1	John Surtees	Ferrari	r	2	r	r	3	p1	r	p1	2	2	40
2	Graham Hill	BRM	1	4	5r	2	2	2	pr	r	1	11	39 (2)
3	Jim Clark	Lotus-Climax	p4r	1	1	pr	p1	r	r	p7r=	r	p5r	32
4	Lorenzo Bandini	Ferrari	10r	r	9	5	3	-	1	3	r	3	23
5	Richie Ginther	BRM	2	11	4	5	8	7	2	4	4	8	23
6	Dan Gurney	Brabham-Climax	r	pr	p6r	1	13	10	r	10	r	1	19
7	Bruce McLaren	Cooper-Climax	r	7	2	6	r	r	r	2	r	7	13
8	Jack Brabham	Brabham-Climax	r	r	3	3	4	12r	9	14r	r	r	11
9	Peter Arundell	Lotus-Climax	3	3	9	4	-	-	-	-	-	-	11
10	Jo Siffert	Lotus-BRM	8	-	-	-	-	-	-	-	-	-	7
		Brabham-BRM	-	13	r	r	11	4	r	7	3	r	
11	Bob Anderson	Brabham-Climax	7r	6	ns	12	7	r	3	11	-	-	5
12	Mike Spence	Lotus-Climax	-	-	-	9	8	r	6	7r=	4	4	4
13	Tony Maggs	BRM	-	ns	ns	-	r	6	4	-	-	-	4
14	Innes Ireland	Lotus-BRM	ns	-	-	-	-	-	-	-	-	-	4
		BRP-BRM	-	-	10	r	10	-	5	5	r	12	
15	Jo Bonnier	Cooper-Climax	5	-	-	-	-	-	-	-	-	-	3
		Brabham-BRM	-	9	r	r	r	-	-	-	-	-	
		Brabham-Climax	-	-	-	-	-	6	12	r	r	-	
16	Chris Amon	Lotus-BRM	nq	5	r	10	r	11r	-	-	r	r	2
		Lotus-Climax	-	-	-	-	r	-	-	-	-	-	
17	Maurice Trintignant	BRM	r	-	-	11	nq	5r	-	r	-	-	2
18	Walt Hansgen	Lotus-Climax	-	-	-	-	-	-	-	-	5	-	2
19	Phil Hill	Cooper-Climax	9r	8	r	7	6	r	r	-	r	9r	1
20	Trevor Taylor	BRP-BRM	r	-	7	r	r	-	r	nq	6	r	1
21	Mike Hailwood	Lotus-BRM	6	12r	-	8	r	r	8	r	8r	r	1
22	Pedro Rodríguez	Ferrari	-	-	-	-	-	-	-	-	-	6	1

1965

Pos	Driver	Car-Engine	ZA	MC	B	F	GB	NL	D	I	USA	MEX	Points
1	Jim Clark	Lotus-Climax	p1	-	1	p1	p1	1	p1	p10r	r	pr	54
2	Graham Hill	BRM	3	p1	p5	5	2	p4	2	2	p1	r	40 (7)
3	Jackie Stewart	BRM	6	3	2	2	5	2	r	1	r	r	33 (1)
4	Dan Gurney	Brabham-Climax	r	-	10	r	6	3	3	3	2	2	25
5	John Surtees	Ferrari	2	4r	3	3	7	r	r	-	-	-	17
6	Lorenzo Bandini	Ferrari	15r	2	9	8r	r	9	6	4	4	8	13
7	Richie Ginther	Honda	-	r	6	r	6	-	14r	7	r	1	11
8	Mike Spence	Lotus-Climax	4	-	7	7	4	8	r	11r	r	3	10
9	Bruce McLaren	Cooper-Climax	5	5	3	r	10	r	r	5	r	r	10
10	Jack Brabham	Brabham-Climax	8	r	4	-	ns	-	5	-	3	r	9
11	Denny Hulme	Brabham-Climax	-	8	-	4	r	5	r	r	-	-	5
12	Jo Siffert	Brabham-BRM	7	6	8	6	9	13	r	r	11	4	5
13	Jochen Rindt	Cooper-Climax	r	nq	11	r	14r	r	4	8	6	r	4
14	Pedro Rodríguez	Ferrari	-	-	-	-	-	-	-	-	5	7	2
15	Ronnie Bucknum	Honda	-	-	r	r	r	-	-	-	13	5	2
16	Richard Attwood	Lotus-BRM	-	r	14r	-	13	12	r	6	10	6	2

1966

Pos	Driver	Car-Engine	MC	B	F	GB	NL	D	I	USA	MEX	Points
1	Jack Brabham	Brabham-Repco	r	4	1	p1	p1	1	r	pr	2	42 (3)
2	John Surtees	Ferrari	r	p1	-	-	-	-	-	-	-	28
		Cooper-Maserati	-	-	r	r	r	2	r	3	p1	
3	Jochen Rindt	Cooper-Maserati	r	2	4	5	r	3	4	2	r	22 (2)
4	Denny Hulme	Brabham-Climax	r	r	-	-	-	-	-	-	-	18
		Brabham-Repco	-	-	3	2	r	r	3	r	3	
5	Graham Hill	BRM	3	r	r	3	2	4	r	r	r	17
6	Jim Clark	Lotus-Climax	pr	r	ns	4	3	pr	-	-	-	16
		Lotus-BRM	-	-	-	-	-	-	1	r	r	
7	Jackie Stewart	BRM	1	r	-	r	4	5	r	r	r	14
8	Mike Parkes	Ferrari	-	-	2	-	r	r	p2	-	-	12
9	Lorenzo Bandini	Ferrari	2	3	pnc	-	6	6	r	r	-	12
10	Lodovico Scarfiotti	Ferrari	-	-	-	-	-	r	1	-	-	9
11	Richie Ginther	Cooper-Maserati	r	5	-	-	-	-	-	-	-	5
		Honda	-	-	-	-	-	-	r	nc	4	
12	Dan Gurney	Eagle-Climax	-	nc	5	r	r	7	-	-	5	4
		Eagle-Weslake	-	-	-	-	-	-	r	-	r	
13	Mike Spence	Lotus-BRM	r	r	r	r	5	r	5	r	ns	4
14	Bob Bondurant	BRM	4	r	-	9	-	r	7	-	-	3
		Eagle-Climax	-	-	-	-	-	-	-	dq	-	
		Eagle-Weslake	-	-	-	-	-	-	-	-	r	
15	Jo Siffert	Brabham-BRM	r	-	-	-	-	-	-	-	-	3
		Cooper-Maserati	-	r	r	nc	-	r	r	4	r	
16	Bruce McLaren	McLaren-Ford	r	-	-	-	-	-	-	5	r	3
		McLaren-Serenissima	-	ns	-	6	ns	-	-	-	-	
17	Peter Arundell	Lotus-BRM	-	ns	r	r	r	8	8r	-	7	1
		Lotus-Climax	-	-	-	-	-	-	6	-	-	
18	Bob Anderson	Brabham-Climax	r	-	7	nc	r	r	6	-	-	1
	Jo Bonnier	Cooper-Maserati	nc	r	-	-	7	r	r	nc	6	1
		Brabham-Climax	-	-	nc	r	-	-	-	-	-	
20	John Taylor*	Brabham-BRM	-	-	6	8	8	r	-	-	-	1

1967

Pos	Driver	Car-Engine	ZA	MC	NL	B	F	GB	D	A	I	USA	MEX	Total
1	Denny Hulme	Brabham-Repco	4	1	3	r	2	2	1	2	r	3	3	51
2	Jack Brabham	Brabham-Repco	p6	pr	2	r	1	4	2	1	2	5	2	46 (2)
3	Jim Clark	Lotus-BRM	r	-	-	-	-	-	-	-	-	-	-	41
		Lotus-Climax	-	r	-	-	-	-	-	-	-	-	-	
		Lotus-Ford Cosworth	-	-	1	p6	r	p1	pr	pr	p3	1	p1	
4	John Surtees	Honda	3	r	r	r	-	6	4	-	1	r	4	20
5	Chris Amon	Ferrari	-	3	4	3	r	3	3	6	7	r	9	20
6	Pedro Rodríguez	Cooper-Maserati	1	5	r	9r	6	5	8	-	-	-	6	15
7	Graham Hill	Lotus-BRM	r	2	-	-	-	-	-	-	-	-	-	15
		Lotus-Ford Cosworth	-	-	pr	r	pr	r	r	4	r	p2	r	
8	Dan Gurney	Eagle-Climax	r	-	-	-	-	-	-	-	-	-	-	13
		Eagle-Weslake	-	r	r	1	r	r	r	3	r	r	r	
9	Jackie Stewart	BRM	r	r	r	2	3	r	r	r	r	r	r	10
10	Mike Spence	BRM	r	6	8	5	r	r	r	5	5	r	5	9
11	John Love	Cooper-Climax	2	-	-	-	-	-	-	-	-	-	-	6
12	Jo Siffert	Cooper-Maserati	r	r	10	7	4	r	r	ns	r	4	12r	6
13	Jochen Rindt	Cooper-Maserati	r	r	r	4	r	r	r	r	4	r	r	6
14	Bruce McLaren	McLaren-BRM	-	4	r	-	-	-	-	7	r	r	r	3
		Eagle-Weslake	-	-	-	-	r	r	r	-	-	-	-	
15	Jo Bonnier	Cooper-Maserati	r	-	-	r	-	r	5	8	r	6	10	3
16	Chris Irwin	Lotus-BRM	-	-	7	-	-	-	-	-	-	-	-	2
		BRM	-	-	-	r	5	7	7	r	r	r	r	
17	Bob Anderson *	Brabham-Climax	5	nq	9	8	r	-	-	-	-	-	-	2
18	Mike Parkes	Ferrari	-	-	5	r	-	-	-	-	-	-	-	2
19	Guy Ligier	Cooper-Maserati	-	-	-	10	nc	-	-	-	-	-	-	1
		Brabham-Repco	-	-	-	-	-	10	6	-	r	r	11	
20	Lodovico Scarfiotti	Ferrari	-	-	6	nc	-	-	-	-	-	-	-	1
		Eagle-Weslake	-	-	-	-	-	-	-	-	r	-	-	
	Jacky Ickx	Matra-Ford Cosworth	-	-	-	-	-	-	(F2)r	-	-	-	-	1
		Cooper-Maserati	-	-	-	-	-	-	-	-	6	r	-	

1968

Pos	Driver	Car-Engine	ZA	E	MC	B	NL	F	GB	D	I	CDN	USA	MEX	Total
1	Graham Hill	Lotus-Ford Cosworth	2	1	p1	r	9r	r	pr	2	r	4	2	1	48
2	Jackie Stewart	Matra-Ford Cosworth	r	-	-	4	1	3	6	1	r	6	1	7	36
3	Denny Hulme	McLaren-BRM	5	-	-	-	-	-	-	-	-	-	-	-	33
		McLaren-Ford Cosworth	-	2	5	r	r	5	4	7	1	1	r	r	
4	Jacky Ickx	Ferrari	r	r	-	3	4	1	3	p4	3	ns	-	r	27
5	Bruce McLaren	McLaren-Ford Cosworth	-	r	r	1	r	8	7	13	r	2	6	2	22
6	Pedro Rodríguez	BRM	r	r	r	2	3	nc	r	6	r	3	r	4	18
7	Jo Siffert	Cooper-Maserati	7	-	-	-	-	-	-	-	-	-	-	-	12
		Lotus-Ford Cosworth	-	r	r	7r	r	11	1	r	r	r	5	p6	
8	John Surtees	Honda	8	r	r	r	r	2	5	r	pr	r	3	r	12
9	Jean-Pierre Beltoise	Matra-Ford Cosworth	6	5	-	-	-	-	-	-	-	-	-	-	11
		Matra	-	-	r	8	2	9	r	r	5	r	r	r	
10	Chris Amon	Ferrari	4	pr	-	pr	p6	10	2	r	r	r	r	r	10
11	Jim Clark *	Lotus-Ford Cosworth	p1	-	-	-	-	-	-	-	-	-	-	-	9
12	Jochen Rindt	Brabham-Repco	3	r	r	r	r	pr	r	3	r	pr	r	r	8
13	Richard Attwood	BRM	-	-	2	r	7	7	r	14	-	-	-	-	6
14	Johnny Servoz-Gavin	Matra-Ford Cosworth	-	-	r	-	-	-	-	-	2	r	-	r	6
		Cooper-BRM	-	-	-	-	-	r	-	-	-	-	-	-	
15	Jackie Oliver	Lotus-Ford Cosworth	-	-	r	5r	nc	ns	r	11	r	r	ns	3	6
16	Lodovico Scarfiotti *	Cooper-Maserati	r	-	-	-	-	-	-	-	-	-	-	-	6
		Cooper-BRM	-	4	4	-	-	-	-	-	-	-	-	-	
17	Lucien Bianchi	Cooper-BRM	-	-	3	6	r	-	-	r	-	nc	nc	r	5
18	Vic Elford	Cooper-BRM	-	-	-	-	-	4	r	r	r	5	r	8	5
19	Brian Redman	Cooper-Maserati	r	-	-	-	-	-	-	-	-	-	-	-	4
		Cooper-BRM	-	3	-	r	-	-	-	-	-	-	-	-	
20	Piers Courage	BRM	-	r	r	r	r	6	8	8	4	r	r	r	4
21	Dan Gurney	Eagle-Weslake	r	-	r	-	-	-	r	9	r	r	4	r	3
		Brabham-Repco	-	-	-	r	-	-	-	-	-	-	-	-	
22	Jo Bonnier	Cooper-Maserati	r	-	-	-	-	-	-	-	-	-	-	-	3
		McLaren-BRM	-	-	nq	r	8	-	r	-	6	r	nc	-	
		Honda	-	-	-	-	-	-	-	-	-	-	-	5	
23	Jack Brabham	Brabham-Repco	r	ns	r	r	r	r	r	5	r	r	r	10r	2
24	Silvio Moser	Brabham-Repco	-	-	nq	-	5	-	nc	ns	nq	-	-	-	2
	Mario Andretti	Lotus-Ford Cosworth	-	-	-	-	-	-	-	-	exc	-	pr	-	

1969

Pos	Driver	Car-Engine	ZA	E	MC	NL	F	GB	D	I	CDN	USA	MEX	Points
1	Jackie Stewart	Matra-Ford Cosworth	1	1	pr	1	p1	1	2	1	r	r	4	63
2	Jacky Ickx	Brabham-Ford Cosworth	r	6r	r	5	3	2	p1	10r	p1	r	2	37
3	Bruce McLaren	McLaren-Ford Cosworth	5	2	5	r	4	3	3	4	5	ns	r	26
4	Jochen Rindt	Lotus-Ford Cosworth	r	pr	-	pr	r	p4	r	p2	3	p1	r	22
5	Jean-Pierre Beltoise	Matra-Ford Cosworth	6	3	r	8	2	9	6r	3	4	r	5	21
6	Denny Hulme	McLaren-Ford Cosworth	3	4	6	4	8	r	r	7	r	r	1	20
7	Graham Hill	Lotus-Ford Cosworth	2	r	1	7	6	7	4	9r	r	r	-	19
8	Piers Courage	Brabham-Ford Cosworth	-	r	2	r	r	5	r	5	r	2	10	16
9	Jo Siffert	Lotus-Ford Cosworth	4	r	3	2	9	8	5r	8r	r	r	r	15
10	Jack Brabham	Brabham-Ford Cosworth	pr	r	r	6	-	-	-	r	2	4	p3	14
11	John Surtees	BRM	r	5	r	9	-	r	ns	nc	r	3	r	6
12	Chris Amon	Ferrari	r	r	r	3	r	r	-	-	-	-	-	4
13	Richard Attwood	Lotus-Ford Cosworth	-	-	4	-	-	-	-	-	-	-	-	3
		Brabham-Ford Cosworth	-	-	-	-	-	-	(F2)2	-	-	-	-	
14	Vic Elford	Cooper-Maserati	-	-	7	-	-	-	-	-	-	-	-	3
		McLaren-Ford Cosworth	-	-	-	10	5	6	r	-	-	-	-	
15	Pedro Rodríguez	BRM	r	r	r	-	-	-	-	-	-	-	-	3
		Ferrari	-	-	-	-	-	-	-	6	r	5	7	
16	Silvio Moser	Brabham-Ford Cosworth	-	-	r	r	7	-	-	r	r	6	11r	1
17	Jackie Oliver	BRM	7	r	r	r	-	r	r	r	r	r	6	1
18	Johnny Servoz-Gavin	Matra-Ford Cosworth	-	-	-	-	-	-	(F2)r	-	6	nc	8	1

1970

Pos	Driver	Car-Engine	ZA	E	MC	B	NL	F	GB	D	A	I	CDN	USA	MEX	Points
1	Jochen Rindt*	Lotus-Ford Cosworth	13r	r	1	r	p1	1	p1	1	pr	ns	-	-	-	45
2	Jacky Ickx	Ferrari	r	r	r	8	3	pr	r	p2	1	pr	1	p4	1	40
3	Clay Regazzoni	Ferrari	-	-	-	-	4	-	4	r	2	1	2	13	p2	33
4	Denny Hulme	McLaren-Ford Cosworth	2	r	4	-	-	4	3	3	r	4	r	7	3	27
5	Jackie Stewart	March-Ford Cosworth	p3	1	pr	pr	2	9	r	r	r	2	-	-	-	25
		Tyrrell-Ford Cosworth	-	-	-	-	-	-	-	-	-	-	pr	r	r	
6	Jack Brabham	Brabham-Ford Cosworth	1	pr	2	r	11	3	2	r	13	r	r	10	r	25
7	Pedro Rodríguez	BRM	9	r	6	1	10	r	r	r	4	r	4	2	6	23
8	Chris Amon	March-Ford Cosworth	r	r	r	2	r	2	5	r	8	7	3	5	4	23
9	Jean-Pierre Beltoise	Matra Simca	4	r	r	3	5	13r	r	r	6	3	8	r	5	16
10	Emerson Fittipaldi	Lotus-Ford Cosworth	-	-	-	-	-	-	8	4	15	ns	-	1	r	12
11	Rolf Stommelen	Brabham-Ford Cosworth	r	r	nq	5	nq	7	ns	5	3	5	r	12	r	10
12	Henri Pescarolo	Matra Simca	7	r	3	6r	8	5	r	6	14	r	7	8	9	8
13	Graham Hill	Lotus-Ford Cosworth	6	4	5	r	nc	10	6	r	-	ns	nc	r	r	7
14	Bruce McLaren *	McLaren-Ford Cosworth	r	2	r	-	-	-	-	-	-	-	-	-	-	6
15	Mario Andretti	March-Ford Cosworth	r	3	-	-	-	r	r	r	-	-	-	-	-	4
	Reine Wisell	Lotus-Ford Cosworth	-	-	-	-	-	-	-	-	-	-	-	3	nc	4
17	Ignazio Giunti	Ferrari	-	-	-	4	-	14	-	-	7	r	-	-	-	3
18	John Surtees	McLaren-Ford Cosworth	r	r	r	-	6	-	-	-	-	-	-	-	-	3
		Surtees-Ford Cosworth	-	-	-	-	-	-	r	9r	r	r	5	r	8	
19	John Miles	Lotus-Ford Cosworth	5	nq	nq	r	7	8	r	r	r	ns	-	-	-	2
20	Jackie Oliver	BRM	r	r	r	r	r	r	r	r	5	r	nc	r	7	2
21	Johnny Servoz-Gavin	March-Ford Cosworth	r	5	nq	-	-	-	-	-	-	-	-	-	-	2
22	François Cevert	March-Ford Cosworth	-	-	-	-	r	11	7	7	r	6	9	r	r	1
23	Peter Gethin	McLaren-Ford Cosworth	-	-	-	-	r	-	-	r	10	nc	6	14	r	1
24	Dan Gurney	McLaren-Ford Cosworth	-	-	-	-	r	6	r	-	-	-	-	-	-	1
	Derek Bell	Brabham-Ford Cosworth	-	-	-	r	-	-	-	-	-	-	-	-	-	1
		Surtees-Ford Cosworth	-	-	-	-	-	-	-	-	-	-	-	6	-	

1971

Pos	Driver	Car-Engine	ZA	E	MC	NL	F	GB	D	A	I	CDN	USA	Points
1	Jackie Stewart	Tyrrell-Ford Cosworth	p2	1	p1	11	p1	1	p1	r	r	p1	p5	62
2	Ronnie Peterson	March-Ford Cosworth	10	r	2	4	-	2	5	8	2	2	3	33
		March-Alfa Romeo	-	-	-	-	r	-	-	-	-	-	-	
3	François Cevert	Tyrrell-Ford Cosworth	r	7	r	r	2	10	2	r	3	6	1	26
4	Jacky Ickx	Ferrari	8	p2	3	p1	r	r	r	r	r	8	r	19
5	Jo Siffert *	BRM	r	r	r	6	4	9	r/dq	p1	9	9	2	19
6	Emerson Fittipaldi	Lotus-Ford Cosworth	r	r	5	-	3	3	r	2	-	7	nc	16
		Lotus-Pratt & Whitney	-	-	-	-	-	-	-	-	8	-	-	
7	Clay Regazzoni	Ferrari	3	r	r	3	r	pr	3	r	r	r	6	13
8	Mario Andretti	Ferrari	1	r	nq	r	-	-	4	-	-	13	ns	12
9	Peter Gethin	McLaren-Ford Cosworth	r	8	r	nc	9	r	r	-	-	-	-	9
		BRM	-	-	-	-	-	-	-	10	1	14	9	
10	Pedro Rodríguez *	BRM	r	4	9	2	r	-	-	-	-	-	-	9
11	Chris Amon	Matra Simca	5	3	r	r	5	r	r	-	p6	10	12	9
12	Reine Wisell	Lotus-Ford Cosworth	4	nc	r	dq	6	-	8	4	-	5	r	9
		Lotus-Pratt & Whitney	-	-	-	-	-	nc	-	-	-	-	-	
13	Denny Hulme	McLaren-Ford Cosworth	6	5	4	12	r	r	r	r	-	4	r	9
14	Tim Schenken	Brabham-Ford Cosworth	-	9	10	r	12r	12r	6	3	r	r	r	5
15	Howden Ganley	BRM	r	10	nq	7	10	8	r	r	5	ns	4	5
16	Mark Donohue	McLaren-Ford Cosworth	-	-	-	-	-	-	-	-	-	3	ns	4
17	Henri Pescarolo	March-Ford Cosworth	11	r	8	nc	r	4	r	6	r	ns	r	4
18	Mike Hailwood	Surtees-Ford Cosworth	-	-	-	-	-	-	-	-	4	-	15r	3
19	John Surtees	Surtees-Ford Cosworth	r	11	7	5	8	6	7	r	r	11	17	3
20	Rolf Stommelen	Surtees-Ford Cosworth	12	r	6	dq	11	5	10	7	ns	r	-	3
21	Graham Hill	Brabham-Ford Cosworth	9	r	r	10	r	r	9	5	r	r	7	2
22	Jean-Pierre Beltoise	Matra Simca	-	6	r	9	7	7	-	-	-	r	8	1

1972

Pos	Driver	Car-Engine	RA	ZA	E	MC	B	F	GB	D	A	I	CDN	USA	Points
1	Emerson Fittipaldi	JPS Lotus-Ford Cosworth	r	2	1	p3	p1	2	1	r	p1	1	11	r	61
2	Jackie Stewart	Tyrrell-Ford Cosworth	1	pr	r	4	-	1	2	11r	7	r	1	p1	45
3	Denny Hulme	McLaren-Ford Cosworth	2	1	r	15	3	7	5	r	2	3	3	3	39
4	Jacky Ickx	Ferrari	3	8	p2	2	r	11	pr	p1	r	pr	12	5	27
5	Peter Revson	McLaren-Ford Cosworth	r	3	5	-	7	-	3	-	3	4	p2	18r	23
6	François Cevert	Tyrrell-Ford Cosworth	r	9	r	nc	2	4	r	10	9	r	r	2	15
7	Clay Regazzoni	Ferrari	4	12	3	r	r	-	-	2	r	r	5	8	15
8	Mike Hailwood	Surtees-Ford Cosworth	-	r	r	r	4	6	r	r	4	2	-	17r	13
9	Ronnie Peterson	March-Ford Cosworth	6	5	r	11	9	5	7r	3	12	9	dq	4	12
10	Chris Amon	Matra Simca	ns	15	r	6	6	p3	4	15	5	r	6	15	12
11	Jean-Pierre Beltoise	BRM	-	r	r	1	r	15	11	9	8	8	r	r	9
12	Mario Andretti	Ferrari	r	4	r	-	-	-	-	-	-	7	-	6	4
13	Howden Ganley	BRM	9	nc	r	r	8	ns	-	4	6	11	10	r	4
14	Brian Redman	McLaren-Ford Cosworth	-	-	-	5	-	9	-	5	-	-	-	-	4
		BRM	-	-	-	-	-	-	-	-	-	-	-	r	
15	Graham Hill	Brabham-Ford Cosworth	r	6	10	12	r	10	r	6	r	5	8	11	4
16	Carlos Reutemann	Brabham-Ford Cosworth	p7	r	-	-	13	12	8	r	r	r	4	r	3
17	Andrea de Adamich	Surtees-Ford Cosworth	r	nc	4	7	r	14	r	13	14	r	r	r	3
18	Carlos Pace	March-Ford Cosworth	-	17	6	17	5	r	r	nc	nc	r	9r	r	3
19	Tim Schenken	Surtees-Ford Cosworth	5	r	8	r	r	17	r	14	11	r	7	r	2
20	Arturo Merzario	Ferrari	-	-	-	-	-	-	6	12	-	-	-	-	1
21	Peter Gethin	BRM	r	nc	r	dq	r	ns	r	-	13	6	r	r	1

1973

Pos	Driver	Car-Engine	RA	BR	ZA	E	B	MC	S	F	GB	NL	D	A	I	CDN	USA	Points
1	Jackie Stewart	Tyrrell-Ford Cosworth	3	2	1	r	1	p1	5	p4	10	1	p1	2	4	5	ns	71
2	Emerson Fittipaldi	JPS Lotus-Ford Cosworth	1	1	3	1	3	2	12r	r	r	r	6	p11r	2	2	6	55
3	Ronnie Peterson	JPS Lotus-Ford Cosworth	r	pr	11	pr	pr	3	p2	1	p2	p11r	r	1	p1	pr	p1	52
4	François Cevert *	Tyrrell-Ford Cosworth	2	10	nc	2	2	4	3	2	5	2	2	r	5	r	ns	47
5	Peter Revson	McLaren-Ford Cosworth	8	r	2	4	r	5	7	-	1	4	9	r	3	1	5	38
6	Denny Hulme	McLaren-Ford Cosworth	5	3	p5	6	7	6	1	8	3	r	12	8	15	13	4	26
7	Carlos Reutemann	Brabham-Ford Cosworth	r	11	7	r	r	r	4	3	6	r	r	4	6	8	3	16
8	James Hunt	March-Ford Cosworth	-	-	-	-	-	9r	-	6	4	3	-	r	ns	7	2	14
9	Jacky Ickx	Ferrari	4	5	r	12	r	r	6	5	8	-	-	-	8	-	-	12
		McLaren-Ford Cosworth	-	-	-	-	-	-	-	-	-	-	3	-	-	-	-	
		Iso Marlboro-Ford Cosworth	-	-	-	-	-	-	-	-	-	-	-	-	-	-	7	
10	Jean-Pierre Beltoise	BRM	r	r	r	5	r	r	r	11	r	5	r	5	13	4	9	9
11	Carlos Pace	Surtees-Ford Cosworth	r	r	r	r	8	r	10	13	r	7	4	3	r	18r	r	7
12	Arturo Merzario	Ferrari	9	4	4	-	-	r	-	7	-	-	-	7	r	15	16	6
13	George Follmer	Shadow-Ford Cosworth	-	-	6	3	r	ns	14	r	r	10	r	r	10	17	14	5
14	Jackie Oliver	Shadow-Ford Cosworth	-	-	r	r	r	10	r	r	r	r	8	r	11	3	15	4
15	Andrea de Adamich	Surtees-Ford Cosworth	-	-	8	-	-	-	-	-	-	-	-	-	-	-	-	3
		Brabham-Ford Cosworth	-	-	-	r	4	7	-	r	r	-	-	-	-	-	-	
16	Wilson Fittipaldi	Brabham-Ford Cosworth	6	r	r	10	r	11r	r	16r	r	r	5	r	r	11	nc	3
17	Niki Lauda	BRM	r	8	r	r	5	r	13	9	12	r	r	ns	r	r	r	2
18	Clay Regazzoni	BRM	p7	6	r	9	10r	r	9	12	7	8	r	6	r	-	8	2
19	Howden Ganley	Iso Marlboro-Ford Cosworth	nc	7	10	r	r	r	11	14	9	9	ns	nc	nc	6	12	1
20	Gijs van Lennep	Iso Marlboro-Ford Cosworth	-	-	-	-	-	-	-	-	-	6	-	9	r	-	-	1
21	Chris Amon	Tecno	-	-	-	-	6	r	-	-	r	r	-	ns	-	-	-	1
		Tyrrell-Ford Cosworth	-	-	-	-	-	-	-	-	-	-	-	-	-	10	ns	

1974

Pos	Driver	Car-Engine	RA	BR	ZA	E	B	MC	S	NL	F	GB	D	A	I	CDN	USA	Points
1	Emerson Fittipaldi	McLaren-Ford Cosworth	10	p1	7	3	1	5	4	3	r	2	r	r	2	p1	4	55
2	Clay Regazzoni	Ferrari	3	2	r	2	p4	4	r	2	3	4	1	5	r	2	11	52
3	Jody Scheckter	Tyrrell-Ford Cosworth	r	13	8	5	3	2	1	5	4	1	2	r	3	r	r	45
4	Niki Lauda	Ferrari	2	r	p16r	p1	2	pr	r	p1	p2	p5	pr	pr	pr	r	r	38
5	Ronnie Peterson	JPS Lotus-Ford Cosworth	p13	6	r	r	r	1	r	8	1	10	4	r	1	3	r	35
6	Carlos Reutemann	Brabham-Ford Cosworth	7r	7	1	r	r	r	r	12	r	6	3	1	r	9	p1	32
7	Denny Hulme	McLaren-Ford Cosworth	1	12	9	6	6	r	r	r	6	7	r/dq	2	6	6	r	20
8	James Hunt	March-Ford Cosworth	r	9	-	-	-	-	-	-	-	-	-	-	-	-	-	15
		Hesketh-Ford Cosworth	-	-	r	10	r	r	3	r	r	r	r	3	r	4	3	
9	Patrick Depailler	Tyrrell-Ford Cosworth	6	8	4	8	r	9	p2	6	8	r	r	r	11	5	6	14
10	Jacky Ickx	JPS Lotus-Ford Cosworth	r	3	r	r	r	r	r	11	5	3	5	r	r	13	r	12
11	Mike Hailwood	McLaren-Ford Cosworth	4	5	3	9	7	r	r	4	7	r	15r	-	-	-	-	12
12	Carlos Pace	Surtees-Ford Cosworth	r	4	11	13	r	r	r	-	-	-	-	-	-	-	-	11
		Brabham-Ford Cosworth	-	-	-	-	-	-	-	-	nq	9	12	r	5	8	2	
13	Jean-Pierre Beltoise	BRM	5	10	2	r	5	r	r	r	10	12	r	r	r	nc	nq	10
14	Jean-Pierre Jarier	Shadow-Ford Cosworth	r	r	-	nc	13	3	5	r	12	r	8	8	r	r	10	6
15	John Watson	Brabham-Ford Cosworth	12	r	r	11	11	6	11	7	16	11	r	4	7	r	5	6
16	Hans-Joachim Stuck	March-Ford Cosworth	r	r	5	4	r	r	-	r	nq	r	7	11r	r	r	nq	5
17	Arturo Merzario	Iso Marlboro-Ford Cosworth	r	r	6	r	r	r	ns	r	9	r	r	r	4	r	r	4
18	Graham Hill	Lola-Ford Cosworth	r	11	12	r	8	7	6	r	13	13	9	12	8	14	8	1
19	Tom Pryce	Token-Ford Cosworth	-	-	-	-	r	-	-	-	-	-	-	-	-	-	-	1
		Shadow-Ford Cosworth	-	-	-	-	-	-	r	r	8	6	r	10	r	nc		
20	Vittorio Brambilla	March-Ford Cosworth	-	-	10	ns	9	r	10r	10	11	r	13	6	r	nq	r	1

1975

Pos	Driver	Car-Engine	RA	BR	ZA	E	MC	B	S	NL	F	GB	D	A	I	USA	Points
1	Niki Lauda	Ferrari	6	5	5	pr	p1	p1	1	p2	p1	8	p3	p6	p3	p1	64.5
2	Emerson Fittipaldi	McLaren-Ford Cosworth	1	2	nc	ns	2	7	8	r	4	1	r	9	2	2	45
3	Carlos Reutemann	Brabham-Ford Cosworth	3	8	2	3	9	3	2	4	14	r	1	14	4	r	37
4	James Hunt	Hesketh-Ford Cosworth	2	6	r	r	r	r	r	1	2	4r	r	2	5	4	33
5	Clay Regazzoni	Ferrari	4	4	16r	nc	r	5	3	3	r	13	r	7	1	r	25
6	Carlos Pace	Brabham-Ford Cosworth	r	1	p4	r	3	8	r	5	r	2r	r	r	r	r	24
7	Jody Scheckter	Tyrrell-Ford Cosworth	11	r	1	r	7	2	7	16r	9	3r	r	8	8	6	20
8	Jochen Mass	McLaren-Ford Cosworth	14	3	6	1	6	r	r	r	3	7r	r	4	r	3	20
9	Patrick Depailler	Tyrrell-Ford Cosworth	5	r	3	r	5	4	12	9	6	9r	9	11	7	r	12
10	Tom Pryce	Shadow-Ford Cosworth	12r	r	9	r	r	6	r	6	r	pr	4	3	6	nc	8
11	Vittorio Brambilla	March-Ford Cosworth	9	r	r	5	r	r	pr	r	r	6	r	1	r	7	6.5
12	Jacques Laffite	Williams-Ford Cosworth	r	11	nc	-	nq	r	-	r	11	r	2	r	r	ns	6
13	Ronnie Peterson	JPS Lotus-Ford Cosworth	r	15	10	r	4	r	9	15r	10	r	r	5	r	5	6
14	Mario Andretti	Parnelli-Ford Cosworth	r	7	17r	r	r	-	4		5	12	10r	r	r	r	5
15	Mark Donohue *	Penske-Ford Cosworth	7	r	8	r	r	11	5	8	r	-	-	-	-	-	4
		March-Ford Cosworth	-	-	-	-	-	-	-	-		5r	r	ns	-	-	
16	Jacky Ickx	JPS Lotus-Ford Cosworth	8	9	12	2	8	r	15	r	r	-	-	-	-	-	3
17	Alan Jones	Hesketh-Ford Cosworth	-	-	-	r	r	r	11	-	-	-	-	-	-	-	2
		Hill-Ford Cosworth	-	-	-	-	-	-	-	13	16	10	5	-	-	-	
18	Jean-Pierre Jarier	Shadow-Ford Cosworth	pns	pr	r	4	r	r	r	r	8	14r	r	-	-	r	1.5
		Shadow-Matra	-	-	-	-	-	-	-	-	-	-	-	r	r	-	
19	Tony Brise *	Williams-Ford Cosworth	-	-	-	7	-	-	-	-	-	-	-	-	-	-	1
		Hill-Ford Cosworth	-	-	-	-	-	r	6	7	7	15r	r	15	r	r	
20	Gijs van Lennep	Ensign-Ford Cosworth	-	-	-	-	-	-	-	10	15	-	6		-	-	1
21	Lella Lombardi	March-Ford Cosworth	-	-	r	6	nq	r	r	14	18	r	7	17	r	-	0.5
		Williams-Ford Cosworth	-	-	-	-	-	-	-	-	-	-	-	-	-	ns	

Half points were awarded in Spain and Austria where the races were stopped early.

1976

Pos	Driver	Car-Engine	BR	ZA	USAW	E	B	MC	S	F	GB	D	A	NL	I	CDN	USAE	J	Points
1	James Hunt	McLaren-Ford Cosworth	pr	p2	r	p1	r	r	5	p1	dq	p1	p4	1	r	p1	p1	3	69
2	Niki Lauda	Ferrari	1	1	2	2	p1	p1	3	r	p1	r	-	-	4	8	3	r	68
3	Jody Scheckter	Tyrrell-Ford Cosworth	5	4	r	r	4	2	p1	6	2	2	r	5	5	4	2	r	49
4	Patrick Depailler	Tyrrell-Ford Cosworth	2	9	3	r	r	3	2	2	r	r	r	7	6	2	r	2	39
5	Clay Regazzoni	Ferrari	7	r	p1	11	2	14r	6	r	r/dq	9	-	2	2	6	7	5	31
6	Mario Andretti	JPS Lotus-Ford Cosworth	r	-	-	r	r	-	r	5	r	12	5	3	r	3	r	p1	22
		Parnelli-Ford Cosworth	-	6	r	-		-	-	-	-	-	-	-	-	-	-	-	
7	John Watson	Penske-Ford Cosworth	r	5	nc	r	7	10	r	3	3	7	1	r	11	10	6	r	20
8	Jacques Laffite	Ligier-Matra	r	r	4	12	3	12r	4	14	r/dq	r	2	r	p3	r	r	7	20
9	Jochen Mass	McLaren-Ford Cosworth	6	3	5	r	6	5	11	15	r	3	7	9	r	5	4	r	19
10	Gunnar Nilsson	JPS Lotus-Ford Cosworth	-	r	r	3	r	r	r	r	r	5	3	r	13	12	r	6	11
11	Ronnie Peterson	JPS Lotus-Ford Cosworth	r	-	-	-	-	-	-	-	-	-	-	-	-	-	-	-	10
		March-Ford Cosworth	-	r	10	r	r	r	7	19r	r	r	6	pr	1	9	r	r	
12	Tom Pryce	Shadow-Ford Cosworth	3	7	r	8	10	7	9	8	4	8	r	4	8	11	r	r	10
13	Hans-Joachim Stuck	March-Ford Cosworth	4	12	r	r	r	4	r	7	r	r	r	r	r	r	5	r	8
14	Carlos Pace	Brabham-Alfa Romeo	10	r	9	6	r	9	8	4	8	4	r	r	r	7	r	r	7
15	Alan Jones	Surtees-Ford Cosworth	-	-	nc	9	5	r	13	r	5	10	r	8	12	16	8	4	7
16	Carlos Reutemann	Brabham-Alfa Romeo	12r	r	r	4	r	r	r	11	r	r	r	r	-	-	-	-	3
		Ferrari	-	-	-	-	-	-	-	-	-	-	-	-	9	-	-	-	
17	Emerson Fittipaldi	Copersucar-Ford Cosworth	13	17r	6	r	nq	6	r	r	6	13	r	r	15	r	9	r	3
18	Chris Amon	Ensign-Ford Cosworth	-	14	8	5	r	13	r	-	r	r	-	-	-	-	-	-	2
		Wolf Williams-Ford Cosworth	-	-	-	-	-	-	-	-	-	-	-	-	ns	-	-	-	
19	Vittorio Brambilla	March-Ford Cosworth	r	8	r	r	r	r	10	r	r	r	r	6	7	14	r	r	1
20	Rolf Stommelen	Brabham-Alfa Romeo	-	-	-	-	-	-	-	-	6	-	-	r	-	-	-	-	1
		Hesketh-Ford Cosworth	-	-	-	-	-	-	-	-	-	-	-	12	-	-	-	-	

1977

Pos	Driver	Car-Engine	RA	BR	ZA	USAW	E	MC	B	S	F	GB	D	A	NL	I	USAE	CDN	J	Points
1	Niki Lauda	Ferrari	r	3	1	p2	ns	2	2	r	5	2	1	p2	1	2	4	-	-	72
2	Jody Scheckter	Wolf-Ford Cosworth	1	r	2	3	3	1	r	r	r	r	p2	r	3	r	3	1	10	55
3	Mario Andretti	JPS Lotus-Ford Cosworth	5r	r	r	1	p1	5	pr	p6	p1	14r	r	r	pr	1	2	p9r	pr	47
4	Carlos Reutemann	Ferrari	3	1	8	r	2	3	r	3	6	15	4	4	6	r	6	r	2	42
5	James Hunt	McLaren-Ford Cosworth	pr	p2	p4	7	r	r	7	12	3	p1	r	r	r	pr	p1	r	1	40
6	Jochen Mass	McLaren-Ford Cosworth	r	r	5	r	4	4	r	2	9	4	r	6	r	4	r	3	r	25
7	Alan Jones	Shadow-Ford Cosworth	-	-	-	r	r	6	5	17	r	7	r	1	r	3	r	4	4	22
8	Gunnar Nilsson	JPS Lotus-Ford Cosworth	ns	5	12	8	5	r	1	19r	4	3	r	r	r	r	r	r	r	20
9	Patrick Depailler	Tyrrell-Ford Cosworth	r	r	3	4	r	r	8	4	r	r	r	13	r	r	14	2	3	20
10	Jacques Laffite	Ligier-Matra	nc	r	r	9r	7	7	r	1	8	6	r	r	2	8	7	r	5r	18
11	Hans-Joachim Stuck	March-Ford Cosworth	-	-	r	-	-	-	-	-	-	-	-	-	-	-	-	-	-	12
		Brabham-Alfa Romeo	-	-	-	r	6	r	6	10	r	5	3	3	7	r	r	r	7	
12	Emerson Fittipaldi	Copersucar-Ford Cosworth	4	4	10	5	14	r	r	18	11	r	nq	11	4	nq	13	r	-	11
13	John Watson	Brabham-Alfa Romeo	r	r	6	dq	r	pr	r	5	2	r	r	8	r	12	r	r	-	9
14	Ronnie Peterson	Tyrrell-Ford Cosworth	r	r	r	r	8	r	3	r	12	r	9r	5	r	6	16	r	r	7
15	Carlos Pace *	Brabham-Alfa Romeo	2	r	13	-	-	-	-	-	-	-	-	-	-	-	-	-	-	6
16	Vittorio Brambilla	Surtees-Ford Cosworth	7r	r	7	r	r	8	4	r	13	8	5	15	12r	r	19	6r	8	6
17	Clay Regazzoni	Ensign-Ford Cosworth	6	r	9	r	r	nq	r	7	7	nq	r	r	r	5	5	r	r	5
18	Patrick Tambay	Surtees-Ford Cosworth	-	-	-	-	-	-	-	nq	-	-	-	-	-	-	-	-	-	5
		Ensign-Ford Cosworth	-	-	-	-	-	-	-	-	r	6	r	5r	r	nq	5	r		
19	Jean-Pierre Jarier	Penske-Ford Cosworth	-	-	-	6	nq	11	11	8	r	9	r	14	r	r	-	-	-	1
		Shadow-Ford Cosworth	-	-	-	-	-	-	-	-	-	-	-	-	-	-	9			
		Ligier-Matra	-	-	-	-	-	-	-	-	-	-	-	-	-	-	-	-	r	
20	Riccardo Patrese	Shadow-Ford Cosworth	-	-	-	-	9	r	-	-	r	-	r	10r	-	13	r	-	10r	6	1
21	Renzo Zorzi	Shadow-Ford Cosworth	r	6	r	r	r	-	-	-	-	-	-	-	-	-	-	-	-	1

1978

Pos	Driver	Car-Engine	RA	BR	ZA	USAW	MC	B	E	S	F	GB	D	A	NL	I	USAE	CDN	Points
1	Mario Andretti	JPS Lotus-Ford Cosworth	p1	4	7	2	11	p1	p1	pr	1	r	p1	r	p1	p6	pr	10	64
2	Ronnie Peterson *	Lotus-Ford Cosworth	5	pr	1	4	r	2	2	3	2	pr	r	p1	2	r	-	-	51
3	Carlos Reutemann	Ferrari	7	1	r	p1	p8	3	r	10	18	1	r	dq	7	3	1	3	48
4	Niki Lauda	Brabham-Alfa Romeo	2	3	pr	r	2	r	r	1	r	2	r	r	3	1	r	r	44
5	Patrick Depailler	Tyrrell-Ford Cosworth	3	r	2	3	1	r	r	r	r	4	r	2	r	11	r	5	34
6	John Watson	Brabham-Alfa Romeo	r	8	3	r	4	r	5	r	p4	3	7	7	4	2	r	r	25
7	Jody Scheckter	Wolf-Ford Cosworth	10	r	r	r	3	r	4	r	6	r	2	r	12	12	3	2	24
8	Jacques Laffite	Ligier-Matra	16r	9	5	5	r	5r	3	7	7	10	3	5	8	4	11	r	19
9	Gilles Villeneuve	Ferrari	8	r	r	r	r	4	10	9	12	r	8	3	6	7	r	1	17
10	Emerson Fittipaldi	Copersucar-Ford Cosworth	9	2	r	8	9	r	r	6	r	r	4	4	5	8	5	r	17
11	Alan Jones	Williams-Ford Cosworth	r	11	4	7	r	10	8	r	5	r	r	r	r	13	2	9	11
12	Riccardo Patrese	Arrows-Ford Cosworth	-	10	r	6	6	r	r	2	8	r	9	r	r	r	r	4	11
13	James Hunt	McLaren-Ford Cosworth	4	r	r	r	r	r	6	8	3	r	dq	r	10	r	7	r	8
14	Patrick Tambay	McLaren-Ford Cosworth	6	r	r	12r	7	-	r	4	9	6	r	9	5	6	8	r	8
15	Didier Pironi	Tyrrell-Ford Cosworth	14	6	6	r	5	6	12	r	10	r	5	r	r	r	10	7	7
16	Clay Regazzoni	Shadow-Ford Cosworth	15	5	nq	10	nq	r	15r	5	r	r	nq	nc	nq	nc	14	nq	4
17	Jean-Pierre Jabouille	Renault	-	-	r	r	10	nc	13	r	r	r	r	r	r	r	4	12	3
18	Hans-Joachim Stuck	Shadow-Ford Cosworth	17	r	nq	ns	r	r	r	11	11	5	r	r	r	r	r	r	2
19	Vittorio Brambilla	Surtees-Ford Cosworth	18	nq	12	r	nq	13r	7	r	17	9	r	6	dq	r	-	-	1
20	Derek Daly	Hesketh-Ford Cosworth	-	-	-	npq	npq	nq	-	-	-	-	-	-	-	-	-	-	1
		Ensign-Ford Cosworth	-	-	-	-	-	-	-	-	nq	r	-	dq	r	10	8	6	
21	Hector Rebaque	Lotus-Ford Cosworth	nq	r	10	npq	npq	npq	r	12	nq	r	6	r	11	nq	r	nq	1
	Jean-Pierre Jarier	ATS-Ford Cosworth	12	ns	8	11	nq	-	-	-	-	-	nq	-	-	-	-	-	
		JPS Lotus-Ford Cosworth	-	-	-	-	-	-	-	-	-	-	-	-	-	-	15r	pr	

1979

Pos	Driver	Car-Engine	RA	BR	ZA	USAW	E	B	MC	F	GB	D	A	NL	I	CDN	USAE	Points
1	Jody Scheckter	Ferrari	r	6	2	2	4	1	p1	7	5	4	4	2	1	4	r	51 (9)
2	Gilles Villeneuve	Ferrari	12r	5	1	p1	7	7r	r	2	14r	8	2	r	2	2	1	47 (6)
3	Alan Jones	Williams-Ford Cosworth	9	r	r	3	r	r	r	4	pr	1	1	1	9	p1	pr	40 (3)
4	Jacques Laffite	Ligier-Ford Cosworth	p1	p1	r	r	pr	p2	r	8	r	3	3	3	r	r	r	36
5	Clay Regazzoni	Williams-Ford Cosworth	10	15	9	r	r	r	2	6	1	2	5	r	3	3	r	29 (3)
6	Patrick Depailler	Ligier-Ford Cosworth	4	2	r	5	1	r	5r	-	-	-	-	-	-	-	-	20 (2)
7	Carlos Reutemann	Lotus-Ford Cosworth	2	3	5	r	2	4	3	13r	8	r	r	r	7	r	r	20 (5)
8	René Arnoux	Renault	r	r	r	ns	9	r	r	3	2	r	p6	pr	r	r	2	17
9	John Watson	McLaren-Ford Cosworth	3	8	r	r	r	6	4	11	4	5	9	r	r	6	6	15
10	Didier Pironi	Tyrrell-Ford Cosworth	r	4	r	dq	6	3	r	r	10	9	7	r	10	5	3	14
11	Jean-Pierre Jarier	Tyrrell-Ford Cosworth	r	ns	3	6	5	11	r	5	3	-	-	r	6	r	r	14
12	Mario Andretti	Lotus-Ford Cosworth	5	r	4	4	3	r	r	r	r	r	r	r	5	10r	r	14
13	Jean-Pierre Jabouille	Renault	r	10	pr	ns	r	r	8	p1	r	pr	r	r	p14r	r	r	9
14	Niki Lauda	Brabham-Alfa Romeo	r	r	6	r	r	r	r	r	r	r	r	r	4	-	-	4
		Brabham-Ford Cosworth	-	-	-	-	-	-	-	-	-	-	-	-	-	ew	-	
15	Elio de Angelis	Shadow-Ford Cosworth	7	12	r	7	r	r	nq	16	12	11	r	r	r	r	4	3
16	Nelson Piquet	Brabham-Alfa Romeo	r	r	7	8	r	r	7r	r	r	12r	r	4	r	-	-	3
		Brabham-Ford Cosworth	-	-	-	-	-	-	-	-	-	-	-	-	-	r	8r	
17	Jacky Ickx	Ligier-Ford Cosworth	-	-	-	-	-	-	-	r	6	r	r	5	r	r	r	3
18	Jochen Mass	Arrows-Ford Cosworth	8	7	12	9	8	r	6	15	r	6	r	6	r	nq	nq	3
19	Hans-Joachim Stuck	ATS-Ford Cosworth	ns	r	r	dq	14	8	r	ns	nq	r	r	r	11	r	5	2
20	Riccardo Patrese	Arrows-Ford Cosworth	ns	9	11	r	10	5	r	14	r	r	r	r	13r	r	r	2
21	Emerson Fittipaldi	Copersucar-Ford Cosworth	6	11	13	r	11	9	r	r	r	r	r	r	8	8	7	1

1980

Pos	Driver	Car-Engine	RA	BR	ZA	USAW	B	MC	F	GB	D	A	NL	I	CDN	USAE	Points
1	Alan Jones	Williams-Ford Cosworth	p1	3	r	r	p2	r	1	1	p3	2	11	2	1	1	67 (4)
2	Nelson Piquet	Brabham-Ford Cosworth	2	r	4	p1	r	3	4	2	4	5	1	1	pr	r	54
3	Carlos Reutemann	Williams-Ford Cosworth	r	r	5	r	3	1	6	3	2	3	4	3	2	2	42 (7)
4	Jacques Laffite	Ligier-Ford Cosworth	r	r	2	r	11	2	p3	r	1	4	3	9	8r	5	34
5	Didier Pironi	Ligier-Ford Cosworth	r	4	3	6	1	pr	2	pr	r	r	r	6	3	3	32
6	René Arnoux	Renault	r	1	1	9	4	r	5	nc	r	p9	p2	p10	r	7	29
7	Elio de Angelis	Lotus-Ford Cosworth	r	2	r	r	10r	9r	r	r	16r	6	r	4	10	4	13
8	Jean-Pierre Jabouille	Renault	r	pr	pr	10	r	r	r	r	r	1	r	r	r	-	9
9	Riccardo Patrese	Arrows-Ford Cosworth	r	6	r	2	r	8	9	9	9	14	r	r	r	r	7
10	Keke Rosberg	Fittipaldi-Ford Cosworth	3	9	r	r	7	nq	r	nq	r	16	nq	5	9	10	6
11	John Watson	McLaren-Ford Cosworth	r	11	11	4	nc	nq	7	8	r	r	r	4	nc		6
12	Derek Daly	Tyrrell-Ford Cosworth	4	14	r	8	9	r	11	4	10	r	r	r	r	r	6
13	Jean-Pierre Jarier	Tyrrell-Ford Cosworth	r	12	7	r	5	r	14	5	15	r	5	13r	7	nc	6
14	Gilles Villeneuve	Ferrari	r	16r	r	r	6	5	8	r	6	8	7	r	5	r	6
15	Emerson Fittipaldi	Fittipaldi-Ford Cosworth	nc	15	8	3	r	6	13r	12	r	11	r	r	r	r	5
16	Alain Prost	McLaren-Ford Cosworth	6	5	ns	-	r	r	r	6	11	7	6	7	r	ns	5
17	Jochen Mass	Arrows-Ford Cosworth	r	10	6	7	r	4	10	13	8	nq	ew	-	11	r	4
18	Bruno Giacomelli	Alfa Romeo	5	13	r	r	r	r	r	r	5	r	r	r	r	pr	4
19	Jody Scheckter	Ferrari	r	r	r	5	8	r	12	10	13	13	9	8	nq	11	2
20	Mario Andretti	Lotus-Ford Cosworth	r	r	12	r	r	7	r	r	7	r	8r	r	r	6	1
21	Hector Rebaque	Brabham-Ford Cosworth	-	-	-	-	-	-	-	7	r	10	r	r	6	r	1

1981

Pos	Driver	Car-Engine	USAW	BR	RA	RSM	B	MC	E	F	GB	D	A	NL	I	CDN	LV	Points
1	Nelson Piquet	Brabham-Ford Cosworth	3	p12	p1	1	r	pr	r	3	r	1	3	2	6r	p5	5	50
2	Carlos Reutemann	Williams-Ford Cosworth	2	1	2	3	p1	r	4	10	2	r	5	r	3	10	p8	49
3	Alan Jones	Williams-Ford Cosworth	1	2	4	12	r	2	7	17	r	11	4	3	2	r	1	46
4	Jacques Laffite	Talbot Ligier-Matra	r	6	r	r	2	3	p2	r	3	3	1	r	r	1	6	44
5	Alain Prost	Renault	r	r	3	r	r	r	r	1	r	p2	r	p1	1	r	2	43
6	John Watson	McLaren-Ford Cosworth	r	8	r	10	7	r	3	2	1	6	6	r	r	2	7	27
7	Gilles Villeneuve	Ferrari	r	r	r	p7	4	1	1	r	r	10	r	r	r	3	dq	25
8	Elio de Angelis	Lotus-Ford Cosworth	r	5	6	-	5	r	5	6	r	7	7	5	4	6	r	14
9	René Arnoux	Renault	8	r	5	8	nq	r	9	p4	p9r	13	p2	r	pr	r	r	11
10	Hector Rebaque	Brabham-Ford Cosworth	r	r	r	4	r	nq	r	9	5	4	r	4	r	r	r	11
11	Riccardo Patrese	Arrows-Ford Cosworth	pr	3	7	2	r	r	r	14	10r	r	r	r	r	r	11	10
12	Eddie Cheever	Tyrrell-Ford Cosworth	5	nc	r	r	6	5	nc	13	4	5	nq	r	r	12r	r	10
13	Didier Pironi	Ferrari	r	r	r	5	8	4	15	5	r	r	9	r	5	r	9	9
14	Nigel Mansell	Lotus-Ford Cosworth	r	11	r	-	3	r	6	7	nq	r	r	r	r	r	4	8
15	Bruno Giacomelli	Alfa Romeo	r	nc	10r	r	9	r	10	15	r	15	r	r	8	4	3	7
16	Marc Surer	Ensign-Ford Cosworth	r	4	r	9	11	6	-	-	-	-	-	-	-	-	-	4
		Theodore-Ford Cosworth	-	-	-	-	-	-	-	12	11r	14r	r	8	nq	9	r	
17	Mario Andretti	Alfa Romeo	4	r	8	r	10	r	8	8	r	9	r	r	r	7	r	3
18	Andrea de Cesaris	McLaren-Ford Cosworth	r	r	11	6	r	r	r	11	r	r	8	ns	7r	r	12	1
19	Patrick Tambay	Theodore-Ford Cosworth	6	10	r	11	nq	7	13	-	-	-	-	-	-	-	-	1
		Talbot Ligier-Matra	-	-	-	-	-	-	-	r	r	r	r	r	r	r	r	
20	Slim Borgudd	ATS-Ford Cosworth	-	-	-	13	nq	npq	nq	nq	6	r	r	10	r	r	nq	1
21	Eliseo Salazar	March-Ford Cosworth	nq	nq	nq	r	nq	npq	-	-	-	-	-	-	-	-	-	1
		Ensign-Ford Cosworth	-	-	-	-	-	-	14	r	nq	nc	r	6	r	r	nc	

1982

Pos	Driver	Car-Engine	ZA	BR	USAW	RSM	B	MC	DET	CDN	NL	GB	F	D	A	CH	I	LV	Points
1	Keke Rosberg	Williams-Ford Cosworth	5	dq	2	-	2	r	4	r	3	pr	5	3	2	1	8	5	44
2	Didier Pironi	Ferrari	18	6	r	1	ns	2r	3	p9	1	2	3	pns	-	-	-	-	39
3	John Watson	McLaren-Ford Cosworth	6	2	6	-	1	r	1	3	9	r	r	r	r	13	4	2	39
4	Alain Prost	Renault	1	p1	r	r	pr	7r	pnc	r	r	6	2	r	8r	p2	r	p4	34
5	Niki Lauda	McLaren-Ford Cosworth	4	r	1	-	dq	r	r	r	4	1	8	ns	5	3	r	r	30
6	René Arnoux	Renault	p3	r	r	pr	r	pr	10	r	pr	r	p1	2	r	16r	1	r	28
7	Patrick Tambay	Ferrari	-	-	-	-	-	-	-	-	8	3	4	1	4	ns	2	ns	25
8	Michele Alboreto	Tyrrell-Ford Cosworth	7	4	4	3	r	10r	r	r	7	nc	6	4	r	7	5	1	25
9	Elio de Angelis	Lotus-Ford Cosworth	8	r	5	-	4	5	r	4	r	4	r	r	1	6	r	r	23
10	Riccardo Patrese	Brabham-BMW	r	-	-	-	r	-	-	-	15	r	r	r	r	5	r	r	21
		Brabham-Ford Cosworth	-	r	3	-	-	1	r	2	-	-	-	-	-	-	-	-	
11	Nelson Piquet	Brabham-BMW	r	-	-	-	5	r	nq	1	2	r	r	r	pr	4	r	r	20
		Brabham-Ford Cosworth	-	dq	r	-	-	-	-	-	-	-	-	-	-	-	-	-	
12	Eddie Cheever	Talbot Ligier-Matra	r	r	r	-	3	r	2	10r	nq	r	16	r	r	nc	6	3	15
13	Derek Daly	Theodore-Ford Cosworth	14	r	r	-	-	-	-	-	-	-	-	-	-	-	-	-	8
		Williams-Ford Cosworth	-	-	-	-	r	6r	5	7r	5	5	7	r	r	9	r	6	
14	Nigel Mansell	Lotus-Ford Cosworth	r	3	7	-	r	4	r	r	-	r	-	9	r	8	7	r	7
15	Carlos Reutemann	Williams-Ford Cosworth	2	r	-	-	-	-	-	-	-	-	-	-	-	-	-	-	6
	Gilles Villeneuve *	Ferrari	r	r	dq	2	ns	-	-	-	-	-	-	-	-	-	-	-	6
17	Andrea de Cesaris	Alfa Romeo	13	r	pr	r	r	3r	r	6r	r	r	r	r	r	10	10	9	5
18	Jacques Laffite	Talbot Ligier-Matra	r	r	r	-	9	r	6	r	r	r	14	r	3	r	r	r	5
19	Mario Andretti	Williams-Ford Cosworth	-	-	r	-	-	-	-	-	-	-	-	-	-	-	-	-	4
		Ferrari	-	-	-	-	-	-	-	-	-	-	-	-	-	-	p3	r	
20	Jean-Pierre Jarier	Osella-Ford Cosworth	r	9	r	4	r	nq	r	r	14	r	r	r	nq	r	r	ns	3
21	Marc Surer	Arrows-Ford Cosworth	-	-	-	-	7	9	8	5	10	r	13	6	r	15	r	7	3
22	Bruno Giacomelli	Alfa Romeo	11	r	r	r	r	r	r	r	11	7	9	5	r	12	r	10	2
23	Eliseo Salazar	ATS-Ford Cosworth	9	r	r	5	r	r	r	r	13	nq	r	r	nq	14	9	nq	2
24	Manfred Winkelhock	ATS-Ford Cosworth	10	5	r	dq	r	r	r	nq	12	nq	11	r	r	r	nq	nc	2
25	Mauro Baldi	Arrows-Ford Cosworth	nq	10	nq	-	r	nq	r	8	6	9	r	r	6	nq	12	11	2
26	Chico Serra	Fittipaldi-Ford Cosworth	17	r	nq	-	6	npq	11	nq	r	r	nq	11	7	nq	11	nq	1

1983

Pos	Driver	Car-Engine	BR	USAW	F	RSM	MC	B	DET	CDN	GB	D	A	NL	I	EUR	ZA	Points
1	Nelson Piquet	Brabham-BMW	1	r	2	r	2	4	4	r	2	13r	3	pr	1	1	3	59
2	Alain Prost	Renault	7	11	p1	2	p3	p1	8	5	1	4	1	r	r	2	r	57
3	René Arnoux	Ferrari	10	3	7	p3	r	r	pr	p1	p5	1	2	1	2	9	r	49
4	Patrick Tambay	Ferrari	5	pr	4	1	4	2	r	3	3	pr	pr	2	4	r	pr	40
5	Keke Rosberg	Williams-Ford Cosworth	pdq	r	5	4	1	5	2	4	11	10	8	r	11	r	-	27
		Williams-Honda	-	-	-	-	-	-	-	-	-	-	-	-	-	-	5	
6	John Watson	McLaren-Ford Cosworth	r	1	r	5	nq	r	3	6	9	5	9	3	-	-	-	22
		McLaren-TAG Porsche	-	-	-	-	-	-	-	-	-	-	-	-	r	r	dq	
7	Eddie Cheever	Renault	r	13r	3	r	r	3	r	2	r	r	4	r	3	10	6	22
8	Andrea de Cesaris	Alfa Romeo	exc	r	12	r	r	r	r	r	8	2	r	r	r	4	2	15
9	Riccardo Patrese	Brabham-BMW	r	10r	r	13r	r	r	r	r	r	3	r	9	pr	7	1	13
10	Niki Lauda	McLaren-Ford Cosworth	3	2	r	r	nq	r	r	r	6	dq	6	-	-	-	-	12
		McLaren-TAG Porsche	-	-	-	-	-	-	-	-	-	-	-	r	r	r	11r	
11	Jacques Laffite	Williams-Ford Cosworth	4	4	6	7	r	6	5	r	12	6	r	r	nq	nq	-	11
		Williams-Honda	-	-	-	-	-	-	-	-	-	-	-	-	-	-	r	
12	Michele Alboreto	Tyrrell-Ford Cosworth	r	9	8	r	r	14	1	8	13	r	r	6	r	r	r	10
13	Nigel Mansell	Lotus-Ford Cosworth	12	12	r	12r	r	r	6	r	-	-	-	-	-	-	-	10
		Lotus-Renault	-	-	-	-	-	-	-	-	4	r	5	r	8	3	nc	
14	Derek Warwick	Toleman-Hart	8	r	r	r	r	7	r	r	r	r	r	4	6	5	4	9
15	Marc Surer	Arrows-Ford Cosworth	6	5	10	6	r	11	11	r	17	7	r	8	10	r	8	4
16	Mauro Baldi	Alfa Romeo	r	r	r	10r	6	r	12	10	7	r	r	5	r	r	r	3
17	Danny Sullivan	Tyrrell-Ford Cosworth	11	8	r	r	5	12	r	dq	14	12	r	r	r	r	7	2
18	Elio de Angelis	Lotus-Ford Cosworth	dq	-	-	-	-	-	-	-	-	-	-	-	-	-	-	2
		Lotus-Renault	-	r	r	r	r	9	r	r	r	r	r	r	5	pr	r	
19	Bruno Giacomelli	Toleman-Hart	r	r	13r	r	nq	8	9	r	r	r	r	13	7	6	r	1
20	Johnny Cecotto	Theodore-Ford Cosworth	14	6	11	r	npq	10	r	r	nq	11	nq	nq	12	-	-	1

1984

Pos	Driver	Car-Engine	BR	ZA	B	RSM	F	MC	CDN	DET	DAL	GB	D	A	NL	I	EUR	P	Points
1	Niki Lauda	McLaren-TAG Porsche	r	1	r	r	1	r	2	r	9r	1	2	1	2	1	4	2	72
2	Alain Prost	McLaren-TAG Porsche	1	2	r	1	7	p1	3	4	r	r	p1	r	p1	r	1	1	71.5
3	Elio de Angelis	Lotus-Renault	p3	7	5	3r	5	5	4	2	3	4	r	r	4	r	r	5	34
4	Michele Alboreto	Ferrari	r	11r	p1	r	r	6	r	r	r	5	r	3	r	2	2	4	30.5
5	Nelson Piquet	Brabham-BMW	r	pr	9r	pr	r	r	p1	p1	r	p7	r	p2	r	pr	p3	p6	29
6	René Arnoux	Ferrari	r	r	3	2	4	3	5	r	2	6	6	7	11r	r	5	9	27
7	Derek Warwick	Renault	r	3	2	4	r	r	r	r	r	2	3	r	r	r	11r	r	23
8	Keke Rosberg	Williams-Honda	2	r	4r	r	6	4	r	r	1	r	r	r	8r	r	r	r	20.5
9	Ayrton Senna	Toleman-Hart	r	6	6	nq	r	2	7	r	r	3	r	r	r	r	r	3	13
10	Nigel Mansell	Lotus-Renault	r	r	r	r	3	r	6	r	p6r	r	4	r	3	r	r	r	13
11	Patrick Tambay	Renault	5r	r	7	r	p2	r	ew	r	r	8r	5	r	6	r	r	7	11
12	Teo Fabi	Brabham-BMW	r	r	r	r	9	-	-	3	-	r	r	4	5	r	r	r	9
13	Riccardo Patrese	Alfa Romeo	r	4	r	r	r	r	r	r	r	12r	r	10r	r	3	6	8	8
14	Jacques Laffite	Williams-Honda	r	r	r	r	8	8	r	5	4	r	r	r	r	r	r	14	5
15	Thierry Boutsen	Arrows-Ford Cosworth	6	12	-	5	-	-	-	-	-	-	-	-	-	-	-	-	5
		Arrows-BMW	-	-	r	-	11	nq	r	r	r	r	5	r	10	9r	r		
16	Eddie Cheever	Alfa Romeo	4	r	r	7r	r	nq	11r	r	r	r	r	r	13r	9r	r	17	3
17	Stefan Johansson	Tyrrell-Ford Cosworth	-	-	-	-	-	-	-	-	dq	dq	nq	dq	-	-	-	-	3
		Toleman-Hart	-	-	-	-	-	-	-	-	-	-	-	-	-	4	r	11	
18	Andrea de Cesaris	Ligier-Renault	r	5	r	6r	10	r	r	r	r	10	7	r	r	r	7	12	3
19	Piercarlo Ghinzani	Osella-Alfa Romeo	r	ns	r	nq	12	7	r	r	5	9	r	r	r	7r	r	r	2
20	Marc Surer	Arrows-Ford Cosworth	7	9	8	-	r	nq	r	r	-	-	-	-	-	-	-	-	1
		Arrows-BMW	-	-	-	r	-	-	-	-	r	11	r	6	r	r	r	r	
	Jo Gartner	Osella-Alfa Romeo	-	-	-	r	-	-	-	-	-	r	r	r	12	5	12r	16r	- (2)
	Gerhard Berger	ATS-BMW	-	-	-	-	-	-	-	-	-	-	-	12r	-	6	r	13	- (1)

Half points were awarded in Monaco where the race was stopped early. The points for Jo Gartner and Gerhard Berger were not valid for the championship because their constructors had only entered one car each for the season.

All points scored by Tyrrell were redistributed due to an infringement of the rules (points originally scored were Martin Brundle 8 and Stefan Bellof 7).

1985

Pos	Driver	Car-Engine	BR	P	RSM	MC	CDN	DET	F	GB	D	A	NL	I	B	EUR	ZA	AUS	Points
1	Alain Prost	McLaren-TAG Porsche	1	r	dq	1	3	r	3	1	2	p1	2	1	p3	4	3	r	73 (3)
2	Michele Alboreto	Ferrari	p2	2	r	2	1	3	r	2	1	3	4	13r	r	r	r	r	53
3	Keke Rosberg	Williams-Honda	r	r	r	8	4	1	p2	pr	12r	r	r	r	4	3	2	1	40
4	Ayrton Senna	Lotus-Renault	r	p1	p7r	pr	16	pr	r	10r	r	2	3	p3	1	p2	r	pr	38
5	Elio de Angelis	Lotus-Renault	3	4	1	3	p5	5	5	nc	r	5	5	6	r	5	r	dq	33
6	Nigel Mansell	Williams-Honda	r	5	5	7	6	r	ns	r	6	r	6	11r	2	1	p1	r	31
7	Stefan Johansson	Tyrrell-Ford Cosworth	7	8	6r	r	2	2	4	r	9	4	r	5r	r	r	4	5	26
8	Nelson Piquet	Brabham-BMW	r	r	8r	r	r	6	1	4	r	r	p8	2	5	r	r	r	21
9	Jacques Laffite	Ligier-Renault	6	r	r	6	8	12	r	3	3	r	r	r	11r	r	-	2	16
10	Niki Lauda	McLaren-TAG Porsche	r	r	4	r	r	r	r	r	5	r	1	r	ns	-	r	r	14
11	Thierry Boutsen	Arrows-BMW	11	r	2	9	9	7	9	r	4	8	r	9	10r	6	6	r	11
12	Patrick Tambay	Renault	5	3	3	r	7	r	6	r	r	10r	r	7	r	12	-	r	11
13	Marc Surer	Brabham-BMW	-	-	-	-	15	8	8	6	r	6	10r	4	8	r	r	r	5
14	Derek Warwick	Renault	10	7	10	5	r	r	7	5	r	r	r	r	6	r	-	r	5
15	Philippe Streiff	Ligier-Renault	-	-	-	-	-	-	-	-	-	-	-	10	9	8	-	3	4
		Tyrrell-Renault	-	-	-	-	-	-	-	-	-	-	-	-	-	-	-	r	-
16	Stefan Bellof *	Tyrrell-Ford Cosworth	-	6	r	nq	11	4	13	11	-	-	-	-	-	-	-	-	4
		Tyrrell-Renault	-	-	-	-	-	-	-	-	8	7r	r	-	-	-	-	-	-
17	Andrea de Cesaris	Ligier-Renault	r	r	r	4	14	10	r	r	r	r	r	r	-	-	-	-	3
18	René Arnoux	Ferrari	4	-	-	-	-	-	-	-	-	-	-	-	-	-	-	-	3
	Ivan Capelli	Tyrrell-Renault	-	-	-	-	-	-	-	-	-	-	-	-	r	-	-	4	3
20	Gerhard Berger	Arrows-BMW	r	r	r	r	13	11	r	8	7	r	9	r	7	10	5	6	3
	Teo Fabi	Toleman-Hart	-	-	-	r	r	r	14r	r	pr	r	r	12	r	r	r	r	-

1986

Pos	Driver	Car-Engine	BR	E	RSM	MC	B	CDN	DET	F	GB	D	H	A	I	P	MEX	AUS	Points
1	Alain Prost	McLaren-TAG Porsche	r	3	1	p1	6	2	3	2	3	6r	r	1	r/dq	2	2	1	72 (2)
2	Nigel Mansell	Williams-Honda	r	2	r	4	1	p1	5	1	1	3	3	r	2	1	5	pr	70 (2)
3	Nelson Piquet	Williams-Honda	1	r	2	7	pr	3	r	3	p2	1	1	r	1	3	4	2	69
4	Ayrton Senna	Lotus-Renault	p2	p1	pr	3	2	5	p1	pr	r	2	p2	r	r	p4r	p3	r	55
5	Stefan Johansson	Ferrari	r	r	4	10	3	r	r	r	r	11r	4	3	3	6	12r	3	23
6	Keke Rosberg	McLaren-TAG Porsche	r	4	5r	2	r	4	r	4	r	p5r	r	9r	4	r	r	r	22
7	Gerhard Berger	Benetton-BMW	6	6	3	r	10	r	r	r	r	10	r	7	5	r	1	r	17
8	Jacques Laffite	Ligier-Renault	3	r	r	6	5	7	2	6	r	-	-	-	-	-	-	-	14
9	Michele Alboreto	Ferrari	r	r	10r	r	4	8	4	8	r	r	r	2	r	5	r	r	14
10	René Arnoux	Ligier-Renault	4	r	r	5	r	6	r	5	4	4	r	10	r	7	15r	7	14
11	Martin Brundle	Tyrrell-Renault	5	r	8	r	r	9	r	10	5	r	6	r	10	r	11	4	8
12	Alan Jones	Lola-Hart	r	r	-	-	-	-	-	-	-	-	-	-	-	-	-	-	4
		Lola-Ford Cosworth	-	-	r	r	11r	10	r	r	r	9	r	4	6	r	r	r	
13	Johnny Dumfries	Lotus-Renault	9	r	r	nq	r	r	7	r	7	r	5	r	r	9	r	6	3
14	Philippe Streiff	Tyrrell-Renault	7	r	r	11	12	11	9	r	6	r	8	r	9	r	r	5r	3
15	Patrick Tambay	Lola-Hart	r	8	r	-	-	-	-	-	-	-	-	-	-	-	-	-	2
		Lola-Ford Cosworth	-	-	-	r	r	ns	-	r	r	8	7	5	r	nc	r	nc	
16	Teo Fabi	Benetton-BMW	10	5	r	r	7	r	r	r	r	r	r	pr	pr	8	r	10	2
17	Riccardo Patrese	Brabham-BMW	r	r	6r	r	8	r	6	7	r	r	r	r	r	r	13r	r	2
18	Christian Danner	Osella-Alfa Romeo	r	r	r	nq	r	r	-	-	-	-	-	-	-	-	-	-	1
		Arrows-BMW	-	-	-	-	-	-	r	11	r	r	r	6	8	11	9	r	
19	Philippe Alliot	Ligier-Renault	-	-	-	-	-	-	-	-	r	9	r	r	r	6	8		1

1987

Pos	Driver	Car-Engine	BR	RSM	B	MC	DET	F	GB	D	H	A	I	P	E	P	MEX	J	Points
1	Nelson Piquet	Williams-Honda	2	ns	r	2	2	2	p2	1	1	p2	p1	3	p4	2	15r	r	73 (3)
2	Nigel Mansell	Williams-Honda	p6	1	pr	pr	p5	p1	1	pr	p14r	1	3	r	1	p1	ns	-	61
3	Ayrton Senna	Lotus-Honda	r	p2	r	1	1	4	3	3	2	5	2	7	5	r	2	dq	57
4	Alain Prost	McLaren-TAG Porsche	1	r	1	9r	3	3	r	7r	3	6	15	1	2	r	7	r	46
5	Gerhard Berger	Ferrari	4	r	r	4	4	r	r	r	r	r	4	p2	r	r	p1	p1	36
6	Stefan Johansson	McLaren-TAG Porsche	3	4	2	r	7	8r	r	2	r	7	6	5	3	r	3	r	30
7	Michele Alboreto	Ferrari	8r	3	r	3	r	r	r	r	r	r	r	r	15r	r	4	2	17
8	Thierry Boutsen	Benetton-Ford Cosworth	5	r	r	r	r	r	7	r	4	4	5	14	16r	r	5	3	16
9	Teo Fabi	Benetton-Ford Cosworth	r	r	r	8	r	5r	6	r	r	3	7	4r	r	5	r	r	12
10	Eddie Cheever	Arrows-Megatron	r	r	4	r	6r	r	r	r	8	r	r	6	8r	4	9	r	8
11	Jonathan Palmer	Tyrrell-Ford Cosworth	10	r	r	5	11	7	8	5	7	14	14	10	r	7	8	4	7
12	Satoru Nakajima	Lotus-Honda	7	6	5	10	r	nc	4	r	r	13	11	8	9	r	6	r	7
13	Riccardo Patrese	Brabham-BMW	r	9	r	r	9	r	r	r	5	r	r	r	13	3	11r	-	6
		Williams-Honda	-															9r	
14	Andrea de Cesaris	Brabham-BMW	r	r	3r	r	r	r	r	r	r	r	r	r	r	r	r	8r	4
15	Philippe Streiff	Tyrrell-Ford Cosworth	11	8	9	r	r	6	r	4	9	r	12	12	7	8	12	r	4
16	Derek Warwick	Arrows-Megatron	r	11r	r	r	r	r	5	r	6	r	r	13	10	r	10	r	3
17	Philippe Alliot	Lola-Ford Cosworth	-	10	8	r	r	r	r	6	r	12	r	r	6	6	r	r	3
18	Martin Brundle	Zakspeed	r	5	r	7	r	r	nc	nc	r	dq	r	r	11	r	r	r	2
19	Ivan Capelli	March-Ford Cosworth	ns	r	r	6	r	r	r	r	10	11	13	9	12	r	r	r	1
20	René Arnoux	Ligier-Megatron	-	ns	6	11	10	r	r	r	r	10	10	r	r	r	r	r	1
21	Roberto Moreno	AGS-Ford Cosworth	-	-	-	-	-	-	-	-	-	-	-	-	-	-	r	6	1
	Yannick Dalmas	Lola-Ford Cosworth	-	-	-	-	-	-	-	-	-	-	-	-	-	9	14r	5	- (2)

Points scored by Yannick Dalmas were not valid for the championship because the constructor had only entered one car for the season.

1988

Pos	Driver	Car-Enginer	BR	RSM	MC	MEX	CDN	DET	F	GB	D	H	B	I	P	E	J	AUS	Points
1	Ayrton Senna	McLaren-Honda	pdq	p1	pr	p2	p1	p1	2	1	p1	p1	p1	p10r	6	p4	p1	p2	90 (4)
2	Alain Prost	McLaren-Honda	1	2	1	1	2	2	p1	r	2	2	2	r	p1	1	2	1	87 (18)
3	Gerhard Berger	Ferrari	2	5	2	3	r	r	4	p9	3	4	r	1	r	6	4	r	41
4	Thierry Boutsen	Benetton-Ford Cosworth	7	4	8	8	3	3	r	r	6	3	dq	6	3	9	3	5	27
5	Michele Alboreto	Ferrari	5	18r	3	4	r	r	3	17r	4	r	r	2	5	r	11	r	24
6	Nelson Piquet	Lotus-Honda	3	3	r	r	4	r	5	5	r	8	4	r	r	8	r	3	22
7	Ivan Capelli	March-Judd	r	r	10	16	5	ns	9	r	5	r	3	5	2	r	r	6	17
8	Derek Warwick	Arrows-Megatron	4	9	4	5	7	r	r	6	7	r	5	4	4	r	r	r	17
9	Nigel Mansell	Williams-Judd	r	r	r	r	r	r	r	2	r	r	-	-	r	2	r	r	12
10	Alessandro Nannini	Benetton-Ford Cosworth	r	6	r	7	r	r	6	3	18	r	dq	9	r	3	5	r	12
11	Riccardo Patrese	Williams-Judd	r	13	6	r	r	r	r	8	r	6	r	7	r	5	6	4	8
12	Eddie Cheever	Arrows-Megatron	8	7	r	6	r	r	11	7	10	r	6	3	r	r	r	r	6
13	Mauricio Gugelmin	March-Judd	r	15	r	r	r	r	8	4	8	5	r	8	r	7	10	r	5
14	Jonathan Palmer	Tyrrell-Ford Cosworth	r	14	5	nq	6	5	r	r	11	r	12r	nq	r	r	12	r	5
15	Andrea de Cesaris	Rial-Ford Cosworth	r	r	r	r	9r	4	10	r	13	r	r	r	r	r	r	8r	3
16	Satoru Nakajima	Lotus-Honda	6	8	nq	r	11	nq	7	10	9	7	r	r	r	r	7	r	1
17	Pierluigi Martini	Minardi-Ford Cosworth	-	-	-	-	-	6	15	15	nq	r	nq	r	r	r	13	7	1

1989

Pos	Driver	Car-Engine	BR	RSM	MC	MEX	USA	CDN	F	GB	D	H	B	I	P	E	J	AUS	Points
1	Alain Prost	McLaren-Honda	2	2	2	5	1	pr	p1	1	2	4	2	1	2	3	r	r	76 (5)
2	Ayrton Senna	McLaren-Honda	p11	p1	p1	p1	pr	7r	r	pr	p1	2	p1	pr	pr	p1	pdq	pr	60
3	Riccardo Patrese	Williams-Renault	r	r	15	2	2	2	3	r	4	pr	r	4	r	5	2	3	40
4	Nigel Mansell	Ferrari	1	r	r	r	r	dq	2	2	3	1	3	r	r/dq	-	r	r	38
5	Thierry Boutsen	Williams-Renault	r	4	10	r	6	1	r	10	r	3	4	3	r	r	3	1	37
6	Alessandro Nannini	Benetton-Ford Cosworth	6	3	8	4	r	dq	r	3	r	r	5	r	4	r	1	2	32
7	Gerhard Berger	Ferrari	r	r	-	r	r	r	r	r	r	r	r	2	1	2	r	r	21
8	Nelson Piquet	Lotus-Judd	r	r	r	11	r	4	8	4	5	6	nq	r	r	8	4	r	12
9	Jean Alesi	Tyrrell-Ford Cosworth	-	-	-	-	-	-	4	r	10	9	-	5	-	4	r	r	8
10	Derek Warwick	Arrows-Ford Cosworth	5	5	r	r	r	r	-	9	6	10	6	r	r	9	6	r	7
11	Eddie Cheever	Arrows-Ford Cosworth	r	9	7	7	3	r	7	nq	12r	5	r	nq	r	r	8	r	6
12	Stefan Johansson	Onyx-Ford Cosworth	npq	npq	npq	r	r	dq	5	npq	r	r	8	npq	3	npq	npq	npq	6
13	Michele Alboreto	Tyrrell-Ford Cosworth	10	nq	5	3	r	r	-	-	-	-	-	-	-	-	-	-	6
		Lola-Lamborghini	-	-	-	-	-	-	-	-	r	r	r	r	11	npq	nq	npq	
14	Johnny Herbert	Benetton-Ford Cosworth	4	11	14	15	5	nq	-	-	-	-	-	-	-	-	-	-	5
		Tyrrell-Ford Cosworth	-	-	-	-	-	-	-	-	-	-	-	r	nq	-	-	-	
15	Pierluigi Martini	Minardi-Ford Cosworth	r	r	r	r	r	r	r	5	9	r	9	7	5	r	-	6	5
16	Mauricio Gugelmin	March-Judd	3	r	r	nq	dq	r	nc	r	r	r	7	r	10	r	7	7	4
17	Andrea de Cesaris	Dallara-Ford Cosworth	13r	10	13	r	8r	3	nq	r	7	r	11	r	r	7	10	r	4
18	Stefano Modena	Brabham-Judd	r	r	3	10	r	r	r	r	r	11	r	exc	14	r	r	8	4
19	Alex Caffi	Dallara-Ford Cosworth	npq	7	4	13	r	6	r	npq	r	7	r	11r	r	r	9	r	4
20	Martin Brundle	Brabham-Judd	r	r	6	9	r	npq	npq	r	8	12	r	6	8	r	5	r	4
21	Satoru Nakajima	Lotus-Judd	8	nc	nq	r	r	nq	r	8	r	r	nq	10	7	r	r	4	3
22	Christian Danner	Rial-Ford Cosworth	14r	nq	nq	12	4	8	nq	nq	nq	nq	nq	nq	nq	-	-	-	3
23	Emanuele Pirro	Benetton-Ford Cosworth	-	-	-	-	-	-	9	11	r	8	10	r	r	r	r	5	2
24	René Arnoux	Ligier-Ford Cosworth	nq	nq	12	14	nq	5	r	nq	11	nq	r	9	13	nq	nq	r	2
25	Jonathan Palmer	Tyrrell-Ford Cosworth	7	6	9	r	9r	r	10	r	r	13	14	r	6	10	r	nq	2
26	Olivier Grouillard	Ligier-Ford Cosworth	9	dq	r	8	nq	nq	6	7	r	nq	13	r	nq	r	r	r	1
27	Gabriele Tarquini	AGS-Ford Cosworth	-	8	r	6	7r	r	r	nq	npq	npq	npq	npq	npq	npq	npq	npq	1
28	Luis Sala	Minardi-Ford Cosworth	r	r	r	nq	r	r	nq	6	nq	r	15	8	12	r	r	nq	1
29	Philippe Alliot	Lola-Lamborghini	12	r	r	nc	r	r	r	r	r	npq	16r	r	9	6	r	r	1

1990

Pos	Driver	Car-Engine	USA	BR	RSM	MC	CDN	MEX	F	GB	D	H	B	I	P	E	J	AUS	Points
1	Ayrton Senna	McLaren-Honda	1	p3	pr	p1	p1	20r	3	3	p1	2	p1	p1	2	pr	pr	pr	78
2	Alain Prost	Ferrari	r	1	4	r	5	1	1	1	4	r	2	2	3	1	r	3	71 (2)
3	Nelson Piquet	Benetton-Ford Cosworth	4	6	5	dq	2	6	4	5	r	3	5	7	5	r	1	1	43 (1)
4	Gerhard Berger	McLaren-Honda	pr	2	2	3	4	p3	5	14r	3	16r	3	3	4	r	r	4	43
5	Nigel Mansell	Ferrari	r	4	r	r	3	2	p18r	pr	r	17r	r	4	p1	2	r	2	37
6	Thierry Boutsen	Williams-Renault	3	5	r	4	r	5	r	2	6	p1	r	r	r	4	5	5	34
7	Riccardo Patrese	Williams-Renault	9	13r	1	r	r	9	6	r	5	4	r	5	7	5	4	6	23
8	Alessandro Nannini	Benetton-Ford Cosworth	11	10	3	r	r	4	16r	r	2	r	4	8	6	3	-	-	21
9	Jean Alesi	Tyrrell-Ford Cosworth	2	7	6	2	r	7	r	8	11r	r	8	r	8	r	ns	8	13
10	Ivan Capelli	Leyton House-Judd	r	nq	r	r	10	nq	2	r	7	r	7	r	r	r	r	r	6
11	Roberto Moreno	EuroBrun-Judd	13	npq	r	nq	nq	exc	npq	npq	npq	npq	npq	npq	npq	npq	-	-	6
		Benetton-Ford Cosworth	-	-	-	-	-	-	-	-	-	-	-	-	-	-	2	7	
12	Aguri Suzuki	Lola-Lamborghini	r	r	r	r	12	r	7	6	r	r	r	r	14r	6	3	r	6
13	Éric Bernard	Lola-Lamborghini	8	r	13r	6	9	r	8	4	r	6	9	r	r	r	r	r	5
14	Derek Warwick	Lotus-Lamborghini	r	r	7	r	6	10	11	r	8	5	11	r	r	r	r	r	3
15	Satoru Nakajima	Tyrrell-Ford Cosworth	6	8	r	r	11	r	r	r	r	r	r	6	ns	r	6	r	3
16	Alex Caffi	Arrows-Ford Cosworth	-	r	nq	5	8	nq	r	7	9	9	10	9	13r	-	9	nq	2
17	Stefano Modena	Brabham-Judd	5	r	r	r	7	11	13	9	r	r	17r	r	r	r	r	12	2
18	Mauricio Gugelmin	Leyton House-Judd	14	nq	r	nq	nq	nq	r	ns	r	8	6	r	12	8	r	r	1

1991

Pos	Driver	Car-Engine	USA	BR	RSM	MC	CDN	MEX	F	GB	D	H	B	I	P	E	J	AUS	Points
1	Ayrton Senna	McLaren-Honda	p1	p1	p1	p1	r	3	3	4r	7r	p1	p1	p2	2	5	2	p1	96
2	Nigel Mansell	Williams-Renault	r	r	r	2	6r	2	1	p1	p1	2	r	1	dq	1	r	2	72
3	Riccardo Patrese	Williams-Renault	r	2	r	r	p3	p1	p5	r	2	3	5	r	p1	3	3	5	53
4	Gerhard Berger	McLaren-Honda	r	3	2	r	r	r	r	2	4	4	2	4	r	pr	p1	3	43
5	Alain Prost	Ferrari	2	4	ns	5	r	r	2	3	r	r	r	3	r	2	4	-	34
6	Nelson Piquet	Benetton-Ford Cosworth	3	5	r	r	1	r	8	5	r	r	3	6	5	11	7	4	26.5
7	Jean Alesi	Ferrari	12r	6	r	3	r	r	4	r	3	5	r	r	3	4	r	r	21
8	Stefano Modena	Tyrrell-Honda	4	r	r	r	2	11	r	7	13	12	r	r	r	16	6	10	10
9	Andrea de Cesaris	Jordan-Ford Cosworth	npq	r	r	r	4	4r	6	r	5	7	13r	7	8	r	r	8	9
10	Roberto Moreno	Benetton-Ford Cosworth	r	7	13r	4	r	5	r	r	8	8	4	-	-	-	-	-	8
		Jordan-Ford Cosworth	-	-	-	-	-	-	-	-	-	-	-	r	10	-	-	-	
		Minardi-Ferrari	-	-	-	-	-	-	-	-	-	-	-	-	-	-	-	16	
11	Pierluigi Martini	Minardi-Ferrari	9r	r	4	12	7	r	9	9	r	r	12	r	4	13	r	r	6
12	J J Lehto	Dallara-Judd	r	r	3	11	r	r	r	13	r	r	r	r	r	8	r	12	4
13	Bertrand Gachot	Jordan-Ford Cosworth	10r	13r	r	8	5	r	r	6	6	9	-	-	-	-	-	-	4
		Lola-Ford Cosworth	-	-	-	-	-	-	-	-	-	-	-	-	-	-	-	nq	
14	Michael Schumacher	Jordan-Ford Cosworth	-	-	-	-	-	-	-	-	-	-	r	-	-	-	-	-	4
		Benetton-Ford Cosworth	-	-	-	-	-	-	-	-	-	-	-	5	6	6	r	r	
15	Satoru Nakajima	Tyrrell-Honda	5	r	r	r	10	12	r	8	r	15	r	r	13	17	r	r	2
16	Mika Häkkinen	Lotus-Judd	r	9	5	r	r	9	nq	12	r	14	r	14	14	r	r	19	2
17	Martin Brundle	Brabham-Yamaha	11	12	11	exc	r	r	r	r	11	r	9	13	12	10	5	nq	2
18	Emanuele Pirro	Dallara-Judd	r	11	npq	6	9	npq	npq	10	10	r	8	10	r	15	r	7	1
19	Mark Blundell	Brabham-Yamaha	r	r	8	r	nq	r	r	r	12	r	6	12	r	r	npq	17	1
20	Ivan Capelli	Leyton House-Ilmor	r	r	r	r	r	r	r	r	r	6	r	8	17r	r	-	-	1
21	Éric Bernard	Lola-Ford Cosworth	r	r	r	9	r	6	r	r	r	r	r	r	nq	r	nq	-	1
22	Aguri Suzuki	Lola-Ford Cosworth	6	ns	r	r	r	r	r	r	r	r	nq	nq	r	nq	r	nq	1
	Julian Bailey	Lotus-Judd	nq	nq	6	nq	-	-	-	-	-	-	-	-	-	-	-	-	1
24	Gianni Morbidelli	Minardi-Ferrari	r	8	r	r	r	7	r	11	r	13	r	9	9	14r	r	-	0.5
		Ferrari	-	-	-	-	-	-	-	-	-	-	-	-	-	-	-	6	

Half points were awarded in Australia where the race was stopped early.

1992

Pos	Driver	Car-Engine	ZA	MEX	BR	E	RSM	MC	CDN	F	GB	D	H	B	I	P	J	AUS	Points
1	Nigel Mansell	Williams-Renault	p1	p1	p1	p1	p1	p2	r	p1	p1	p1	2	p2	pr	p1	pr	pr	108
2	Riccardo Patrese	Williams-Renault	2	2	2	r	2	3	r	2	2	8r	pr	3	5	r	1	r	56
3	Michael Schumacher	Benetton-Ford Cosworth	4	3	3	2	r	4	2	r	4	3	r	1	3	7	r	2	53
4	Ayrton Senna	McLaren-Honda	3	r	r	9r	3	1	pr	r	r	2	1	5	1	3	r	r	50
5	Gerhard Berger	McLaren-Honda	5	4	r	4	r	r	1	r	5	r	3	r	4	2	2	1	49
6	Martin Brundle	Benetton-Ford Cosworth	r	r	r	r	4	5	r	3	3	4	5	4	2	4	3	3	38
7	Jean Alesi	Ferrari	r	r	4	3	r	r	3	r	r	5	r	r	r	r	5	4	18
8	Mika Häkkinen	Lotus-Ford Cosworth	9	6	10	r	nq	r	r	4	6	r	4	6	r	5	r	7	11
9	Andrea de Cesaris	Tyrrell-Ilmor	r	5	r	r	14r	r	5	r	r	r	8	8	6	9	4	r	8
10	Michele Alboreto	Footwork-Mugen Honda	10	13	6	5	5	7	7	7	7	9	7	r	7	6	15	r	6
11	Erik Comas	Ligier-Renault	7	9	r	r	9	10	6	5	8	6	r	nq	r	r	r	r	4
12	Karl Wendlinger	March-Ilmor	r	r	r	8	12	r	4	r	r	16	r	11	10	r	-	-	3
13	Ivan Capelli	Ferrari	r	r	r	10r	r	r	r	r	9	r	6	r	r	r	-	-	3
14	Thierry Boutsen	Ligier-Renault	r	10	r	r	r	12	10	r	10	7	r	r	r	8	r	5	2
15	Johnny Herbert	Lotus-Ford Cosworth	6	7	r	r	r	r	r	6	r	r	r	13r	r	r	r	13	2
16	Pierluigi Martini	Dallara-Ferrari	r	r	r	6	6	r	8	10	15	11	r	r	8	r	10	r	2
17	Stefano Modena	Jordan-Yamaha	nq	r	r	nq	r	r	r	r	r	nq	r	15	nq	13	7	6	1
18	Christian Fittipaldi	Minardi-Lamborghini	r	r	r	11	r	8	13r	nq	-	-	-	nq	nq	12	6	9	1
19	Bertrand Gachot	Venturi Larrousse	r	11	r	r	r	6	dq	r	r	14	r	18r	r	r	r	r	1

1993

Pos	Driver	Car-Engine	ZA	BR	EUR	RSM	E	MC	CDN	F	GB	D	H	B	I	P	J	AUS	Points
1	Alain Prost	Williams-Renault	p1	pr	p3	p1	p1	p4	p1	1	p1	p1	p12	p3	p12r	2	p2	2	99
2	Ayrton Senna	McLaren Ford Cosworth	2	1	1	r	2	1	18r	4	5r	4	r	4	r	r	1	p1	73
3	Damon Hill	Williams-Renault	r	2	2	r	r	2	3	p2	r	15r	1	1	1	p3	4	3	69
4	Michael Schumacher	Benetton-Ford Cosworth	r	3	r	2	3	r	2	3	2	2	r	2	r	1	r	r	52
5	Riccardo Patrese	Benetton-Ford Cosworth	r	r	5	r	4	r	r	10	3	5	2	6	5	16r	r	8r	20
6	Jean Alesi	Ferrari	r	8	r	r	r	3	r	r	9	7	r	r	2	4	r	4	16
7	Martin Brundle	Ligier-Renault	r	r	r	3	r	6	5	5	14r	8	5	7	r	6	9r	6	13
8	Gerhard Berger	Ferrari	6r	r	r	r	6	14r	4	14	r	6	3	10r	r	r	r	5	12
9	Johnny Herbert	Lotus-Ford Cosworth	r	4	4	8r	r	r	10	r	4	10	r	5	r	r	11	r	11
10	Mark Blundell	Ligier-Renault	3	5	r	r	7	r	r	r	7	3	7	11r	r	r	7	9	10
11	Michael Andretti	McLaren-Ford Cosworth	r	r	r	r	5	8	14	6	r	r	r	8	3	-	-	-	7
12	Karl Wendlinger	Sauber-Ilmor	r	r	r	r	r	13	6	r	r	9	6	r	4	5	r	15r	7
13	J J Lehto	Sauber-Ilmor	5	r	r	4r	r	r	7	r	8	r	r	9	r	7	8	r	5
14	Christian Fittipaldi	Minardi-Ford Cosworth	4	r	7	r	8	5	9	8	12r	11	r	r	8r	9	-	-	5
15	Mika Häkkinen	McLaren-Ford Cosworth	-	-	-	-	-	-	-	-	-	-	-	-	-	r	3	r	4
16	Derek Warwick	Footwork-Mugen Honda	7r	9	r	r	13	r	16	13	6	17	4	r	r	15r	14r	10	4
17	Philippe Alliot	Larrousse-Lamborghini	r	7	r	5	r	12	r	9	11	12	8	12	9	10	-	-	2
18	Rubens Barrichello	Jordan-Hart	r	r	10r	r	12	9	r	7	10	r	r	r	r	13	5	11	2
19	Fabrizio Barbazza	Minardi-Ford Cosworth	r	r	6	6	r	11	r	r	-	-	-	-	-	-	-	-	2
20	Alessandro Zanardi	Lotus-Ford Cosworth	r	6	8	r	14r	7	11	r	r	r	r	ns	-	-	-	-	1
21	Erik Comas	Larrousse-Lamborghini	r	10	9	r	9	r	8	16r	r	r	r	r	6	11	r	12	1
22	Eddie Irvine	Jordan-Hart	-	-	-	-	-	-	-	-	-	-	-	-	-	-	6	r	1

1994

Pos	Driver	Car-Engine	BR	PAC	RSM	MC	E	CDN	F	GB	D	H	B	I	P	EUR	J	AUS	Points
1	Michael Schumacher	Benetton-Ford Cosworth	1	1	1	p1	p2	p1	p1	dq	r	p1	dq	-	-	p1	p2	r	92
2	Damon Hill	Williams-Renault	2	r	6	r	1	2	p2	p1	8	2	1	1	1	2	1	r	91
3	Gerhard Berger	Ferrari	r	2	r	3	r	4	3	r	p1	12r	r	2	pr	5	r	2	41
4	Mika Häkkinen	McLaren-Peugeot	r	r	3	r	r	r	r	3	r	-	2	3	3	3	7	12r	26
5	Jean Alesi	Ferrari	3	-	-	5	4	3	r	2	r	r	r	pr	r	10	3	6	24
6	Rubens Barrichello	Jordan-Hart	4	3	nq	r	r	7	r	4	r	r	pr	4	4	12	r	4	19
7	Martin Brundle	McLaren-Peugeot	r	r	8	2	11r	r	r	r	r	4r	r	5	6	r	r	3	16
8	David Coulthard	Williams-Renault	-	-	-	-	r	5	-	5	r	r	4	6r	2	-	-	-	14
9	Nigel Mansell	Williams-Renault	-	-	-	-	-	-	r	-	-	-	-	-	-	r	4	1	13
10	Jos Verstappen	Benetton-Ford Cosworth	r	r	-	-	-	-	r	8	r	3	3	r	5	r	-	-	10
11	Olivier Panis	Ligier-Renault	11	9	11	9	7	12	r	12	2	6	7	10	dq	9	11	5	9
12	Mark Blundell	Tyrrell-Yamaha	r	r	9	r	3	10r	10	r	r	5	5	r	r	13	r	r	8
13	Heinz Harald Frentzen	Sauber-Mercedes-Benz	r	5	7	ns	r	r	4	7	r	r	r	r	r	6	6	7	7
14	Nicola Larini	Ferrari	-	r	2	-	-	-	-	-	-	-	-	-	-	-	-	-	6
15	Christian Fittipaldi	Footwork-Ford Cosworth	r	4	13r	r	r	dq	8	9	4	14r	r	r	8	17	8	8	6
16	Eddie Irvine	Jordan-Hart	r	-	-	-	6	r	r	ns	r	r	13r	r	7	4	5	r	6
17	Ukyo Katayama	Tyrrell-Yamaha	5	r	5	r	r	r	r	6	r	r	r	r	r	7	r	r	5
18	Éric Bernard	Ligier-Renault	r	10	12	r	8	13	r	13	3	10	10	7	10	-	-	-	4
		Lotus-Mugen Honda	-	-	-	-	-	-	-	-	-	-	-	-	-	18	-	-	
19	Karl Wendlinger	Sauber-Mercedes-Benz	6	r	4	ns	-	-	-	-	-	-	-	-	-	-	-	-	4
	Andrea de Cesaris	Jordan-Hart	-	-	r	4	-	-	-	-	-	-	-	-	-	-	-	-	4
		Sauber-Mercedes-Benz	-	-	-	-	r	6	r	r	r	r	r	r	r	r	-		
21	Pierluigi Martini	Minardi-Ford Cosworth	8	r	r	r	5	9	5	10	r	r	8	r	12	15	r	9	4
22	Gianni Morbidelli	Footwork-Ford Cosworth	r	r	r	r	r	r	r	r	5	r	6	r	9	11	r	r	3
23	Erik Comas	Larrousse-Ford Cosworth	9	6	r	10	r	r	11r	r	6	8	r	8	r	r	9	-	2
24	J J Lehto	Benetton-Ford Cosworth	-	-	r	7	r	6	-	-	-	-	-	9	r	-	-	-	1
		Sauber-Mercedes-Benz	-	-	-	-	-	-	-	-	-	-	-	-	-	-	r	10	
25	Michele Alboreto	Minardi-Ford Cosworth	r	r	r	6	r	11	r	r	r	7	9	r	13	14	r	r	1
	Ayrton Senna*	Williams-Renault	pr	pr	pr	-	-	-	-	-	-	-	-	-	-	-	-	-	

1995

Pos	Driver	Car-Engine	BR	RA	RSM	E	MC	CDN	F	GB	D	H	B	I	P	EUR	PAC	J	AUS	Points
1	Michael Schumacher	Benetton-Renault	1	3	pr	p1	1	p5	1	r	1	11r	1	r	2	1	1	p1	r	102
2	Damon Hill	Williams-Renault	pr	1	1	4	p2	r	p2	pr	pr	p1	2	r	3	r	3	r	p1	69
3	David Coulthard	Williams-Renault	2	pr	4	r	r	r	3	3	2	2	r	pr	p1	p3	p2	r	r	49
4	Johnny Herbert	Benetton-Renault	r	4	7	2	4	r	r	1	4	4	7	1	7	5	6	3	r	45
5	Jean Alesi	Ferrari	5	2	2	r	r	1	5	2	r	r	r	r	5	2	5	r	r	42
6	Gerhard Berger	Ferrari	3	6	3	3	3	11r	12	r	3	3	pr	r	4	r	4	r	r	31
7	Mika Häkkinen	McLaren-Mercedes-Benz	4	r	5	r	r	r	7	r	r	r	r	2	r	8	-	2	ns	17
8	Olivier Panis	Ligier-Mugen Honda	r	7	9	6	r	4	8	4	r	6	9	r	r	r	8	5	2	16
9	Heinz Harald Frentzen	Sauber-Ford Cosworth	r	5	6	8	6	r	10	6	r	5	4	3	6	r	7	8	r	15
10	Mark Blundell	McLaren-Mercedes-Benz	6	r	-	-	5	r	11	5	r	r	5	4	9	r	9	7	4	13
11	Rubens Barrichello	Jordan-Peugeot	r	r	r	7	r	2	6	11r	r	7	6	r	11	4	r	r	r	11
12	Eddie Irvine	Jordan-Peugeot	r	r	8	5	r	3	9	r	9r	13r	r	r	10	6	11	4	r	10
13	Martin Brundle	Ligier-Mugen Honda	-	-	-	9	r	10r	4	r	-	r	3	r	8	7	-	-	r	7
14	Gianni Morbidelli	Footwork-Hart	r	r	13	11	9	6	14	-	-	-	-	-	-	-	r	r	3	5
15	Mika Salo	Tyrrell-Yamaha	7	r	r	10	r	7	15	8	r	r	8	5	13	10	12	6	5	5
16	Jean-Christophe Boullion	Sauber-Ford Cosworth	-	-	-	-	8r	r	r	9	5	10	11	6	12	r	r	-	-	3
17	Aguri Suzuki	Ligier-Mugen Honda	8	r	11	-	-	-	-	-	6	-	-	-	-	-	r	ns	-	1
18	Pedro Lamy	Minardi-Ford Cosworth	-	-	-	-	-	-	-	-	-	9	10	r	r	9	13	11	6	1

1996

Pos	Driver	Car-Engine	AUS	BR	RA	EUR	RSM	MC	E	CDN	F	GB	D	H	B	I	P	J	Points
1	Damon Hill	Williams-Renault	1	p1	p1	p4	1	r	pr	p1	1	pr	p1	2	5	pr	p2	1	97
2	Jacques Villeneuve	Williams-Renault	p2	r	2	1	11r	r	3	2	2	1	3	1	p2	7	1	pr	78
3	Michael Schumacher	Ferrari	r	3	r	2	p2	pr	1	r	pns	r	4	p9r	1	1	3	2	59
4	Jean Alesi	Benetton-Renault	r	2	3	r	6	r	2	3	3	r	2	3	4	2	4	r	47
5	Mika Häkkinen	McLaren-Mercedes-Benz	5	4	r	8	8r	6r	5	5	5	3	r	4	3	3	r	3	31
6	Gerhard Berger	Benetton-Renault	4	r	r	9	3	r	r	r	4	2	13r	r	6	r	6	4	21
7	David Coulthard	McLaren-Mercedes-Benz	r	r	7	3	r	2	r	4	6	5	5	r	r	r	13	8	18
8	Rubens Barrichello	Jordan-Peugeot	r	r	4	5	5	r	r	r	9	4	6	6	r	5	r	9	14
9	Olivier Panis	Ligier-Mugen Honda	7	6	8	r	r	1	r	r	7	r	7	5	r	r	10	7	13
10	Eddie Irvine	Ferrari	3	7	5	r	4	7r	r	r	r	r	r	r	r	r	5	r	11
11	Martin Brundle	Jordan-Peugeot	r	12r	r	6	r	r	r		6	8	6	10	r	4	9	5	8
12	Heinz Harald Frentzen	Sauber-Ford Cosworth	8	r	r	r	r	4	4	r	r	8	8	r	r	r	7	6	7
13	Mika Salo	Tyrrell-Yamaha	6	5	r	dq	r	5r	dq	r	10	7	9	r	7	r	11	r	5
14	Johnny Herbert	Sauber-Ford Cosworth	r	r	9	7	r	3	r	7	dq	9	r	r	9r	8	10		4
15	Pedro Diniz	Ligier-Mugen Honda	10	8	r	10	7	r	6	r	r	r	r	r	r	6	r	r	2
16	Jos Verstappen	Footwork-Hart	r	r	6	r	r	r	r	r	r	10	r	r	r	8	r	11	1

1997

Pos	Driver	Car-Engine	AUS	BR	RA	RSM	MC	E	CDN	F	GB	D	H	B	I	A	L	J	EUR	Points
1	Jacques Villeneuve	Williams-Renault	pr	p1	p1	pr	r	p1	r	4	p1	r	1	p5	5	p1	1	pdq	p3	81
2	Heinz Harald Frentzen	Williams-Renault	8r	9	r	1	pr	8	4	2	r	r	r	3	3	3	3	2	6	42
3	David Coulthard	McLaren-Mercedes-Benz	1	10	r	r	r	6	7	7	4	r	r	r	1	2	r	10r	2	36
4	Jean Alesi	Benetton-Renault	r	p6	7	5	r	3	2	5	2	6	11	8	p2	r	2	5	13	36
5	Gerhard Berger	Benetton-Renault	4	2	p6	r	9	10	-	-	-	p1	8	6	7	10	4	8	4	27
6	Mika Häkkinen	McLaren-Mercedes-Benz	3	4	5	6	r	7	r	r	r	3	r	dq	9	r	pr	4	1	27
7	Eddie Irvine	Ferrari	r	16	2	3	3	12	r	3	r	r	9r	10r	8	r	r	3	5	24
8	Giancarlo Fisichella	Jordan-Peugeot	r	8	r	4	6	9	3	9	7	11r	r	2	4	r	7	11		20
9	Olivier Panis	Prost-Mugen Honda	5	3	r	8	4	2	11r	-	-	-	-	-	-	-	6	r	7	16
10	Johnny Herbert	Sauber-Petronas	r	7	4	r	r	5	5	8	r	r	3	4	r	8	7	6	8	15
11	Ralf Schumacher	Jordan-Peugeot	r	r	3	r	r	r	r	6	5	5	5	r	5	r	9	r		13
12	Damon Hill	Arrows-Yamaha	ns	17r	r	r	r	r	9	12	6	8	2	13r	r	7	8	11	r	7
13	Rubens Barrichello	Stewart-Ford Cosworth	r	r	r	r	2	r	r	r	r	r	r	13	14r	r	r	r		6
14	Alexander Wurz	Benetton-Renault	-	-	-	-	-	r	r	3	-	-	-	-	-	-	-	-	-	4
15	Jarno Trulli	Minardi-Hart	9	12	9	ns	r	15	r	-	-	-	-	-	-	-	-	-	-	3
		Prost-Mugen Honda	-	-	-	-	-	-	-	10	8	4	7	15	10	-	-	-	-	
16	Pedro Diniz	Arrows-Yamaha	10	r	r	r	r	r	8	r	r	r	r	7	r	13r	5	12	r	2
17	Mika Salo	Tyrrell-Ford Cosworth	r	13	8	9	5	r	r	r	r	r	13	11	r	r	10	r	12	2
18	Shinji Nakano	Prost-Mugen Honda	7	14	r	r	r	r	6	r	11r	7	6	r	11	r	r	r	10	2
19	Nicola Larini	Sauber-Petronas	6	11	r	7	r	-	-	-	-	-	-	-	-	-	-	-	-	1
	Michael Schumacher	Ferrari	2	5	r	2	1	4	p1	p1	r	2	p4	1	6	6	r	1	r	78

Michael Schumacher was stripped of his second place in the championship as punishment for the European Grand Prix incident where he collided with Jacques Villeneuve. He retained his points!

1998

Pos	Driver	Car-Engine	AUS	BR	RA	RSM	E	MC	CDN	F	GB	A	D	H	B	I	L	J	Points
1	Mika Häkkinen	McLaren-Mercedes-Benz	p1	p1	2	r	p1	p1	r	p3	p2	1	p1	p6	pr	4	1	1	100
2	Michael Schumacher	Ferrari	r	3	1	2	3	10	1	1	1	3	5	1	r	p1	p2	pr	86
3	David Coulthard	McLaren-Mercedes-Benz	2	2	p6	p1	2	r	pr	6	r	2	2	2	7	r	3	3	56
4	Eddie Irvine	Ferrari	4	8	3	3	r	3	3	2	3	4	8	r	r	2	4	2	47
5	Jacques Villeneuve	Williams-Mecachrome	5	7	r	4	6	5	10	4	7	6	3	3	r	r	8	6	21
6	Damon Hill	Jordan-Mugen Honda	8	dq	8	10r	r	8	r	r	r	7	4	4	1	6	9	4	20
7	Heinz Harald Frentzen	Williams-Mecachrome	3	5	9	5	8	r	r	15r	r	r	9	5	4	7	5	5	17
8	Alexander Wurz	Benetton-Playlife	7	4	4	r	4	r	4	5	4	9	11	16r	r	r	7	9	17
9	Giancarlo Fisichella	Benetton-Playlife	r	6	7	r	r	2	2	9	5	pr	7	8	r	8	6	8	16
10	Ralf Schumacher	Jordan-Mugen Honda	r	r	r	7	11	r	r	16	6	5	6	9	2	3	r	r	14
11	Jean Alesi	Sauber-Petronas	r	9	5	6	10	12r	r	7	r	r	10	7	3	5	10	7	9
12	Rubens Barrichello	Stewart-Ford Cosworth	r	r	10	r	5	r	5	10	r	r	r	r	r	10	11	r	4
13	Mika Salo	Arrows	r	r	r	9	r	4	r	13	r	r	14	r	r	r	14	r	3
14	Pedro Diniz	Arrows	r	r	r	r	r	6	9	14	r	r	r	11	5	r	r	r	3
15	Johnny Herbert	Sauber-Petronas	6	11r	r	r	7	7	r	8	r	8	r	10	r	r	r	10	1
16	Jan Magnussen	Stewart-Ford Cosworth	r	10	r	r	12	r	6	-	-	-	-	-	-	-	-	-	1
17	Jarno Trulli	Prost-Peugeot	r	r	11	r	9	r	r	r	r	10	12	r	6	13	r	12	1

1999

Pos	Driver	Car-Engine	AUS	BR	RSM	MC	E	CDN	F	GB	A	D	H	B	I	EUR	MAL	J	Points
1	Mika Häkkinen	McLaren-Mercedes-Benz	pr	p1	pr	p3	p1	1	2	pr	p3	pr	p1	p2	pr	5	3	1	76
2	Eddie Irvine	Ferrari	1	5	r	2	4	3	6	2	1	1	3	4	6	7	1	3	74
3	Heinz Harald Frentzen	Jordan-Mugen Honda	2	3r	r	4	r	11r	1	4	4	3	4	3	1	pr	6	4	54
4	David Coulthard	McLaren-Mercedes-Benz	r	r	2	r	2	7	r	1	2	5	2	1	5	r	r	r	48
5	Michael Schumacher	Ferrari	8	2	1	1	3	pr	5	r	-	-	-	-	-	-	p2	p2	44
6	Ralf Schumacher	Williams-Supertec	3	4	r	r	5	4	4	3	r	4	9	5	2	4	r	5	35
7	Rubens Barrichello	Stewart-Ford Cosworth	5	r	3	9r	dq	r	p3	8	r	r	5	10	4	3	5	8	21
8	Johnny Herbert	Stewart-Ford Cosworth	ns	r	10r	r	r	5	r	12	14	11r	11	r	r	1	4	7	15
9	Giancarlo Fisichella	Benetton-Playlife	4	r	5	5	9	2	r	7	12r	r	r	11	r	r	11	14r	13
10	Mika Salo	BAR-Supertec	-	-	7r	r	8	-	-	-	-	-	-	-	-	-	-	-	10
		Ferrari	-	-	-	-	-	-	-	-	9	2	12	7	3	r	-	-	
11	Jarno Trulli	Prost-Peugeot	r	r	r	7	6	r	7	9	7	r	8	12	r	2	ns	r	7
12	Damon Hill	Jordan-Mugen Honda	r	r	4	r	7	r	r	5	8	r	6	6	10	r	r	r	7
13	Alexander Wurz	Benetton-Playlife	r	7	r	6	10	r	r	10	5	7	7	14	r	r	8	10	3
14	Pedro Diniz	Sauber-Petronas	r	r	r	r	r	6	r	6	6	r	r	r	r	r	r	11	3
15	Olivier Panis	Prost-Peugeot	r	6	r	r	r	9	8	13	10	6	10	13	11r	9	r	r	2
16	Jean Alesi	Sauber-Petronas	r	r	6	r	r	r	r	14	r	8	16r	9	9	r	7	6	2
17	Pedro de la Rosa	Arrows	6	r	r	r	11	r	11	r	r	r	15	r	r	r	r	13	1
18	Marc Gené	Minardi-Ford Cosworth	r	9	9	r	r	8	r	15	11	9	17	16	r	6	9	r	1

2000

Pos	Driver	Car-Engine	AUS	BR	RSM	GB	E	EUR	MC	CDN	F	A	D	H	B	I	USA	J	MAL	Points
1	Michael Schumacher	Ferrari	1	1	1	3	p5	1	pr	p1	pr	r	r	p2	2	p1	p1	p1	p1	108
2	Mika Häkkinen	McLaren-Mercedes-Benz	pr	pr	p2	2	1	2	6	4	2	p1	2	1	p1	2	r	2	4	89
3	David Coulthard	McLaren-Mercedes-Benz	r	dq	3	1	2	p3	1	7	1	2	p3	3	4	r	5	3	2	73
4	Rubens Barrichello	Ferrari	2	r	4	pr	3	4	2	2	3	3	1	4	r	r	2	4	3	62
5	Ralf Schumacher	Williams-BMW	3	5	r	4	4	r	r	14r	5	r	7	5	3	3	r	r	r	24
6	Giancarlo Fisichella	Benetton-Playlife	5	2	11	7	9	5	3	3	9	r	r	r	r	11	r	14	9	18
7	Jacques Villeneuve	BAR-Honda	4	r	5	16r	r	r	7	15r	4	4	8	12	7	r	4	6	5	17
8	Jenson Button	Williams-BMW	r	6	r	5	17r	10r	r	11	8	5	4	9	5	r	r	5	r	12
9	Heinz Harald Frentzen	Jordan-Mugen Honda	r	3	r	17r	6	r	10r	r	7	r	r	6	6	r	3	r	r	11
10	Jarno Trulli	Jordan-Mugen Honda	r	4	15r	6	12	r	r	6	6	r	9	7	r	r	r	13	12	6
11	Mika Salo	Sauber-Petronas	dq	ns	6	8	7	r	5	r	10	6	5	10	9	7	r	10	8	6
12	Jos Verstappen	Arrows-Supertec	r	7	14	r	r	r	r	5	r	r	r	13	15	4	r	r	10	5
13	Eddie Irvine	Jaguar-Ford Cosworth	r	r	7	13	11	r	4	13	13	ew	10	8	10	r	7	8	6	4
14	Ricardo Zonta	BAR-Honda	6	9	12	r	8	r	8	r	r	r	r	14	12	6	6	9	r	3
15	Alexander Wurz	Benetton-Playlife	7	r	9	9	10	12r	r	9	r	10	r	11	13	5	10	r	7	2
16	Pedro de la Rosa	Arrows-Supertec	r	8	r	r	r	6	r	r	r	r	6	16	16	r	r	12	r	2

2001

Pos	Driver	Car-Engine	AUS	MAL	BR	RSM	E	A	MC	CDN	EUR	F	GB	D	H	B	I	USA	J	Points
1	Michael Schumacher	Ferrari	p1	p1	p2	r	p1	p2	1	p2	p1	1	p2	r	p1	1	4	p2	p1	123
2	David Coulthard	McLaren-Mercedes-Benz	2	3	1	p2	5	1	p5	r	3	4	r	r	3	2	r	3	3	65
3	Rubens Barrichello	Ferrari	3	2	r	3	r	3	2	r	5	3	3	2	2	5	2	15r	5	56
4	Ralf Schumacher	Williams-BMW	r	5	r	1	r	r	r	1	4	p2	r	1	4	7	3	r	6	49
5	Mika Häkkinen	McLaren-Mercedes-Benz	r	6	r	4	9r	r	r	3	6	ns	1	r	5	4	r	1	4	37
6	Juan Pablo Montoya	Williams-BMW	r	r	r	r	2	r	r	r	2	r	4	pr	8	pr	p1	r	2	31
7	Jacques Villeneuve	BAR-Honda	r	r	7	r	3	8	4	r	9	r	8	3	9	8	6	r	10	12
8	Nick Heidfeld	Sauber-Petronas	4	r	3	7	6	9	r	r	r	6	6	r	6	r	11	6	9	12
9	Jarno Trulli	Jordan-Honda	r	8	5	5	4	dq	r	11r	r	5	r	r	r	r	r	4	8	12
10	Kimi Räikkönen	Sauber-Petronas	6	r	r	r	8	4	10	4	10	7	5	r	7	r	7	r	r	9
11	Giancarlo Fisichella	Benetton-Renault	13	r	6	r	14	r	r	r	11	11	13	4	r	3	10	8	17r	8
12	Eddie Irvine	Jaguar-Ford Cosworth	11	r	r	r	r	7	3	r	7	r	9	r	r	r	r	5	r	6
13	Heinz Harald Frentzen	Jordan-Honda	5	4	11r	6	r	r	r	ew	r	8	7	-	-	-	-	-	-	6
		Prost-Acer	-	-	-	-	-	-	-	-	-	-	-	-	r	9	r	10	12	
14	Olivier Panis	BAR-Honda	7	r	4	8	7	5	r	r	r	9	r	7	r	11	9	11	13	5
15	Jean Alesi	Prost-Acer	10	9	8	9	10	10	6	5	15r	12	11	6	-	-	-	-	-	5
		Jordan-Honda	-	-	-	-	-	-	-	-	-	-	-	-	10	6	8	7	r	
16	Pedro de la Rosa	Jaguar-Ford Cosworth	-	-	-	-	r	r	r	6	8	14	12	r	11	r	5	12	r	3
17	Jenson Button	Benetton-Renault	14r	11	10	12	15	r	7	r	13	16r	15	5	r	r	r	9	7	2
18	Jos Verstappen	Arrows-Asiatech	9	7	r	r	12	6	8	10r	r	13	10	9	12	10	r	r	15	1

2002

Pos	Driver	Car-Engine	AUS	MAL	BR	RSM	E	A	MC	CDN	EUR	GB	F	D	H	B	I	USA	J	Points
1	Michael Schumacher	Ferrari	1	p3	1	p1	p1	1	2	1	2	1	1	p1	2	p1	2	p2	p1	144
2	Rubens Barrichello	Fearrari	pr	r	r	2	ns	p2	7	3	1	2	ns	4	p1	2	1	1	2	77
3	Juan Pablo Montoya	Williams-BMW	2	2	p5	4	2	3	pr	pr	pr	p3	p4	2	11	3	pr	4	4	50
4	Ralf Schumacher	Williams-BMW	r	1	2	3	11r	4	3	7	4	8	5	3	3	5	r	16	11r	42
5	David Coulthard	McLaren-Mercedes-Benz	r	r	3	6	3	6	1	2	r	10	3	5	5	4	7	3	r	41
6	Kimi Räikkönen	McLaren-Mercedes-Benz	3	r	12r	r	r	r	r	4	3	r	2	r	4	r	r	r	3	24
7	Jenson Button	Renault	r	4	4	5	12r	7	r	15r	5	12r	6	r	r	r	5	8	6	14
8	Jarno Trulli	Renault	r	r	r	9	10r	r	4	6	8	r	r	r	8	r	4	5	r	9
9	Eddie Irvine	Jaguar-Ford Cosworth	4	r	7	r	r	r	9	r	r	r	r	r	r	6	3	10	9	8
10	Nick Heidfeld	Sauber-Petronas	r	5	r	10	4	r	8	12	7	6	7	6	9	10	10	9	7	7
11	Giancarlo Fisichella	Jordan-Honda	r	13	r	r	r	5	5	5	r	7	ew	r	6	r	8	7	r	7
12	Jacques Villeneuve	BAR-Honda	r	8	10r	7	7	10r	r	r	12	4	r	r	r	8	9	6	r	4
13	Felipe Massa	Sauber-Petronas	r	6	r	8	5	r	r	9	6	9	r	7	7	r	r	-	r	4
14	Olivier Panis	BAR-Honda	r	r	r	r	r	r	r	8	9	5	r	r	12	12r	6	12	r	3
15	Takuma Sato	Jordan-Honda	r	9	9	r	r	r	r	10	16	r	r	8	10	11	12	11	5	2
16	Mark Webber	Minard-Asiatech	5	r	11	11	ew	12	11	11	15	F	8	r	16	r	r	r	10	2
17	Mika Salo	Toyota	6	12	6	r	9	8	r	r	r	r	r	9	15	7	11	14	8	2
18	Heinz Harald Frentzen	Arrows-Ford Cosworth	dq	11	r	r	6	11	6	13	13	r	nq	r	-	-	-	-	-	2
		Sauber-Petronas	-	-	-	-	-	-	-	-	-	-	-	-	-	-	-	13	-	

2003

Pos	Driver	Car-Engine	AUS	BR	RA	EUR	RSM	MC	E	CDN	F	GB	D	H	B	I	P	J	Points
1	Michael Schumacher	Ferrari	p4	6	r	p1	p1	p1	3	1	5	3	4	7	8	p1	1	8	93
2	Kimi Räikkönen	McLaren-Mercedes-Benz	3	1	2	2	r	2	2	6	pr	4	3	r	2	4	p2	2	91
3	Juan Pablo Montoya	Williams-BMW	2	12r	r	7	4	r	1	3	2	2	2	p1	3	2	6	r	82
4	Rubens Barrichello	Ferrari	r	2	pr	3	3	3	8	5	3	7	p1	r	r	3	r	p1	65
5	Raalf Schumacher	Williams-BMW	8	4	7	4	5	6	p4	p2	1	p1	9	r	4	ns	r	12	58
6	Fernando Alonso	Renault	7	p3	3	6	2	r	5	4	4	r	r	4	p1	8	r	r	55
7	David Coulthard	McLaren-Mercedes-Benz	1	r	4	5	r	5	7	r	15r	5	5	2	5	r	r	3	51
8	Jarno Trulli	Renault	5	5	8	13	r	8	6	r	r	r	6	3	7	r	4	5	33
9	Jenson Button	BAR-Honda	10	7	r	8	9	4	ns	r	7	r	8	8	10	r	r	4	17
10	Mark Webber	Jaguar-Ford Cosworth	r	r	9r	r	7	7	r	7	6	6	14	11r	6	7	r	11	17
11	Heinz Harald Frentzen	Sauber-Petronas	6	9	5	11	r	r	r	r	9	12	12	r	r	13r	3	r	13
12	Giancarlo Fisichella	Jordan-Ford Cosworth	12r	r	1	15r	r	r	10	r	12	r	r	13r	r	10	7	r	12
13	Cristiano da Matta	Toyota	r	11	10	12	6	10	9	11r	r	11	7	6	11	r	9	7	10
14	Nick Heidfeld	Sauber-Petronas	r	8	r	10	10	r	11	r	8	13	17	10	9	9	5	9	6
15	Olivier Panis	Toyota	r	r	r	9	r	r	13	8	r	8	11	5	r	r	r	10	6
16	Jacques Villeneuve	BAR-Honda	9	ns	6	r	r	12	r	r	r	9	10	9	r	6	r	-	6
17	Marc Gené	Williams-BMW	-	-	-	-	-	-	-	-	-	-	-	-	-	5	-	-	4
18	Takuma Sato	BAR-Honda	-	-	-	-	-	-	-	-	-	-	-	-	-	-	-	6	3
19	Ralph Firman	Jordan-Ford Cosworth	r	10			8	11	12	r	11	15	13	r	ns	-	r	14	1
20	Justin Wilson	Minardi-Ford Cosworth	r	r	r	r	11	13	r	r	13	14	16	-	-	-	-	-	1
		Jaguar-Ford Cosworth	-	-	-	-	-	-	-	-	-	-	-	r	r	r	8	13	

2004

Pos	Driver	Car-Engine	AUS	MAL	BRN	RSM	E	MC	EUR	CDN	USA	F	GB	D	H	B	I	CH	J	BR	Points
1	Michael Schumacher	Ferrari	p1	p1	p1	1	p1	r	p1	1	1	1	1	p1	p1	2	2	12	p1	7	148
2	Rubens Barrichello	Ferrari	2	4	2	6	2	3	2	2	p2	3	3	12	2	3	p1	p1	r	p3	114
3	Jenson Button	BAR-Honda	6	3	3	p2	8	2	3	3	r	5	4	2	5	r	3	2	3	r	85
4	Fernando Alonso	Renault	3	7	6	4	4	r	5	r	r	p2	10	3	3	r	r	4	5	4	59
5	Juan Pablo Montoya	Williams-BMW	5	2	13	3	r	4	8	dq	dq	8	5	5	4	r	5	5	7	1	58
6	Jarno Trulli	Renault	7	5	4	5	3	p1	4	r	4	4	r	11	r	p9	10	-	-	-	46
		Toyota	-	-	-	-	-	-	-	-	-	-	-	-	-	-	-	-	11	12	
7	Kimi Räikkönen	McLaren-Mercedes-Benz	r	r	r	8	11	r	r	5	6	7	p2	r	r	1	r	3	6	2	45
8	Takuma Sato	BAR-Honda	9	15r	5	16r	5	r	r	r	3	r	11	8	6	r	4	6	4	6	34
9	Ralf Schumacher	Williams-BMW	4	r	7	7	6	10r	r	pdq	r	-	-	-	-	-	-	r	2	5	24
10	David Coulthard	McLaren-Mercedes-Benz	8	6	r	12	10	r	r	6	7	6	7	4	9	7	6	9	r	11	24
11	Giancarlo Fisichella	Sauber-Petronas	10	11	11	9	7	r	6	4	9r	12	6	9	8	5	8	7	8	9	22
12	Felipe Massa	Sauber-Petronas	r	8	12	10	9	5	9	r	r	13	9	13	r	4	12	8	9	8	12
13	Mark Webber	Jaguar-Ford Cosworth	r	r	8	13	12	r	7	r	r	9	8	6	10	r	9	10	r	r	7
14	Olivier Panis	Toyota	13	12	9	11	r	8	11	dq	5	15	r	14	11	8	r	14	14	-	6
15	Antônio Pizzonia	Williams-BMW	-	-	-	-	-	-	-	-	-	-	-	7	7	r	7	-	-	-	6
16	Christian Klien	Jaguar-Ford Cosworth	11	10	14	14	r	r	12	9	r	11	14	10	13	6	13	r	12	14	3
17	Cristiano da Matta	Toyota	12	9	10	r	13	6	r	dq	r	14	13	r	-	-	-	-	-	-	3
18	Nick Heidfeld	Jordan-Ford Cosworth	r	r	15	r	r	7	10	8	r	16	15	r	12	11	14	13	13	r	3
19	Timo Glock	Jordan-Ford Cosworth	ap	ap	ap	ap	ap	ap	ap	7	ap	ap	ap	ap	ap	ap	15	15	15		2
20	Zsolt Baumgartner	Minardi-Ford Cosworth	r	16	r	15	r	9	15	10	8	r	r	16	15	r	15	16	r	16	1

2005

Pos	Driver	Car-Engine	AUS	MAL	BRN	RSM	E	MC	EUR	CDN	USA	F	GB	D	H	TR	I	B	BR	J	CHN	Points
1	Fernando Alonso	Renault	3	p1	p1	1	2	4	p1	r	ns	p1	p2	1	11	2	2	2	p3	3	p1	133
2	Kimi Räikkönen	McLaren-Mercedes-Benz	8	9	3	pr	p1	p1	11r	1	ns	2	3	pr	1	p1	4	1	2	1	2	112
3	Michael Schumacher	Ferrari	r	7	r	2	r	7	5	2	1	3	6	5	p2	r	10	r	4	7	r	62
4	Juan Pablo Montoya	McLaren-Mercedes-Benz	6	4	-	-	7	5	7	r	ns	r	1	2	r	3	1	p14r	1	r	r	60
5	Giancarlo Fisichella	Renault	p1	r	r	r	5	12	6	r	ns	6	4	4	9	4	3	r	5	2	4	58
6	Ralf Schumacher	Toyota	12	5	4	9	4	6	r	6	ns	7	8	6	3	12	6	7	8	p8	3	45
7	Jarno Trulli	Toyota	9	2	2	5	3	10	8	r	pns	5	9	14r	4	6	5	r	13	r	15	43
8	Rubens Barrichello	Ferrari	2	r	9	r	9	8	3	3	2	9	7	10	10	10	12	5	6	11	12	38
9	Jenson Button	BAR-Honda	11r	r	r	dq	-	-	10	pr	ns	4	5	3	5	5	8	3	7	5	8	37
10	Mark Webber	Williams-BMW	5	r	6	7	6	3	r	5	ns	12	11	nc	7	r	14	4	nc	4	7	36
11	Nick Heidfeld	Williams-BMW	r	3	r	6	10	2	p2	r	ns	14	12	11	6	r	-	-	-	-	-	28
12	David Coulthard	Red Bull-Cosworth	4	6	8	11	8	r	4	7	ns	10	13	7	r	7	15	r	r	6	9	24
13	Felipe Massa	Sauber-Petronas	10	10	7	10	11r	9	14	4	ns	r	10	8	14	r	9	10	11	10	6	11
14	Jacques Villeneuve	Sauber-Petronas	13	r	11r	4	r	11	13	9	ns	8	14	15	r	11	11	6	12	12	10	9
15	Christian Klien	Red Bull-Cosworth	7	8	ns	ap	ap	ap	ap	8	ns	r	15	9	r	8	13	9	9	9	5	9
16	Tiago Monteiro	Jordan-Toyota	16	12	10	13	12	13	15	10	3	13	17	17	13	15	17	8	r	13	11	7
17	Alexander Wurz	McLaren-Mercedes-Benz	-	-	ap	3	-	ap	ap	-	-	-	-	ap	ap	-	-	ap	ap	-	-	6
18	Narain Karthikeyan	Jordan-Toyota	15	11	r	12	13	r	16	r	4	15	r	16	12	14	20	11	15	15	r	5
19	Christijan Albers	Minardi-Cosworth	r	13	13	r	r	14	17	11	5	r	18	13	r	r	19	12	14	16	16	4
20	Pedro de la Rosa	McLaren-Mercedes-Benz	ap	ap	5	ap	ap	-	-	ap	ap	ap	ap	-	-	ap	ap	-	-	ap	ap	4
21	Patrick Friesacher	Minardi-Cosworth	17	r	12	r	r	r	18	r	6	r	19	-	-	-	-	-	-	-	-	3
22	Antônio Pizzonia	Williams-BMW	-	-	-	-	-	-	-	-	-	-	-	-	-	-	7	15r	r	r	13	2
23	Takuma Sato	BAR-Honda	14r	-	r	dq	-	-	12	r	ns	11	16	12	8	9	16	r	10	dq	r	1
24	Vitantonio Liuzzi	Red Bull-Cosworth	ap	ap	ap	8	r	r	9	-	-	ap	ap	ap	ap	ap	ap	ap	ap	ap	ap	1

2006

Pos	Driver	Car-Engine	BRN	MAL	AUS	RSM	EUR	E	MC	GB	CDN	USA	F	D	H	TR	I	CHN	J	BR	Points
1	Fernando Alonso	Renault	1	2	1	2	p2	p1	p1	p1	p1	5	2	5	r	2	r	p2	1	2	134
2	Michael Schumacher	Ferrari	p2	6	r	p1	1	2	5	2	2	p1	p1	1	8r	3	1	1	r	4	121
3	Felipe Massa	Ferrari	9	5	r	4	3	4	9	5	5	2	3	2	7	p1	9	r	p2	p1	80
4	Giancarlo Fisichella	Renault	r	p1	5	8	6	3	6	4	4	3	6	6	r	6	4	3	3	6	72
5	Kimi Räikkönen	McLaren-Mercedes-Benz	3	r	2	5	4	5	r	3	3	r	5	p3	pr	r	p2	r	5	5	65
6	Jenson Button	Honda	4	3	p10r	7	r	6	11	r	9	r	r	4	1	4	5	4	4	3	56
7	Rubens Barrichello	Honda	15	10	7	10	5	7	4	10	r	6	r	r	4	8	6	6	12	7	30
8	Juan Pablo Montoya	McLaren-Mercedes-Benz	5	4	r	3	r	r	2	6	r	r	-	-	-	-	-	-	-	-	26
9	Nick Heidfeld	BMW Sauber-BMW	12	r	4	13	10	8	7	7	7	r	8	r	3	14	8	7	8	17r	23
10	Ralf Schumacher	Toyota	14	8	3	9	r	r	8	r	r	r	4	9	6	7	15	r	7	r	20
11	Pedro de la Rosa	McLaren-Mercedes-Benz	-	-	-	-	-	-	-	-	-	-	7	r	2	5	r	5	11	8	19
12	Jarno Trulli	Toyota	16	9	r	r	9	10	17r	11	6	4	r	7	12r	9	7	r	6	r	15
13	David Coulthard	Red Bull-Ferrari	10	r	8	r	r	14	3	12	8	7	9	11	5	15r	12	9	r	r	14
14	Mark Webber	Williams-Cosworth	6	r	r	6	r	9	r	r	12	r	r	r	r	10	10	8	r	r	7
15	Jacques Villeneuve	BMW Sauber-BMW	r	7	6	12	8	12	14	8	r	r	11	r	-	-	-	-	-	-	7
16	Robert Kubica	BMW Sauber-BMW	ap	ap	ap	ap	ap	ap	ap	ap	ap	ap	ap	ap	dq	12	3	13	9	9	6
17	Nico Rosberg	Williams-Cosworth	7	r	r	11	7	11	r	9	r	9	14	r	r	r	r	11	10	r	4
18	Christian Klien	Red Bull-Ferrari	8	r	r	r	r	13	r	14	11	r	12	8	r	11	11	-	-	-	2
19	Vitantonio Liuzzi	Toro Rosso-Cosworth	11	11	r	14	r	15r	10	13	13	8	13	10	r	r	14	10	14	13	1

2007

Pos	Driver	Car-Engine	AUS	MAL	BR	E	MC	CDN	USA	F	GB	EUR	H	TR	I	B	J	CHN	BR	Points
1	Kimi Räikkönen	Ferrari	p1	3	3	r	8	5	4	p1	1	pr	2	2	3	p1	3	1	1	110
2	Lewis Hamilton	McLaren-Mercedes-Benz	3	2	2	2	2	p1	p1	3	p3	9	p1	5	2	4	p1	pr	7	109
3	Fernando Alonso	McLaren-Mercedes-Benz	2	1	5	3	p1	7	2	7	2	1	4	3	p1	3	r	2	3	109
4	Felipe Massa	Ferrari	6	p5	p1	p1	3	dq	3	p2	5	2	13	p1	r	2	6	3	2	94
5	Nick Heidfeld	BMW Sauber-BMW	4	4	4	r	6	2	r	5	6	6	3	4	4	5	14r	7	6	61
6	Robert Kubica	BMW Sauber-BMW	r	18	6	4	5	r	-	4	4	7	5	8	5	9	7	r	5	39
7	Heikki Kovalainen	Renault	10	8	9	7	13r	4	5	15	7	8	8	6	7	8	2	9	r	30
8	Giancarlo Fisichella	Renault	5	6	8	9	4	dq	9	6	8	10	12	9	12	r	5	11	r	21
9	Nico Rosberg	Williams-Toyota	7	r	10	6	12	10	16r	9	12	r	7	7	6	6	r	16	4	20
10	David Coulthard	Red Bull-Renault	r	r	r	5	14	r	r	13	11	5	11	10	r	r	4	8	9	14
11	Alexander Wurz	Williams-Toyota	r	9	11	r	7	3	10	14	13	4	14	11	13	r	r	12	-	13
12	Mark Webber	Red Bull-Renault	13	10	r	r	r	9	7	12	r	3	9	r	9	7	r	10	r	10
13	Jarno Trulli	Toyota	9	7	7	r	15	r	6	r	r	13	10	16	11	11	13	13	8	8
14	Sebastian Vettel	BMW Sauber-BMW	ap	ap	-	-	-	-	8	-	-	-	16	19	18	r	r	4	r	6
15	Jenson Button	Honda	15	12	r	12	11	r	12	8	10	r	r	13	8	r	11r	5	r	6
16	Ralf Schumacher	Toyota	8	15	12	r	16	8	r	10	r	r	6	12	15	10	r	r	11	5
17	Takuma Sato	Super Aguri-Honda	12	13	r	8	17	6	r	16	14	r	15	18	16	15	15r	14	12	4
18	Vitantonio Liuzzi	Toro Rosso-Ferrari	14	17	r	r	r	r	17r	r	16r	r	r	15	17	12	9	6	13	3
19	Adrian Sutil	Spyker-Ferrari	17	r	15	13	r	r	14	17	r	r	17	21r	19	14	8	r	r	1

2008

Pos	Driver	Car-Engine	BRN	MAL	AUS	RSM	EUR	E	MC	GB	CDN	USA	F	G	H	TR	I	CHN	J	BR	Points
1	Lewis Hamilton	McLaren-Mercedes-Benz	p1	5	13	3	2	1	pr	10	1	p1	p5	2	p3	7	3	p12	p1	5	98
2	Felipe Massa	Ferrari	r	pr	1	2	p1	p3	5	1	13	3	17r	p1	1	6	p13	7	2	p1	97
3	Kimi Räikkönen	Ferrari	8r	1	2	p1	3	9	r	p2	4	6	3	r	18r	9	15r	3	3	3	75
4	Robert Kubica	BMW Sauber-BMW	r	2	p3	4	4	2	1	5	r	7	8	3	6	3	11	2	6	11	75
5	Fernando Alonso	Renault	4	8	10	r	6	10	r	8	6	11	4	r	4	4	1	1	4	2	61
6	Nick Heidfeld	BMW Sauber-BMW	2	6	4	9	5	14	2	13	2	4	10	9	2	5	6	9	5	10	60
7	Heikki Kovalainen	McLaren-Mercedes-Benz	5	3	5	r	12	8	9	4	p5	5	1	4	10r	2	10	r	r	7	53
8	Sebastian Vettel	Toro Rosso-Ferrari	r	r	r	r	17	5	8	12	r	8	r	6	5	p1	5	6	9	4	35
9	Jarno Trulli	Toyota	r	4	6	8	10	13	6	3	7	9	7	5	16	13	r	5	r	8	31
10	Timo Glock	Toyota	r	r	9	11	13	12	4	11	12	r	2	7	9	11	4	r	7	6	25
11	Mark Webber	Red Bull-Renault	r	7	7	5	7	4	12	6	10	r	9	12	8	8	r	8	14	9	21
12	Nelsinho Piquet	Renault	r	11	r	r	15	r	r	7	r	2	6	11	r	10	r	4	8	r	19
13	Nico Rosberg	Williams-Toyota	3	14	8	r	8	r	10	16	9	10	14	8	12	14	2	11	15	12	17
14	Rubens Barrichello	Honda	dq	13	11	r	14	6	7	14	3	r	16	16	r	17	r	13	11	15	11
15	Kazuki Nakajima	Williams-Toyota	6	17	14	7	r	7	r	15	8	14	13	15	14	12	8	15	12	17	9
16	David Coulthard	Red Bull-Renault	r	9	18	12	9	r	3	9	r	13	11	17	11	16	7	r	10	r	8
17	Sébastien Bourdais	Toro Rosso-Ferrari	7r	r	15	r	r	r	13	17	11	12	18	10	7	18	12	10	13	14	4
18	Jenson Button	Honda	r	10	r	6	11	11	11	r	r	17	12	13	15	15	9	14	16	13	3

2009

Pos	Driver	Car-Engine	AUS	MAL	CHN	BRN	E	MON	TR	GB	D	H	EUR	B	I	SIN	J	BR	ABU	Points
1	Jenson Button	Brawn-Mercedes-Benz	p1	p1	3	p1	p1	p1	1	6	5	7	7	r	2	5	8	5	3	95
2	Sebastian Vettel	Red Bull-Renault	13r	15r	p1	2	4	r	p3	p1	2	r	r	3	8	4	p1	4	1	84
3	Rubens Barrichello	Brawn-Mercedes-Benz	2	5	4	5	2	2	r	3	6	10	1	7	1	6	7	p8	4	77
4	Mark Webber	Red Bull-Renault	12	6	2	11	3	5	2	2	p1	3	9	9	r	r	17	1	2	69.5
5	Lewis Hamilton	McLaren-Mercedes-Benz	dq	7	6	4	9	12	13	16	18	1	p2	r	p12r	p1	3	3	pr	49
6	Kimi Räikkönen	Ferrari	15r	14	10	6	r	3	9	8	r	2	3	1	3	10	4	6	12	48
7	Nico Rosberg	Williams-Toyota	6	8	15	9	8	6	5	5	4	4	5	8	16	11	5	r	9	34.5
8	Jarno Trulli	Toyota	3	4	r	p3	r	13	4	7	17	8	13	r	14	12	2	r	7	32.5
9	Fernando Alonso	Renault	5	11	9	8	5	7	10	14	7	pr	6	r	5	3	10	r	14	26
10	Timo Glock	Toyota	4	3	7	7	10	10	8	9	9	6	14	10	11	2	ns	-	-	24
11	Felipe Massa	Ferrari	r	9	r	14	6	4	6	4	3	ns	-	-	-	-	-	-	-	22
12	Heikki Kovalainen	McLaren-Mercedes-Benz	r	r	5	12	r	r	14	r	8	5	4	6	6	7	11	12	11	22
13	Nick Heidfeld	BMW Sauber-BMW	10	2	12	19	7	11	11	15	10	11	11	5	7	r	6	r	5	19
14	Robert Kubica	BMW Sauber-BMW	14r	r	13	18	11	r	7	13	14	13	8	4	r	8	9	2	10	17
15	Giancarlo Fisichella	Force India-Mercedes-Benz	11	18r	14	15	14	9	r	10	11	14	12	2	-	-	-	-	-	8
		Ferrari	-	-	-	-	-	-	-	-	-	-	-	-	9	13	12	10	16	
16	Sébastien Buemi	Toro Rosso-Ferrari	7	16r	8	17	r	r	15	18	16	16	r	12	13	r	r	7	8	6
17	Adrian Sutil	Force India-Mercedes-Benz	9	17	17r	16	r	14	17	17	15	r	10	11	4	r	13	r	17	5
18	Kamui Kobayashi	Toyota	-	-	-	-	-	-	-	-	-	-	-	-	-	-	ap	9	6	3
19	Sébastien Bourdais	Toro Rosso-Ferrari	8	10	11	13	r	8	18	r	r	-	-	-	-	-	-	-	-	2

Half points were awarded in Malaysia where the race was stopped early.

World Champion Drivers

Year	Driver	Car
1950	Giuseppe Farina	Alfa Romeo
1951	Juan Manuel Fangio	Alfa Romeo
1952	Alberto Ascari	Ferrari
1953	Alberto Ascari	Ferrari
1954	Juan Manuel Fangio	Maserati/Mercedes-Benz
1955	Juan Manuel Fangio	Mercedes-Benz
1956	Juan Manuel Fangio	Ferrari
1957	Juan Manuel Fangio	Maserati
1958	Mike Hawthorn	Ferrari
1959	Jack Brabham	Cooper Climax
1960	Jack Brabham	Cooper Climax
1961	Phil Hill	Ferrari
1962	Graham Hill	BRM
1963	Jim Clark	Lotus Climax
1964	John Surtees	Ferrari
1965	Jim Clark	Lotus Climax
1966	Jack Brabham	Brabham Repco
1967	Denny Hulme	Brabham Repco
1968	Graham Hill	Lotus Ford Cosworth
1969	Jackie Stewart	Matra Ford Cosworth
1970	Jochen Rindt	Lotus Ford Cosworth
1971	Jackie Stewart	Tyrrell Ford Cosworth
1972	Emerson Fittipaldi	Lotus Ford Cosworth
1973	Jackie Stewart	Tyrrell Ford Cosworth
1974	Emerson Fittipaldi	McLaren Ford Cosworth
1975	Niki Lauda	Ferrari
1976	James Hunt	McLaren Ford Cosworth
1977	Niki Lauda	Ferrari
1978	Mario Andretti	Lotus Ford Cosworth
1979	Jody Scheckter	Ferrari
1980	Alan Jones	Williams Ford Cosworth
1981	Nelson Piquet	Brabham Ford Cosworth
1982	Keke Rosberg	Williams Ford Cosworth
1983	Nelson Piquet	Brabham BMW
1984	Niki Lauda	McLaren TAG Porsche
1985	Alain Prost	McLaren TAG Porsche
1986	Alain Prost	McLaren TAG Porsche
1987	Nelson Piquet	Williams Honda
1988	Ayrton Senna	McLaren Honda
1989	Alain Prost	McLaren-Honda
1990	Ayrton Senna	McLaren-Honda
1991	Ayrton Senna	McLaren-Honda
1992	Nigel Mansell	Williams-Renault
1993	Alain Prost	Williams-Renault
1994	Michael Schumacher	Benetton-Ford Cosworth
1995	Michael Schumacher	Benetton-Renault
1996	Damon Hill	Williams-Renault
1997	Jacques Villeneuve	Williams-Renault
1998	Mika Häkkinen	McLaren-Mercedes-Benz
1999	Mika Häkkinen	McLaren-Mercedes-Benz
2000	Michael Schumacher	Ferrari
2001	Michael Schumacher	Ferrari
2002	Michael Schumacher	Ferrari
2003	Michael Schumacher	Ferrari
2004	Michael Schumacher	Ferrari
2005	Fernando Alonso	Renault
2006	Fernando Alonso	Renault
2007	Kimi Räikkönen	Ferrari
2008	Lewis Hamilton	McLaren-Mercedes-Benz
2009	Jenson Button	Brawn-Mercedes-Benz

World Champion Constructors

1958	Vanwall
1959	Cooper Climax
1960	Cooper Climax
1961	Ferrari
1962	BRM
1963	Lotus Climax
1964	Ferrari
1965	Lotus Climax
1966	Brabham Repco
1967	Brabham Repco
1968	Lotus Ford Cosworth
1969	Matra Ford Cosworth
1970	Lotus Ford Cosworth
1971	Tyrrell Ford Cosworth
1972	Lotus Ford Cosworth
1973	Lotus Ford Cosworth
1974	McLaren Ford Cosworth
1975	Ferrari
1976	Ferrari
1977	Ferrari
1978	Lotus Ford Cosworth
1979	Ferrari
1980	Williams Ford Cosworth
1981	Williams Ford Cosworth
1982	Ferrari
1983	Ferrari
1984	McLaren TAG Porsche
1985	McLaren TAG Porsche
1986	Williams Honda
1987	Williams Honda
1988	McLaren-Honda
1989	McLaren-Honda
1990	McLaren-Honda
1991	McLaren-Honda
1992	Williams-Renault
1993	Williams-Renault
1994	Williams-Renault
1995	Benetton-Renault
1996	Williams-Renault
1997	Williams-Renault
1998	McLaren-Mercedes-Benz
1999	Ferrari
2000	Ferrari
2001	Ferrari
2002	Ferrari
2003	Ferrari
2004	Ferrari
2005	Renault
2006	Renault
2007	Ferrari
2008	Ferrari
2009	Brawn-Mercedes-Benz